MAN: WHENCE, HOW AND WHITHER

MAN: WHENCE, HOW AND WHITHER

A Record of Clairvoyant Investigation

BY
ANNIE BESANT
CHARLES WEBSTER LEADBEATER

GYAN

ISBN: 978-81-212-1890-0 (HB)
First Published, 1913
Published, 2018
Published by

Gyan Publishing House
5, Ansari Road
Daryaganj, New Delhi-110002
Phone: 011-47034999, 9811692060
www.gyanbooks.com
E-mail: books@gyanbooks.com

Printed at: G. Print Process, Delhi.

FOREWORD

THE idea that clairvoyant observation is possible is no longer regarded as entirely insane. It is not generally accepted, nor indeed is it accepted to any large extent. A constantly growing minority, however, of fairly intelligent people believe clairvoyance to be a fact, and regard it as a perfectly natural power, which will become universal in the course of evolution. They do not regard it as a miraculous gift, nor as an outgrowth from high spirituality, lofty intelligence, or purity of character; any or all of these may be manifested in a person who is not in the least clairvoyant. They know that it is a power latent in all men, and that it can be developed by any one who is able and willing to pay the price demanded for its forcing, ahead of the general evolution.

The use of clairvoyance for research into the past is not new. *The Secret Doctrine* of H. P. Blavatsky is a standing instance of such use. Whether or not the work thus done is reliable is a question which must be left for decision to future generations, possessing the power which is now used for this purpose. We shall, we know, have a large body of readers who are students, who, believing the power to be a reality, and knowing us to be honest, will find this book both interesting and illuminative. For them it has been written. As the number of students increases, so will increase the number of our readers. More than this we cannot hope for. Centuries hence, when people will be able to write much better books, based on similar researches, this will be looked on as an interesting pioneer, considering the time at which it was written.

Proofs of its general accuracy obviously cannot be given, though from time to time discoveries may be made which confirm an occasional statement. The truth of clairvoyant research can no more be proved to the general public, than colour can be demonstrated to a blind man. The general public, so far as it reads the book, will regard it with blank incredulity; some may think it an interesting fabrication; others may find it dull. Most will regard the authors as either self-deceived or fraudulent, according as the judges are kind-hearted or malevolent.

To students we would say: Accept it so far as it helps you in your studies, and throws light on what you already know. Amplification and correction may be made in the future, for we have only given a few fragments of a huge history, and the task has been a very heavy one.

The research work was done at Adyar in the summer of 1910; in the heat of the summer many of the students were away, and we shut ourselves up, so as to be uninterrupted, for five evenings every week; we observed, and said exactly what we saw, and two members, Mrs. Van Hook and Don Fabrizio Ruspoli, were good enough to write down all we said, exactly as we said it; these two sets of notes have been preserved. They are woven into the present story, written partly during the summer of 1911, when a few weeks were stolen for the purpose, and completed in April and May 1912, similarly stolen out of the rush of busy lives. This kind of work cannot be done in the midst of constant interruptions, and the only way to accomplish it is to escape from the world for the time, to 'go into retreat,' as the Roman Catholics call it.

The broad Theosophical outline of evolution has been followed, and it is given among the 'preliminaries' in Chapter I. This governs the whole, and is the ground-plan of the book. The fact of an Occult Hierarchy, which guides and shapes evolution, is throughout taken for granted, and some of its members inevitably appear in the course of the story. In order to throw ourselves back into the earliest stages, we sought for our own consciousnesses, present there, and easier to start from than anything else, since no others were recognisable. They gave us, as it were, a footing in the first and second Chains. From the latter part of the third Chain and onwards, we traced humanity's story by following a group of individuals, except where this group was otherwise occupied during any important stage of evolution—as in the beginnings of the third and fourth sub-races of the fifth Root Race; when that was the case we left it, and followed the main stream of progress. In this record comparatively few details as to persons can be given, the sweep of the story being so large. Many detailed lives, however, have been published in *The Theosophist,* under the general title 'Rents in the Veil of Time'—rents through which glimpses of the past of individuals may be seen. A volume of these, named *Lives of Alcyone,* will shortly be published, and to that will be appended full genealogical tables, showing the relationships in each life of all the characters so far identified. Work of this kind might be done *ad libitum,* if there were people to do it.

As a history cannot be written without names, and as reincarnation is a fact—and therefore the re-appearance of the same individual throughout succeeding ages is also a fact, the individual playing many parts under many names —we have given names to many individuals by which they may be recognised throughout the dramas in which they take part. Irving is the same Irving to us, as Macbeth, Richard III, Shylock, Charles I, Faust, Romeo, Matthias; and in any story of his life as actor he is spoken of as Irving, whatever part he is playing; his continuing individuality is recognised throughout. So a human being, in the long story in which lives are days, plays hundreds of parts but is himself throughout—be he man or woman, peasant, prince, or priest. To this 'himself' we have given a distinguishing name, so that he may be recognised under all the disguises put on to suit the part he is playing. These are mostly names of constellations, or stars. For instance, we have given to Julius Cæsar the name of Corona; to Plato that of Pallas: to Lao-Tze that of Lyra; in this way we can see how different are the lines of evolution, the previous lives which produce a Cæsar and a Plato. It gives to the story a human interest, and teaches the student of reincarnation.

The names of Those who constantly appear in this story as ordinary men and women, but who are now Masters, may make those great Beings more real to some; They have climbed to where They stand on the same ladder of life up which we are climbing now; They have known the common household life, the joys and sorrows, the successes and the failures, which make up human experiences. They are not Gods perfect from unending ages, but men and women who have unfolded the God within themselves and have, along a toilsome road, reached the superhuman. They are the fulfilled promise of what we shall be, the glorious flowers on the plant on which we are the buds.

And so we launch our ship on the stormy ocean of publicity, to face its destiny and find its fate.

SOME OF THE CHARACTERS IN THE STORY

THE FOUR KUṂĀRAS... Four of the Lords of the Flame, still living in Shamballa.

MAHĀGURU ... ... The Boḍhisaṭṭva of the time, appearing as Vyāsa, Thoth (Hermes), Zaraṭhuṣhtra, Orpheus, finally as Gauṭama, who became the Lord Buḍḍha.

SURYA ...	... The Lord Maiṭreya, the present Boḍhisaṭṭva, the Supreme Teacher of the world.
MANU ...	... The Head of a Root Race. If with a prefix, Root-Manu or Seed-Manu, a yet higher Official, presiding over a larger cycle of evolution—a Round or a Chain. The cognomen Vaivasvaṭa is given in Hinḍū books both to the Root-Manu of our Chain and the Manu of the Āryan, or fifth, Root Race.
VIRĀJ ...	... The Mahā-Chohan, a high official, of rank equal to that of a Manu or a Boḍhisaṭṭva.
SATURN ...	... Now a Master, spoken of in some Theosophical books as 'The Venetian'.
JUPITER ...	... Now a Master, residing in the Nilgiri Hills.
MARS ...	... Now the Master M. of the *Occult World*.
MERCURY ...	... Now the Master K. H. of the *Occult World*
NEPTUNE ...	... Now the Master Hilarion.
OSIRIS ...	... Now the Master Serapis.
BṚHASPAṬI ...	... Now the Master Jesus.
VENUS ...	... Now the Master Rāgozci (or Rakovzky), the 'Hungarian

Adept,' the Comte de S. Germain of the eighteenth century.

URANUS ...	... Now the Master D. K.
VULCAN ...	... Now a Master; known in His last earth-life as Sir Thomas More.
ATHENA ...	... Now a Master; known on earth as Thomas Vaughan, 'Eugenius Philalethes'.

ALBA	... Ethel Whyte.
ALBIREO ...	... Maria-Luisa Kirby.
ALCYONE ...	... J. Krishnamurti.
ALETHEIA ...	... Johan van Manen.
ALTAIR ...	... Herbert Whyte.
ARCOR ...	... A. J. Willson.
AURORA ...	... Count Bubna-Licics.
CAPELLA ...	... S. Maud Sharpe.
CORONA ...	... Julius Cæsar.
CRUX	... The Hon. Otway Cuffe.
DENEB ...	... Lord Cochrane (Tenth Earl of Dundonald).
EUDOXIA ...	... Louisa Shaw.
FIDES	... G. S. Arundale.
GEMINI ...	... E. Maud Green.
HECTOR ...	... W. H. Kirby.
HELIOS ...	... Marie Russak.
HERAKLES ...	... Annie Besant.
LEO	... Fabrizio Ruspoli.
LOMIA	... J. I. Wedgwood.

LUTETIA ... ... Charles Bradlaugh.

LYRA ... ... Lao-Tze.

MIRA ... ... Carl Holbrook.

MIZAR ... ... J. Nityananda.

MONA ... ... Piet Meuleman.

NORMA ... ... Margherita Ruspoli.

OLYMPIA ... ... Damodar K. Mavalankar.

PALLAS ... ... Plato.

PHOCEA ... ... W. Q. Judge.

PHŒNIX ... ... T. Pascal.

POLARIS ... ... B. P. Wadia.

PROTEUS ... ... The Teshu Lama.

SELENE ... ... C. Jinarajadasa.

SIRIUS ... ... C. W. Leadbeater.

SIWA ... ... T. Subba Rao.

SPICA ... ... Francesca Arundale.

TAURUS ... ... Jerome Anderson.

ULYSSES ... ... H. S. Olcott.

VAJRA ... ... H. P. Blavatsky.

VESTA ... ... Minnie C. Holbrook.

A certain number of members of the Theosophical Society have bravely allowed their names to appear in the above list, despite the ridicule it may bring on them. A large number of our friends are just now in Hindū bodies, but we cannot expose them to the mockery and persecution they would be likely to suffer if we named them, so we have not asked their permission.

CONTENTS

MAN: WHENCE, HOW AND WHITHER

INTRODUCTION

THE problem of Man's origin, of his evolution, of his destiny, is one of inexhaustible interest. Whence came he, this glorious Intelligence, on this globe, at least, the crown of visible beings? How has he evolved to his present position? has he suddenly descended from above, a radiant angel, to become the temporary tenant of a house of clay, or has he climbed upwards through long dim ages, tracing his humble ancestry from primeval slime, through fish, reptile, mammal, up to the human kingdom? And what is his future destiny? is he evolving onwards, climbing higher and higher, only to descend the long slope of degeneration till he falls over the precipice of death, leaving behind him a freezing planet, the sepulchre of myriad civilisations? or is his present climbing but the schooling of an immortal spiritual Power, destined in his maturity to wield the sceptre of a world, a system, a congeries of systems, a veritable God in the making?

To these questions many answers have been given, partially or fairly fully, in the Scriptures of ancient religions, in the shadowy traditions handed down from mighty men of old, in the explorations of modern archæologists, in the researches of geologists, physicists, biologists, astronomers, of our own days. The most modern knowledge has vindicated the most ancient records in ascribing to our earth and its inhabitants a period of existence of vast extent and of marvellous complexity; hundreds of millions of years are tossed together to give time for the slow and laborious processes of nature; further and further back 'primeval man' is pushed; Lemuria is seen where now the Pacific ripples, and Australia, but lately rediscovered, is regarded as one of the oldest of lands; Atlantis is posited, where now the Atlantic rolls, and Africa is linked to America by a solid bridge of land, so that the laurels of a discoverer are plucked from the brow of Columbus, and he is seen as following long-perished generations who found their way from Europe to the continent of the setting sun. Poseidonis is no longer the mere fairy-tale told by superstitious Egyptian priests to a Greek philosopher; Minos of Crete is dug out of his ancient grave, a man and not a myth; Babylon, once ancient, is shown as the modern successor of a series of highly civilised cities, buried in stratum after stratum, glooming through the night of time. Tradition is beckoning the explorer to excavate in Turkestan, in Central Asia, and whispering of cyclopean ruins that await but his spade for their unburying.

Amid this clash of opinions, this conflict of theories, this affirmation and repudiation of ever-new hypotheses, it may be that the record of two observers, two explorers—treading a very ancient path that few feet tread to-day, but that will be trodden more and more by thronging students as time shows its stability—may have a chance of being read. Science is to-day exploring the marvels of what it calls the 'subjective mind,' and is finding in it strange powers, strange upsurgings, strange memories. Healthy and balanced, dominating the brain, it shows as genius; out of equilibrium with the brain, vagrant and incalculable, it shows as insanity. Some day Science will realise that what it calls the subjective mind, Religion calls the Soul, and that the exhibition of its powers depends on the physical and super-physical instruments at its command. If these are well-constructed, sound and flexible, and thoroughly under its control, the powers of vision, of audition, of memory, irregularly up-welling from the subjective mind, become the normal and disposable powers of the Soul; if the Soul strive upwards to the Spirit—the Divine Self—veiled in the matter of our System, the true Inner Man, instead of ever clinging to the body, then its powers increase, and knowledge, otherwise unattainable, comes within its reach.

Metaphysicians, ancient and modern, declare that Past, Present, and Future are ever simultaneously existent in the divine Consciousness, and are only successive as they come into manifestation, *i.e.*, under Time, which is verily the succession of states of consciousness. Our limited consciousness, existing in Time, is inevitably bound by this succession; we can only think successively. But we all know, from our experience of dream-states, that *time-measures* vary with this change of state, though succession remains; we know also that time-measures vary even more in the thought-world, and that when we construct mental pictures we can delay, hasten, repeat, the succession of thought-images at will, though still ever bound by succession. Pursuing this line of thought, it is not difficult to conceive of a mind raised to transcendent power, the mind of a LOGOS, or WORD—such a Being, *e.g.*, as is described in the Johannine Gospel, i. 1-4—containing within itself all the mental images embodied in, say, a Solar System, arranged in the order of succession of their proposed manifestation, but all there, all capable of review, as we can review our own thought-images, though we have not yet attained to the divine power, so strikingly voiced by the Prophet Muhammad, as: "He only saith to it: 'Be,' and it is".[1] Yet, as the infant of a day contains within himself the potentialities of his sire, so do we, the offspring of God, contain within ourselves the potentialities of Divinity. Hence, when we resolutely turn the Soul away from earth and concentrate his attention on the Spirit—the substance whereof he is the shadow in the world of matter—the Soul may reach the 'Memory of Nature,' the embodiment in the material world of the Thoughts of the LOGOS, the reflection, as it were, of His Mind. There dwells the Past in

[1] *Al Quran,* xi. 17.

ever-living records; here also dwells the Future, more difficult for the half-developed Soul to reach, because not yet manifested, nor yet embodied, though quite as 'real'. The Soul, reading these records, may transmit them to the body, impress them on the brain, and then record them in words and writings. When the Soul is merged in the Spirit—as in the case of "men made perfect," of Those who have completed human evolution, the Spirits who are 'liberated,' or 'saved'[1]—then the touch with the divine Memory is immediate, direct, ever-available, and unerring. Before that point is reached, the touch is imperfect, mediate, subject to errors of observation and transmission.

The writers of this book, having been taught the method of gaining touch, but being subject to the difficulties involved in their uncompleted evolution, have done their best to observe and transmit, but are fully conscious of the many weaknesses which mar their work. Occasional help has been given to them by the Elder Brethren, in the way of broad outlines here and there, and dates where necessary.

As in the case of the related books which have preceded this in the Theosophical movement, the "treasure is in earthen vessels," and, while gratefully acknowledging the help graciously given, they take the responsibility of all errors entirely on themselves.

[1] The terms used by Hindūs and Christians respectively to mark the end of purely human evolution.

MAN:

WHENCE AND HOW

CHAPTER I

PRELIMINARIES

WHENCE comes man and whither goes he? In the fullest answer we can only say: Man, as a spiritual Being, comes forth from God and returns to God; but the Whence and Whither with which we deal here denote a far more modest sweep. It is but a single page of his life-story that is copied out herein, telling of the birth into dense matter of some of the Children of Man—What lies beyond that birthing, O still unpenetrated Night?—and following on their growth from world to world to a point in the near future but some few centuries hence—What lies beyond that cloud-flush in the dawning, O still unrisen Day?

And yet the title is not wholly wrong, for he who comes from God and goes to God is not precisely 'Man'. That Ray of the divine Splendour which comes forth from Divinity at the beginning of a manifestation, that "fragment of Mine own Self, transformed in the world of life into an immortal Spirit,"[1] is far more than Man. Man is but one stage of his unfolding, and mineral, vegetable, animal, are but stages of his embryonic life in the womb of nature, ere he is born as Man. Man is the

[1] *Bhagavaḍ-Giṭā*, xv. 7.

stage in which Spirit and Matter struggle for the mastery, and when the struggle is over and Spirit has become Lord of Matter, Master of life and death, then Spirit enters on his superhuman evolution, and is no longer Man, but rather Superman.

Here then we deal with him only as Man: with Man in his embryonic stage, in the mineral, vegetable and animal kingdoms; with Man in his development in the human kingdom; with Man and his worlds, the Thinker and his field of evolution.

In order to follow readily the story told in this book, it is necessary for the reader to pause for a few minutes on the general conception of a Solar System, as outlined in Theosophical literature,[1] and on the broad principles of the evolution therein carried on. This is not more difficult to follow than the technical terminology of every science, or than other cosmic descriptions, as in astronomy, and a little attention will easily enable the student to master it. In all studies of deep content, there are ever dry preliminaries which have to be mastered. The careless reader finds them dull, skips them, and is, throughout his subsequent reading, in a more or less bewildered and confused condition of mind; he is building his house without a foundation, and must continually be shoring it up. The careful reader faces these difficulties bravely, masters

[1] The student may find it in H. P. Blavatsky's *The Secret Doctrine*, A. P. Sinnett's *Esoteric Buddhism*, and *Growth of the Soul*, Annie Besant's *The Ancient Wisdom*, etc. There are minor differences—such as H. P. Blavatsky's and A. P. Sinnett's naming of the globes of the earth-chain—but the main facts are identical.

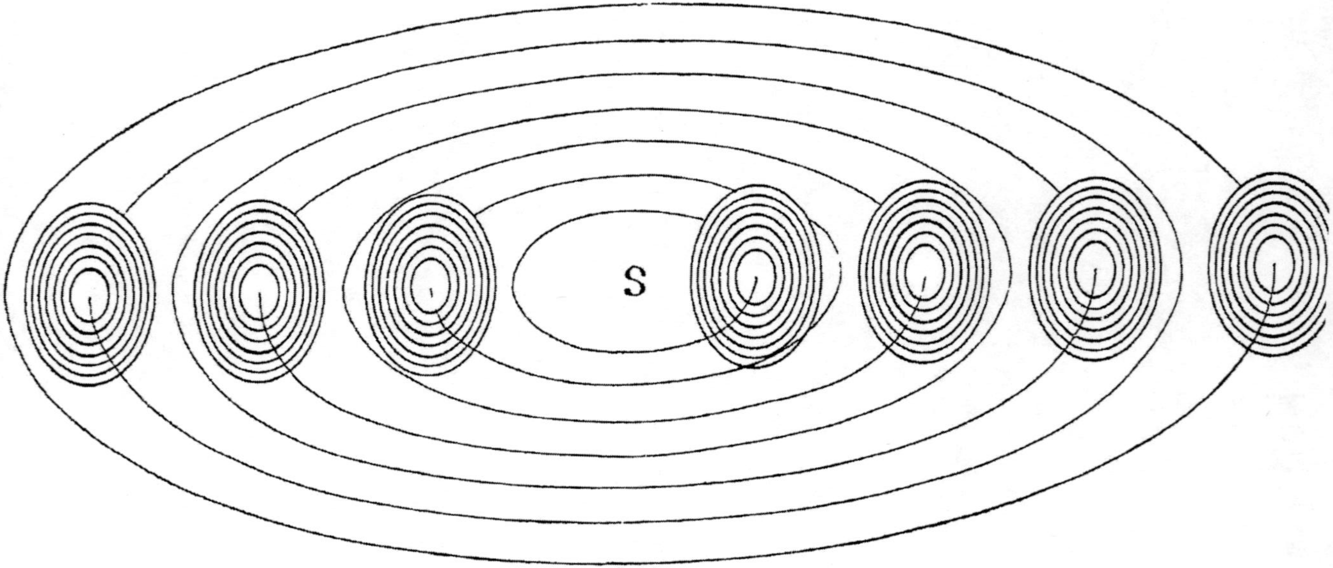

DIAGRAM I

them once for all, and with the knowledge thus gained he goes easily forward, and the details he meets with later fall readily into their places. Those who prefer the first plan, had better miss the present Chapter, and go on to Chapter II; the wiser readers will give an hour to mastering what follows.

That great Sage, Plato, one of the world's master-intellects, whose lofty ideas have dominated European thought, makes the pregnant statement: "God geometrises." The more we know of Nature, the more we realise this fact. The leaves of plants are set in a definite order of succession, $\frac{1}{2}$, $\frac{1}{3}$, $\frac{2}{5}$, $\frac{3}{8}$, $\frac{5}{13}$, and so on. The vibrations that make the successive notes of a scale may be correspondently figured in a regular series. Some diseases follow a definite cycle of days, and the 7th, the 14th, the 21st, mark the crises that result in continued physical life or in death. It is useless to multiply instances.

There is, then, nothing surprising in the fact that we find, in the order of our Solar System, the continual recurrence of the number Seven. Because of this, it has been called a 'sacred number'; a 'significant number' would be a better epithet. The moon's life divides itself naturally into twice seven days of waxing and an equal number of waning, and its quarters give us our week of seven days. And we find this seven as the root-number of our Solar System, dividing its departments into seven, and these again divided into subsidiary sevens, and these into other sevens, and so on. The religious student will think of the seven Ameshaspentas of the Zoroastrian, of the seven Spirits before the throne of God of the Christian; the Theosophist of the supreme Triple LOGOS of the system, with His Ministers, the "Rulers of seven Chains,"[1] round Him, each ruling His own department of the system, as a Viceroy for an Emperor. We are concerned here with but one department in detail. The Solar System contains ten of these, for while rooted in the seven, it develops ten departments, ten being, therefore, by Mystics, called the 'perfect number'. Mr. A. P. Sinnett has well named these departments 'Schemes of Evolution,' and within each of these Schemes humanities are evolving or will evolve. We will now confine ourselves to our own, though never forgetting that the others exist, and that very highly evolved Intelligences may pass from one to another. In fact, such visitors came to our earth at one stage of its evolution, to guide and help our newly-born humanity.

A Scheme of Evolution passes through seven great evolutionary stages, each of which is called a Chain. This name is derived from the fact that a Chain consists of seven Globes, mutually interrelated; it is a chain of seven links, each link a globe. The seven Schemes are shown in Diagram I, around the central sun, and at any one period of time only one of the rings in each Scheme will be active; each ring of each of these seven Schemes is composed of seven globes; these

[1] These have been called Planetary Logoi, but the name often causes confusion, and is therefore here dropped.

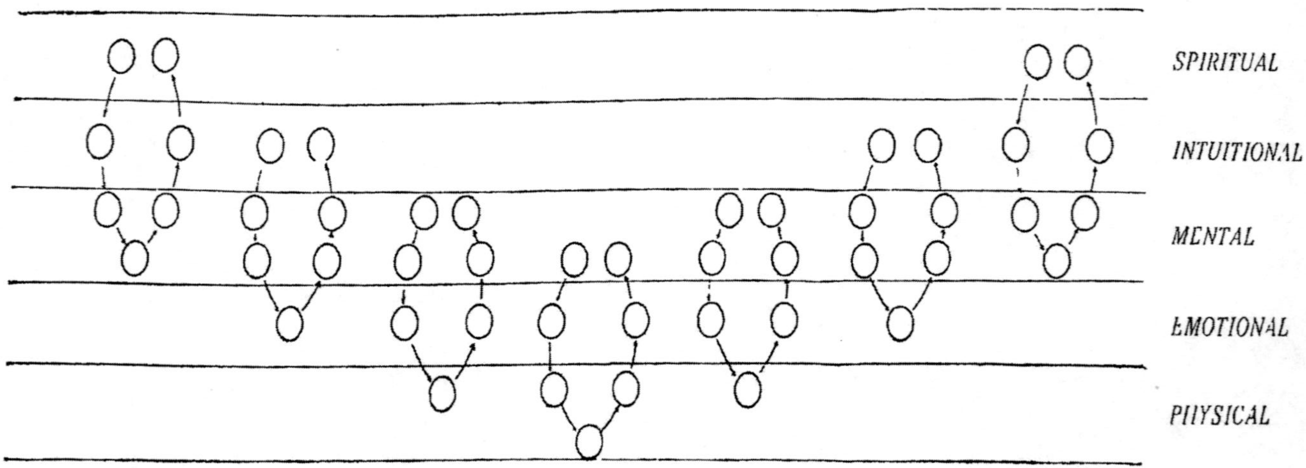

DIAGRAM II

are not figured separately but form what we here have drawn as a ring, in order to save space. The globes are shown in the next Diagram.

In Diagram II we have a single Scheme, figured in the seven stages of its evolution, *i.e.,* in its seven successive Chains; it is now shown in relation to five of the seven spheres, or types, of matter existing in the Solar System; matter of each type is composed of atoms of a definite kind, all the solids, liquids, gases, and ethers of one type of matter being aggregations of atoms of a single kind;[1] this matter is named according to the mood of consciousness to which it responds: physical, emotional, mental, intuitional, spiritual.[2] In the first Chain, its seven Worlds, A, B, C, D, E, F, G, are seen arranged:[3] A and G, the root-world and the seed-world, are on the spiritual plane, for all descends from the higher to the lower, from the subtle to the dense, and climbs again to the higher, enriched with the gains of the journey, the gains serving as seed for the next Chain; B and F are on the intuitional plane, one gathering and the

[1] See *Occult Chemistry,* Annie Besant and C. W. Leadbeater, pp. 5—11.

[2] Physical matter is the matter with which we are daily dealing in our waking life. Emotional matter is that which is set vibrating by desires and emotions, and is called astral in our older books, a name we retain to some extent. Mental matter is that which similarly answers to thoughts. Intuitional matter (buḍḍhic, in Samskṛt) is that which serves as medium for the highest intuition and all-embracing love. Spiritual matter (āṭmic) is that in which the creative Will is potent.

[3] The top left-hand globe is A; the next lower is B; and so on up to G, the top right-hand globe.

other assimilating; C and F are on the higher mental, in similar relationship; D, the turning point, the point of balance between the ascending and descending arcs, is in the lower part of the mental plane. These pairs of globes in every Chain are ever closely allied, but the one is the rough sketch, the other the finished picture. In the second Chain, the globes have all sunk one stage lower into matter, and D is on the emotional plane. In the third Chain, they have sunk yet one stage further, and D reaches the physical plane. In the fourth Chain, and on the fourth only, the midmost Chain of the seven, the most deeply involved in densest matter, the turning point of the Chains as is D of the globes, there are three of the globes—C, D, and E—on the physical plane. On the return journey, as it were, the ascent resembles the descent: in the fifth Chain, as in the third, there is one physical globe; in the sixth, as in the second, globe D is emotional; in the seventh, as in the first, globe D is mental. With the ending of the seventh Chain the Scheme has worked itself out, and its fruitage is harvested.

The seven Schemes of our Solar System may, for convenience sake, be named after the globe D of each, this being the globe best known to us; these are: Vulcan, Venus, Earth, Jupiter, Saturn, Uranus, Neptune (see Diagram I). In the Scheme to which our Earth belongs, the Chain which preceded our terrene Chain was the third of its series, and its one physical globe, globe D, was the globe which is now our Moon; hence the third Chain is called the lunar, while the second

THE SUCCESSIVE LIFE-WAVES

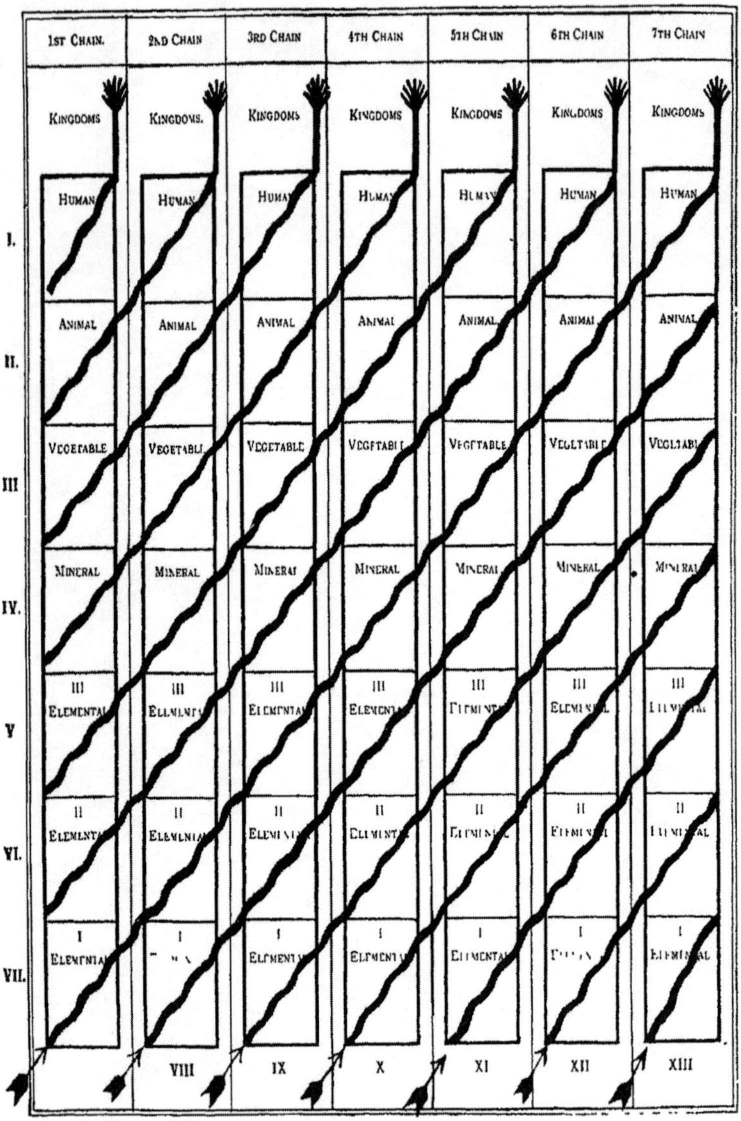

DIAGRAM III.

and first Chains are designated only by numbers; our Earth Chain, or terrene Chain, is the fourth in succession, and has therefore three of its seven globes in physical manifestation, its third globe, C, being what is called the planet Mars, and its fifth globe, E, what is called the planet Mercury. The Neptunian Scheme also, with Neptune as its globe D, has three globes of its Chain in physical manifestation—C and E being the two physical planets connected with it, the existence of which was mentioned in Theosophical literature before they were recognised by Science—and hence has reached the fourth Chain of its series. The Venusian Scheme is reaching the end of its fifth Chain, and Venus has consequently lately lost her Moon, the globe D of the preceding Chain.[1] It is possible that Vulcan, which Herschel saw, but which, it is said, has now disappeared, is in its sixth Chain, but on that we have no information, either direct or mediate. Jupiter is not yet inhabited, but its moons are, by beings with dense physical bodies.

Diagrams III and IV represent the relationships between the seven Chains within a Scheme, showing the evolutionary progress from Chain to Chain. Diagram III should be first studied; it is merely a simplification of Diagram IV, which is a copy of one drawn by a Master; this—though at first sight somewhat bewildering—will be found very illuminative when understood.

Diagram III places the seven Chains in a Scheme as columns standing side by side, in order that

[1] It may be remembered that the Moon of Venus was seen by Herschel.

the divine Life-Streams, figured by the arrows, may be traced from kingdom to kingdom in their ascent. Each section in a column represents one of the seven kingdoms of nature—three elemental, mineral, vegetable, animal, human.[1] Follow Life-Stream 7, the only one which goes through the seven kingdoms within the Scheme; it enters the first Chain at the first Elemental Kingdom, and there develops during the life-period of the Chain; it passes into the second Elemental Kingdom on the second Chain, and develops therein during its life-period; it appears in the third Elemental Kingdom on the third Chain, and enters the Mineral on the fourth; it then successively develops through the Vegetable and Animal Kingdoms on the fifth and sixth Chains, and attains the Human in the seventh. The whole Scheme thus provides a field of evolution for a stream of the divine Life from its ensouling of matter up to man.[2] The remaining streams have either commenced in another

[1] The 'elemental' kingdoms are the three stages of life on its descent into matter—involution—and the seven kingdoms might be figured on a descending and ascending arc, like Chains and globes:

1st Elemental		Human
2nd Elemental		Animal
3rd Elemental		Vegetable
	Mineral	

[2] These seven Life-Streams and the six additional ingresses for the lowest Elemental Kingdom in the remaining six Chains, thirteen in all, are the successive impulses which make up, for this Scheme, what Theosophists call the 'second Life-wave,' *i.e.*, the form-evolving current of Life from the second LOGOS, the Viṣhṇu of the Hinḍū, the Son of the Christian, Trinities.

Scheme and enter this at the point of evolution therein reached, or enter this too late to reach the human kingdom herein.

The study of Diagram IV must be begun by realising that the coloured circles are not seven Chains of *globes,* as might be expected, but the seven Kingdoms of Nature in each successive Chain, and therefore correspond with the sections of columns in Diagram III. We have here a whole Scheme of Evolution, with the place of each Kingdom shown in each Chain. The student should select a line of any colour in the first circle and trace it carefully onwards.

Let us take the blue circle at the top left-hand, pointed out by the arrow; it represents the first Elemental Kingdom on the first Chain. Leaving the first Chain for the second—the next ring of coloured circles—this blue stream divides on arriving there; its least advanced part, which is not ready to go on into the second Elemental Kingdom, breaks off from the main stream and goes again into the first Elemental Kingdom of this second Chain, joining the new Life-stream—coloured yellow and marked with an arrow—which enters on its evolution in that Chain, and being merged in it; the main blue stream goes on into the second Elemental Kingdom of this second Chain, receiving into itself some laggards from the second Elemental Kingdom of the first Chain, assimilating them, and carrying them on with itself; it will be noticed that only a blue stream leaves this Kingdom, the foreign elements having been completely assimilated. The blue stream flows on into the third Chain, divides, leaves its laggards to continue in the second Elemental Kingdom in the third Chain, while the bulk goes on to form the third Elemental Kingdom of this third Chain; again it receives some laggards from the third Elemental Kingdom of the second Chain, assimilates them, and carries them on with itself, an undiluted blue stream, into the Mineral Kingdom of the fourth Chain; as before, it leaves some laggards to evolve themselves in the third Elemental Kingdom of the fourth Chain, and receives some from the Mineral Kingdom of the third Chain, assimilating them as before. It has now reached its densest point in evolution, the Mineral Kingdom. Leaving this—we still follow the blue line—it climbs into the Vegetable Kingdom of the fifth Chain, sending off its laggards to the Mineral Kingdom of this Chain, and taking up the laggards of the Vegetable Kingdom of the fourth Chain. Again it climbs upwards, now into the Animal Kingdom of the sixth Chain, leaving its insufficiently developed vegetables to complete that stage of their evolution in the Vegetable Kingdom of the sixth Chain, and receiving undeveloped animals from the fifth Chain into its own Kingdom. Lastly, it completes its long evolution by entering the Human Kingdom on the seventh Chain, dropping its too undeveloped animals into the Animal Kingdom of the seventh Chain, receiving some human beings from the Human Kingdom of the sixth Chain, carrying them on with itself to its triumphant conclusion, where human evolution is perfected and the superhuman begins, along one or another of the seven paths, indicated in the blue plume at the end. In another

Scheme, those we left as laggards in the Animal Kingdom of the seventh Chain will appear in the Human Kingdom of the first Chain of that new Scheme, and therein reach perfection as men. They will be in the circle corresponding to the grey-brown circle with its plume in the first Chain of the present Diagram.

Each line can be followed in this way from Kingdom to Kingdom in successive Chains. The life in the second, the orange, circle, representing the second Elemental Kingdom in the first Chain—and having therefore, one stage of life in a Chain behind it, or, in other words, having entered the stream of evolution as the first Elemental Kingdom in the seventh Chain of a previous Scheme (see the top left-hand circle with arrow in the seventh Chain in our Diagram)—reaches the Human Kingdom in the sixth Chain and passes on. That in the third circle, purple, with two Kingdoms behind it in a previous Scheme, reaches the Human Kingdom in the fifth Chain and passes on. That in the fourth, the Mineral Kingdom, passes out in the fourth Chain. That in the Vegetable Kingdom passes out in the third Chain; that in the Animal in the second; that in the Human in the first.

The student who will thoroughly master this diagram will find himself in possession of a plan into the compartments of which he can pack any number of details without, in the midst of their complexity, losing sight of the general principles of æonian evolution.

Two points remain: the sub-elemental and the superhuman. The Life-Stream from the LOGOS ensouls matter first in the first, or lowest, Elemental Kingdom; hence when that same stream from the first Chain enters the second Elemental Kingdom on the second Chain, the matter which is to be that of the first Elemental Kingdom on that second Chain has to be ensouled by a new Life-Stream from the LOGOS, and so on with each of the remaining Chains.[1]

When the Human Kingdom is traversed, and man stands on the threshold of His superhuman life, a liberated Spirit, seven paths open before Him for His choosing: He may enter into the blissful omniscience and omnipotence of Nirvāṇa, with activities far beyond our knowing, to become, perchance, in some future world an Avaṭāra, or divine Incarnation: this is sometimes called, 'taking the Ḍharmakāya vesture'. He may enter on 'the Spiritual Period'—a phrase covering unknown meanings, among them probably that of 'taking the Sambhogakāya vesture'. He may become part of that treasure-house of spiritual forces on which the Agents of the LOGOS draw for Their work, 'taking the Nirmāṇakāya vesture'. He may remain a member of the Occult Hierarchy which rules and guards the world in which He has reached perfection. He may pass on to the next Chain, to aid in building up its forms. He may enter the splendid Angel—Ḍeva—Evolution. He may give Himself to the immediate service of the LOGOS, to be used by Him in any part of the Solar System, His

[1] "My Father worketh hitherto and I work." *S. John* v. 17. See in Chapter v. the description of this on our Earth, when the Spirit of the Moon incarnates therein

Servant and Messenger, who lives but to carry out His will and do His work over the whole of the system which He rules. As a General has his Staff, the members of which carry his messages to any part of the field, so are These the Staff of Him who commands all, "Ministers of His that do His pleasure".[1] This seems to be considered a very hard Path, perhaps the greatest sacrifice open to the Adept, and is therefore regarded as carrying with it great distinction. A member of the General Staff has no physical body, but makes one for Himself by Kriyāshakṭi—the 'power to make'—of the matter of the globe to which He is sent. The Staff contains Beings at very different levels, from that of Arhaṭship[2] upwards. There are some who dedicated themselves to it on reaching Arhaṭship in the Moon-Chain; others who are Adepts;[3] others who have passed far beyond this stage in human evolution.

The need for the provision of such a Staff arises probably, among many other reasons unknown to us, from the fact that in the very early stages of the evolution of a Chain—especially of one on the downward arc—or even of a globe, more help from outside is needed than is required later. On the first Chain of our Scheme, for instance, the attainment of the first of the Great Initiations was the appointed level of achievement, and none of its humanity attained Adeptship, which is itself nowhere near Buḍḍhahood; it would therefore

[1] *Psalms*, ciii. 21.

[2] Those who have passed the fourth Great Initiation.

[3] Those who have passed the fifth Great Initiation.

be necessary to supply the higher offices from outside. So again later Chains were helped, and our Earth will have to provide high Officials for the earlier Chains of other Schemes, as well as yielding the normal supply for the later globes and Rounds of our own Chain. Already from our own Occult Hierarchy two Members, within our own knowledge, have left our Earth, either to join the General Staff, or lent by the Head of our Hierarchy to the Head of the Hierarchy of some other globe outside our Scheme.

The human beings who, in any Chain, do not reach by a certain time the level appointed for the Humanity of the Chain, are its 'failures'; the 'failure' may be due to youth and consequent lack of time, or to lack of due exertion, and so on; but, whatever the cause, those who fail to reach a point from which they can progress sufficiently, during the remaining life of a Chain, to attain the required level by its end, drop out of its evolution before that evolution is completed, and are obliged to enter the succeeding Chain at a point determined by the stage already reached, that they may complete their human course. There are others who succeed in passing this crucial point, the 'Day of Judgment' for the Chain, but who yet do not progress with sufficient rapidity to reach the level from which the seven Paths open out. These, though not 'failures,' have not wholly succeeded, and they therefore also pass on into the next Chain and lead its humanity, when that humanity has reached a stage at which the bodies are sufficiently evolved to serve as vehicles for their further progress. We shall find these various classes in our study, and this is but a bird's-eye view of them; the details will make them come out more clearly. Only in the first Chain we noticed no failures dropping out of its evolution. There were some there who did not succeed, but if that Chain had its Day of Judgment, we failed to observe it.

In a single Chain the evolutionary wave sweeps from A to G, using each globe in turn as the field of growth; this circling round the Chain is appropriately named a Round, and seven times the wave sweeps round, ere the life of the Chain is over, its work complete. Then the results are gathered up and garnered, and all form the seed for the succeeding Chain, save Those who, having finished Their course as men, and become Super-men, elect to serve in other ways than in guiding that coming Chain upon its way, and who enter on another of the seven Paths.

To conclude these preliminaries. In the Monadic Sphere, on the super-spiritual level, dwell the Divine Emanations, the Sons of God, who are to take flesh and become Sons of Man in the coming universe. They ever behold the Face of the Father, and are the Angel-Counterparts of men. This divine Son in his own world is technically called a 'Monad,' a Oneness. He it is that, as said on p. 1, is "transformed in the world of life into an immortal Spirit". The Spirit is the Monad veiled in matter, triple therefore in his aspects of Will, Wisdom, and Activity, being the very Monad himself, after he has appropriated the atoms of matter of the spiritual, intuitional and mental sphere, round which his future bodies will be formed. In the Monad wells up the intarissable fount of life; the Spirit, or himself veiled, is his manifestation in a universe. As he gains mastery over matter in the lower sphere, he takes more and more control of the evolutionary work, and all the great choices which decide a man's destiny are made by his Will, guided by his Wisdom, and achieved by his Activity.

CHAPTER II

THE FIRST AND SECOND CHAINS

WE have to face what is practically the only great difficulty of our study at the very outset—the evolutionary cycles on the first and second Chains of our Scheme. A Master said smilingly as to this: "Well, you will be able to see it, but it is doubtful how far you will be able to describe it in intelligible language, so that others may understand." The conditions are so different from all that here we know: the forms are so tenuous, so subtle, so changing; the matter so utterly "the stuff which dreams are made of," that clear voicing of the things seen is well-nigh impossible. Yet however imperfect the description, some description must be essayed, in order to render intelligible the later growth and unfolding; poor as it must be, it may be better than none.

A real 'beginning' may not be found; in the endless chain of living things a link may be studied, fairly complete in itself; but the metal thereof has somewhere slept in the bosom of the earth, has been dug out from some mine, smelted in some furnace, wrought in some workshop, shaped by some hands, ere it appears as a link in a chain. And so with our Scheme. Without previous Schemes it could not be, for its higher inhabitants began not here their evolution. Suffice it, that some of the fragments of Deity, eternal Spirits, who otherwhere had passed through the downward arc—involving themselves in ever-densifying matter through the Elemental Kingdoms, and reaching their lowest point—began in the Mineral Kingdom of this first Chain their upward climbing, their long unfolding in evolving matter; and in that Chain, learning our first evolutionary lessons in that Mineral Kingdom, were we—the humanity of our present earth. It is these consciousnesses that we propose to trace from their life in minerals in the first Chain to their life in men in the fourth. Ourselves part of the humanity of the earth, it is easier to trace this than to trace something entirely alien from ourselves. For in this we are but evoking from the Eternal Memory scenes in which we ourselves played our part, with which we are indissolubly linked, and which we therefore can more easily reach.

Seven centres are seen, forming the first Chain, the first and seventh, as already said, on the spiritual level,[1] the second and sixth on the intuitional,[2] the third and fifth on the higher mental, the fourth on the lower mental. We name them in the fashion of later globes, A and G, B and F, C and E, and in the centre D, the turning point of the cycle. In the first Round of the fourth Chain, which is to some extent a coarse copy of the first Chain, the *Occult Commentary* quoted in *The Secret Doctrine* says of the Earth

[1] Nirvāṇic.

[2] Buḍḍhic.

that it was "a fœtus in the matrix of Space," and the simile recurs to the mind. This Chain is the future worlds in the matrix of thought, the worlds that later are to be born into denser matter. We can scarcely call these centres 'globes'; they are like centres of light in a sea of light, foci of light through which light is rushing, wrought of the very substance of light and only light, yet modified by the flood of light which courses through them; they are as vortex-rings, yet the rings are but light, only distinguishable by their whirling, by the difference of their motion, like whirlpools made only of water in the midst of water; but these are whirlpools of light in the midst of light. The first and seventh centres are both modifications of spiritual matter, the seventh the perfected out-working of the broad outlines visible in the first, the finished picture outwrought from the rough sketch of the divine Artist. There is a humanity there, a very glorified humanity, product of some previous evolution, which is here to complete its human course on this Chain (see the top right hand circle in the first Chain in Diagram IV); hereon each entity will acquire his lowest body—in the fourth globe of each Round—the body of mental matter which is the densest the Chain can give. The level fixed for achievement on this Chain—the non-attainment of which would imply the necessity for rebirth on the following Chain—is the first of the great Initiations, or what corresponds to it there. On this first Chain there are—so far as we could see—none who drop out as failures, and some, as always seems to be the case in later

Chains also, pass far beyond the appointed level; in the seventh Round the members of that humanity who became Initiates entered on one or other of the seven Paths before-mentioned.

All stages of ego-hood appear to be present on this Chain, but the absence of the lower levels of matter to which we are accustomed makes one notable difference in the evolutionary methods that strikes the observer: everything not only starts but also progresses 'above,' there being no below and no 'forms' in the ordinary sense of the word, but only centres of life, living beings without stable forms; there are no physical and emotional worlds—in the first three globes not even a lower mental—from which impulses can surge upwards, calling down the higher in response to ensoul and use the forms already existing on the lower levels. The nearest approach to such action is on globe D, where the animal-like thought-forms reach upwards, attracting the attention of the subtle centres floating above them; then more of the life of the Spirit pulses out into the centres, and they anchor themselves to the thought-forms and ensoul them, and the thought-forms become human.

It is difficult to mark off the successive Rounds; they seem to fade one into the other like dissolving views,[1] and are marked only by slight increases and diminutions of light. Progress is very slow; one recalls the Saṭya Yuga of the Hinḍū Scriptures, where a life lasts for many thousands of

[1] It may be remembered that the first and second Races on our present world also showed something of this peculiarity, though on a level so much lower.

years without much change.[1] The entities unfold very slowly, as rays of magnetised light play upon them; it is like a gestation, like growth within an egg, or of a flower-bud within its sheath. The chief interest of the Chain is in the evolution of the Shining Ones—the Ḍevas, or Angels—those who live habitually on these high levels; while the lower evolutions seem to play a subsidiary part. Humanity is much influenced by these, mostly by their mere presence and by the atmosphere created by them, and occasionally a Shining One may be seen to take a human being almost as a toy or as a pet. The vast angelic evolution helps humanity by its very existence; the vibrations set up by these glorious Spirits play on the lower human types, strengthening and vivifying them. Looking at the Chain as a whole, we saw it as a field for this Angel Kingdom primarily, and only secondarily for humanity; but perchance that may ever be so, and that it is because we are human that we regard the world as so specially our own.

On the fourth globe, now and again a Shining One may be seen deliberately to aid a human being, transferring matter from his own body into the human, and thus increasing the responsiveness and susceptibility of the latter. Such helpers belong to the class of Form-Angels—Rūpa-Ḍevas—who live normally in the lower mental world.

[1] The Hinḍūs divide time into cycles composed of four Yugas, or Ages, that succeed each other, the Saṭya, the first of the series, being the most spiritual and the longest. When the fourth is ended, a new cycle opens, again with a Saṭya.

When we turn to the mineral kingdom, we are among those some of whom will become men on the Moon Chain, and some on the Earth Chain. The consciousness asleep in these minerals is to awaken gradually and to unfold through long stages into the human.

The vegetable kingdom is a little more awake, but very dull and sleepy still; the normal progress herein will carry the ensouling consciousness into the animal kingdom on the second Chain, and into the human on the third.

At present, while we must needs speak of these kingdoms as mineral and vegetable, they are really composed of mere thoughts—thoughts of minerals, thoughts of vegetables, with the Monads who dream in them, as it were, floating over them, sending down faint thrills of life into these airy forms; these Monads are, it would seem, forced now and again to turn attention to them, to feel through them, to sense through them, when some external touch compels a drowsy notice. These thought-forms are as models in the Mind of the Ruler of the Seven Chains, living within Him, products of His meditation, a world of thoughts, of ideas; we see that the Monads who have acquired permanent atoms in some previous Scheme, and who are floating over these thought-forms, attach themselves to them, and become vaguely conscious in and through them. Vague as this consciousness is there are differences in it: the lowest grade can scarcely be called consciousness, the life in the thought-forms of types resembling what we should now call earth, rocks, stones. Monads touching these can scarcely be said to be aware of anything through them, save of pressure, drawing from them a dull stirring of life, showing itself as resistance to the pressure, and thus different from the yet duller life in the chemical molecules unattached to Monads, and sensing no pressure. In the next grade, in the thought-forms resembling what we should now call metals, the sense of pressure is stronger and the resistance to it a little more definite; there is almost an effort to push outwards against it, a reaction causing expansion. When this sub-conscious reaction is in several directions, the thought-model of a crystal is formed. We noticed that when our own consciousness was *in* the mineral, we felt only the sub-conscious re-action; but passing out, and trying to feel the re-action from outside, it figured itself in our consciousness as a vague discontent at the pressure, and a dull resentful effort to resist and push against it. "I feel a discontented sort of mineral," one of us remarked. Probably the Monadic life, seeking expression, did vaguely feel displeasure at its frustration, and this we felt when we came out of the mineral, feeling it in ourselves as we felt it in that part of our consciousness which was at that time outside the rigid form. If we glance hastily forward, we may see that Monads attached to crystals do not enter the next Chain in the lowest forms of vegetable life, but only in the higher, and, passing through those, enter the Moon Chain at its middle point as mammals, becoming individualised there, and taking human birth in its fifth Round.

One most disconcerting fact for observers is that these 'thoughts of minerals' are not immobile, but mobile; a hill, which one expects to be steady, will turn over or float away, or change its form; there is no solid earth, but a shifting panorama. It requires no faith to move these mountains, for they move of themselves.

At the end of this first Chain, all who attained the appointed level set for it—that which, as said before, corresponded to our first Initiation—entered on one or other of the seven Paths, one of these leading to work on the second Chain as the builders of the forms of its humanity, playing to it a part similar to that played later on our earth by the 'Lords of the Moon'.[1] These are called by H. P. Blavatsky 'Asuras,' *i.e.*, 'living beings'; later the term was confined by usage to living beings in whom intellect, but not emotion was developed.[2] Those who did not succeed in reaching this level entered the second Chain for their own further evolution

[1] The Barhiṣhaḍ Piṭṛs of *The Secret Doctrine*.

[2] These Asuras acted on the second Chain as Barhiṣhaḍ Piṭṛs, and on the third as Agniṣhvāṭṭa Piṭṛs, and formed one of the highest classes of the superhuman Mānasapuṭras who came to our earth, according to *The Secret Doctrine*. It must be remembered that these stages are all superhuman; they apparently indicate the superhuman stages of the fifth of the seven Paths named on p. 12. In *The Secret Doctrine* a difficulty is created by the use of this same name of Asuras for those who left the lunar Chain from the first globe of its seventh Round, and who caused trouble on Earth by 'refusing to create'. Readers of *The Pedigree of Man* must correct it by this, and by details given later, for I was led into a mistake by the double use of the word in *The Secret Doctrine*. The human beings can never exist, *as such*, on more than two successive Chains. They must have become Supermen, for such appearance.—A. B.

at its midmost point and led its humanity, at the close of that Chain reaching liberation and being among its 'Lords'; some of these Lords, in turn, worked on the third Chain in building the forms of its humanity.[1] The early humanity on the second Chain was drawn from the animal kingdom of the first; the animal kingdom of the second Chain from the vegetable of the first; while the vegetable kingdom of the second came from the mineral of the first. The three elemental kingdoms on the downward arc of the first Chain passed similarly into the second Chain, filling the mineral kingdom and two of the elemental, while the first elemental kingdom was formed from a new impulse of life from the LOGOS.

In the second Chain, the further descent into matter gives us a globe on the emotional plane, an astral globe, and the denser material makes things a little more coherent and comprehensible. We have then A and G on the intuitional level, B and F on the higher mental, C and E on the lower mental, and D on the emotional. On this lowest globe, things were a little more like those to which we are accustomed though still very strange and weird. Thus things with the general appearance of vegetables moved about with the freedom of animals, though apparently with little, if any, sentiency. They were not anchored to physical matter, and hence were very mobile. The young humanity here lived in close contact with the Shining Ones, who still dominated the evolutionary field, and the

[1] In the nomenclature of the *S. D.* becoming its Barhiṣhaḍ Pitṛs.

Form-Angels and the Desire-Angels—Rūpa Ḍevas and Kāma Ḍevas—strongly, but for the most part unintentionally, influenced human evolution. Passion showed itself in many who now had emotional bodies on globe D, and its germs were visible in animals. Differences were noticeable in the capacity to respond to vibrations sent out, consciously and unconsciously, by the Shining Ones, but changes were very gradual and progress was slow. Later, when the intuitional consciousness unfolded, there was communication between this Scheme and the Scheme of which Venus is now the physical globe; that Scheme is a Chain ahead of ours, and some came to our second Chain from there; but whether they belonged to the Venus humanity, or were members of the 'Staff,' we could not tell.

Great surging clouds of matter, splendid in colour, were a noticeable feature on globe D in the first Round; they became in the following Round denser, more brilliantly coloured, more responsive to vibrations which shaped them into forms, whether vegetable or animal it is hard to say. Much of the work was on the higher levels, a vitalising of subtle matter for future use, showing but little effect on the lower forms. Just as now elemental essence is used to build emotional and mental bodies, so then the Form- and Desire-Angels were seeking to differentiate themselves more fully by using these clouds of matter and living in them. They came down, sub-plane by sub-plane, into denser matter, but were not in this using the human kingdom. Even at the present time a Ḍeva, or Angel, may ensoul a whole country-side, and such action was very general then; the emotional and lower-mental matter formed the bodies of these Angels, changing, intermingling: and incidentally permanent atoms of vegetables, minerals, and even animals, rooting themselves in such Angel-bodies, grew and evolved. The Angels seemed to take no particular interest in them, any more than we interest ourselves in the evolution of microbes within ourselves; now and then, however, some interest was shown in an animal, and its capacity to respond increased rapidly under such conditions.

Studying vegetable consciousness in the second Chain—in which we, who now are human, were living in the vegetable world—we find a dim awareness of forces playing on it, and a certain sense of compulsion towards growth. In some, there was a feeling of the want to grow, the wish to grow; as one of the investigators remarked: "I am trying to flower." In others there was a slight resistance to the line of growth impressed, and a vague groping after another self-chosen direction. Some seemed to try to *use* any forces that contacted them, and in their germinal consciousness held that all around existed for them. Some tried to push out in a direction which attracted them, and were frustrated and became vaguely resentful; one, forming part of a Ḍeva, was observed to be thus hindered, since the Ḍeva was naturally arranging things to suit himself, and not any constituents of his body. On the other hand, from the obscure view-point of the vegetable, the Deva's proceedings were as incomprehensible as the weather is to us in these days, and often as troublesome.

Towards the end of the Chain, the more highly developed vegetables were showing a little mind, in fact a fair baby intelligence, recognising the existence of external animals, liking the neighbourhood of some and shrinking from others. And there was a craving for more cohesion, evidently the result of the downward push of life into matter of greater density, the Will working in Nature for descent into denser levels. Without the physical anchorage the emotional forms were very unstable, and tended to float about vaguely and without purpose.

In the seventh Round of this Chain a considerable number dropped out from its humanity as failures, having fallen too far behind to find suitable forms; and they went on later into the third, the Moon Chain, as men. Others reached the level now marked by the third Initiation, the level appointed for success on the second Chain, and entered on one of the seven Paths, one, as before, leading to the next Chain for work thereon. Those who were not failures, but had not reached perfect success, went on to the third Chain, entering it at the Round suitable for the stage previously reached. The foremost from the animal kingdom individualised on the second Chain, and began their human evolution on the Moon Chain, passing through its lower kingdoms very rapidly and becoming men; they then led evolution on that Chain until the classes already mentioned--first the failures, and then those who had not achieved perfect success dropped in from the second Chain and became successively the leaders. The foremost from the second Chain vegetable kingdom entered the Moon Chain Animal Kingdom as mammals, in its fourth Round, not passing through the infusoria and lower animal types—fishes and reptiles; the rest came in, in its first Round, as animals of the lower types. The consciousnesses in the second Chain Mineral Kingdom passed on into the Vegetable Kingdom in the Moon Chain, and the Mineral Kingdom was filled from the highest Elemental Kingdom of the second Chain. As before, the lowest Elemental Kingdom was filled by a new wave of life from the LOGOS.

An important principle may here be mentioned; each of the seven sub-planes which make up a plane is again divided into seven; hence a body, while containing matter of all the sub-planes in its constitution, will show activity only in the subdivisions corresponding to the number of the Chains or Rounds already experienced, or in the course of being experienced. A man working in the second Round of the second Chain will be able to use in his emotional and mental bodies only the first and second subdivisions of each sub-plane of astral and mental matter; in the third Round he will be able to use the first, second and third, though not so fully as regards the third as he will do when he shall be in the third Round of the third Chain, and so on. Thus later on, in our Earth Chain, man in the second Round was working at and through the first and second subdivisions of each of the sub-planes, and feebly in the third and fourth, as he was in the fourth Chain; so that, while he had matter of all the sub-planes in him, it was only the two lower subdivisions of the two lower sub-planes that were fully active, and through these only could his consciousness fully work. Not until the seventh Race of our seventh Round will man possess the splendid body in which every particle will thrill responsive to himself, and even then not as perfectly as in later Chains.

CHAPTER III

EARLY TIMES ON THE MOON CHAIN

ON the Moon Chain—the third in succession—there is a deeper plunge into matter, and the middle globe is on the physical plane; A and G are on the higher mental, B and F on the lower mental, C and E on the emotional, and D on the physical. This middle globe, the scene of the greatest activity in the Chain, is still surviving as the Moon, but the Moon is only what is left of it after much loss ot material, its inner core, as it were, after the disintegration of the crust, a globe much diminished in size, on its way to total wreck—a corpse, in fact.

Following the evolving consciousnesses which we have seen as minerals on the first Chain, as vegetables on the second, we find the crest of the advancing wave which bears us within it entering the third Chain as mammals at its middle point, appearing on globe D, the Moon, in the fourth Round. These mammals are curious creatures, small but extraordinarily active; the most advanced of them are monkey-like in form, making enormous leaps. The fourth Round creatures are as a rule at first scaly in skin, and later the skin is frog-like; then the more advanced types develop bristles, which form a very coarse harsh fur. The air is altogether different from our present atmosphere, heavy and stifling, reminding one of choke-damp, but it obviously suits the Moon inhabitants. The consciousnesses we are following take the bodies of small mammals, long in body and short in legs, a mixture of weasel, mongoose and prairie-dog, with a short scrubby tail, altogether clumsy and ill-finished; they are red-eyed, and able to see in the darkness of their holes; coming out of the holes, they raise themselves on their hind legs, which form a tripod with the short strong tail, and turn their heads from side to side, sniffing. These animals are fairly intelligent, and the relations between the lunar animals and men, in this district at least, seem more friendly than between wild animals and men on our earth; these creatures are not domesticated, but do not scuttle away when men appear on the scene. In other parts, where men are mere savages, eating their enemies when they can get them, and animals when man-flesh is unobtainable, the wild creatures are timid, and fly from human neighbourhood.

After this first stage of animal life, comes a spell as creatures that live much in the trees, the limbs double-jointed, the feet padded; the feet are curiously modified, with a thumb-like projection at right-angles to the limb, like the spur of a cock, armed with a curving claw; running rapidly along the underside of branches, the animal uses this to hold on by, the remaining part of the feet being useless; but when moving on the ground it walks on the pads, and the spur sticks out behind, above the ground level, and does not impede movement.

Other animals, more highly developed than these and far more intelligent, monkey-like in form, live habitually in human settlements, and attach themselves strongly to the men of their time, serving them in various ways. These become individualised on globe D of this fourth Round, and on globes E, F and G develop human, emotional and mental bodies, the causal, though fully formed, showing but little growth. These will leave the Moon Chain in the middle of the seventh Round, as we shall see, and thus go through, on the Moon Chain, three Rounds of development as men. Among these, individualised in a small community living in the country, are observed the present Masters, Mars and Mercury, who are now at the head of the Theosophical Society, and who are to be the Manu and Bodhisattva[1] of the sixth Root Race on our earth, in the present fourth Round of the terrene Chain.

The consciousnesses of the animals we are following, after the death of their last bodies on globe D, practically slept through the remainder of the fourth Round and through the first three globes of the fifth; losing their emotional and inchoate mental bodies very shortly after the death of the physical ones, and having no causal, they remained sleeping in a sort of heaven with pleasant dreams, without touch with the manifested worlds, the gulf between them and those worlds

[1] The official titles of the Heads—the King and the Priest, the Ruler and the Teacher—of a Root Race.

unbridged. On globe D of the fifth Round, they were again thrown down into bodies and appeared as large monkey-like creatures, leaping forty feet at a bound, and appearing to enjoy making tremendous springs high into the air. In the time of the fourth human race on this globe D they became domesticated, acting as guardians of their masters' property and as playmates of the children of the household, much as faithful watch-dogs may be now, carrying the children on their backs and in their arms, and developing intense affection for their human masters; the children nestled delightedly in their thick soft fur, and enjoyed the huge bounds of their faithful guardians. One scene may act as a type of the individualisation of such creatures.

There is a hut in which dwells a Moon-man, his wife and children; these we know in later times under the names of Mars and Mercury, the Mahāguru and Sūrya.[1] A number of these monkey-creatures live round the hut, and give to their owners the devotion of faithful dogs; among them we notice the future Sirius, Herakles, Alcyone and Mizar, to whom we may give their future names for the purpose of recognition, though they are still

[1] See 'Rents in the Veil of Time' in *The Theosophist* of 1910, 1911. The Mahāguru is the Lord Gauṭama, Sūrya is the Lord Maiṭreya. Why did these animals come into this close connection with those who were to be their Masters on the then far-off Earth? Had they been plants tended by them, as we tend our plants now, in the higher cases—for the Lords Gauṭama and Maiṭreya were men on the second Chain—or in the lower cases animals and plants that had an affinity for each other?

non-human. Their astral and mental bodies have grown under the play of their owners' human intelligence, as those of domesticated animals now develop under our own; Sirius is devoted chiefly to Mercury, Herakles to Mars; Alcyone and Mizar are passionately attached servants of the Mahāguru and Sūrya.

One night there is an alarm; the hut is surrounded by savages, supported by their domesticated animals, fierce and strong, resembling furry lizards and crocodiles. The faithful guardians spring up around their masters' hut and fight desperately in its defence; Mars comes out and drives back the assailants, using some weapon they do not possess; but, while he drives them backward, a lizard-like creature darts behind him into the hut, and catching up the child Sūrya, begins to carry him away. Sirius springs at him, bears him down, and throws the child to Alcyone, who carries him back into the hut, while Sirius grapples with the lizard, and, after a desperate struggle, kills it, falling senseless, badly mangled, over its body. Meanwhile a savage slips behind Mars and stabs at his back, but Herakles, with one leap, flings himself between his master and the weapon, and receives the blow full on his breast, and falls, dying. The savages are now flying in all directions, and Mars, feeling the fall of some creature against his back, staggers, and, recovering himself, turns. He recognises his faithful animal defender, bends over his dying servant, and places his head in his lap.

The poor monkey lifts his eyes, full of intense devotion, to his master's face, and the *act* of service done, with passionate desire to save, calls down a stream of response from the Will aspect of the Monad in a fiery rush of power, and in the very moment of dying the monkey individualises, and thus he dies—a man.

Our damaged monkey, Sirius, has been very much chewed up by his lizard-enemy, but is still living, and is carried within the hut; he lives for a considerable time, a crippled wreck, and can only drag himself about with difficulty. It is touching to see his dumb fidelity to his mistress; his eyes follow her everywhere as she moves about; the child Sūrya nurses him tenderly, and his monkey comrades, Alcyone and Mizar, hang round him; gradually his intelligence, fed by love, grows stronger, until the lower mind, reaching up, draws down response from the higher, and the causal body flashes into being, shortly before his death. Alcyone and Mizar live on after his death for some time, one-pointed devotion to the Mahāguru and Sūrya their most marked characteristic, until the emotional body, instinct with this pure fire, calls down an answer from the intuitional plane, and they also reach individualisation, and pass away.

These cases are good instances of the three great types of methods of individualisation,[1] in each of which the downflow of the higher life is through one aspect of the Triple Spirit, through Will, through Wisdom, through active Intellect. Action reaches up and calls down Will; Love reaches up and calls down Wisdom; Mind reaches up and

[1] See on this C. W. Leadbeater's 'Modes of Individualisation,' in *The Inner Life*, vol. ii, § 6.

calls down Intellect. These are the three 'Right Ways' of Individualisation. Others there are, that we shall turn to in a moment, reflexions of these in denser matter, but these are 'Wrong Ways' and lead to much sorrow.

Henceforth these consciousnesses that we have been specially following are definitely human, and have the same causal bodies which they still use; they are in globe E as human beings, but are not taking any definite part in its ordinary life. They float about in its atmosphere like fishes in water, but are not sufficiently advanced to share in its normal activities. The new emotional body on globe E is produced by a kind of protuberance formed round the emotional permanent atom; the newly individualised are not born as children of its inhabitants, who, it may be said in passing, are not prepossessing in appearance; their real progress as human beings cannot be said to begin until they land again on globe D in the sixth Round. Some consolidation and improvement there certainly is—in the emotional body floating in the atmosphere of globe E, in the mental similarly floating in that of globe F, and in the causal likewise in that of globe G. This improvement is shown in the descent through the atmospheres of globes A, B and C of the sixth Round, wherein the matter drawn into each body is better of its kind, and is more coherent. But, as said, the effective progress is on globe D, whereon physical matter is once more donned.

Among the advanced animals in this fifth Round, living in contact with primitive human beings, there are some who are of interest because they later drift together into a type founded on a similarity of the method of individualisation. They individualise in one of the 'Wrong Ways' aforesaid. They try to imitate the human beings among whom they are, in order to gain credit for superiority with their fellow-animals, strutting about, full of vanity, and constantly 'showing off'. They are monkey-like creatures, much like those previously observed, but distinctly cleverer and with more imaginative, or, at least, imitative faculty, and they play at being human beings, as children play at being grown up. They individualise by this intense vanity, which stimulates the imitative faculty to an abnormal degree, and causes a strong feeling of separation, an emphasising of the dawning 'I' of the animal, until the effort to be distinguished from others calls down an answer from the higher levels, and the ego is formed. But the effort to rise above their fellows, without either admiration or love for any one above them, to rise only in order that they may look down, does nothing to change animal passions into human emotions, and lays no foundation for future harmonious growth of the emotional and intellectual natures. They are independent, self-centred, self-sufficient, each thinking of himself only, with no thought of co-operation, or union for a common purpose. When they die, after becoming individualised, they dream away the interval between death and re-birth on globe D in the sixth Round, much in the same way as did the other individualised animals described, but with one difference—a difference of enormous import to the lines of growth—that in the previous cases the new human beings had their minds fixed lovingly on their adored owners of globe D, and their emotions were thus strengthened and improved, whereas those individualised by vanity fixed their minds only on themselves and their own excellences, and hence had no emotional growth of love.

Another set of animals is individualised by admiration of the human beings with whom they come into contact, and they also seek to imitate them, not because they wish to outstrip their fellows, but because they regard the human beings as superior and wish to be like them. There is no strong love of them or wish to serve them, but there is much desire to be taught and great readiness to obey, growing out of the admiration felt for them as superior beings. They are trained by their owners, first to perform tricks and then to do trifling services, and in this way they grow into a certain sense of co-operation with their owners; they try to please them and to win their approval, not because they care specially for them, but because the permitted co-operation, resulting from the approval won, brings them nearer to the greater beings with whom they work. When they individualise through the growth of intelligence, the intellect is ready to submit to discipline, to cooperate, to see the advantages of united effort, and the necessity for obedience. They carry into their intermediate existence this sense of united work and willingness to submit to direction, to their own great advantage in the future.

Another type is developed along a most unfortunate line, that of mind rendered keen and alert by fear; animals hunted for food or owned by savage types of men, and often cruelly treated, may reach individualisation by efforts to escape cruelty, by planning how to escape when chased; they develop craft and cunning and similar faculties, showing a distorted ingenuity bred of fear, with much suspicion, distrust and revengefulness. When the mind has been thus strengthened to a certain point in contact with man, albeit along most undesirable lines, individualisation results; in one case we observed that a creature's mate was killed, and there was a great rush of hatred and passionate revenge, causing individualisation; in another a lynx-like animal individualised by an intense desire to inflict pain, as yielding a sense of power over others; but here again the stimulus was a malign human influence and example. The long interval between individualisation and re-birth is in these cases filled with dreams of successful escapes, of treacherous revenges, and of cruelties inflicted on those who misused them during their last animal lives. The unfortunate result throws responsibility on the man who caused it, and makes a link in future lives; it would perhaps be not unreasonable to regard all such individualisations as premature —"taking the human shape too soon". We shall find these types again in the sixth Round, working out their new humanity along the lines determined by their respective methods of individualisation. It would seem as though only the three kinds of individualisations caused by a downflow from above were in the Plan, and that the forcing upward from below was brought about by the wrong-doing of man.

Ere following both these and our friends of other types into their lives on globe D on the sixth Round, we may glance at the higher civilisation of the cities of the Moon Chain in this, its fifth, Round. There were many communities scattered over the globe leading distinctly primitive lives; some, like those in the hut already mentioned, who were kindly, although little developed, fighting vigorously when attacked, while others were savage, quarrelsome and continually at war, apparently for the mere lust of blood-shedding and cruelty. In addition to these various communities, some large, some small, some nomad, some pastoral, there were more highly civilised people, living in cities, carrying on trades, ruled by settled governments. There did not appear to be much in the way of what we should call a nation; a city and a considerable—sometimes a very extensive—area around it, with scattered villages, formed a separate State, and these States entered into fluctuating agreements with each other as to trade, mutual defence, etc.

One sample may serve as illustration. Near what corresponds to the Equator is a great city—but it looks more like a cemetery—with a large extent of cultivated land round it. The city is built in separate quarters, according to the class of inhabitants. The poorer people live out of doors during the day, and at night, or when it rains, crawl under flat roofs, reminding one of dolmens, which lead into oblong holes, or chambers, cut out of the rocks. These are like underground burrows going a long way and communicating with each other, a regular labyrinth; the entrance-door is made of a huge slab of stone, resting on upright smaller stones as pillars. These rooms are massed together—thousands of them—lining the two sides of one long circular street, and forming the outside ring of the city.

The higher classes live in the domed houses within this ring, built on a higher level, with a wide terrace in front, forming a ring right round like the road below; the domes are supported on short strong pillars, carved all over, the carving showing a fairly well-advanced civilisation. An immense number of these domes are joined together at the lower edge, and make a kind of community city, a belt, with again a circular terrace above its inner edge. The centre of the city is its highest part, and there the houses themselves are taller, with three domes, rising one above another; the central one has five domes, one on the top of the other, each successive dome being smaller than the one below it. The upper ones are reached by steps inside one of the pillars on the ground floor, and winding round the central pillar above. It seems as though these had been hewn out of a pinnacle of living rock. In the higher domes no provision seems to be made for light and air. The highest dome has a kind of hammock hanging from the centre, and this is the prayer room; it appears that any one who is praying must not touch the ground during his prayer.

This is evidently the highest humanity of the Moon, who will later become the Lords of the Moon, reaching the Arhaṭ level, the goal set for the lunar evolution. They are already civilised, and in one room a boy is writing, in a script which is wholly unintelligible to us.

Those of the lunar humanity who in this Round were entering on the Path were in touch with a loftier band of Beings, the Hierarchy of the time, who had come over from the second Chain to help evolution on the third. These lived on a lofty and practically inaccessible mountain, but Their presence was realised by those on the Path, and was generally accepted as a fact by the intelligent humanity of the time. Their disciples reached Them when out of the body, and occasionally one of Them descended into the plains, and lived for a while among men. The dwellers in the central house of the city just described were in touch with These, and were influenced by Them in matters of serious concern.

CHAPTER IV

THE SIXTH ROUND ON THE MOON CHAIN

WE come again to Globe D, but now in the sixth Round, and our individualised animals are born into it as men of a simple and primitive, but not savage and brutal, type. They are not handsome according to our present ideas of beauty—hair ragged, lips thick, noses squat, and wide at the base. They are living on an island, and food has run short, so that, in his first fully human life, Herakles appears on the scene engaged in a vigour-ous struggle with another savage for the corpse of an eminently undesirable-looking animal. Fighting among the islanders themselves does not seem usual, and only occurs when food runs short; but there is much of it in repulsing, from time to time, the invasions from the mainland, where the savages are particularly brutal cannibals, fiendishly cruel, and much dreaded by their gentler neigh-bours. These unpleasant neighbours cross the straits on primitive looking rafts, and pour over the island, destroying as they go. They are regarded as demons by the islanders, who nevertheless fight fiercely in self-defence. The islanders kill all whom they take prisoners, but do not, like the mainland savages, either torture them living, or eat them dead.

These savages of the mainland are from those who became individualised by fear in the fifth Round, and among them may be recognised Scorpio, whose hatred of Herakles, so prominent in future lives, may here have had its root, as even in this very primitive humanity they are in opposed tribes and fight furiously against each other. Scorpio, in Herakles' second life in this community, leads an attack on a tribe inhabiting the island, presently to be mentioned, and Herakles was in a rescue party, which assailed the savages on their return home, and succeeded in crushing them, and in saving a wounded captive of a much more evolved type, who was being kept for torture.

Among the islanders at this same time we find Sirius, and also Alcyone and Mizar; there do not seem to be any special relationships—life is communal, and people live promiscuously—beyond those which are formed by personal attractions in any one life. The intervals between death and re-birth are very short, a few years at most, and our savages are re-born in the same community. The second life shows advance, for help comes from outside which quickens their evolution.

A stranger lands upon the island, a man of much higher type and lighter complexion—a clear bright blue—than the muddy-brown islanders, who cluster round him with much curiosity and admiration. He comes to civilise the islanders, who are docile and teachable, in order to incorporate them in the Empire, from the capital city of which he has come. He begins by astonishing them. He puts water into a bowl made of the shell of a fruit, and, taking a small seed-like ball out of his pocket, he drops it into the water; it catches fire and he lights some dry leaves and presently has a blazing fire, the first fire seen by the savages, who promptly run away and climb up trees, gazing down with terrified eyes at this strange leaping shining creature. He coaxes them down gradually, and they approach timidly, and, finding that nothing harmful ensues, and that the fire is pleasant at night, they incontinently decide that he is a God, and proceed to worship him, and also the fire. His influence being thus established, he further teaches them to cultivate the ground, and they grow a vegetable, like a species of cactus, but red-leaved, which produces underground tubers, somewhat resembling yams; he cuts open the thick stems and leaves, dries them in the sun, and shows them how to make a kind of thick soup with them. The inside pith of the stems is a little like arrowroot, and the juice, squeezed out, yields a coarse sweet sugar. Herakles and Sirius are close comrades, and in their clumsy ignorant way discuss this stranger's proceedings, both feeling much attracted to him.

Meanwhile, a party of savages from the mainland had attacked a tribe living at some distance from the settlement of our tribe, had killed most of the men, carrying off a few as prisoners, with all the women of marriageable age and the children, and killing the elder women; the children were carried off as animals might have been—merely as specially delicious food. A wounded fugitive arrived at the village with the news, and implored the fighting men to rescue the unhappy captives; Herakles and a troop went off, not averse to a fray, and falling on the savages when they were heavy with gormandising, succeeded in killing the whole band, with the exception of Scorpio, who was absent. In a hut they found a wounded man, evidently, from his colour, of the same race as the stranger who had come to the island, who was being kept with a view to torture, and subsequent feasting on what remained of him. He was lifted on a litter of crossed spears—if long sharpened sticks may be so designated—and carried back to the island, with two or three rescued captives, and the younger women who had been kept alive. Sorely wounded as he was, he gave a cry of joy on recognising the stranger, a well-loved friend from the same city as himself, and he was taken into the stranger's hut. There he remained until well, and recounted how he had been sent to exterminate the savage tribes on the mainland coasts; his army had been surrounded and annihilated instead, himself and some of his officers and men having been captured alive. They had been put to death with horrible tortures, but he was left for awhile to gain strength, being too weak to promise amusement by long resistance to torture, and had thus been saved. Herakles nursed him in his rude way with dog-like devotion, and sat for hours listening as the friends—Mars and Mercury—talked together in a tongue to him wholly unknown. Mercury was something of a doctor, and his friend grew rapidly better under his care, his wounds healing and his strength returning.

The people were becoming a little more civilised under the influence of Mercury, and when Mars, recovered, decided to return to the city, Mercury resolved to remain awhile with the devoted tribe he was educating. An expedition was sent off to convoy Mars through the dangerous belt inhabited by the man-eating savages, and a small escort accompanied him as far as the city, Herakles insisting on becoming his servant, and refusing to leave him. There was much rejoicing in the city on his return, as the people had thought him dead; the news of the destruction of his army and of his own narrow escape roused great excitement, and preparations for a new expedition were at once set on foot.

The city was distinctly civilised, with large and handsome buildings in the better quarters, and an immense number of shops. There were many domesticated animals, some of them used for draught purposes and for riding. Commerce was carried on with other cities, and there was a system of canals connecting the city with many at great distances. The city itself was divided into quarters, the different classes inhabiting different parts of it; in the centre of it the people were of a distinctly high type and blue complexion, and the ruler and his highest nobles were in touch with a group of people living secluded in a somewhat inaccessible region. These people, some of whom will be known later as the Lords of the Moon, were themselves pupils of still more exalted Beings, who had come thither from some other sphere. Some of the humanity of the Moon succeeded in going beyond the Arhaṭ Initiation, and their superiors were evidently from a humanity which had reached a far higher stage.

It was from These that an order reached the Ruler of the city—which was the capital of a large Empire—for the extermination of the savages of the mainland coasts; the expedition was led by Virāj—who looked much like a North American Indian—with Mars under him, and was an overwhelming force. Against such a body the poorly armed and undisciplined savages had no chance, and they were completely annihilated; Scorpio, once more, was the chief of a band, and he and the men with him fought desperately to the last. Herakles followed Mars as his servant and fought under him, and when the battles were over, and it was decided to transplant the docile savages from the island to the mainland, and to incorporate them as a colony of the Empire, Sirius and Herakles met again, to their mutual delight, as great according to their small capacity as the deeper joy of Mars and Mercury on their higher level. Mercury took his people over to the mainland and established them there as cultivators of the soil, and then returned to the city with Mars, Herakles persuading Sirius—who was nothing loth—to accompany them. Thus the two became dwellers in the city, and there lived to a great age, attaching themselves very decidedly to their respective masters, whom they regarded as Deities, as belonging to a divine race and omnipotent.

The extermination of the savages—though done in obedience to an order that none dared to disobey—was regarded by the soldiers, and even by most of the officers, as only part of a political plan of conquest, intended to enlarge the borders of the Empire; these tribes stood in the way, and therefore had to be cleared out of it. From the higher standpoint, a stage had been reached beyond which these savages were incapable of advancing on the Moon Chain, bodies suitable to their low stage of evolution being no longer available. Hence, as they died, or were killed off, they were not re-born, but passed into a condition of sleep; many bodies of similarly low types were annihilated by seismic catastrophes which laid whole districts waste, and the population of the globe was very much diminished. It was the 'Day of Judgment' of the Moon Chain, the separation between those who were capable and those who were incapable of further progress on that Chain, and from that time forward all was directed towards the pressing forward as rapidly as possible of those who remained; it was a preparation of the remaining population for evolution on another Chain.

It may be noted that, at this time, the year was, roughly, of about the same length as at present; the relation of the globe to the sun was similar, but was different as regards the constellations.

The whole tribe partially civilised by Mercury escaped the dropping out, while in the city, Herakles and Sirius, together with the households and dependents of Mars and Mercury[1] also just slipped over the

[1] In the household of Mars were: Herakles, Siwa, Corona, Vajra, Capella, Pindar, Beatrix, Lutetia, Theodoros, Ulysses, Aurora. In the household of Mercury: Sirius, Alcyone, Mizar, Orion, Achilles, Hector, Albireo, Olympia, Aldebaran, Leo, Castor, Rhea.

dividing line, by virtue of their attachment to their respective leaders; they married—if the term may be applied to the loose connections of that time—into the low-class city population, and incarnation succeeded incarnation in the lower classes of the more civilised people of the time, with very little progress, intelligence being very poor and development very slow. Sirius, in one birth, was observed as a small tradesman, the shop being a hole ten feet square, in which he sold things of various kinds. Herakles, twelve lives further on, was seen as a woman labouring in the fields, advanced enough to cook her rats and other edibles instead of eating them raw, and with a whole pack of brothers as husbands—Capella, Pindar, Beatrix, Lutetia. Women were scarce at the time, and a plurality of husbands was very common.

Very many lives later, improvement was visible; the members of the above-named groups were no longer so primitive, and others had come up below them, but they were only very small employers of labour, shop-people and farmers, and they did not go much beyond that stage on the Moon. In one life to which our attention was attracted by the curious agricultural proceedings, Sirius was the wife of a small farmer, who employed other men. The harvest was rather a nightmare. Much of the vegetation belonged to what we should now call the fungus family, but gigantic and monstrous. There were trees which grew to a great height in a single year, and which were semi-animal. The cut-off branches writhed like snakes and coiled round the axe-wielders, contracting as they died; red sap, like blood, gushed out under the strokes of the axe, and the texture of the tree was fleshy; it was carnivorous, and during its growth, seized any animal that touched it, coiling its branches round it like an octopus, and sucking it dry. The harvesting of this crop was considered to be very dangerous, and only very strong and skilful men took part in it. When the tree was cut down and the branches lopped off, they were left to die; then, when all movement had ceased, the rind was stripped off and was made into a kind of leather, and the flesh cooked and eaten.

Many of the growths we must call plants were semi-animal and semi-vegetable; one had a large umbrella-like top, with a slit in the middle which allowed the two halves, armed with teeth, to open out; it bent over, with these jaws gaping open, hanging above the ground, and any animal brushing against it was seized, and the two halves closed over it; then the stem straightened itself, and the closed halves again formed the umbrella surface, while the animal within them was slowly sucked dry. These were cut down when the jaws were above and closed, and the skill required consisted in leaping out of reach, as the top swooped downwards to seize the aggressor.

Insect life was voluminous and gigantic, and served largely as food to the carnivorous trees. Some insects were fully two feet long, and of most formidable aspect, and were greatly dreaded by the human inhabitants. The houses were built as quadrangles, enclosing very large courtyards; these were covered in with strong network, and in the seasons when the large insects were about, the children were not allowed to go outside these enclosures.

Those who individualised in the fifth Round by vanity were born for the most part into city populations, and life after life they tended to drift together by similarity of tastes and contempt for others, even though their dominating idiosyncrasy of vanity led to much quarrelling and often-repeated ruptures among themselves. Separateness became much intensified, the mental body strengthening in an undesirable way, and becoming more and more of a shell, shutting out others. The emotional body, as they repressed animal passions, grew less powerful, for the animal passions were starved out by a hard and cold asceticism, instead of being transmuted into human emotions; sex-passion, for instance, was destroyed instead of being changed into love. The result was that they had less feeling, birth after birth, and physically tended towards sexlessness, and while they developed individualism to a high point, this very development led to constant quarrels and rioting. They formed communities, but these broke up again, because no one would obey; each wanted to rule. Any attempt to help or guide them, on the part of more highly developed people, led to an outburst of jealousy and resentment, it being taken as a plan to manage or belittle them. Pride grew stronger and stronger, and they became cold and calculating, without pity and without remorse. When the tide of life flowed onwards into the fifth globe—of emotional matter—they remained in activity for but a short time, the emotional body being dwarfed until it became atrophied, and on the sixth globe the mental body became hardened and lost plasticity, leading to a curious truncated effect, by no means attractive—reminding one, indeed, oddly, of a man who had lost his legs from the knee downwards, and had his trousers sewn up over the stumps.

The type which in the previous Round individualised by admiration, and was docile and teachable, also tended to come mostly into city populations, and formed the better class of labourers at first, rising through the lower middle class to the upper, and developing intelligence to a very considerable extent. They were free from the excessive pride of the preceding type—the pride which deeply tinged their auras with orange—and showed a clear, bright, and rather golden yellow. They were not devoid of emotion, but their emotions, while leading them to co-operation and to obedience to those wiser than themselves, were selfish rather than loving. They saw clearly that co-operation brought about better results than strife, and they co-operated for their own advantage rather than with any desire to spread happiness among others. They were much more intelligent than the people whom we have been specially following, and their orderliness and discipline quickened their evolution. But they gave the impression of having developed in their mental bodies (by a clear vision of what was most to their own advantage) the qualities which should have had their roots in their emotional bodies, founded in and nourished by love and devotion. Hence the emotional bodies were insufficiently developed, though not atrophied as in the previously mentioned type. But they also profited little by their sojourn on globe E, while considerably improving their mental bodies on globe F.

Globes E, F and G, were most useful to the groups of egos who had individualised in one of the three 'Right Ways,' and were hence developing in an all-round, rather than in a lop-sided, fashion, as was the case with those who individualised in the 'Wrong Ways,' so far as intelligence was concerned; but, after all, these egos would be compelled later to develop the emotions they had in the early days stunted or neglected. In the long run, all powers have to be completely developed; and in gazing at the huge sweep of evolution from nescience to omniscience, the progress or the methods at any particular stage lose the immense importance which they appear to have as they loom through the mists of our ignorance and propinquity.

As these three globes on the ascending arc of the sixth Round came successively into activity, very great emotional and mental progress was made by the more advanced egos. As only those were embodied on them who had passed over the critical period, the 'Day of Judgment' on the Moon Chain, there were no hopeless laggards to be a clog on evolution, and growth was steady and more rapid than before. When the Round was over, preparations began to be made for the exceptional conditions of the final Round, the seventh, during which all the inhabitants, and much of the substance, of the Moon Chain were to be transferred to its successor, that in which our Earth is the fourth, or central, globe.

CHAPTER V

THE SEVENTH ROUND ON THE MOON CHAIN

THE Seventh Round of a Chain differs from the preceding Rounds in that its globes, one by one, pass into quiescence on the way to disintegration, as their inhabitants leave them for the last time. When the period arrives for this final departure from each globe, such of its inhabitants as are capable of further evolution on the Chain pass on, as in earlier Rounds, to the next globe; while the others, for whom the conditions of the later globes are unsuitable, leave the Chain altogether when they leave the globe, and remain in a state hereafter to be described, awaiting re-embodiment on the next Chain. Thus the stream of departures from each globe on this Round—leaving out any who may have attained the Arhaṭ level—divides into two, some going on as usual to the globe next in succession, while others take ship to sail over an ocean, the further shore of which is the next Chain.

Normally, a man is free to leave a Chain—unless dropped out as temporarily hopeless—only when he has reached the level appointed for the humanity evolved on the Chain. That level in the Moon Chain, we have already seen, was equivalent to that which we now call the fourth, or Arhaṭ, Initiation. But we found, much to our surprise, that, on the seventh Round, groups of emigrants departed from globes A, B and C, while the huge mass of the population of globe D left the Moon Chain finally as the life-wave quitted that globe to roll onwards to globe E. Only a comparatively small number remained behind to carry on their evolution on the three remaining globes, and of these some departed finally from the Chain as each globe dropped into inactivity.

It appears that, in a seventh Round, the mighty Being to whom has been given the title of the 'Seed-Manu of a Chain' takes into His charge the humanity and lower forms of living beings which have been evolving thereon. A Chain Seed-Manu gathers up into Himself, takes within His mighty far-reaching aura, all these results of the evolutions on the Chain, transporting them into the Inter-Chain sphere, the Nirvāṇa for the inhabitants of the dying Chain, nourishing them within Himself, and finally handing them over at the appointed time to the Root-Manu of the next Chain, who, following out the plan of the Seed-Manu, determines the times and places of their introduction into His kingdom.

The Seed-Manu of the Moon Chain appeared to have a vast plan, according to which he grouped the Moon-creatures, dividing them, after their last deaths, into classes, and sub-classes, and sub-sub-classes, in a quite definite way, apparently by some kind of magnetisation; this set up particular rates of vibration, and the people who could work best at one such rate were grouped together, and those who worked best at another rate were similarly grouped, and so on, when He was dealing with huge multitudes, as on globe D. These groups appeared to form themselves automatically in the heaven-world of globe D, as figures on a vibrating disc form themselves under the impact of a musical note; but on the three earlier globes more easily distinguished lines of cleavage appeared, and people were sent off by a great Official, evidently working on a definite plan. The Seed-Manu was aided in His gigantic task by many great Beings, who carried out His directions, and the whole vast plan was worked out with an order and an inevitableness which were unspeakably impressive. He appeared, among other things, to be choosing out the Officials for the next Chain, those who, in the long course of evolution, would pass ahead of their fellows, and become Masters, Manus, Boḍhisaṭṭvas, in the various Rounds and Races. He evidently selected many more than would be needed, as a gardener chooses out many plants for special culture, out of which a later selection may be made. Most, if not all, of this choosing was done on globe D, and we shall return to it when we reach that world. Meanwhile we will consider globes A, B and C.

On globe A of the Moon Chain, we see that a part of the humanity is not taken on to globe B, but is compelled to leave the Chain because it can make no further progress on it. The great Official who has charge of the globe has not been able to evolve some of the people in the way He desired—has, in fact, found some of the human material too rigid for further evolution, and so He ships it off when the life of the globe is over. This boat-load, as we call it, for the number is not large, consists of our friends with the orange-hued auras, who have brought their mental bodies to a point beyond which they cannot develop on the Moon Chain, except mischievously; they have so shut themselves into their mental shell, and have so starved the germs of their emotional bodies, that they cannot safely descend any further; moreover they are far too proud to wish to do so. The causal bodies are a rigid shell, not a living expanding form, and to let them pass on into globe B would only mean a fatal hardening of the lower mental. They are very clever, but quite selfish, and have cut themselves off from further progress for the time, save a progress which would be harmful. The Official is clearly dissatisfied with these orange-hued people, and does His best for them by shipping them off; glancing forward, we see that we shall meet some of these again in Atlantis, as Lords of the Dark Face, priests of the Dark Worship, leaders against the White Emperor, and so on. Meanwhile, they will rest in the Inter-Chain sphere, self-centred as ever.

The group of people before-mentioned, whose auras showed the golden-yellow of disciplined intellect, together with the rest of the inhabitants of the Chain, passed on to globe B, including some who had reached the Arhaṭ level on globe A, and who on globe B became Adepts. From globe B the golden-yellow group was shipped off, for they also had not sufficiently nourished the emotional side to make the formation of a fairly developed emotional body possible for them on globe C. Their willingness to obey shaped for them a fairer future than that of the orange people, and we meet them again in Atlantis as priests of the White temples, gradually forming emotional bodies of a good type. Both these first boat-loads enter on the terrene evolution at its fourth Round, being too advanced to take part in its earlier stages. It seems that it is necessary on each globe to develop the qualities which will need for their full expression a body of the material of the next; so our yellow people could go no further, but had to be shipped off to the Inter-Chain sphere.

From globe C went off a small number who had reached the Arhaṭ level, who had developed to a lofty point both intellect and emotion, and who needed no further evolution on the Moon Chain; they therefore left it by any one of the usual seven Paths. One group of these is specially interesting to us, because they formed part of one division of the 'Lords of the Moon'—the group called Barhiṣhaḍ Piṭṛs in *The Secret Doctrine*—who superintended the evolution of forms on our Earth Chain. On leaving globe C, they went towards the region where the Earth Chain was building, to be joined later by a number of others who also gave themselves to this work. Globe A of the terrene Chain began to form as the life-wave left globe A of the lunar Chain. The Spirit of a globe, when its life is over, takes a new incarnation, and, as it were, transfers the life with himself to the corresponding globe of the next Chain. The inhabitants, after leaving the Chain, have long to wait ere their new home is ready for them, but the preparation of that home begins when the Spirit of the first globe leaves it and it becomes a dead body, while he enters on a new cycle of life and a new globe begins to form round him. Molecules are built up under the direction of Ḍevas, humanity not being at all involved. The Spirit of a globe is probably on the line of this class of Ḍevas, and members of it perform the work of building globes all through the system. A great wave of life from the LOGOS builds up atoms in a system by the intermediary of such a Ḍeva; then molecules are built, then cells, and so on. Living creatures are like parasites on the surface of the Spirit of the earth, and he does not concern himself with them, and is probably not normally conscious of their existence, though he may feel them slightly when they make very deep mines. The Arhaṭs who, leaving globe C of the Moon Chain, selected the path which leads to the Earth Chain, passed, as said, to the region where globe A of the Earth Chain was forming; it commenced with the first Elemental Kingdom, which flowed upwards from the middle of the globe—the workshop of the Third LOGOS—as water wells up in an artesian boring, and flows over the edge on all sides. It came from the heart of the Lotus, as sap comes up into a leaf. These Lords of the Moon took no active part at this stage, but seemed to be looking on at the building of a world-to-be. Æons later they were joined by some of the Lords of the Moon from globe G of the lunar Chain, and these made the original forms on globe A—giving their Chhāyās, or Shadows, to make these, as *The Secret Doctrine* phrases it—and then the Lives came and occupied the forms in succession. Globes B and C were similarly built up round their respective Spirits, as the latter left their lunar predecessors. Our physical Earth was formed when the inhabitants left globe D of the Moon Chain; the Spirit of the globe left the Moon, and the Moon then began to disintegrate, a very large part of its substance passing over to build up the Earth. When the inhabitants began to leave the Moon finally, globes A, B and C of the terrene Chain were already formed, but globe D, our Earth, could not go far in its formation till its congener, globe D of the lunar Chain, the Moon, had died.

The groups—which were, as said, small in number—which left the Chain from globes A and B were, as we have seen, people who had shot on ahead intellectually, but who had been individualised in the fifth Round. The Arhaṭs who left globe C had been individualised in the fourth Round among a city population, and thus were brought into a civilisation where the pressure quickened their evolution; surrounded by more highly advanced people, they were stimulated into more rapid growth. To be ready to take advantage of these conditions it is evident that their development as animals on the previous Chain must have reached a higher point than that of those who individualised in the same Chain in primitive country districts. It seems as though the humanity of a Chain can only advance towards and enter the Path, when the individualising of animals on that Chain has practically ceased, and when only exceptional cases of individualisation will occur in the future. When the door of the human kingdom is shut against animals, then the door to the Path is opened to humanity.

As said, the groups which left the Chain from globes A, B and C, were small in number, the mass of the population on each globe passing on to the next in the usual way. But on globe D, things became very different; there the immense majority of the population, when the period for the death of the globe was approaching, after leaving their physical bodies for the last time, were not prepared for transference to globe E, but were shipped off to the Inter-Chain sphere, the lunar Nirvāṇa, to await their transference to the new Chain preparing for them. If we compare the other groups launched on the ocean of space to boat-loads, we have now a huge fleet of ships launched on that same ocean. The general fleet leaves the Moon; only a small population is left, set aside for reasons which will presently appear, and these leave globes E, F and G in small groups, boat-loads only—to keep up our metaphor.

The group of egos that we have been following as samples of the lower humanity of the Moon shows marks of distinct improvement on globe D; the causal body is well marked, the intelligence is more developed, and the affection for their superiors has deepened and intensified; instead of a passion, it has now become a settled emotion, and is their most distinguishing characteristic. To this group may be given the name of Servers—for although the instinct is still blind and half-conscious, yet to serve and please the higher people to whom they have devoted themselves is now the dominating motive in their lives; looking forward, we see that this remains their characteristic through the long series of lives to come on earth, and they do much rough pioneer work in the future. They love their superiors and are ready to obey them, "without cavil or delay". A marked change has come over their physical bodies in this Round; they are now bright blue, instead of being muddy brown as before. They are brought together physically during their last incarnations on the Moon, and much arranging is going on for a considerable time before this: the strengthening of ties between groups of egos is brought about by guiding them to re-birth in communities, and a very large number, indeed most, of the characters in *Rents in the Veil of Time* appear here; and it seems likely that the remainder, were we able to recognise them, would be among friends of later days, for these are all Servers, ready to do whatever they are told, to go whithersoever they are sent. They are marked out by a slight downpour of the higher life, which causes a little expansion of a thread of intuitional matter, connecting the intuitional and mental permanent atoms, and makes it a little broader above than below, like a small funnel; large numbers of people far more intelligent than they are do not show this, and it is connected with the germinal desire to serve, absent in those otherwise more advanced people. The group includes many types, and does not consist, as might be expected, of people of one Ray, or temperament; there are persons who became individualised in any one of the three Right Ways, through the aspects of Will, Wisdom, and active Intellect,[1] each stimulated into action by devotion to a superior. The method of individualisation comes in only as a cause of subdivision within the group, and affects the length of the interval between death and rebirth, but does not affect the characteristic of serviceableness. It affects the rate of vibration of the causal body, which is formed in the several cases by an endeavour to serve: (1) by an act of devotion; (2) by a great outburst of pure devotion; and (3) by devotion causing an effort to understand and appreciate. The actual formation of the causal body is always sudden; it comes into existence as by a flash; but the preceding circumstances differ and affect the rate of vibration of the body thus formed. An act of sacrifice in the physical body calls on the Will, and there is a pulsation in spiritual matter; devotion, working in the emotional body[2] calls on Wisdom, and there is a pulsation in intuitional matter; activity in the lower mind calls on the Active Intellect, and there is a pulsation in higher mental matter. We shall presently find our group of Servers subdivided into two by these differences, the first two forming a sub-group, with intervals of an average of seven hundred years between births, and the third forming a second group

[1] Āṭmā, Buḍḍhi, Manas.

[2] The vehicle of desire, Kāma.

with intervals of an average of one thousand two hundred years. This difference will come out on the Earth Chain at a more advanced stage of evolution, and the two sub-groups reach the Earth in the fourth Round with an interval of 400,000 years between them, apparently planned to bring them to birth together at a certain period, when their joint services would all be required; so minute in its details is the Great Plan. This division does not affect the relation between Masters and disciples, as pupils of each of the two Masters who are to be the Manu and Boḍhisaṭṭva of the sixth Root Race, were found in both sub-groups. Thus the germinal desire to serve, seen by the higher Authorities, is the mark of this whole group, and the differences in individualisation, affecting the interval between death and re-birth, subdivide the group into two.[1]

At the head of this group stand many whom we know as Masters now, and high above them are many who were already Arhaṭs, who transmit to those below them the orders received from far mightier Beings. The Manu of the Race—it is the seventh Race of the globe—is in charge, and He is obeying the orders, carrying out the plan, of the Seed-Manu, who directs all the preparations

[1] It will, of course, be understood that the seven hundred and one thousand two hundred years' intervals are 'averages,' and the 'exact' length of each interval will depend on the length and conditions of the preceding life. There is this marked difference between the sub-groups; as though the members of the one lived with greater intensity than the other in the heaven-world, and thus crowded a similar amount into a briefer time.

for the transfer of the huge population. Some of the advanced people know vaguely that some great changes are impending, but these changes, though far-reaching, are too slow to draw much attention; some co-operate, unconsciously but effectively, while thinking that they are carrying out great schemes of their own. There is one man, for instance, who has an ideal community in his mind, and who gathers together a number of people in order to form it; he is trying to please a Master who is an Arhaṭ of the Moon, and people are attracted by him and collect round him, forming a definite group with a common aim, thus subserving the Great Plan. We, at our low level, look up to the Arhaṭs and higher people as Gods, and try, in our very humble way, to fall in with any indications of their wishes that we can catch.

This group of Servers, as its numbers die out for the last time, having reached the required level on globe D, is regathered on the mental plane, the heavenly world, and its members remain there for an enormous time, having always before them the images of those they love, notably of the more advanced egos to whom they are especially devoted. It is this rapt devotion which so much helps their development, and brings out their higher qualities, so that later on they are more receptive to the influences which play upon them in the Inter-Chain sphere. They are included in the general mass of the egos called by H. P. Blavatsky 'Solar Piṭṛs,' and by A. P. Sinnett 'First-class Piṭṛs'. Other huge multitudes are also reaching the mental world—none being re-born who have reached an appointed level, which appears to be the possession of a fully formed causal body—and are falling into great groups under the play of the powerful magnetic force before mentioned, rayed down upon them by the Seed-Manu. As strings at different tensions answer to different notes, so do the causal bodies of these people—and none, as just said, are here except those whose causal bodies are fully formed—answer to the chord He strikes, and they are thus separated off. People who come forth through the same Planetary Ruler are drafted into different groups; friends fall into different groups; none of the ordinary ties seem to count. The egos are automatically sorted out and wait on in their own places, as a crowd, in continental countries, is sorted off into waiting-rooms, to await the arrival of their own particular train—in this case, to use our former image, to await their own ship.

We noticed especially two of the ship-loads, because we ourselves formed part of them; one included the coming Manu and Boḍhisaṭṭva, those who are now Chohans and Masters, together with many of the Servers who are now disciples, or approaching that level. These all apparently belonged to the sub-group with the seven hundred years' average between earth-lives. Another included many who are now Masters and disciples, with perhaps half the persons mentioned in the *Rents in the Veil of Time,* all belonging to the sub-group with the one thousand two hundred years' average. These two ship-loads contained many, if not all, of those who are to form the Heavenly Man, and they were then divided into the two sub-groups.

Vaivasvaṭa Manu and the present Boḍhisaṭṭva were seen together on globe D, but they passed on to the higher globes of the Moon Chain.

This great mass includes: (1) the Servers aforesaid, a very mixed lot of many grades, united by one common characteristic. Then (2) there is a large group of highly developed egos who are approaching the Path—on the line of Service, therefore, but too far ahead of the former group to be classed with it—and who are yet not near enough to the Path to reach it within the remaining life of the Chain. Then (3) a huge group of very good people, but people who have no wish to serve, and are not therefore yet turned towards the Path, and who will form the bulk of the population of Atlantis during its good period. (4) A small but striking group of egos, united by the common characteristic of highly developed intellectual power, future geniuses, varied as to character and morals, a group manifestly destined to leadership in the future, but not dedicating themselves to Service, nor turning their faces to the Path. Then three very large groups: (5) good, and often religious, people—merchants, soldiers, etc., fairly clever, self-centred, thinking mainly of their own development and advancement, knowing nothing of the Path, and therefore with no wish to enter it; (6) bourgeois-commonplace-weak, a very large group of the type described by the naming; (7) undeveloped, well-meaning, uneducated folk, the lowest class who have the causal body fully formed.

These are all in the heaven-world of the Moon, awaiting their despatch to the Inter-Chain sphere.

As convulsions begin to rend the Moon, preparatory to the disruption of its crust, other types pass also into this world; a very considerable number of the Solar Piṭṛs, or First-class Piṭṛs—who are capable of making further progress on the remaining globes of the Chain, where we shall meet them again—come on into the heaven-world to await transference in due course to globe E.

Below these first-class Piṭṛs comes an immense class of egos who have not fully formed the causal body, Mr. Sinnett's 'Second-class Piṭṛs'; a network has formed itself, connecting the ego and the lower mind, and, from the appearance of this, the name of 'Basket-works' has been given to them. The mass of these, when the Moon begins to approach dissolution, pass out of the body for the last time on the Moon Chain, and are gathered together in the emotional world. There they fall asleep, for they cannot function therein; when this emotional world of the Moon becomes uninhabitable, they lose their emotional bodies, and remain inward-turned, like bulbs awaiting shipment to another land, to be in due course shipped off to the Inter-Chain sphere, to sleep through ages, until the third Round of the Earth Chain offers a suitable field for their growth. There are some Basket-works, however, who show a capacity for further evolution on the Moon Chain, and they will pass on to the higher globes when these come into activity, and there form the causal body, re-inforcing the Solar, or First-class Piṭṛs.

The last class above the animals are the Animal-Men, Madame Blavatsky's 'First-class Lunar

Piṭṛs,' Mr. Sinnett's 'Third-class Piṭṛs'. These are distinguishable by delicate lines of matter which link the germinal ego to the dawning lower mind. They are gathered up, like the Basket-works, in the emotional world, when they pass out of the body for the last time on the Moon, and remain unconscious in the mental world; they are in due time shipped off, and sleep away æons of time, and finally reach the Earth Chain and begin the long work of building on globe A, working through all the kingdoms up to the human, and then remaining human through the succeeding globes of the Round, and through the following Rounds. Some of these 'Lines,' as we may name them for distinction, are also held back when the mass is shipped off, and are sent on to globe E for further evolution, and become Basket-works, joining thus the class which was above them.

So far we have followed the fate of the varied classes of lunar Humanity. Some part of it dropped out, the failures, in the sixth Round, and were 'hung-up' until the next Chain gave a suitable field for further evolution. Some, the orange-hued, left globe A in the seventh Round. Some, the golden-yellow, left globe B. Some Arhaṭs left from globes A, B, and C, and some of them went over to the forming Earth Chain from globe C. Then we have the classes that left globe D; those with fully formed causal bodies, those with basket-work, those with lines. Those that remained passed on to globes E, F, and G, some leaving each globe, when they had made all the progress of which they were capable; some Basket-works, higher-class

Piṭṛs and Arhaṭs thus went away from each globe. Most of the animals went off to the Inter-Chain Nirvāṇa—a regular Noah's Ark; a few, who were capable of becoming Animal-men, were taken on to the later globes.

The determining cause of these different causal bodies lies in the stage at which individualisation occurred. In the lower parts of the animal kingdom very many animals are attached to a single group-soul, and the number diminishes as they climb towards humanity, till in the higher class of animals there are but ten or twenty attached to a group-soul. Contact with man may bring about individualisation at a comparatively low stage; if the animal, say a dog, has been for a long time in contact with man, and is one of a small group of ten or twenty, then, on individualising, a complete causal body is formed. If there are about one hundred in the group—the sheep-dog stage—a basket-work causal body would be formed; if there were several hundreds—pariah dogs, as in Constantinople or India—he would have the indication of the causal body made by the connecting lines.

These stages remind us of somewhat similar differences in the vegetable kingdom; the more highly developed members of the vegetable world pass directly into the mammalian animal kingdom. The decent gentle animal does not become a cruel and brutal savage, but only a pleasantly primitive man. The kingdoms overlap, and a really nice animal may be a more agreeable companion than some human beings.

An entity may stop for a shorter time in the animal stage and a longer time in the human, or *vice versa*. It does not seem really to matter, as it always 'gets there' in the end, just as longer or shorter times in the heaven-world work out to the same stage of progress among men. It is probably a mere human folly which makes one feel that it is pleasanter to be the best of one's kind at the time, and that one would rather have been a banyan-tree or an oak-tree than a flight of mosquitoes, a splendid mastiff than a clay-eating or man-eating savage.

To return. Globes E, F, and G seem to have been used as a kind of forcing-houses for special cultures, for enabling some to reach the Path, or attain Arhaṭship, who could not accomplish it on globe D, although in a fair way towards it, and to permit some, who were approaching a higher stage, to enter it. They were centres more than globes. Their population was small, since the bulk of human and animal kind had been shipped off from globe D, and was further diminished by the sending off successively of a boat-load from each globe as it passed into quiescence. The boat-load from globe E consisted of some who were already on the Path and who had there become Arhaṭs, some Basket-works who had completed the causal body, and some Lines who had become Basket-works. When these left globe E, the remaining population, consisting of those below the Arhaṭ level who could bear the strain of further forcing, were carried over into globe F. Those who left passed into the Inter-Chain Nirvāṇa, and were there sorted out into the classes they had attained, as late letters with an extra stamp are sorted into the heaps to which they belong.

A similar process went on upon globe F, and it was deeply interesting to notice that the Lord Gauṭama Buḍḍha and the Lord Maiṭreya were among those who passed onwards, both from globe E and globe F, and reached the first great Initiation on globe G. They had dropped out in the seventh round of the second Chain, not being able to bear the forcing process on globes E, F, and G of that Chain, the conditions being too strenuous, and only suitable for those who could attain the prescribed level of success for that Chain, or could pass from the class they were in to the class above. They entered globe D of the Moon Chain in the fourth Round as primitive men, with the animals of the second Chain who were nearly ready for individualisation.

They took together, on globe F, their vow to become Buḍḍhas, but the arrangements were not the same as on our earth. There was a kind of Heavenly Council in a heavenly world—the Buḍḍhist Sukhāvaṭi—and the great Being to whom they made their vow and who, as the acting Buḍḍha, accepted it, was He who is called Ḍīpāṅkara in the books. They reached Arhaṭship on globe G, ere leaving the Chain.

The Lord Buḍḍha Ḍīpāṅkara came from the fourth Chain of the Venus Scheme; the physical globe of that Chain was the Moon of Venus, which was seen by Herschel but which has disappeared since his time. He was one of the members of the General Staff, spoken of on p. 13, who may be sent to any Chain needing help. The Lord Ḍīpāṅkara was followed in the great office of the Buḍḍha by the Buḍḍhas of the Earth Chain; we know of the Lord Kashyapa, for instance, the Boḍhisaṭṭva of the third Root Race, taking Buḍḍhahood in the fourth; and the Lord Gauṭama Himself, the Boḍhisaṭṭva of the fourth Root Race, taking Buḍḍhahood in the fifth. He was succeeded by the Lord Maiṭreya, the Boḍhisaṭṭva of the fifth Root Race, who will take Buḍḍhahood in the sixth. He will be followed by the coming Boḍhisaṭṭva of the sixth Root Race—now known as the Master K. H.—who will take Buḍḍhahood in the seventh.

It must be remembered that a Buḍḍha is an Official who has to superintend much more than a humanity; He is the Teacher of Ḍevas, Angels, as well as of men, so the fact that a given humanity may be at a very low stage of evolution does not do away with the need for that high office.

We noted also the Master Jupiter among those who entered the Path on globe G.

THE INTER-CHAIN NIRVĀṆA

The human mind reels before the enormous periods of time concerned in evolution, and one takes refuge in the old—and modern—idea that time has no fixed existence, but is long or short according to the working of the consciousness of the being concerned.[1] In the Inter-Chain Nirvāṇa the really working consciousnesses were those of the Seed-Manu of the lunar Chain and the Root-Manu

[1] See the suggestive little book, *Two New Worlds*, by E. E. Fournier d'Albe.

of the terrene. What time may be to Their consciousnesses who may pretend to guess?

The Great Plan is in the mind of the Seed-Manu, and the Root-Manu receives it from Him and works it out in the new Chain over which He presides. The results of the evolution in the Chain whose life is over are gathered up within the aura of the Seed-Manu, and are arranged, tabulated, filed—if one may use terms drawn from our common life—in perfect order. On these intelligences of many grades, inward-turned, living a strange slow subjective life, without idea of time, He pours intermittent streams of His stimulating magnetism. A continuous stream would break them into pieces, so it plays on them and stops, and they doze on for perhaps a million years, slowly assimilating it; and then another stream plays on them, and so on and on, for millions upon millions of years. As we watched that strange scene, many analogies rose up in our minds; bulbs laid carefully on shelves, inspected from time to time by a gardener; cots in a hospital, visited day by day by a physician. The time drew nearer and nearer when the great Gardener was to give out His bulbs for the planting, and the planting ground was the Earth Chain and the bulbs were living souls.

CHAPTER VI

EARLY TIMES ON THE EARTH CHAIN

MEANWHILE the Earth Chain had been slowly forming, and the Lords of the Moon had been looking on at the building as we saw[1]; the time had come for shipping off to the new Chain the first of those who were to evolve in it during the coming ages. The Seed-Manu determined the contents of each shipload and the order of its going, and the Root-Manu distributed them as they arrived successively on globe A of the terrene Chain.

The Occult Government of the Chain may here be briefly sketched, though only in broad outline, so that the student may realise something of the greatness of the evolutionary Plan which he is to survey.

At the head is the Seed-Manu of the preceding Chain, Chakṣhushas, something of whose vast work we have seen in the lunar Chain. He is aided by Officials who report to Him how the members of any special division have responded to the influences He has thrown upon them during their stay in the Inter-Chain Nirvāṇa. Just as the least advanced in 'age' are sent out to perform the task of inhabiting the most primitive forms,

[1] See *Ante,* p. 61.

and the more advanced follow when the forms have evolved to a higher state, so, out of any special division brought over from the Moon and stored in the Inter-Chain Nirvāṇa, those who have progressed least under His influence during the time of retirement are sent out first of their class into the new world.

The Root-Manu of the terrene Chain, Vaivasvaṭa,[1] who directs the whole order of its evolution, is a mighty Being from the fourth Chain of the Venus Scheme; two of His Assistants come from the same Chain, and a third is a high Adept who attained early in the lunar Chain.[2] A Root-Manu of a Chain must achieve the level fixed for the Chain or Chains on which He is human, and become one of its Lords; then He becomes the Manu of a Race; then a Praṭyeka Buḍḍha; then a Lord of the World; then the Root-Manu, then the Seed-Manu of a Round, and only then the Root-Manu of a Chain. He directs the Manus of Rounds, who distribute the work among the Manus of Races. Further, each Chain yields a number of successful human beings, 'the Lords of the Chain,' some of whom devote Themselves to the work of the new Chain, under its Root-Manu.

[1] The Root-Manu Vaivasvaṭa must not be confused with the Manu Vaivasvaṭa of the Āryan Root Race. The former was a far loftier Being, as will be seen from the statement of His long ascent, made in this same paragraph.

[2] It must be remembered that when a man reaches the level appointed for the Chain on which he is evolving, he may remain upon it and proceed on his further evolution, as Adepts, attaining now on our globe, may, without leaving it, reach the higher levels of the Hierarchy.

We thus find, for our Chain, seven classes of Lords of the Moon, working under our Root-Manu, drawn from the seven globes of the Moon Chain; they form one of the two great classes of Helpers from outside, who are concerned in the guiding of the general evolution of the Earth Chain. The second important class of Helpers from outside are Those known as the Lords of the Flame, who arrive from Venus on the fourth globe, in the fourth Round, in the middle of the third Root-Race, to quicken mental evolution, to found the Occult Hierarchy of the Earth, and to take over the government of the globe. It is They whose tremendous influence so quickened the germs of mental life that these burst into growth, and there followed the great downrush through the Monad that we call the third Life-Wave, causing the formation of the causal body, the 'birth' or 'descent of the ego' for all those who had come up from the animal kingdom; so instantaneous was the response of the myriad inhabitants of Earth that They are sometimes said to have 'given,' to have 'projected' the spark of mind; but the spark was fanned into flame, not projected; the nature of the gift was the quickening of the germ already present in nascent humanity, the effect of a sun-ray on a seed, not a giving of a seed.[1] By the Lords of the Flame was concentrated the power of the LOGOS upon the Monads, as the sun-rays might be concentrated by a lens, and under that influence the responsive spark appeared. These are the true Mānasapuṭras, the Sons of Mind—coming, as They did from the

[1] *The Secret Doctrine*, iii, 560.

fifth, the mental Round of Venus—the Sons of the Fire, the Lords of the Flame.[1]

The seven classes of the Lords of the Moon were distributed by the Root-Manu over the Earth Chain to take charge of the Rounds and globes, while the Manus of Races took special care of the evolution of Races, each of one Root Race.

THE FIRST ROUND

The Lords of the Moon from globes A, B, and C of the lunar Chain were the three classes who watched over, without partaking in, the physical construction of the globes of our Chain, as they were formed successively round the Spirit of each globe, as before described.[2] They appear to have superintended the detailed work of the Lords who attained later. The lowest class, from globe G, made the primitive archetypal forms on globe A of the Earth Chain in the first Round, and guided the Lines who came in to fill them, and to evolve therein. The next class, from globe F, superintended the evolution of forms in the second Round; that from globe E the similar evolution in the third; and that from globe D the similar evolution in the fourth.[3] Further, we find some of the Lords

[1] The word Mānasaputra is used in *The Secret Doctrine* to indicate not only These, but also all egos who are sufficiently advanced to quicken into activity the germ of mind in others, as we may now do with animals. The word thus covers a huge class, containing many varying grades in evolution.

[2] See *Ante*, p. 61.

[3] All these are included under the name Barhiṣhaḍ Piṭṛs in *The Secret Doctrine*.

from globe E working on Mars in the fourth Round, while those from globe D become active later on the Earth.

When the despatch of the first entities from the Inter-Chain Nirvāṇa began, the first ships brought the Lines, and the great mass of animals from globe D of the Moon Chain; the first shiploads succeeded each other at intervals of about one hundred thousand years, and then the supply stopped, and an immense period followed, during which the new arrivals, the pioneers on our Earth Chain, were pursuing their long journey of the first and second Rounds and part of the third.

The worlds are curious, like churning whirlpools; our Earth, the most solid, is hot, muddy, sticky, and much of its territory does not seem to be anchored down very firmly. It is seething, and constantly changing in consistency; huge cataclysms engulf great multitudes from time to time, and in their embryonic condition they do not seem very much the worse for the engulfing, but increase and multiply in huge caves and caverns, as though they were living on the surface.

The first Round of the Earth Chain had its globes on the same levels as the seventh Round of the Moon Chain; globe A was on the higher mental plane, with some of the matter scarcely awakened; globe B was on the lower mental; globe C on the emotional; globe D on the physical; globe E on the emotional again; globe F on the lower mental; globe G on the higher mental. In the second Round the whole Chain descended, and three globes became physical, C, D, and E; but the living things on them were etheric in substance, and pudding-baggy—to borrow H. P. Blavatsky's graphic epithet—in form. Globes C and E, which we now call Mars and Mercury, had at that time physical matter, but in a glowing gaseous state.

The human bodies on the Earth during the first Round were amœboid, cloudy, drifting things, mostly etheric, and thus indifferent to the heat; they multiplied by fission. They seemed to succeed each other in Races but without separate incarnations, each form lasting for a Race. There were no births and no deaths; they enjoyed an amœba-immortality, and were under the care of Lords of the Moon who had achieved Arhaṭship on globe G. Some etheric floating things appeared to be trying, but not very successfully, to be dreams of vegetables.

The minerals were somewhat more solid, for they were largely pelted on to the Earth by the Moon in a molten condition; the temperature might be anything above 3,500 C. (6,332 F.), for copper was in the condition of vapour, and it volatilises in an electrical furnace at this temperature. Silicon was visible, but most of the substances were proto-elements, not elements, and the present combinations seemed to be very rare; the earth was surrounded by huge masses of vapour shutting in the heat, and hence cooled very slowly. At the Pole there was some boiling mud, which gradually settled down, and after some thousands of years a green scum appeared, which was vegetable; or perhaps it would be more accurate to say that it would become vegetable later on.

SECOND ROUND

In the second Round the temperature of globe D had dropped considerably, and the copper had cooled down and become liquid, in some places solid. There was some land near the Poles, but flames burst out if a hole was made, as at some points on the sides of the cone of Vesuvius. The pudding-bag creatures did not seem to mind the heat, but floated about indifferently, reminding one in their shape of wounded soldiers who had lost their legs and had had their clothes sewn round the trunk; a blow made an indentation, which slowly filled up again, like the flesh of a person suffering from dropsy; the fore part of the thing had a kind of sucking mouth, through which it drew in food, and it would fasten on another and draw it in, as though sucking an egg through a hole, whereupon the sucked one grew flabby and died; a struggle was noticed in which each had fixed its mouth on the other, and sucked away diligently. They had a kind of flap-hand, like the flap of a seal, and they made a cheerful kind of chirruping trumpeting noise, expressing pleasure—pleasure being a sort of general sense of *bien-être,* and pain a massive discomfort, nothing acute, only faint likes and dislikes. The skin was sometimes serrated, giving shades of colour. Later on, they became a little less shapeless and more human, and crawled on the ground like caterpillars. Later still, near the North Pole, on the cap of land there, these creatures were developing hands and feet, though unable to stand up, and more intelligence was noticeable. A Lord of the Moon—an Arhaṭ who had attained on globe F of the Moon Chain—was observed, who had magnetised an island and shepherded on to it a flock of these creatures, reminding one of sea-cows or porpoises, though with no formed heads; they were taught to browse, instead of sucking each other, and when they did eat each other they chose some parts in preference to others, as though developing taste. The depression which served for mouth grew deeper into a kind of funnel, and a stomach began to develop, which was promptly turned inside out if any alien matter which was disapproved of found its way in. One turned himself entirely inside out, and seemed none the worse. The surface of the Earth being still very uncertain, they occasionally got burnt or partially cooked; this they evidently disliked, and if it went too far they collapsed. The heavy atmosphere made floating their usual method of locomotion, and this was pleasanter to look at than the writhing motion adopted on the ground, recalling the "loathly worm". Reproduction was by budding; a protuberance appeared, grew, and after a while broke off, and led an independent existence.

Their intelligence was infantile, and one was seen who had aimed at a neighbour with his mouth, and, missing him, had caught hold of his own lower end, and then went on sucking contentedly till, presumably becoming uncomfortable, he spat himself out again. One fellow found out that by rolling his lower end in mud, he could float upright instead of lengthwise, and appeared to be very proud of himself. Gradually the end which contained the funnel tapered off somewhat, and a small centre appeared in it, which, in far future ages, might become a brain. A small protuberance appeared, and the habit was formed of drifting forward, with this in front, as carrying the mouth, and impacts being constantly made on this, development was promoted.

Vegetable life developed during this period, aided by the heavy choking atmosphere; there were forest-like growths, much resembling grass, but forty feet high and proportionately thick. They grew in the warm mud, and flourished exceedingly.

Towards the end of this period, some of the Earth was quite solid and only reasonably warm. There was much tumultuous cracking, apparently due to shrinkage, and every hill was an active volcano.

Mars became more solid, cooling more rapidly in consequence of its smaller size, but life on it was much like that on the Earth.

Third Round

In the third Round Mars was quite solid and firm, and some animals began to develop, though at first they looked rather like clumsy chunks of wood, sawed off a log. They recalled sketches made by children who had not learned how to draw; but as time went on, there were beings who were distinctly human, though more like gorillas than men.

The configuration then was very different from that of the Mars now known to us.[1] The water question had not arisen, for about three-fourths of the surface was water and only one-fourth dry land. Hence there were no canals, as now, and the general physical condition much resembled that of the Earth of to-day.

The people who began with the linear indication of the causal body had by this time developed basket-work of a kind coarser, we noticed, than that which had been developed on the Moon. When this stage was reached the Basket-works from the Moon came streaming in, ship-loads again being sent off by the Seed-Manu to the Earth.

Looking at the Inter-Chain Nirvāṇa, in order to trace out the coming of the Basket-works to Mars, we came upon an interesting point. The 'shelves' on which the 'bulbs' were stored were clearly of the higher mental matter; but the bulbs brought over in the Seed-Manu's aura were brought over through the spiritual sphere, and the basket-work of Moon mental matter would thus be disintegrated, and would need to be reformed before these entities began their terrene career. They would have slept for ages in the spiritual sphere, and then would have been reclothed in basket-work of the equivalent terrene mental matter. There is no continuity of mental matter between Chains. The distance, of course, may be disregarded, as the terrene Chain occupies much the same position as the lunar, but the discontinuity of the mental matter renders necessary the disintegration and reintegration of the basket-work causal bodies.

We saw a Manu coming over to Mars with a ship-load of Basket-works, reminding us of the stories in the Hindū Purāṇas of the Manu crossing the ocean in a ship, bearing with Him the seeds of a new world, and those in the Hebrew records of Noah, preserving in an ark all that was needed to repopulate the Earth after a flood. The legends preserved in the Scriptures of religions are often stories containing the records of the past, and the Manu truly came to the Martian world to give a new impulse to evolution. Arriving on Mars, He founded a colony of His Basket-works thereon.

Tracing back this particular set, the first arrival of Basket-works in the terrene Chain, we found that they had come from globe G of the lunar Chain, having thereon become Basket-works. They were the least developed of the Basket-work crowd, having been the last to reach that stage; the Manu guided them to take birth in the most promising third-Race families on Mars, and, as they grew, He led them off to His colony, where they would more quickly develop into fourth-Race people. In the colony the people moved by a central will like bees in a hive, the central will being that of the Manu; He sent out streams of force and directed all. Two other sets of these Basket-work bees came to Mars, those who reached this stage on globes E and F of the Moon Chain; they arrived in reverse order from that of their leaving the Moon, those from globe F forming the fourth Race on Mars, and those from globe E the fifth. They developed some affection and some intelligence under the fostering care of the Manu; at first living in caves, they soon began to build, and to teach the aborigines to build under them, even

Basket-works becoming leaders at this stage of evolution.

These people were hermaphrodite, but one sex was usually developed more than the other, and two individuals were necessary for reproduction. Other forms of reproduction also existed among the lower types, and there were some embryonic human beings of the hydra kind who reproduced by budding and others by exudation, while some were oviparous. But these were not found among the Basket-works.

In the fifth-Race the social arrangements changed, as more intelligence was developed; the bee system disappeared, but they still had little individuality, and moved rather in flocks and herds, shepherded by their Manu. The baskets became more closely woven, and represented what could be done by the unfolding life in those who were emphatically self-made men, unaided by the great stimulus given in the fourth Round by the Lords of the Flame. This type which moves in flocks is still largely represented among us by the people who hold conventional ideas because others hold them, and are wholly dominated by Mrs. Grundy. These are often quite good people, but are very sheepy and flocky, and are appallingly monotonous. There are differences among them, but they are like the differences between people who buy tea by the quarter-pound or by the ounce, noticeable chiefly by themselves.

One fierce type of Basket-work was observed, not living in communities, but wandering about in forests in pairs; their heads ran up to a point behind matching the chin in front, and the head ending in two points looked odd and unattractive. They fought by butting against each other like goats, the top of the head being of very hard bone. There were some yet lower types, curious reptilian creatures, living in trees. They were larger than the Lines and far less intelligent, and ate the latter when they had the chance.

There were also on Mars some carnivorous brutes; a huge crocodile-like animal was seen fiercely attacking a man, who rushed at it with a club, which did not seem a very effective weapon. However, he stumbled over a rock and fell headlong into the creature's jaws, and so came to an untimely end.

The third Round on the Earth much resembled that on Mars, the people being smaller and denser, but, from our present standpoint, still huge and gorilla-like. The bulk of the Basket-works from globe D of the lunar Chain arrived on our Earth in this Round, and led the human evolution; the Basket-works from Mars fell in behind them, and the whole resembled fairly intelligent gorillas. The animals were very scaly, and even the creatures we must call birds were covered with scales rather than feathers; they all seemed to be made of a job-lot of fragments stuck together, half-bird, half-reptile, and wholly unattractive. Still, it was a little more like a world than the preceding globes, in fact than anything we had seen since we left the Moon; and later on cities were built. The work of the Lords of the Moon—who in this Round were Arhaṭs from globe E—resembled the training of animals more than the evolution of a humanity. But it is noticeable that they were working on sections, as it were, of the different bodies, physical and subtle. The third sub-planes of the physical, astral and mental spheres were being specially worked through, and the spirillæ of the atoms on these sub-planes were being vivified.[1]

The methods of reproduction on our Earth during the third Round were those which are now confined to the lower kingdoms of nature. In the first and second Races, not thoroughly densified, fission still occurred, but in the third and onwards the methods were: budding-off like hydræ in the less organised; the exuding of cells from different organs of the body, which reproduced similar organs, and grew into a miniature duplication of the parent; the laying of eggs, within which the young human being developed. These were hermaphrodite, and gradually one sex predominated, but never sufficiently to represent a definite male and female.

The passing of the life-wave from one globe to another is gradual and there is considerable overlapping; it will be remembered that globe A of the terrene Chain began to form when globe A of the lunar Chain was in process of disintegration, the passing of the Spirit of the globe being the signal of the transference of activity.[2] Thus life-activity is continuous, though egos have long periods of rest. A globe 'passes into obscuration' when the attention of the LOGOS is turned away from it, and thus His Light is withdrawn. It passes into a kind of coma, and there is a residuum of living creatures, left behind;

[1] See *Ante*, pp. 29, 30 [2] See *Ante*, pp. 60, 61

these creatures do not seem to increase in number during this period. But while the Races die out, the egos inhabiting them having passed on, the globe becomes a field for the Inner Round, a place to which egos in a transition state can be transferred for special treatment in order to quicken their evolution. The globe to which the attention of the LOGOS is turned starts into active life, and receives the streams of egos ready to go forward on their journey.

Another point that may be noted is the recurrence of types at a higher level of evolution. in which they form but transitional stages. As in the development of the human embryo of to-day, the fish-, reptile-, and lower mammalian-types appear, repeating in a few months the æonic evolution of the past, so do we see in each Round that a period of repetition precedes that of new advance. The third Round laboriously worked out in detail that which the third Race in the fourth Round would reproduce with comparative swiftness, while the second Race would similarly reflect the second Round, and the first Race the first Round. This broad principle once grasped, study becomes more easy, as the outline is clear into which details are to be fitted.

CHAPTER VII

EARLY STAGES OF THE FOURTH ROUND

In taking a preliminary bird's-eye-view of the fourth Round, one important and far-reaching change is apparent in the surroundings amid which human evolution is to proceed. In the three preceding Rounds the elemental essence was practically untouched by man, and was affected only by the Ḍevas, or Angels, by whose influences it evolved. Man was not sufficiently developed to affect it to any serious extent. But in this Round man's influence plays a very important part, and his self-centred thoughts create swirls in the elemental essence surrounding him. The elementals, also, begin to show more hostility to him, as he emerges from the animal state into the dominating human, for he is, from their standpoint, no longer an animal among animals, but an independent and domineering entity, likely to be hostile and aggressive.

Another most important characteristic of the fourth Round, the midmost of the seven, is that, in it, the door was shut against the animal kingdom, and the door was opened to the Path. Both statements are general; here and there an animal, by very special help, may still be evolved to a point where a human incarnation is possible for it, but in almost all cases no human body can now be found of sufficiently low development for its embodiment; so also might a man who had attained Arhaṭship or more on the Moon Chain climb yet higher, but all below that rank who had complete causal bodies did not enter into evolution on the Earth Chain until the later third and early fourth Root Races.

On Mars in the fourth Round we find a number of savages who had not been sufficiently advanced to leave that globe for the Earth when the mass of the egos went on in the preceding Round. On each globe some fail to go on, and remain behind as the globe begins its period of obscuration; and they return to this same globe when again it recommences full activity, and form a very backward class; these were Basket-works of a very poor kind, and were savages of the brutal and cruel type, some of those who had individualised through fear and anger.

Mars, in the fourth Round, felt the stress of scarcity of water, and it was the Lords of the Moon—Arhaṭs who had attained on Globe E—who planned out the system of canals, and the Basket-works who executed them under Their direction. The Martian seas are not salt, and the polar snow-caps, as they melt, supply the water necessary for irrigation, and thus enable the ground to be cultivated, and crops to be raised.

The fifth Martian Root Race was white, and made considerable progress, and the Basket-work developed into a complete causal body. They were good, well-meaning, and kindly, though not capable of any large ideas, of widely spread feelings of affection, or of self-sacrifice. At a quite early stage, they began to divide food instead of fighting over it, developing the social feeling to some extent.

The first and second Root Races on the Earth were going on before Mars was deserted, some entities being available for these primitive conditions whom Mars in its later stages was too advanced to accommodate, and the full attention of the LOGOS not being turned on to the Earth in these early times. The Lords of the Moon—Arhaṭs who had achieved on globe D of the lunar Chain—brought into these early Races a number of backward entities, so that these served as special coaches for the laggards, many of whom repaid the care bestowed upon them, and entered the first sub-race of the third Root Race, as its lowest types; they were egg-headed, with an eye at the top of their heads, a roll like a sausage representing a forehead, and prognathous jaws. The egg-headed type persisted for a very long time, but became much modified in the later sub-races of this third Root Race, and specimens of them are found in later Lemurian times. The blue people who formed the powerful sixth sub-race, and the white who composed the seventh sub-race, were finer types, but were still Lemurian, and showed a trace of egg-headedness, due to the retreating foreheads.[1] The population of the Earth during the

[1] While this is going through the press a report has appeared in the newspapers of the discovery of some skulls of this type, but no particulars are yet available. See *The Theosophist* for August, 1912, in 'On the Watch-Tower,' p. 631.

first and second Root Races was very limited, and this special help appears to have been given because in the fourth globe of the fourth Chain "the door is shut". Furthermore, everything possible was done to bring forward all of whom anything could be made, before the coming of the Lords of the Flame, in the middle of the third Root Race, should make the gulf well-nigh impassable between the human and animal kingdoms.

Mars, at the end of its seventh Root Race, had a very considerable population to pour into the Earth, and these came streaming in for the third Root Race, to head it until the more advanced egos from the Moon Chain should come in to take over the leadership. These Basket-works, whose causal bodies were now completed, had made considerable progress on Mars, and they now prepared the way for the more advanced people who were soon to arrive. It was they who fought with the savage reptilian creatures, slimy and backboneless, who were the "water-men terrible and bad" of the Stanzas of Dzyān, the re-embodied remnants of the previous Rounds, who had been 'water-men,' *i. e.,* amphibious, scaly, half-human animals, on Mars.

The many schemes of reproduction characteristic of the third Round re-appear in this third Root Race, and run simultaneously in various parts of the Earth. The bulk of the population passed on through the successive stages and became mostly oviparous, but there were various little side-shows in which earlier methods persisted. It seems as though the various schemes of reproduction were suitable to egos at different stages of evolution, and were kept going for laggards after the bulk of the people had passed beyond them. The egg-scheme was dropped very slowly; the shell became thinner and thinner, the human being within developing into a hermaphrodite; then he became a hermaphrodite with one sex predominant; and then a unisexual being. These changes began some sixteen and a half million years ago, and occupied some five and a half to six million years, physical bodies changing very slowly and reversion frequently occurring. Moreover the original number was small, and needed time for multiplication. When this last type became quite stable, then the egg was preserved within the feminine body, and reproduction assumed the form which still persists.

To sum up: we have the first Root Race, repeating the first Round, etheric clouds drifting about in a hot heavy atmosphere, which enclosed a world rent by recurrent cataclysms; these multiplied by fission. The second Root Race, repeating the second Round, was of the 'pudding-bag' type, described under the second Round; these multiplied by budding. The early third Root Race, repeating the third Round, was human-gorilla in form, and reproduction was at first by extrusion of cells, the 'sweat-born' of *The Secret Doctrine.* Then comes the oviparous stage, and finally the unisexual.

Some very special treatment was applied to some of the eggs; they were taken away by the Lords of the Moon, and were carefully magnetised and kept at an equable temperature, until the human form, at this stage a hermaphrodite, broke out; it was then specially fed and carefully developed, and when ready, was taken possession of by one of the Lords of the Moon, many of whom became incarnate in order to work on the physical plane, and they used these carefully prepared bodies for a long period of time; some Ḍevas also took some of these prepared bodies. This seems to have been only a few centuries before the separation of the sexes.

While the later Egg-borns were in possession, the very best of the Basket-works came in, straight from the Inter-Chain Nirvāṇa, and these were quickly followed by the lowest of those who had gained complete causal bodies on the Moon. Between the highest of the first and the lowest of the second there was but little difference. The first boat-load of the latter consisted of those who had responded but little to the influence of the Seed-Manu, from globes G, F, and E of the lunar Chain, the majority being from G, the stupidest of those who had gained complete causal bodies. The second boat-load had a large number from globe G, a low section from globe F, and a still lower from globe E. The third contained the best from globe G, with some fairly good from globe F, and good from globe E. The fourth boat-load had the best from globe F, and all but the very best of globe E. The fifth boat-load brought the best of globe E, with a few from globe D. These all seemed to be sorted out by 'age' rather than by 'type,' and were, in fact, of all types. One individual was noticed who was a chief in the savage mainland tribe which took Mars prisoner on the Moon, one who had individualised through fear. All these incarnated among the Egg-borns, some hundreds of thousands of them.

Then came, from ten to eleven million years ago, when separation of the sexes was fully established, the important stage when some of these incarnated Lords of the Moon descended on the seven-pointed Lemurian Polar Star, and formed etheric images of themselves, which were then materialised into greater density, multiplying these for the use of the incoming egos; the Lords were of different types, the "seven men each on his lot," and gave bodies suited to the seven Rays, or temperamental types of humanity, making the forms on the points of the Star.

At this stage there were four human classes, pressing on each other to obtain better human forms. These were: (1) the set of the best Basket-works above-named, with the five boatloads from globes G, F, and E, possessing complete causal bodies; then (2) the Basket-works from Mars; then (3) the Lines, who had been here all the time; then (4) the last, composed of those who were only now coming up out of the animals. Below these were the animals, plants, and minerals, with which we need not concern ourselves.

The coming of these into the etheric forms provided by the Lords of the Moon was something of a struggle, for there were often many claimants for a single form, and the one who succeeded in gaining it could not always hold it for more than a few moments; the scene recalls the Greek idea that the Gods made the world amid shouts of laughter, for it decidedly had its comic element, as the egos struggled for the forms and could not manage them when they had obtained them. It is one of the descents into matter, the final materialisation of the body of man, the completion of 'the fall of man'. Gradually they became accustomed to the new 'coats of skin,' and settled down to reproduce the seven great temperamental types. In various parts of the world other ways of reproduction continued for long periods of time; the successive stages overlapped very much, owing to the great differences in evolution, and the classes that came in from other Rounds had not been in the two early Root Races on Earth; the tribes following the early methods gradually became sterile, while the true men and women multiplied greatly, until humanity, as we know it now, was definitely established all over the world.

The forms as thrown off by the Lords of the Moon were fairly good-looking, but being etheric they were very readily modifiable, and the incoming egos much distorted them; the children born of them were distinctly ugly; probably those using them were accustomed to think of the egg-shaped head and sausage-roll forehead, and hence these reappeared.

After many generations of well-established human beings, descended from the etheric materialised forms, had been evolved, the Arhaṭs urged on those who had left globes A, B, and C of the lunar Chain—because they could make no further progress on it—that they should descend and take incarnation in the bodies now ready for their indwelling. There were three boat-loads of these;

more than two million orange people from globe A, rather less than three million golden-yellow from globe B, and rather more than three million pink from globe C—about nine millions in all; they were guided to different areas of the world's surface, with the view that they should form tribes. The orange, on seeing the bodies offered to them, refused to enter, not out of any wickedness but from pride, disdaining the unattractive forms, and perhaps also from their ancient hatred of sexual unions; but the yellow and pink were docile and obeyed, gradually improving the bodies they inhabited. These made the fourth Lemurian sub-race, the first which was in any sense, except the embryonic, human; and it may be dated from the giving of the forms. It is interesting to notice that H. P. Blavatsky in *The Secret Doctrine* speaks of this fourth sub-race as 'yellow,' apparently noting the incoming of the golden-yellow people from globe B of the Moon Chain; she can hardly have been referring to the established colour of the fourth sub-race, as that was black, and the black continued even in the lower classes of the sixth sub-race, in which the higher classes were of a quite respectable blue. Yet even in those there was an underlying tinge of black.

The area allotted to the orange tribe was thus left open, and the bodies they should have used were gladly seized upon by the entities just emerging from the animal kingdom, the lowest of the classes before mentioned, the very poorest human type; these, not unnaturally, felt little difference between themselves and the ranks from which they had just emerged, and hence arose the "sin of the mindless".

It is interesting to note the karma of this refusal of the orange people to take their due place in the work of peopling the world. Later, the law of evolution forced them into incarnation, and they had to take lower and coarser bodies, the Lords of the Moon having gone on into other work; they thus became a backward race, cunning but not good, and passed through many unpleasant experiences; they diminished in number by constantly coming into collision with the common order, and being hammered, largely by suffering, into ordinary folk. A few—strong, remorseless and unscrupulous—became Lords of the Dark Face in Atlantis; some were seen among the North American Indians with refined but hard faces; some few still persist, even down to our own day—the unscrupulous among the kings of finance, statesmen like Bismarck, conquerors like Napoleon; but they are gradually disappearing, for they have learned many bitter lessons. Those who are wanting in heart, who are always fighting, always opposing everything everywhere, on general principles, must ultimately, in a realm of law, be beaten into shape; a very few may end in black magic, but the steady pressure is too great for the majority. It is a hard road to choose for progress!

The Coming of the Lords of the Flame

The great Lemurian Polar Star was still perfect, and the huge Crescent still stretched along the equator, including Madagascar. The sea which occupied what is now the Gobi Desert still broke against the rocky barriers of the northern Himālayan slopes, and all was being prepared for the most dramatic moment in the history of the Earth —the Coming of the LORDS OF THE FLAME.

The Lords of the Moon and the Manu of the third Root Race had done all that was possible to bring men up to the point at which the germ of mind could be quickened, and the descent of the ego could be made. All the laggards had been pushed on; there were no more in the animal ranks capable of rising into man. The door against further immigrants into the human kingdom from the animal was only shut when no more were in sight, nor would be capable of reaching it without a repetition of the tremendous impulse only given once in the evolution of a Scheme, at its midmost point.

A great astrological event, when a very special collocation of planets occurred and the magnetic condition of the Earth was the most favourable possible, was chosen as the time. It was about six and a half million years ago. Nothing more remained to be done, save what only They could do.

Then, with the mighty roar of swift descent from incalculable heights, surrounded by blazing masses of fire which filled the sky with shooting tongues of flame, flashed through the aerial spaces the chariot of the Sons of the Fire, the Lords of the Flame from Venus; it halted, hovering over the 'White Island,' which lay smiling in the bosom of the Gobi Sea; green was it, and radiant with masses of fragrant many-coloured blossoms, Earth offering her best and fairest to welcome her coming King. There He stood, "the Youth of sixteen summers," Sanaṭ Kumāra, the 'Eternal Virgin-Youth,' the new Ruler of Earth, come to His kingdom, His Pupils, the three Kumāras, with Him, His Helpers around Him; thirty mighty Beings were there, great beyond Earth's reckoning, though in graded order, clothed in the glorious bodies They had created by Kriyāshakṭi, the first Occult Hierarchy, branches of the one spreading Banyan-Tree, the nursery of future Adepts, the centre of all occult life. Their dwelling-place was and is the Imperishable Sacred Land, on which ever shines down the Blazing Star, the symbol of Earth's Monarch, the changeless Pole round which the life of our Earth is ever spinning.[1]

A *Catechism* says: "Out of the seven Kumāras, four sacrificed themselves for the sins of the world, and the instruction of the ignorant, to remain till the end of the present Manvanṭara ... These are the Head, the Heart, the Soul and the Seed of undying knowledge." H. P. Blavatsky adds: "Higher than the 'Four' is only ONE on Earth as in Heaven—that still more mysterious and solitary Being"—the Silent Watcher.[2]

Until the Coming of the Lords the shiploads from the Inter-Chain Nirvāṇa had arrived separately,

[1] The use of these occult symbols misled the readers of *The Secret Doctrine,* (perhaps even its writer) into the mistake that the 'Pole' and 'Star' mentioned in the Occult Commentary were the physical North Pole and North Star. I followed this mistaken idea in my *Pedigree of Man.*—A. B.

[2] *The Secret Doctrine,* ii, 294, 295.

but now, with the tremendous stimulus given, fecundity increased rapidly like everything else, and perfect fleets were wanted to bring in egos to inhabit the bodies; these came pouring in, while others of lower types took possession of all the animals with the germs of mind who were individualised at the Coming, the Lords of the Flame doing in a moment for millions what we now do by long care for units.

And now the Arhaṭs from globes A, B, and C came into incarnation, to help the Manu in founding and civilising the fifth, sixth and seventh sub-races of the Lemurians. The fourth sub-race continued, the very egg-headed one, with a stature of from twenty-four to twenty-seven feet in height, loosely and clumsily built, and black in colour; one whom we measured was twenty-five feet in height.[1] Their buildings were proportionate to their size, cyclopean in structure, made of enormous stones.

The Arhaṭs became Kings in the later sub-races, the King-Initiates of the myths which are truer than history.

A King-Initiate would gather a number of persons round Him, forming a clan, and then would

[1] Some curiosity may arise as to how we measured him: first by standing by him, when we came, respectively, a little below and level with his knee; then by setting him against a first-floor balcony at Headquarters, where he could rest his raised hands on the parapet and put his chin on them. We later measured the height of the parapet. The poor image was not made welcome when he put his head over the balcony: "Take him away," said the owner of the balcony; "he is very ugly and enough to frighten anybody." Perhaps he was, poor thing.

teach this clan some of the arts of civilisation, and direct and help them in the building of a city. One large city was erected under such instruction on what is now the island of Madagascar, and many others were similarly built over the great Crescent. The style of architecture was, as said above, cyclopean, impressive from its hugeness.

During the long period thus occupied, the physical appearance of the Lemurians was changing. The central eye at the top of the head was retreating, as it ceased to function, from the surface to the interior of the head, to form the pineal gland, while the two eyes—at first one on each side of it—were becoming active. The Greek legend of Cyclops is evidently a tradition from the early Lemurian age.

There was some domestication of animals; one egg-headed Lemurian was seen leading about a scaly monster, almost as unattractive as his master. Animals of all sorts were eaten raw—among some tribes human flesh was not despised—and creatures of the grade of our slugs, snails and worms, much larger than their degenerate descendants, were regarded with peculiar favour as toothsome morsels.

While the sixth sub-race was developing, a large number of Initiates and their disciples were sent off from the Inter-Chain Nirvāṇa to the Earth,[1] to help the Manu of the fourth Root Race by incarnating in the best bodies He had so far

[1] It may be noted that while the general rule was that the less evolved should be sent first to the Earth, exceptions were made where help was wanted, as in this case with this special boat-load.

evolved. The very best bodies being given to those who had exhausted their karma, their occupants were able to improve them, and to get out of them everything which they were capable of yielding. These Arhaṭs and their pupils worked under the Lords of the Moon and the Manus of the third and fourth Root Races; the seventh sub-race, the bluish-white, was evolved by their help, and furnished men and women of a better type for further moulding by the Manu of the fourth.

CHAPTER VIII

THE FOURTH ROOT RACE

THE Head of the Hierarchy began, almost immediately after His coming, to make arrangements for the founding of the fourth Root Race, employing the future Manu to pick out the smallest, densest and best of the Lemurian types available; and while the founding and growth of civilisation under the King-Initiates were going forward among the Lemurians, the Manu of the coming Race was diligently seeking for the egos suitable for His purpose, and selecting for them appropriate incarnations. He gathered together, in one case, thousands of people, and finally selected one, after tests that lasted over many years, evidently experiencing much difficulty in finding desirable ancestors for His Race. Tribes were set apart, their members inter-marrying for long periods, and the Manu chose promising specimens and transplanted them; He and His disciples incarnated in the progeny of these to raise the physical level. He carried on various experiments simultaneously on the points of the Star, utilising the differences of climate. It looked at first a hopeless task, as though negroes and mulattoes should inter-marry to make a white race; but after generations of selection within a tribe, He would take away one or two, and pair them off with another one or two, similarly selected from another tribe. The third-Race Manu had evolved a blue type for His sixth sub-race, and a bluish-white for His seventh, though the masses of the Lemurians remained black; some of the fourth sub-race also mixed in with the blue, and slowly, very slowly, the general Lemurian type improved. It is noticeable also that when, in other parts of the world a lighter-coloured or better type appeared, it was sent off to the Manu, and He tried to find for it a suitable husband or wife; we observed one that was thus sent in from the Madagascan city, and others similarly came in from elsewhere.

More rapid progress was made after the arrival of the Initiates, mentioned at the close of the last chapter, the best of the bodies improved by their indwelling being taken by the Manu for the shaping of His first sub-race; the fourth Race had thus, ultimately, a very fine founding and nursing, thanks to the large number of developed people who took the lead and pressed things forward. The Manu was able, finally, to take the bodies of the seventh sub-race, improved by the Initiates using them, as the nucleus of His first sub-race, the Rmoahal, of the fourth Root Race. All who were taken on into the fourth Root Race were the Initiates and their disciples in these bodies, and none at this stage were taken from those who had previously been evolving on the Earth Chain.

Subba Rao distinguished the Lemurians as blue-black, the Atlanteans as red-yellow, and the Āryans as brown-white. We find the fourth Race Manu eliminating the blue from the colour of His people, passing through purple into the red of the Rmoahal sub-race, and then, by mixing in the blue-white of the seventh Lemurian sub-race, He obtained the first sub-race which seemed to be fully human, and that we could imagine as living among ourselves. After the race-type was fully established, He thus had the materials for the rich red-brown of the Toltec, the third sub-race, the most splendid and imperial of the Atlantean peoples, which ruled the world for tens of thousands of years. After a long period of patient working, about a million years having been spent in taking stupendous trouble and care, He reached a fair resemblance to the type given to Him to produce; then He definitely founded the Race, He Himself taking incarnation, and calling His disciples to take bodies in His own family, His posterity thus forming the Race. In the most literal sense the Manu of a Race is its Progenitor, for the whole Race has its Manu as its physical ancestor.

Even the Manu's immediate descendants, however, were not a very attractive-looking crowd, judging by our present standard, although a vast improvement on the surrounding population. They were smaller, but had no nervous organisation worth speaking of, and their astral bodies were shapeless. It is extraordinary what He made of such a body for Himself, moulding and shaping it after His own astral and mental bodies, and modifying the pigment in the skin, till He worked it into more of the colour that He wished for His Race.

After this many generations passed before the young Race took possession of its continent, Atlantis, but from this point onwards ship-loads of egos begin to come in from the Inter-Chain Nirvāṇa, to inhabit the fourth Race bodies. The Manu arranged with the Root-Manu to send Him large numbers of egos ready for incarnation—those from globe D of the Moon Chain who had complete causal bodies, and who had individualised in the lunar fourth and fifth Rounds. Some of these came into the Tlavatli sub-race, and some later into the Toltec, when it was evolved; and then He again incarnated in the latter, and founded the City of the Golden Gates, the first of many successive cities of that name. The founding was about one million years ago, one hundred and fifty thousand years before the first great catastrophe which rent the continent of Atlantis.

The Toltec was at this time the ruling Race, by virtue of its great superiority. It was a warrior race, going all over the world and subduing its inhabitants, but its pure types never formed the lower classes anywhere. Even in the City of the Golden Gates, only the aristocracy and the middle class were Toltec; the lower classes were of mixed blood, and were largely composed of men and women taken captive in wars with other sub-races, and reduced to servitude by their conquerors.

At this time arrived on Earth a ship-load of egos, in a group of whom—which kept much together—we are specially interested, as it contained many old friends, Sirius, Orion, Leo and others; some of these were ear-marked on their arrival by Vaivasvaṭa Manu—the Manu of the fifth Race—as part of His future materials. Hence H. P. Blavatsky speaks of the founding of the fifth Race as occurring one million years ago, though it was only led out from Atlantis 79,997 B. C. These, later, formed the group with an average 1,200 to 1,000 years' interval between death and re-birth.[1]

The interval between death and re-birth was at this time naturally somewhat shorter, for the material gathered in these primitive lives was not enough to make a long interval, however thinly spread out. The people were not yet capable of deep feeling, though making something out of the heaven-life. In the heaven-world these egos kept together, and the filmy beings connected with them in the intuitional sphere showed a strong affinity for each other. In the lower spheres there was apparently a dull, groping, sense of 'want,' as though they were very dimly sensing the absence of the old friends of former lives and of the Inter-Chain interval, who were still sleeping away in the Inter-chain Nirvāṇa, not to arrive on Earth for another 400,000 years. In the intuitional sphere, these 700-year people were in touch with the 1,200-year group, but it was only when the former arrived on the Earth that there was a time of general rejoicing among the egos in the higher mental sphere, due chiefly to the arrival of those who were the most deeply loved and revered—the future Masters. Those immediately

[1] These intervals must be taken provisionally; the intervals between death and re-birth in this group and in the one mentioned below were relatively *about* as these lengths.

connected with some of the earlier group were still in that Nirvāṇa, although others had come to earth with the 1,200-year set, among them the two future Masters who now wear English bodies.[1] A good deal of slight retarding or hastening of re-birth was resorted to, in order to keep the group together in incarnation.

In one of these early lives, Corona[2]—a very fine fighter—came from the City of the Golden Gates, and conquered the Tlavatli tribe in which our friends had incarnated. Unconscious as he was of the tie between them, he was yet influenced by it, and treated the tribe kindly: instead of carrying them off as slaves, he introduced various improvements, and incorporated the tribe into the Toltec Empire. Sirius took several births in the Tlavatli sub-race, and then passed into the Toltec. Glancing forward, we saw him once incarnated among the Rmoahals, in order to be with Ursa and others, then several lives were passed in the Turanian, the fourth sub-race—a Chinese stage—and a number in the Akkadian, the sixth; he was observed trading among a people who resembled the Phœnicians of later times. He did not take the sub-races in any special order, and it is difficult, at present, to generalise on this question.

Shiploads of egos continued to arrive, and the main cause of separation seemed to be the method of individualisation. Egos of all Rays, or temperaments, of similar general development were mixed

[1] They were once Sir Thomas More and 'Philalethes' Thomas Vaughan.

[2] Known in later history as Julius Cæsar.

up, but those of different intervals between re-births were not. Nor was there any mingling of the large classes of the Moon-Men and Animal-Men. Unless an individual had been taken through the Inner Round, and had undergone its special forcing, when he passed into the class ahead of him, the broad lines of distinction remained, and one class did not overtake another. Even when the Basket-works had completed their causal bodies, the basket origin remained discernible.

The first ship-load containing the 700-year group arrived on Earth about 600,000 B. C., some 250,000 years after the first great cataclysm which rent the continent of Atlantis. With it came the future Masters, Mars and Mercury and others, and Mars was born in the north in the Tlavatli sub-race, with Sūrya and Mercury for his father and mother. Herakles was also in the family, as an elder sister. Sūrya was the Chief of the tribe, and Mars, his eldest son, soon became its foremost warrior.[1] At the age of fifteen, he was left for dead on a battle-field, but was searched for and found by his sister, who was passionately devoted to him, and who nursed him back to health. He succeeded his father as Chief, and had his first experience of earthly rule.

There was one quite small but interesting group, only 105 in number, who arrived about the same period, 600,000 B. C., but who did not come from the Moon. It was a contingent arranged for specially by the Head of the Hierarchy, and seemed to consist of some who in Venus had been pet

[1] See the Proem for these and other names.

animals of the Lords of the Flame, and were so strongly linked to Them by affection, that without Them they would not have evolved. They had individualised on Venus, and were brought over here, and He placed them all in the first and second Rays. There were other small groups, abnormal in evolution. Thus one little group, belonging to the third Round, was sent over to Mercury, for the special treatment possible under Mercury conditions, and was then brought back here. Some underwent treatment of this kind in preparation for the fifth Root Race. It may be noted that H. P. Blavatsky speaks of some who came to the Earth from Mercury.

Herakles' third birth on earth was in the same tribe, in which many members of the group were re-united. They had a certain amount of civilisation, but the houses were mere huts, and—the climate being warm—the clothing was scanty. The life was marked by the re-knitting of the undesirable link with Scorpio, and has therefore a certain importance for those concerned. The tribe in which Herakles was a warrior was attacked by a very savage tribe to which Scorpio belonged; the plan of the latter was to surprise the other tribe and slaughter it as a sacrifice to their deity, or, failing that, to commit suicide, and thereby gain power to torment their enemies from the other world. They performed magical rites of an Obeah-like nature, which, though done in secret, seem to have become known to Herakles. The final suicide was essential to the success of the whole plan of after-death activity, and the weird spells, with many tremendous 'curses and swears,' became then effective: the result of these was apparently as much dreaded by their foes as it was valued by themselves. The attack failed, and they proceeded to carry out the alternative to victory, a general suicide with gruesome rites. Herakles, partly because his religion did not permit suicide, partly moved by superstitious fears, and partly by the thought that the savages would make nice brawny slaves, interfered and saved a number of them whom he captured and bound. Later on these folk plotted to assassinate him, and he had them executed; thus began again, this time on earth, a long series of antagonisms not yet exhausted.

It may be noted, as bearing on the closeness of ties set up between individuals and enduring for hundreds of lives, that from this time forward a set of persons within the large groups of 1,200- and 700-years' people—a set which we may, for the sake of distinction, dub 'the Clan'—while visiting almost every country in the world, kept generally together, and Sirius, especially, was rarely found to marry outside this little group. Taking a bird's-eye-view, we notice that there were occasional gatherings of the whole big Clan, as in the City of the Golden Gates when Mars was King, in Peru when he was Emperor, in the mainland near the White Island under the Manu, and in the second and third sub-races at their beginnings and their migrations—to take a few instances out of many. Herakles turned out to be a fighting sort of person, clinging closely to Mars; Sirius a more peaceful one, following Mercury continually; Alcyone is also of that ilk, with Mizar. A good many belonging to the larger groups with whom we were very familiar in those early days, however, seem to have dropped out by the way, and we have not met them in this life; some may be just now in the heaven-world. The Theosophical Society is another instance of the gathering of this same Clan, and people are coming into it all the time, who turn out to be old friends. Some again, like Corona, are just now awaiting a favourable opportunity for incarnation.

The ship-loads continued to come in for a long time, only ceasing with the catastrophe of 75,000 B.C., so the phrase as to shutting the door evidently applies only to the animals coming up into humanity, and not to those whose causal bodies were already developed. The anthropoid apes, of whom H. P. Blavatsky spoke as still admissible to human bodies, would belong to the animal kingdom of the Moon, not to that of the Earth; they took up bodies produced by the "sin of the mindless," and are the gorillas, chimpanzees, orang-utangs, baboons, and gibbons. They might be looked for in Africa, and might incarnate there in the still existing very low human races of Lemurian type.

Coming down to 220,000 B. C., to the City of the Golden Gates, we find Mars there ruling as Emperor, and bearing by inheritance the title of 'Divine Ruler,' transmitted from Those who had ruled in the past, the great Initiates of earlier days. Mercury was the chief Hierophant, the head of the State religion. It is remarkable how these two come down together through the ages, one always the Ruler, the Warrior, the other always the Teacher, the Priest. Noteworthy also is the fact that we never saw Mars in a woman's body, whereas Mercury did take one from time to time.

There was quite a gathering of the Clan at this time. The Crown Prince was then Vajra, and Ulysses, who had been a successful leader on the frontier, was Captain of the Imperial Guard. This Guard formed a picked body of men, even the privates being of the upper classes, and they had charge of the Palace; they were not supposed to go out to war, but rather to strut about in gorgeous uniforms, to attend on the person of the Monarch during ceremonials, and increase his splendour. Later, however, after the death of Ulysses, Vajra became Captain of the Guard, and he persuaded his father to allow him to take his troop off into a campaign; being always a turbulent and restless person, he was not content to lead a life of show and luxury, and his soldiers, who adored him for his dash and courage, were willing enough to exchange their golden breastplates for the severer armament of war. Among them we find a number of our Clan: Herakles was there, with Pindar, Beatrix, Gemini, Capella, Lutetia, Bellona, Apis, Arcor, Capricorn, Theodoros, Scotus and Sappho. Herakles had as servant-boys three Tlavatli youths, captured in battle by his father and given to him—Hygeia, Boötes, and Alcmene. The soldiers were distinctly rowdy, indulging in orgies of eating and drinking, and then rioting about the city; but they had the merit of respecting learning, paid reverence to the priests. and attended religious ceremonies as part of their Palace duty. They had a certain code of honour among themselves and kept it very rigidly, and in this was included the protection of the weak. Their homes were not unrefined, after a fashion, though not squaring with modern ideas.

The death of Ulysses, the Captain of the Guard, must not be passed by unnoticed, for it linked in indissoluble bonds the three persons chiefly concerned. The Emperor Mars had placed in the Captain's hands the care of his son Vajra, a daring, reckless lad; for the times were dangerous, conspiracies were rife in the Golden City, and the capture of the person of the Crown Prince would have been a great triumph for the conspirators. Hence Ulysses would not allow the Prince to leave the Palace grounds, much to that young man's disgust. One day the Captain and the Prince were sitting at some little distance from the Palace, and a band of conspirators, greatly daring, crept up under the shelter of some bushes, and suddenly pounced upon the two. The Prince was struck down senseless, but Ulysses, bestriding his body, fought fiercely against the assailants, shouting for help. His cries were heard, and as he fell bleeding across the body of his young master, pierced by many wounds, some soldiers of the Guard came rushing up, and the conspirators took to their heels. The two unconscious bodies were lifted on to stretchers, carried to the Throne-room of the Palace, where the Emperor was sitting, and there laid at his feet. The dying Captain raised his eyes to his Emperor: "Sire, forgive; I did my best."

The Emperor stooped down, and dipped his finger in the blood welling up from the Captain's breast; he touched with it the forehead of the dying man, his own forehead and his feet, and musically his voice fell upon the silence: "By the blood that was shed for me and mine, the bond between us shall never be broken. Depart in peace, faithful servant and friend."

The words reached the ears already becoming dull; Ulysses smiled, and died. The young Prince, who was only stunned, revived. And the bond lasted on, millennium after millennium, and became the bond between Master and disciples, for ever unbreakable.

The lives of Herakles were not remarkable in any way for a long time. They were spent in fighting, when the body was that of a man, in having very numerous babies when it was that of a woman.

The spread of black magic in Atlantis led up to the second great catastrophe of 200,000 B. C., which left as remnants of the great continent which had joined Europe and Africa to America the huge islands of Ruṭa and Ḍaiṭya. They endured until the catastrophe of 75,025 B. C.[1] overwhelmed them beneath the waters of the ocean we now call the Atlantic.

During the next hundred thousand years, the people of Atlantis flourished abundantly, and built up a mighty, but over-luxurious, civilisation. Its centre was in the City of the Golden Gates—the name was preserved—but it spread far and wide over the world, both over Africa and the West. Unhappily with the civilisation spread again also

[1] Usually given roughly as the 80,000 B. C. catastrophe.

the knowledge giving control over nature which, used for selfish purposes, becomes black magic.

Members of the Clan came into it, more or less, sometimes being born into families immersed in it, and breaking away; sometimes dallying with it and being a little tarred therewith. Some experiences of Alcyone's that often tormented him in the form of dreams in a later life may here be put on record.[1] They happened in a life that occurred about 100,000 B. C., Corona was then the White Emperor at the City of the Golden Gates; Mars was a general under him, and Herakles was the wife of Mars. A great rebellion was being plotted, and a man of strange and evil knowledge,—a 'Lord of the Dark Face,' leagued with the dark Earth-Spirits who form the 'Kingdom of Pan,' the semi-human, semi-animal creatures who are the originals of the Greek satyrs—was gradually gathering round himself a huge army which followed him as Emperor, the Emperor of the Midnight Sun, the Dark Emperor, set over against the White. The worship he established, with himself as central idol—huge images of himself being placed in the temples—was sensual and riotous, holding men through the gratification of their animal passions. Against the White Cave of Initiation in the City of the Golden Gates was set up the Dark Cave in which the mysteries of Pan, the Earth-God, were celebrated. All was working up toward another great catastrophe.

Alcyone, some one hundred and twenty lives back, was the son of a man who followed the hideous

[1] See 'Rents in the Veil of Time,' *The Theosophist,* May, 1910.

rites of this dark cult, but he held himself much aloof, shrinking from the wild orgies of animalism that enchained the bulk of the worshippers. But, as is too often the case, he fell into the trap baited by a woman's beauty, and met a grievous fate. The story may be told, as it throws light on the conditions which brought down later upon Atlantis the heavy doom pronounced by the Occult Hierarchy.

CHAPTER IX

BLACK MAGIC IN ATLANTIS

AN EPISODE

ALCYONE is lying half asleep, half awake, on a grassy bank sloping down to a rippling brooklet. His face is perplexed, even anxious, the reflex of his troubled mind. He is the son of a wealthy and powerful family, belonging to the priesthood, the 'Priesthood of the Midnight Sun,' vowed to the service of the Gods of the Nether World, whom the priests sought in the gloom of night, in dark earth-caverns opening into passages that led down, down, into unknown depths.

At this time, the great civilised nations of Atlantis had drawn into two opposed camps: the one, looking to the ancient City of the Golden Gates as their sacred metropolis, maintained the traditional worship of their race, the worship of the Sun—the Sun in the beauty of his rising, clad in the bright colours of the dawning, encircled with the radiant youths and maidens of his court; the Sun in the zenith of his glory, the blazing strength of his mid-heaven, scattering abroad his brilliant rays of life and heat; the Sun in the splendid couch of his setting, touching into rarest softest hues the clouds he left as promise of his return. The people worshipped him with choral dances, with incense and with flowers, with joyous songs, and with offerings of gold and gems, with laughter and with minstrelsy, with joyous games and sports. Over these children of the Blazing Sun the White Emperor bore rule, and his race had for long millennia held unchallenged sway. But gradually the outlying kingdoms, ruled by his lieutenants, had become independent, and they were beginning to join together into a Federation, rallying round a man who had appeared among them, a remarkable but sinister figure.

This man, Oduarpa by name, ambitious and crafty by nature, had realised that, in order to give stability to the Federation and to make head against the White Emperor, it was necessary to call to his aid the resources of the darker magic, to make compact with the denizens of the Nether World, and to establish a worship which would attract the people by its sensuous pleasures, and by the weird unholy powers it placed within the reach of its adepts. He had himself, by such compact, extended his life over an abnormal period, and, when going into battle, rendered himself impervious to spear or sword-thrust by materialising a metallic coating over his body, which turned weapons aside as would a shirt of mail. He aimed at supreme power, and was in a fair way to reach it, and he dreamed of himself as sitting crowned in the Palace of the City of the Golden Gates.

The father of our youth was among the most intimate of his friends, and privy to his most secret designs, and both hoped that the lad would devote himself to the forwarding of their ambitions. But the youth had dreams and hopes of his own, nourished silently within his own heart; he had seen in the visions of the night the stately figure of Mars, a general of the White Emperor, Corona, had gazed into his deep compelling eyes, had heard, as from afar, his words: "Alcyone, thou art mine, of my people, and surely thou shalt come to me, and know thyself as mine. Pledge not thyself to mine enemies, thou who art mine." And he had vowed himself his subject, as vassal to his lord.

Of this was Alcyone thinking, as he lay musing by the stream. For another influence was playing upon him, and his blood ran hotly in his veins. Ill-pleased at his indifference to their worship—nay, at his shrinking from it, even in its outward rites of animal sacrifice and poured out oblations of strong drink—his father and Oduarpa had conceived the plan of drawing him into the secret mysteries by the allurements of a maiden, Cygnus, dark and beauteous as the midnight sky star-studded, who loved him deeply, but had so far failed to win his young heart with her charms. Between her dusky brilliant eyes and his half-fascinated gaze would float the splendid face of his vision, and he would hear again the thrilling whisper: "Thou art mine."

At length, however, she had so far won him—persuaded to the task by her mother, a veritable witch-hag, who had told her that thus alone might she gain his love—as to obtain from him a promise that he would accompany her to the underground caves in which the magical rites were performed, which drew the denizens of the Nether World from their retreats, and gained from them the forbidden knowledge which changed the human into the animal form, thus giving opportunity for free play to the passions of the brute hidden in man, passions of lust and slaughter. Cygnus had played upon his heart with skill taught by her own passion, and had fanned his indifference into fire, not enduring, indeed, but warm while it lasted. And to-day the passion was hot upon him, and the power of her allurements swayed him. For she had just left him, after coaxing him to promise to meet her after sunset near the caverns where the mysteries were performed, and he was struggling between his longing to follow her, and his repulsion from the guessed-at scenes in which he would be expected to take part. The sun sank below the horizon and the sky darkened while still Alcyone lay musing; with a shudder he started to his feet, but now his mind was made up, and he turned his steps towards the *rendez-vous*.

To his surprise a considerable company was gathered at the spot; his father was there with his priestly friends, and Cygnus with a crescent moon on her head, the sign of the bride, and a band of maidens round her, all clad in gauzy star-spangled raiment, through which the brown lithe limbs gleamed duskily; a band of youths of his own age, among whom he recognised his nearest friends, were also waiting, with spotted skins of animals for raiment, and light cymbals which they clashed as they danced round him like fauns.

"Hail, Alcyone!" they cried, "favourite of the Dark Sun, child of the Night! See where thy Moon and her Stars await thee. But first thou must win her from us, her defenders."

Suddenly she was whirled away in the midst of the dancers, and vanished in the darkness of the cavern yawning wide in front, and Alcyone was seized, stripped of his garments, a skin like that of the rest thrown over him, and intoxicated, maddened, he fled in her pursuit, amid laughter and cheers: "Hey! young hunter, be swift, lest the hounds pull down thy deer!"

After a few minutes Alcyone, with the shouting crowd at his heels, had raced through the outer caverns, and had reached a vast hall, blazing with crimson light. In the midst rose a huge canopy, red in colour and studded with great carbuncles, that tossed back the light like splashes of fiery blood; beneath the canopy was a copper throne, inlaid with gold, and before it a yawning gulf, out of which flashed tongues of flame, lurid and roaring. Heavy clouds of strange incense filled the air, intoxicating, maddening.

The rush swept him onwards, and he was caught up into a wild tumultuous whirl of dancers, who shouted, yelled, sprang into the air in wild bounds, circling round the canopied throne, and crying: "Oduarpa! Oduarpa! Come, we are craving for thee!"

A low roll of thunder crept muttering round the cavern, growing louder and louder, and ending in a tremendous clap just overhead; the flames leapt up, and amid them rose the mighty form of Oduarpa, steel-grey in his magic sheathing, stern, majestic, with his face grave, even sad, as that of a fallen Archangel, but strong with unbending pride and iron resolution. He took his seat on the throne, where he sat throughout all that followed, silent and sombre, taking no part in the riot; he waved his hand, and the mad orgy recommenced, the wildest dancers bathing in the flames which lapped over the edges of the gulf and tossed themselves high in air. Alcyone had caught sight of Cygnus in the midst of the youths and the girls, and he raced, mad with excitement, in her direction; she eluded him, her escort baffled him, he touched her only to see her whirled out of his reach. At last, panting, wild, he made a desperate rush, and the escort fled with screams of laughter, each youth with a girl, and he leapt on Cygnus and clasped her in his arms.

Wilder and wilder grew the revel; slaves bearing huge pitchers of strong drink appeared, accompanied by others with goblets. Madness of drink was added to madness of motion, and the lurid lights sank low into twilight of redness. The orgy which followed is better hidden than described.

But see! out of the passage whence had emerged Oduarpa, comes a wild procession; hairy bipeds, long-armed and claw-footed, with animals' heads and manes streaming over shoulders, horrent, appalling, non-human, yet horribly human. They hold in their claw-like hands phials and boxes, and as they mingle with the wildest dancers they give these to the revellers most mad with drink and lust. These smear over their limbs the ointment in the boxes, drink the contents of the phials, and lo! they drop senseless, huddled on the ground, but from each huddled heap there springs an animal form, snarling, ravening, and vanishes from the cavern into the darkness of the outside night.

The bright Gods help the wayfarers who meet these bedevilled astral materialisations, fierce and conscienceless as animals, cruel and crafty as men! But the bright Gods are sleeping, and only the hosts of the Midnight Sun, ghosts, goblins and all evil things, are abroad. The creatures return, their jaws dripping with blood, their hides draggled with filth, ere morning dawns, and, crouching on the huddled forms on the floor of the cavern, sink into them and disappear.

Such orgies as these were held from time to time, Oduarpa using them to increase his hold upon the people, and he established similar rites at many places, making himself the central figure in all, becoming a veritable object of worship, and gradually welding the people together in allegiance to himself, until he became the acknowledged Emperor. His relations with the inhabitants of the Nether World—called in latter days, as said above, the 'Kingdom of Pan'—gave him much additional power, and he had trusted lieutenants—bound to him by their common knowledge of, and participation in, the ghastly abominations of that realm—ever prompt to carry out his commands.

He finally succeeded in assembling a very large army and began his march against the White Emperor, directing his course towards the City of the Golden Gates. He hoped to overawe and conquer, not only by fair assault of arms, but by the terror that would be spread by his hellish allies, and the ghastly transformations of the black wizards into animal forms. He himself had a body-guard of magic animals round him, powerful desire-forms materialised into physical bodies, who guarded him and devoured any who approached him with hostile intent. When a battle was raging, and the issue doubtful, Oduarpa would suddenly loose against his foes his horde of demoniacal allies, who would rush into the fray, tearing with teeth and claws, and spread panic among the startled hosts. When his enemies broke into flight, he would send these swift demons in pursuit, and the troops of wizards would likewise take animal forms, gorging themselves on the bodies of the slain.

Thus he fought his way onwards, northward ever, till he came near the City of the Golden Gates, where the last army of the White Emperor lay embattled. Alcyone had fought as a soldier in the army, partly under a spell, and yet awake enough to be sick at heart at his surroundings, and Cygnus, with other ladies, had accompanied the camp. The day of the decisive battle dawned; the imperial army was led by the White Emperor himself, Corona, and the right wing of the army was under the command of his most trusted general, Mars. During the preceding night, Alcyone had been visited once more by his early vision, and had heard the well-loved voice: "Alcyone, thou art fighting against thy true lord, and to-morrow wilt thou meet me, face to face. Break thou then thy rebel sword and yield thee to me; thou shalt die by my side, and it shall yet be well."

And so indeed it happed. For in the fierce shock of battle, as the imperial troops were giving way, the Emperor slain, Alcyone saw, struggling gallantly against overwhelming odds, the face of his vision, the general Mars. With a cry he sprang forward, breaking his sword in two, and catching up a spear, he threw himself at Mars' back, fiercely thrusting through a soldier who struck at Mars from behind. At that moment Oduarpa charged up, mad with fury, and struck Mars down, and with a cry that rang across the field, he summoned Cygnus, by swift spell changing her into a fierce animal, which rushed with bared fangs at Alcyone, fainting from loss of blood. But in the very act, the love which had been her life cried out from Cygnus' soul and wrought her rescue; for its strong flow changed into loving woman the form of ravening hate, and with a dying kiss on Alcyone's dying face she breathed away her life.

Herakles, the wife of Mars, was captured by Oduarpa in the assault on the City of the Golden Gates that followed and completed his victory; she indignantly repulsed his advances, and catching up a dagger stabbed at him with all her strength. The dagger slipped aside on his metallic casing, and, laughing, he struck her down, outraging her as she lay half senseless: when she recovered consciousness, he summoned his horrible animals, and they tore her into pieces and devoured her.

Oduarpa, enthroned on a pile of corpses, and surrounded by his animal and half-animal guards, was crowned Emperor of the City of the Golden Gates, assuming the desecrated title of 'Divine Ruler'. But his triumph was not of long duration, for Vaivasvaṭa Manu marched against him with a great army, and His mere presence put to flight the denizens of the Kingdom of Pan, while He destroyed the artificial thought-forms, created by black magic. A crushing victory scattered the army of the Emperor, and he himself was shut up in a tower whither he had fled in the rout. The building was fired, and he perished miserably, literally boiled to death within his materialised metallic shell.

Vaivasvaṭa Manu purified the City and re-established there the rule of the White Emperor, consecrating to that office a trusted servant of the Hierarchy. For a time things went on well, but slowly the evil again gathered power, and the southern centre once more grew strong; until, at last, the same Lord of the Dark Face, appearing in a new re-incarnation, again fought against the White Emperor of the time, and set up his own throne against him. Then the words of doom were spoken by the Head of the Hierarchy, and, as the *Occult Commentary* tells us: the "Great King of the Dazzling Face"—the White Emperor—sent to his brother Chiefs: "Prepare. Arise, ye men of the Good Law, and cross the land while yet dry." The "Rod of the Four"—the Kumāras—was raised. "The hour has struck, the black night is ready." The "servants of the Great Four" warned their people, and many escaped. "Their Kings reached them in their Vimānas[1] and led them on to the lands of

[1] Chariots which moved in the air—the ancient aeroplanes.

fire and metal [east and north]."[1] Explosions of gas, floods and earthquakes destroyed Ruṭa and Ḍaiṭya, the huge islands of Atlantis, left from the catastrophe of 200,000 B. C., and only the island of Poseidonis remained, the last remnant of the once huge continent of the Atlantic. These islands perished in 75,025 B. C., Poseidonis enduring to 9,564 B. C. when it also was whelmed beneath the ocean.

[1] *The Secret Doctrine,* ii, pp. 445, 446.

CHAPTER X

THE CIVILISATION OF ATLANTIS[1]

ATLANTIS peopled many countries with its sub-races, and built many splendid civilisations. Egypt, Mesopotamia, India, North and South America, knew them, and the Empires they raised endured for long, and reached a point of glory that the Āryan Race has not yet overtopped. The chapters XI—XIII on Peru and Chaldea in the present work shew remnants of their greatness, and these may be supplemented by some additional details.

Mr. Scott-Elliot thus describes the famous City of the Golden Gates: "A beautifully wooded park-like country surrounded the city. Scattered over a large area of this were the villa-residences of the wealthier classes. To the west lay a range of mountains, from which the water-supply of the city was drawn. The city itself was built on the slopes of a hill, which rose from the plain about five hundred feet. On the summit of this hill lay the Emperor's palace and gardens, in the centre of which welled

[1] A good account of this may be read in *The Story of Atlantis* by W. Scott-Elliot. The writers of the present book were among the *collaborateurs* who collected the materials therein so ably arranged and presented, so the ground is very familiar to us.

up from the earth a never-ending stream of water, supplying first the palace and the fountains in the gardens, thence flowing in the four directions, and falling in cascades into a canal or moat which encompassed the palace grounds, and thus separated them from the city which lay below on every side. From this canal four channels led the water through four quarters of the city to cascades which, in their turn, supplied another encircling canal at a lower level. There were three such canals forming concentric circles, the outermost and lowest of which was still above the level of the plain. A fourth canal at this lowest level, but on a rectangular plan, received the constantly flowing waters, and in its turn discharged them into the sea. The city extended over part of the plain, up to the edge of this great outermost moat, which surrounded and defended it with a line of waterways extending about twelve miles by ten miles square.

"It will thus be seen that the city was divided into three great belts, each hemmed in by its canals. The characteristic feature of the upper belt, that lay just below the palace grounds, was a circular race-course and large public gardens. Most of the houses of the court officials also lay on this belt, and here also was an institution of which we have no parallel in modern times. The term 'Strangers' Home' amongst us suggests a mean appearance and sordid surroundings; but this was a palace where all strangers who might come to the city were entertained as long as they might choose to stay—being treated all the time as guests of the Government. The detached houses of the inhabitants and the various temples scattered throughout the city occupied the other two belts. In the days of the Toltec greatness there seems to have been no real poverty—even the retinue of slaves attached to most houses being well fed and clothed—but there were a number of comparatively poor houses in the lowest belt to the north, as well as outside the outermost canal towards the sea. The inhabitants of this part were mostly connected with the shipping, and their houses, though detached, were built closer together than in other districts."

Other large towns, built on the plains, were protected by immense banks of earth, sloping towards the town, and sometimes terraced, while, on the outward side, they were faced with thick plates of metal, clamped together; these were supported on great beams of wood, the uprights being driven deeply into the earth; when these were in place, and connected with heavy crossbars, the plates were attached to them, overlapping like scales, and then the space between the earth-work and the barrier was filled with earth, solidly rammed together. The whole formed a practically impregnable barrier against the spears, swords, and bows and arrows which were the usual weapons of the time. But such a city necessarily lay open to assaults from above, and the Atlanteans carried the making of air-ships—aeroplanes, we should call them now—to a high pitch of excellence; and, if such a city were to be attacked, these birds-of-war were sent to hover over it, and to drop into it bombs which burst in the air, and discharged a rain of heavy poisonous vapour, destructive of human life. Allusions to these may be found in the conflicts related in the great epics and Purāṇas of the Hindūs. They had also weapons which projected sheaves of fire-tipped arrows, which scattered far and wide as they hurtled through the air like deadly rockets, and many others of similar kinds, all constructed by men well-versed in the higher branches of scientific knowledge. Many of these are described in the very ancient books above referred to, and they are mentioned as being given by some superior Being. The knowledge required for their construction was never made common.

The land system of the Toltecs will be described in the chapters on Peru, and the absence of poverty and the general well-being of the population were largely due to the provision therein made for universal primary education. The whole scheme of government was planned out by the Wise for the benefit of all, and not by special classes for their own advantage. Hence the general comfort was immensely higher than in modern civilisations.

Science was carried far, for the use of clairvoyance being habitual, the processes of nature, now invisible to most, were readily observed. Its applications to arts and crafts were also numerous and useful. The rays of sunshine, sent through coloured glass, were used for promoting the growth of plants and animals; scientific breeding was carefully carried out for the improvement of promising species; experiments were tried in crossing—*e.g.*, the crossing of wheat with various grasses produced different kinds of grain; less satisfactory were the attempts which produced wasps from bees, and white ants from ants.[1] The seedless banana was evolved from a melon-like ancestor, containing, like the melon, large quantities of seeds. Forces, the knowledge of which has been lost, were known to the science of the day; one of these was used for the propulsion of both air-and water-ships; another for so changing the relation of heavy bodies to the earth, that the earth repelled instead of attracting them, so making the raising of gigantic stones to a lofty height a matter of the greatest ease. The subtler of these were not applied by machinery, but were controlled by will-power, using the thoroughly understood and developed mechanism of the human body, "the vīṇā of a thousand strings".

Metals were much used and admirably wrought, gold, silver and aurichalcum being those most employed in decoration, and in domestic utensils. They were more often alchemically produced than sought for in the crust of the earth, and were often very artistically introduced to add richness to schemes of decoration, carried out in brilliant colours. Armour was gorgeously inlaid with them, and that used merely for show in pageants and ceremonies

[1] Wheat, bees and ants were brought from Venus by the Lords of the Flame, and the crossing of these with species already existing on the earth brought about the results named. The nature-spirits in charge of some departments of animal and vegetable evolution also attempted on their own account to imitate, with the purely terrestrial resources at their disposal, these importations from another planet. Their efforts, which were only partially successful, are responsible for some of the more unpleasant results above-mentioned.

was often entirely made of the precious metals; golden helmets, breastplates and greaves being worn on such occasions over tunics and stockings of the most brilliant colours—scarlet, orange, and a very exquisite purple.

Food differed in different classes. The masses of the people ate meat, fish, and even reptiles—perhaps one should not say 'even,' remembering the turtle of our City Fathers. The carcase of an animal, with all its contents, was slit down the breast and stomach, and hung up over a large fire; when it was thoroughly cooked through it was removed from the fire, the contents were scooped out and, among the more refined, placed on dishes, while the rougher people gathered round the carcase itself, and plunged their hands into its interior, selecting toothsome dainties—a plan which sometimes led to quarrels; the rest was thrown away or given to domestic animals, the flesh itself being considered as offal. The higher classes partook of similar food, but those belonging immediately to the Court made rather a secret of such banquets. The Divine King, of course, and those closely connected with Him, ate only food composed of grains cooked in various ways, vegetables, fruits, and milk, the latter being drunk as a liquid, or made into many sweet preparations. Fruit-juices were also largely used as drinks. Some of the courtiers and dignitaries, while partaking of these milder comestibles publicly, were observed quietly stealing away to their private chambers and feasting on more toothsome viands, among which fish, as 'high' as modern game, played a not inconspicuous part.

Government was autocratic, and in the palmy days of Toltec civilisation under the Divine Kings, no system could have been happier for the people; but as the unchecked powers They wielded passed into the hands of younger souls, abuses crept in and troubles arose; for here, as everywhere, decay began in the corruption of the highest. The system was that Governors were held accountable for the welfare and happiness of their provinces, and crime or famine was regarded as due to their negligence or incapacity. They were drawn chiefly from the upper classes, but specially promising children were drafted out into the higher schools to be trained for the service of the State, whenever they were found. Sex was no disqualification, as it is now, for any office in the State.[1]

The immense growth of wealth and of luxury gradually undermined the most splendid civilisation that the world has yet seen. Knowledge was prostituted to individual gain, and control over the powers of nature was turned from service to oppression. Hence Atlantis fell, despite the glory of its achievements and the might of its Empires; and the leading of the world passed into the hands of a daughter Race, the Āryan, which, though it has to its credit many magnificent achievements in the past, has not yet reached the zenith of its glory and its power, and will, some centuries

[1] The exclusion of women from political power in England only came, it should be remembered, with the growth of democracy, and the consequent idea that physical force, not intelligence or character, should be the basis of Government. This is the nadir of political life, as the occult system is its zenith.

hence, rise even higher than Atlantis rose in its palmiest days.

We have chosen two daughter civilisations which grew up in later days, far from the great centre of the fourth Root Race—one descended from the third sub-race, the Toltec, the other from the fourth sub-race, the Turanian—in order to give a more vivid and detailed picture of the level reached by the Atlanteans. These did not form part of the investigations made in the summer of 1910, and chronicled in the present book; they were done during the last decade of the nineteenth century by the present writers, working with some other members of the T. S., whose names we are not at liberty to give. One of the present writers put them into the form of articles for *The Theosophical Review,* and these articles are here reprinted in their proper place, as part of a much larger work.

CHAPTER XI

TWO ATLANTEAN CIVILISATIONS[1]

Toltec, in Ancient Peru, B. C. 12,000

THE civilisation of Peru in the thirteenth millennium B. C. so closely resembled that of the Toltec Empire in its zenith, that, having closely studied that period, we utilise it here as an example of Atlantean civilisation. Egypt and India in their Atlantean periods, offered other examples, but, on the whole, the chief features of the Toltec Empire are best reproduced in the Peru which is here described. The Government was autocratic—no other Government in those days was possible.

To show why this was so, we must look back in thought to a period far earlier—to the original segregation of the great fourth Root Race. It will be obvious that when the Manu and His lieutenants—great Adepts from a far higher evolution—incarnated among the youthful Race which They were labouring to develop, They were to those people absolutely as Gods in knowledge and power,

[1] The opening pages of this description of Ancient Peru, as given in the *Theosophical Review*, will be found in Appendix iii, with a brief statement of the circumstances under which it was originally written.

so far were They in advance of them in every conceivable respect. Under such circumstances there could be no form of Government possible but an autocracy, for the Ruler was the only person who really knew anything, and so he had to take the control of everything. These Great Ones became therefore the natural rulers and guides of child-humanity, and ready obedience was ever paid to Them, for it was recognised that wisdom gave authority, and that the greatest help that could be given to the ignorant was that they should be guided and trained. Hence all the order of the new society came, as all true order must ever come, from above and not from below; as the new Race spread the principle persisted, and on this basis the mighty monarchies of remote antiquity were founded, in most cases beginning under great King-Initiates, whose power and wisdom guided Their infant States through all their initial difficulties.

Thus it happened that, even when the original Divine Rulers had yielded Their positions into the hands of Their pupils, the true principle of Government was still understood, and hence, when a new Kingdom was founded, the endeavour was always to imitate as closely as might be, under the new circumstances, the splendid institutions which the Divine Wisdom had already given to the world. It was only as selfishness arose among both peoples and rulers that gradually the old order changed, and gave place to experiments that were not wise, to Governments which were inspired by greed and ambition, instead of by the fulfilment of duty.

At the period with which we have to deal—12,000 B. C.—the earlier Cities of the Golden Gates had been sunk beneath the waves for many thousands of years, and though the chief of the Kings of the Island of Poseidonis still arrogated to himself the beautiful title which had belonged to them, he made no pretence to imitate the methods of Government which had ensured them a stability so far beyond the common lot of human arrangements. Some centuries before, however, a well-conceived attempt to revive—though of course on a much smaller scale—the life of that ancient system had been made by the Monarchs of the country afterwards called Peru, and at the time of which we are speaking this revival was in full working order, and perhaps at the zenith of its glory, though it maintained its efficiency for many centuries after. It is, then, with this Peruvian revival that we are now concerned.

It is a little difficult to give an idea of the physical appearance of the race inhabiting the country, for no race at present existing on earth sufficiently resembles it to suggest a comparison, without misleading our readers in one direction or another. Such representatives of the great third sub-race of the Atlantean Root Race as are still to be seen on earth are degraded and debased, as compared with the Race in its glory. Our Peruvian had the high cheek-bones and the general shape of face which we associate with the highest type of the Red Indian, and yet he had modifications in its contour which made him almost more Āryan than Atlantean; his expression differed fundamentally from that of most modern Red Men, for it was usually frank, joyous, and mild, and in the higher classes keen intellect and great benevolence frequently showed themselves. In colour he was reddish-bronze, lighter on the whole among the upper classes, and darker among the lower, though the intermingling between the classes was such that it is scarcely possible to make even this distinction.

The disposition of the people was on the whole happy, contented, and peaceful. The laws were few, suitable, and well administered, and so the people were naturally law-abiding; the climate was for the most part delightful, and enabled them to do without undue toil all the work connected with the tilling of the land, giving them a bountiful harvest in return for moderate exertion—a climate calculated to make the people contented and disposed to make the best of life. Obviously such a state of mind among their people gave the rulers of the country an enormous advantage to begin with.

As has already been remarked, the Monarchy was absolute, yet it differed so entirely from anything now existing that the mere statement conveys no idea of the facts. The key-note of the entire system was responsibility. The King had absolute power, certainly, but he had also the absolute responsibility for everything; he had been trained from his earliest years to understand that if, anywhere in his vast Empire, an avoidable evil of any kind existed—if a man willing to work could not get the kind of work that suited him, if even a child was ill and could not get proper attention—this was a slur upon his administration, a blot upon his reign, a stain upon his personal honour.

He had a large governing class to assist him in his labours, and he subdivided the whole huge nation in the most elaborate and systematic manner under its care. First of all the Empire was divided into provinces, over each of which was a kind of Viceroy; under them again were what we might call Lord-Lieutenants of counties; and under them again Governors of cities or of smaller districts. Every one of these was directly responsible to the man next above him in rank for the well-being of every person in his division. This subdivision of responsibility went on until we come to a kind of Centurion—an official who had a hundred families in his care, for whom he was absolutely responsible. This was the lowest member of the governing class; but he, on his part, usually aided himself in his work by appointing some one out of every tenth household as a kind of voluntary assistant, to bring him the more instant news of anything that was needed or anything that went wrong.[1]

If any one of this elaborate network of officials neglected any part of his work, a word to his next superior would bring down instant investigation, for that superior's own honour was involved in the perfect contentment and well-being of everyone within his jurisdiction. And this

[1] Readers of ancient Hindū literature will at once recognise the likeness between this system and that prevailing among the Āryans in the early days. This is but natural, since the successive Manus are all members of the same Hierarchy, and are engaged in similar work.

sleepless vigilance in the performance of public duty was enforced not so much by law (though law no doubt there was), as by the universal feeling among the governing class—a feeling akin to the honour of a gentleman, a force far stronger than the command of any mere outer law can ever be, because it is in truth the working of a higher law from within—the dictation of the awakening ego to his personality on some subject which he *knows*.

It will be seen that we are thus introduced to a system which was in every respect founded on the very antithesis of all the ideas which have arrogated to themselves the name of modern progress. The factor which made such a Government, so based, a possible and a workable one, was the existence among all classes of the community of an enlightened public opinion—an opinion so strong and definite, so deeply ingrained, as to make it practically impossible for any man to fail in his duty to the State. Any one who had so failed would have been regarded as an uncivilised being, unworthy of the high privilege of citizenship in this great Empire of 'The Children of the Sun,' as these early Peruvians called themselves; he would have been looked upon with something of the same horror and pity as was an excommunicated person in mediæval Europe.

From this state of affairs—so remote from anything now existing as to be barely conceivable to us—arose another fact almost as difficult to realise. There were practically no laws in old Peru, and consequently no prisons; indeed, our system of punishments and penalties would have appeared absolutely unreasonable to the nation of which we are thinking. The life of a citizen of the Empire was in their eyes the only life worth living; but it was thoroughly well understood that every man held his place in the community only on condition that he fulfilled his duty towards it. If a man in any way fell short of this (an almost unheard-of occurrence, because of the force of opinion which is above described), an explanation would be expected by the officer in charge of his district; and if, on examination, he proved blameworthy, he would be reprimanded by that officer. Anything like continued neglect of duty ranked among the heinous offences, such as murder or theft; and for all these there was only one punishment—that of exile.

The theory upon which this arrangement was based was an exceedingly simple one. The Peruvian held that the civilised man differed from the savage principally in that he understood and intelligently fulfilled his duties towards the State of which he formed a unit; if a man did *not* fulfil those duties he at once became a danger to the State, he showed himself unworthy to participate in its benefits, and he was consequently expelled from it, and left to live among the barbarous tribes on the fringes of the Empire. Indeed, it is perhaps characteristic of the attitude of the Peruvians in this matter that the very word by which these tribes were designated in their language means, when literally translated, 'the lawless ones'.

It was, however, only rarely that it became necessary to resort to this extreme measure of exile; in most cases the officials were revered and beloved, and a hint from one of them was more than sufficient to bring back any unruly spirit to the path of order. Nor were even the few who were exiled irrevocably cast forth from their native country; after a certain period they were allowed to return upon probation to their place among civilised men, and once more to enjoy the advantages of citizenship, as soon as they had shown themselves worthy of them.

Among their manifold functions the officials (or 'fathers,' as they were called) included those of judges, although, as there was practically no law, in our sense of the word, to administer, they perhaps corresponded more closely to our idea of arbitrators. All disputes which arose between man and man were referred to them, and in this case, as in all others, any one who felt dissatisfied with a decision could always appeal to the official next above, so that it was within the bounds of possibility that a knotty point might be carried to the very footstool of the King himself.

Every effort was made by the higher authorities to render themselves readily accessible to all, and part of the plan arranged for this purpose consisted in an elaborate system of visitations. Once in seven years the King himself made a tour of his Empire for this purpose; and in the same way the Governor of a province had to travel over it yearly; and his subordinates in their turn had constantly to see with their own eyes that all was going well with those under their charge, and to give every opportunity for any one who wished to consult them or appeal to them. These various royal and official progresses were made with considerable state, and were always occasions of the greatest rejoicing among the people.

The scheme of Government had at least this much in common with that of our own day, that a complete and careful system of registration was adopted, births, marriages and deaths being catalogued with scrupulous accuracy, and statistics compiled from them in quite the modern style. Each Centurion had a detailed record of the names of all who were under his charge, and kept for each of them a curious little tablet upon which the principal events of his life were entered as they occurred. To *his* superior in turn he reported not names, but numbers—so many sick, so many well, so many births, so many deaths, etc., —and these small reports gradually converged and were added together as they passed higher and higher up the official hierarchy, until an abstract of them all periodically reached the Monarch himself, who had thus a kind of perpetual census of his Empire always ready to his hand.

Another point of similarity between this ancient system and our own is to be found in the exceeding care with which the land was surveyed, parcelled out, and above all *analysed*—the chief object of all this investigation being to discover the exact constitution of the earth in every part of the country, in order that the most appropriate crop might be planted in it, and the most made out of it generally. Indeed, it may be said that almost more importance was attached to the study of what we should now call scientific agriculture than to any other line of work.

This brings us directly to the consideration of perhaps the most remarkable of all the institutions of this ancient race—its land system. So excellently suited to the country was this unique arrangement, that the far inferior race which, thousands of years later, conquered and enslaved the degenerate descendants of our Peruvians, endeavoured to carry it on as well as they could, and the admiration of the Spanish invaders was excited by such relics of it as were still in working order at the time of their arrival. Whether such a scheme could be as successfully carried out in less fertile and more thickly-populated countries may be doubtful, but at any rate it was working capitally at the time and place where we thus find it in action. This system we must now endeavour to explain, dealing first, for clearness' sake, with the broad outline of it only, and leaving many points of vital importance to be treated under other headings.

Every town or village, then, had assigned to it for cultivation a certain amount of such arable land as lay around it—an amount strictly proportioned to the number of its inhabitants. Among those inhabitants were in every case a large number of workers who were appointed to till that land—what we may call a labouring class, in fact; not that all the others did not labour also, but that these were set apart for this particular kind of work. How this labouring class was recruited must be explained later; let it be sufficient for the moment to say that all its members were men in the prime of life and strength, between twenty and five-and-forty years of age—that no old men or children, no sickly or weakly persons, were to be seen among its ranks.

The land assigned for cultivation to any given village was first of all divided into two halves, which we will call the private land and the public land. Both these halves had to be cultivated by the labourers, the private land for their own individual benefit and support, and the public land for the good of the community. That is to say, the cultivation of the public land may be regarded as taking the place of the payment of rates and taxes in our modern State. Naturally the idea will at once occur that a tax which is equivalent to half a man's income, or which takes up half the time and energy that he expends (which in this case is the same thing) is an enormously heavy and most iniquitous one. Let the reader wait until he learns what was done with the produce of that tax, and what part it played in the national life, before he condemns it as an oppressive imposition. Let him realise also that the practical result of the rule was by no means severe; the cultivation of both public and private lands meant far less hard work than falls to the lot of the agriculturalist in England; for while at least twice a year it involved some weeks of steady work from morning till night, there were long intervals when all that was required could easily be done in two hours' work each day.

The private land, with which we will deal first, was divided among the inhabitants with the most scrupulous fairness. Each year, after the harvest had been gathered in, a certain definite amount of land was apportioned to every adult, whether man or woman, though all the cultivation was done by the men. Thus a married man without children would have twice as much as a single man; a widower with, say, two adult unmarried daughters would have three times as much as a single man; but when one of those daughters married, her portion would go with her—that is, it would be taken from her father and given to her husband. For every child born to the couple, a small additional assignment would be made to them, the amount increasing as the children grew older—the intention of course being that each family should always have what was necessary for its support.

A man could do absolutely what he chose with his land, except leave it uncultivated. Some crop or other he must make it produce, but as long as he made his living out of it, the rest was his own affair. At the same time the best advice of the experts was always at his service for the asking, so that he could not plead ignorance if his selection proved unsuitable. A man not belonging to our technical 'labouring class'—that is, a man who was making his living in some other way—could either cultivate his plot in his leisure time, or employ a member of that class to do it for him in addition to his own work; but in this latter case the produce of the land belonged not to the original assignee, but to the man who had done the work. The fact that in this way one labouring man could, and frequently quite voluntarily did, perform two men's work, is another proof that the fixed amount of labour was in reality an extremely light task.

It is pleasant to be able to record that a great deal of good feeling and helpfulness was always shown with regard to this agricultural work. The man who had a large family of children, and therefore an unusually large piece of ground, could always count upon much kindly assistance from his neighbours as soon as they had completed their own lighter labours; and any one who had reason for taking a holiday never lacked a friend to supply his place during his absence. The question of sickness is not touched upon, for reasons which will presently appear.

As to disposing of the produce, there was never any difficulty about that. Most men chose to grow grain, vegetables or fruits which they themselves could use for food; their surplus they readily sold or bartered for clothes and other goods; and at the worst, the Government was always prepared to buy any amount of grain that could be offered, at a fixed rate, a trifle below the market price, in order to store it in the enormous granaries which were invariably kept full in case of famine or emergency.

But now let us consider what was done with the produce of that other half of the cultivated ground which we have called the public land. This public land was itself divided into two equal parts (each of which therefore represented a quarter of the whole arable land of the country), one of which was called the land of the King, the other the land of the Sun. And the law was that the land of the Sun must first be tilled, before any man turned a sod of his own private land; when that was done, each man was expected to cultivate his own piece of land, and only after all the rest of the work was safely over was he required to do his share towards tilling the land of the King—so that if unexpected bad weather delayed the harvest the loss would fall first upon the King, and except in an exceedingly inclement season could scarcely affect the people's private share; while that of the Sun would be safeguarded in almost any possible contingency short of absolute failure of the crops.

In regard to the question of irrigation (always an important one in a country, a great part of which is so sterile), the same order was always observed. Until the lands of the Sun were fully watered, no drop of the precious fluid was directed elsewhere; until every man's private field had all that it needed, there was no water for the lands of the King. The reason of this arrangement will be obvious later on, when we understand how the produce of these various sections was employed.

Thus it will be seen that a quarter of the entire wealth of the country went directly into the hands of the King; for in the case of money derived from manufactures or mining industries the division was still the same—first one-fourth to the Sun, then one-half to the worker, and then the remaining fourth to the King. What then did the King do with this enormous revenue?

First, he kept up the entire machinery of Government to which reference has already been made. The salaries of the whole official class,—from the stately Viceroys of great provinces down to the comparatively humble Centurions—were paid by him, and not only their salaries but all the expenses of their various progresses and visitations.

Secondly, out of that revenue he executed all the mighty public works of his Empire, the mere ruins of some of which are still wonders to us now, fourteen thousand years later. The marvellous roads which joined city to city and town to town throughout the Empire, hollowed out through mountains of granite, carried by stupendous bridges over the most impracticable ravines, the splendid series of aqueducts—which, by feats of engineering skill in no way inferior to that of our own day, were enabled to spread the life-giving fluid over the remotest corners of an often sterile country—all these were constructed and maintained out of the income derived from the lands of the King.

Thirdly, he built and kept always filled a series of huge granaries, established at frequent intervals all over the Empire. For sometimes it would happen that the rainy season failed altogether, and then famine would threaten the unfortunate agriculturalist; so the rule was that there should always be in store two years' provision for the entire nation—a store of food such as perhaps no other race in the world has ever attempted to keep. Yet, colossal as was the undertaking, it was faithfully carried out in spite of all difficulties; though perhaps even the mighty power of the Peruvian

Monarch could not have achieved it, but for the method of concentrating food which was one of the discoveries of his chemists—a method which will be mentioned later.

Fourthly, out of this share he kept up his army—for an army he had, and a highly trained one, though he contrived to utilise it for many other purposes besides mere fighting, of which indeed there was not often much to be done, since the less civilised tribes which surrounded his Empire had learnt to know and respect his power.

It will be better not to pause now to describe the special work of the army, but rather to fill in the remainder of our rough outline of the polity of this ancient State by indicating the place held in it by the great Guild of the Priests of the Sun, so far as the civil side of the work of that priesthood is concerned. How did this body employ their vast revenues, equal in amount to those of the King when his were at their highest point, and far more certain than his not to be diminished in time of distress or scarcity?

The King indeed performed wonders with his share of the country's wealth, but his achievements pale when compared with those of the priests. First, they kept up the splendid temples of the Sun all over the land—kept them up on such a scale that many a small village shrine had golden ornaments and decorations that would now represent many thousands of pounds, while the great cathedrals of the larger cities blazed with a magnificence which has never since been approached anywhere upon earth.

Secondly, they gave free education to the entire youth of the Empire, male and female—not merely an elementary education, but a technical training that carried them steadily through years of close application up to the age of twenty, and sometimes considerably beyond. Of this education details will be given later.

Thirdly (and this will probably seem to our readers the most extraordinary of their functions), they took absolute charge of all sick people. It is not meant that they were merely the physicians of the period (though that they were also), but that the moment a man, woman or child fell ill in any way, he at once came under the charge of the priests, or, as they more gracefully put it, became the 'guest of the Sun'. The sick person was immediately and entirely absolved from all his duties to the State, and, until his recovery, not only the necessary medicines, but also his food, were supplied to him free of all charge from the nearest temple of the Sun, while in any serious case he was usually taken to that temple as to a hospital, in order to receive more careful nursing. If the sick man were the breadwinner of the family, his wife and children also became 'guests of the Sun' until he recovered. In the present day any arrangement even remotely resembling this would certainly lead to fraud and malingering; but that is because modern nations lack as yet that enlightened and universally-diffused public opinion which made these things possible in ancient Peru.

Fourthly—and perhaps this statement will be considered even more astonishing than the last—

the *entire population* over the age of forty-five (except the official class) were also 'guests of the Sun'. It was considered that a man who had worked for twenty-five years from the age of twenty—when he was first expected to begin to take his share of the burdens of the State—had earned rest and comfort for the remainder of his life, whatever that might be. Consequently every person, when he or she attained the age of forty-five, might, if he wished, attach himself to one of the temples and live a kind of monastic life of study, or, if he preferred still to reside with his relatives as before, he might do so, and might employ his leisure as he would. But in any case he was absolved from all work for the State, and his maintenance was provided by the priesthood of the Sun. Of course he was in no way prohibited from continuing to work in any way that he wished, and as a matter of fact most men preferred to occupy themselves in some way, even though it were but with a hobby. Indeed, many most valuable discoveries and inventions were made by those who, being free from all need for constant labour, were at liberty to follow out their ideas, and experimentalise at leisure in a way that no busy man could do.

Members of the official class, however, did not retire from active work at the age of forty-five, except in case of illness, nor did the priests themselves. In those two classes it was felt that the added wisdom and experience of age were too valuable not to be utilised; so in most cases priests and officials died in harness.

It will now be obvious why the work of the priests was considered the most important, and why, whatever else failed, the contributions to the treasury of the Sun must not fall short, for on them depended not only the religion of the people, but the education of the young and the care of the sick and the aged.

What was achieved by this strange system of long ago, then, was this: for every man and woman a thorough education was assured, with every opportunity for the development of any special talent he or she might possess; then followed twenty-five years of work—steady indeed, but never either unsuitable in character or overwhelming in amount—and after that, a life of assured comfort and leisure, in which the man was absolutely free from any sort of care or anxiety. Some, of course, were poorer than others, but what we now call poverty was unknown, and destitution was impossible, while, in addition to this, crime was practically non-existent. Small wonder that exile from that State was considered the direst earthly punishment, and that the barbaric tribes on its borders became absorbed into it as soon as they could be brought to understand its system!

It will be of interest to us to examine the religious ideas of these men of the olden time. If we had to classify their faith among those with which we are now acquainted, we should be obliged to call it a kind of Sun-worship, though of course they never thought for a moment of worshipping the physical sun. They regarded it, however, as something much more than a mere symbol; if we endeavour to express their feeling in Theosophical terminology, we shall perhaps come nearest to it by saying that they looked upon the sun as the physical body of the LOGOS, though that attributes to them a precision of idea which they would probably have considered irreverent. They would have told an enquirer that they worshipped the Spirit of the Sun, from whom everything came, and to whom everything must return—by no means an unsatisfactory presentment of a mighty truth.

It does not seem that they had any clear conception of the doctrine of reincarnation. They were quite certain that man was immortal, and they held that his eventual destiny was to go to the Spirit of the Sun—perhaps to become one with Him, though this was not clearly defined in their teachings. They knew that before this final consummation many other long periods of existence must intervene, but we cannot find that they realised with certainty that any part of that future life would be spent upon this earth again.

The most prominent characteristic of the religion was its joyousness. Grief or sorrow of any kind was held to be absolutely wicked and ungrateful, since it was taught that the Deity wished to see His children happy, and would Himself be grieved if He saw them grieving. Death was regarded not as an occasion for mourning, but rather for a kind of solemn and reverent joy, because the Great Spirit had accounted another of His children worthy to approach nearer to Himself. Suicide, on the other hand, was, in pursuance of the same idea, regarded with the utmost horror, as an act of the grossest presumption; the man who committed suicide thrust himself uninvited into higher realms, for which he was not yet judged fit by the only authority who possessed the requisite knowledge to decide the question. But indeed at the time of which we are writing suicide was practically unknown, for the people as a whole were a most contented race.

Their public services were of the simplest character. Praise was offered daily to the Spirit of the Sun, but never prayer; because they were taught that the Deity knew better than they what was required for their welfare—a doctrine which one would like to see more fully comprehended at the present day. Fruit and flowers were offered in their temples, not from any idea that the Sun-God desired such service, but simply as a token that they owed all to Him; for one of the most prominent theories of their faith was that all light and life and power came from the Sun—a theory which is fully borne out by the discoveries of modern science. On their great festivals splendid processions were organised, and special exhortations and instructions were delivered to the people by the priests; but even in these sermons simplicity was a chief characteristic, the teachings being given largely by means of picture and parable.

It happened once that, in the course of our researches into the life of a particular person, we followed him to one of these assemblies, and heard with him the sermon delivered on that occasion by an old white-haired priest. The few simple words which were then uttered will perhaps give a better idea of the inner spirit of this old-world religion than any description that we can offer. The preacher, robed in a sort of golden cope, which was the symbol of his office, stood at the top of the temple steps and looked round upon his audience. Then he began to talk to them in a gentle yet resonant voice, speaking quite familiarly, more like a father telling a story to his children than like one delivering a set oration.

He spoke to them of their Lord the Sun, calling upon them to remember how everything that they needed for their physical well-being was brought into existence by Him; how without His glorious light and heat the world would be cold and dead, and all life would be impossible; how to His action was due the growth of the fruits and grains which formed the staple of their food, and even the fresh water, which was the most precious and necessary of all. Then he explained to them how the wise men of old had taught that behind this action which all could see, there was always another and still grander action which was invisible, but could yet be felt by those whose lives were in harmony with their Lord's; how what the Sun in one aspect did for the life of their bodies, that same office He also performed, in another and even more wonderful aspect, for the life of their souls. He pointed out that both these actions were absolutely continuous—that though sometimes the Sun was hidden from the sight of His child the earth, yet the cause of such temporary obscuration was to be found in the earth and not in the Sun, for one had only to climb far enough up the mountains in order to rise above the overshadowing clouds, and discover that their Lord was shining on in glory all the time, entirely unaffected by the veil which seemed so dense when seen from below.

From this the transition was easy to the spiritual depression or doubt which might sometimes seem to shut out the higher influences from the soul; and the preacher was most emphatic in his fervent assurance that, despite all appearances to the contrary, the analogy held good here also; that the clouds were always of men's own making, and that they had only to raise themselves high enough in order to realise that He was unchanged, and that spiritual strength and holiness were pouring down all the while, as steadily as ever. Depression and doubt, consequently, were to be cast aside as the offspring of ignorance and unreason, and to be reprobated as showing ingratitude to the Giver of all good.

The second part of the homily was equally practical. The full benefit of the Sun's action, continued the priest, could be experienced only by those who were themselves in perfect health. Now the sign of perfect health on all levels was that men should resemble their Lord the Sun. The man who was in the enjoyment of full physical health was himself a kind of minor sun, pouring out strength and life upon all around, so that by his very presence the weak became stronger, the sick and the suffering were helped. In exactly the same way, he insisted, the man who was in perfect moral health was also a spiritual sun, radiating love and purity and holiness on all who were happy enough to come into contact with him.

This, he said, was the duty of man—to show his gratitude for the good gifts of his Lord, first by preparing himself to receive them in all their fulness, and secondly by passing them undiminished to his fellow-men. And both these objects together could be attained in one way, and in one way only—by that constant imitation of the benevolence of the Spirit of the Sun, which alone drew His children ever nearer and nearer to Him.

Such was this sermon of fourteen thousand years ago, and, simple though it be, we cannot but admit that its teaching is eminently Theosophical, and that it shows a much greater knowledge of the facts of life than many more eloquent addresses which are delivered at the present day. Here and there we notice minor points of especial significance; the accurate knowledge, for example, of the radiation of superfluous vitality from a healthy man seems to point to the possession of clairvoyant faculty among the ancestors from whom the tradition was derived.

It will be remembered that, besides what we may call their purely religious work, the priests of the Sun had entire charge of the education of the country. All education was absolutely free, and its preliminary stages were exactly the same for all classes and for both sexes. The children attended preparatory classes from an early age, and in all these the boys and girls were taught together. Something corresponding to what we now think of as elementary education was given in these, though the subjects embraced differed considerably. Reading, writing, and a certain kind of arithmetic, indeed, were taught, and every child had to attain facility in these subjects, but the system included a great deal more that is somewhat difficult to classify—a sort of rough and ready knowledge of all the general rules and common interests of life, so that no child of either sex arriving at the age of ten or eleven could be ignorant of the way in which the ordinary necessaries of life were obtained, or of how any common work was done. The utmost kindness and affection prevailed in the relations between teachers and children, and there was nothing in the least corresponding to the insane system of impositions and punishments which occupies so prominent and so baneful a position in modern school life.

School hours were long, but the occupations were so varied, and included so much that we should not think of as school work, that the children were never unduly fatigued. Every child, for example, was taught how to prepare and cook certain simple kinds of food, how to distinguish poisonous fruits from wholesome ones, how to find food and shelter if lost in the forest, how to use the simpler tools required in carpentering, in building, or in agriculture, how to make his way from place to place by the positions of the sun and stars, how to manage a canoe, as well as to swim, to climb, and to leap with amazing dexterity. They were also instructed in the method of dealing with wounds and accidents, and the use of certain herbal remedies was explained to them. All this varied and remarkable curriculum was no mere matter of theory for them; they were constantly required to put the whole of it into practice; so that before they were allowed to pass out of this preparatory school they had become exceedingly handy little people, capable of acting for themselves to some extent in almost any emergency that might arise.

They were also carefully instructed in the constitution of their country, and the reasons for its various customs and regulations were explained to them. On the other hand, they were entirely ignorant of many things which European children learn; they were unacquainted with any language except their own, and though great stress was laid upon speaking that with purity and accuracy, facility in this was attained by constant practice rather than by the observance of grammatical rules. They knew nothing of algebra, geometry or history, and nothing of geography beyond that of their own country. On leaving this first school they could have built you a comfortable house, but could not have made a sketch of it for you; they knew nothing whatever of chemistry, but were thoroughly well instructed in the general principles of practical hygiene.

A certain definite standard in all these varied qualifications for good citizenship had to be attained before the children could pass out of this preliminary school. Most of them easily gained this level by the time they were twelve years old; a few of the less intelligent needed several years longer. On the chief teachers of these preparatory schools rested the serious responsibility of determining the pupil's future career; or, rather perhaps, of advising him as to it, for no child was ever forced to devote himself to work which he disliked. Some definite career, however, he had to select, and when this was decided, he was drafted into a kind of technical school, which was specially intended to prepare him for the line of life that he had chosen. Here he spent the remaining nine or ten years of his pupilage, chiefly in practical work of the kind to which he was to devote his energies. This characteristic was prominent all through the scheme of instruction; there was comparatively little theoretical teaching; but, after being shown a thing a few times, the boys or girls were always set to do the thing themselves, and to do it over and over again until facility was acquired.

There was a great deal of elasticity about all these arrangements; a child, for example, who after due trial found himself unsuited for the special work he had undertaken, was allowed, in consultation with his teachers, to choose another vocation and transfer himself to the school appropriate to it. Such transfers, however, seem to have been rare; for in most cases before the child left his first school he had shown a decided aptitude for one or another of the lines of life which lay open before him.

Every child, whatever might be his birth, had the opportunity of being trained to join the governing class of the country if he wished it, and if his teachers approved. The training for this honour was, however, so exceedingly severe, and the qualifications required so high, that the number of applicants was never unduly large. The instructors, indeed, were always watching for children of unusual ability, in order that they might endeavour to fit them for this honourable but arduous position, if they were willing to undertake it.

There were various vocations among which a boy could make his choice, besides the governing class and the priesthood. There were many kinds of manufactures—some with large openings for the development of artistic faculty in various ways; there were the different lines of working in metals, of making and improving machinery, of architecture of all sorts. But perhaps the principal pursuit of the country was that of scientific agriculture.

Upon this the welfare of the nation largely depended, and to this therefore a great deal of attention had always been given. By a long series of patiently conducted experiments, extending over many generations, the capabilities of the various kinds of soil which were to be found in the country had been thoroughly ascertained, so that at the time with which we are dealing there already existed a large body of tradition on this subject. Detailed accounts of all the experiments were kept in what we should now call the archives of the Agricultural Department, but the general results were epitomised for popular use in a series of short maxims, so arranged as to be readily memorised by the students.

Those who adopted farming as a profession were not, however, by any means expected to depend exclusively upon the opinions of their forefathers. On the contrary every encouragement was given to new experiment, and anyone who succeeded in inventing a new and useful manure, or a labour-saving machine, was highly honoured and rewarded by the Government. All over the country were scattered a large number of Government Farms, where young men were carefully trained; and here again, as in the earlier schools, the training was less theoretical than practical, each student learning thoroughly how to do for himself every detail of the work which he would afterwards have to superintend.

It was at these training-farms that all new experiments were tried, at the cost of the Government. The inventor had none of the trouble in securing a patron with capital to test his discovery, which is so often a fatal bar to his success in the present day; he simply submitted his idea to the Chief of his district, who was assisted when necessary by a council of experts, and unless these were able to point out some obvious flaw in his reasoning, his scheme was tried, or his machine constructed, under his own supervision, without any outlay or trouble at all on his part. If experience showed that there was anything in his invention, it was at once adopted by the Government and employed wherever it was likely to be of use.

The farmers had elaborate theories as to the adaptation of various kinds of manure to the different soils. They not only used the material which we now import for that purpose from that very country, but also tried all sorts of chemical combinations, some of which were remarkably successful. They had an ingenious though cumbersome system of the utilisation of sewage, which was, however, quite as effective as anything of that kind which we have at the present day.

They had achieved considerable advances also in the construction and use of machinery, though most of it was simpler and rougher than ours, and they had nothing like the extreme accuracy in the fitting together of minute parts, which is so prominent a characteristic of modern work. On the other hand, though their machinery was often large and cumbrous, it was effective, and apparently not at all liable to get out of order. One example that we noted was a curious machine for sowing seed, the principal part of which looked as though it had been modelled from the ovipositor of some insect. It was something of the shape of a very wide low cart, and as it was dragged across a field it automatically drilled ten lines of holes at a regular distance apart, dropped a seed into each, watered it, and raked the ground even again.

They had evidently some knowledge of hydraulics also, for many of their machines were worked by hydraulic pressure—especially those employed in their elaborate system of irrigation, which was unusually perfect and effective. A great deal of the land was hilly and could not be cultivated to any advantage in its natural state; but these ancient inhabitants carefully laid it out in terraces, much as is done now in the hill country of Ceylon. Anyone who has travelled by rail from Rambukkana to Peradeniya can scarcely have failed to notice many examples of this sort of work. In old Peru every corner of ground near the great centres of population was utilised with the most scrupulous care.

There was a good deal of scientific knowledge among them, but all their science was of a severely practical kind. They had no sort of idea of such an abstract study of science as exists among ourselves. They made a careful study of botany, for example, but not in the least from our point of view. They knew and cared nothing about the classification of plants as endogenous and exogenous, nothing about the number of stamens in a flower, or the arrangement of leaves on a stem; what they wanted to know about a plant was what properties it possessed, what use could be made of it in medicine, as a food-stuff, or to furnish a dye. This they did know, and thoroughly.

In the same way in their chemistry: they had no knowledge as to the number and arrangement of atoms in a carbon compound; indeed, they had no thought of atoms and molecules at all, so far as we could see. What interested them were such chemicals as could be utilised: those which could be combined into valuable manures or plant-foods, those which could be employed in their various manufactures, which would yield them a beautiful dye or a useful acid. All scientific studies were made with some special practical point in view; they were always trying to find out something, but always with a definite object connected with human life, never for the sake of knowledge in the abstract.

Perhaps their nearest approach to abstract science was their study of astronomy; but this was regarded rather as religious than as merely secular knowledge. It differed from the rest in that it was purely traditional, and that no efforts were made to add to their stock of information in this direction. The stock was not a great one, though accurate enough as far as it went. They understood that the planets differed from the rest of the stars, and spoke of them as the sisters of the earth—for they recognised that the earth was one of them—or sometimes 'the elder children of the Sun'. They knew that the earth was globular in shape, that day and night were due to its rotation on its axis, and the seasons to its annual revolution round the sun. They were aware also that the fixed stars were outside the solar system, and they regarded comets as messengers from these other great Beings to their Lord the Sun; but it is doubtful whether they had anything like an adequate conception of the real size of any of the bodies involved.

They were able to predict eclipses both of the sun and moon with perfect accuracy, but this was not done by observation, but by use of a traditional formula; they understood their nature, and do not seem to have attached much importance to them. There is abundant evidence to show that those from whom they inherited their traditions must have been either capable of direct scientific observation, or else in possession of clairvoyant powers which rendered such observation needless; but neither of these advantages appertained to the Peruvians at the date of our examination of them. The only attempt that they were seen to make at anything like personal observation was that the exact moment of noon was found by carefully measuring the shadow of a lofty column in the grounds of the temple, a set of little pegs being moved along stone grooves to mark it accurately. The same primitive apparatus was employed to find the date of the summer and winter solstices, since in connection with these periods there were special religious services.

CHAPTER XII

TWO ATLANTEAN CIVILISATIONS

Toltec, in Ancient Peru, B. C. 12,000

(Continued)

THE architecture of this ancient race differed in many ways from any other with which we are acquainted, and its study would be of extreme interest to any clairvoyant who was possessed of technical knowledge of the subject. Our own lack of such knowledge makes it difficult for us to describe its details accurately, though we may, perhaps, hope to convey something of the general impression which it gives at the first glance to observers of the present century.

It was colossal, yet unpretentious; bearing evidence in many cases of years of patient labour, but distinctly designed for use rather than for show. Many of the buildings were of vast extent, but most of them would seem to a modern eye somewhat out of proportion, the ceilings being nearly always much too low for the size of the rooms. For example, it was no unusual thing to find in the house of a Governor several apartments about the size of Westminster Hall, and yet none of them would measure more than twelve feet or so from floor to ceiling. Pillars were not unknown, but were sparingly used, and what with us would be a graceful colonnade was in old Peru more usually a wall with frequent apertures in it. Such pillars as there were were massive, and often monolithic.

The true arch with the keystone was apparently unknown to them, though windows or doors with a semi-circular top were by no means uncommon. In the larger examples of these a heavy metal semi-circle was sometimes made and fixed upon the side-posts of the aperture; but they generally trusted entirely to the powerful adhesive which they used in the place of mortar. The exact nature of this material we do not know, but it was certainly effective. They cut and fitted their enormous blocks of stone with the greatest accuracy, so that the joint was barely perceptible; then they plastered the outside of each junction with clay, and poured in their 'mortar' in a hot and fluid condition. Minute as were the crevices between the stones, this fluid found and filled them, and when it cooled it set like flint, which, indeed, it closely resembled in appearance. The clay was then scraped off the outside, and the wall was complete; and if after the lapse of centuries a crack in the masonry ever made its appearance it was certainly not at any of the joints, for they were stronger than even the stone itself.

The majority of the houses of the peasantry were built of what we must call brick, since it was manufactured from clay; but the 'bricks' were large cubes, measuring perhaps a yard each way; and the clay was not baked, but mixed with some chemical preparation and left in the open air for some months to harden; so that in consistency and appearance they resembled blocks of cement rather than bricks, and a house built of them was scarcely inferior in any way to one of stone.

All houses, even the smallest, were built on the classical and oriental plan of the central courtyard, and all alike had walls of what would now be considered enormous thickness. The simplest and poorest cottage had only four rooms, one on each of the sides of the tiny courtyard into which they all faced, and as these rooms had usually no external windows the appearance of such houses from outside was dull and bare. Very little attempt at exterior ornament was made in the poorer parts of the city or village; a kind of frieze of a very simple pattern was usually all that broke the monotony of the dead walls of the cottages.

The entrance was always at one corner of the square, and in earlier days the door was simply a huge slab of stone, which ran up, like a portcullis or a modern sash-window, in grooves and by means of counterweights. When the door was shut the counterweights could be rested on shelves and detached, so that the door remained a practically immovable mass, which would have been distinctly discouraging to a burglar, had any such person existed in so well-ordered a State. In better-class houses this door-slab was elaborately carved, and at a later period it was often replaced by a thick plate of metal. The method of working it, however, was but little varied, though a few instances were observed of heavy metal doors which turned on pivots.

The larger houses were originally built on exactly the same plan, though with a good deal more ornamentation, not only in the way of carving the stone into patterns, but also in diversifying its surface with broad bands of metal. In such a climate, dwellings so massively built were almost everlasting, and the majority of the houses in existence and occupation at the time of which we write were of this type. Some later ones, however—evidently built in the centuries when the population had become convinced of the stability of the Government system, and of its power to make the laws respected—had a double set of rooms round their courtyards, as any modern house might have, one set facing into the yard (which in their case was a beautifully-laid-out garden) and the other facing outwards towards the surrounding scenery. This latter set had large windows—or rather openings, for, though several kinds of glass were made, it was not used in windows—which could be closed on the same principle as that of the doors.

Still it will be seen that the general style of the domestic architecture, in large and small houses alike, was somewhat severe and monotonous, though admirably adapted to the climate. The roofs were mostly heavy and nearly flat, and were almost invariably made either of stone, or of sheets of metal. One of the most remarkable features of their house-building was the almost entire absence of wood, which they avoided because of its combustibility;

and in consequence of this precaution conflagrations were unknown in ancient Peru.

The way in which houses were built was peculiar. No scaffolding was employed, but as the house was erected it was filled with earth, so that when the walls had risen to their full height there was a level surface of earth within them. Upon this the stones of the roof were laid, and then the hot cement was poured between them as usual. As soon as that had set, the earth was dug out and the roof left to support its own prodigious weight, which, thanks to the power of that wonderful cement, it seems always to have done with perfect safety. Indeed, the whole structure, roof and walls alike, became, when finished, to all intents and purposes one solid block, as though it had been hollowed out of the living rock—a method, by the way, which was actually adopted in some places upon the mountain-side.

A first-floor had been added to a few of the houses in the capital city, but the idea had not achieved popular favour, and such daring innovations were extremely rare. Something resembling the effect of a series of stories one above the other was indeed obtained in a curious way in some of the erections in which the priests or monks of the Sun were housed, but the arrangement was not one which could ever have been extensively adopted in a crowded city. An immense platform of earth, say a thousand feet square and about fifteen or eighteen feet in height, was first made, and then upon that, but fifty feet in from the edge on each side, another huge platform nine hundred feet square was constructed; upon that there was another having sides measuring eight hundred feet, and above that a fourth measuring seven hundred feet, and so they rose, steadily decreasing in size, until they reached a tenth stage only a hundred feet square, and then in the centre of that final platform they built a small shrine to the Sun.

The effect of the whole was something like a great, flat pyramid rising by broad shallow steps —a sort of Primrose Hill cut into terraces. And out of the upright front of each of these great platforms they hollowed out rooms—cells, as it were, in which the monks and their guests lived. Each cell had an outer and an inner room, the latter being lighted only from the former, which was quite open to the air on the side which faced outwards; indeed it consisted only of three sides and a roof. Both rooms were lined and floored with slabs of stone, cemented into solidity in the usual manner. The terraces in front were laid out in gardens and walks, and altogether the cells were pleasant residences. In several cases a natural elevation was cut into terraces in this manner, but most of these pyramids were artificially erected. Frequently they ran tunnels into the heart of the lowest tier of such a pyramid, and constructed subterranean chambers there, which were used as storehouses for grain and other necessaries.

In addition to these remarkable flattened pyramids there were the ordinary temples of the Sun, some of them of great size and covering a large amount of ground, though all of them had, to European eyes, the universal defect of being too low for their length. They were always surrounded by pleasant gardens, under the trees of which was done most of the teaching for which these temples were so justly famed.

If the exterior of these temples was sometimes less imposing than might have been desired, at any rate the interior more than atoned for any possible defects. The large extent to which the precious metals were used in decoration was a feature of Peruvian life even thousands of years later, when a handful of Spaniards succeeded in dominating the comparatively degenerate race which had taken the place of that whose customs we are trying to describe. At the time of which we write the inhabitants were not acquainted with our art of gilding, but they were exceedingly clever in hammering out metal into large thin plates, and it was no uncommon thing for the greater temples to be literally lined with gold and silver. The plates covering the walls were often as much as a quarter of an inch in thickness, and yet were moulded over delicate reliefs in the stone as though they had been so much paper, so that from our modern point of view a temple was frequently the depository of untold wealth.

The race which built the temples regarded all this not as wealth in our sense at all, but merely as fit and proper decoration. It must be remembered that ornament of this nature was by no means confined to the temples; all houses of any consideration had their walls lined with some kind of metal, just as ours now are papered, and to have the bare stone showing in the interior was with them equivalent to a white-washed wall with us—practically confined to outhouses or the dwellings of the peasantry. But only the palaces of the King and the chief Governors were lined with pure gold like the temples; for ordinary folk, all kinds of beautiful and serviceable alloys were made, and rich effects were produced at comparatively little cost.

In thinking of their architecture we must not forget the chain of fortresses which the King erected round the boundaries of his Empire, in order that the barbarous tribes beyond the frontier might be kept in check. Here again for accurate description and for criticism that shall be worth anything we need the services of an expert; but even the veriest civilian can see that in many cases the situation of these forts was admirably chosen, and that, short of artillery, they must have been practically impregnable. The height and thickness of their walls was in some cases enormous, and they had the peculiarity (as indeed had all high walls in the country) that they gradually tapered from a thickness of many feet at the base to a much more ordinary size at a height of twenty or thirty yards. Look-out chambers and secret passages were hollowed out in the heart of these wonderful walls, and the interior of the fort was so arranged and so fully provisioned that the garrison must have been able to stand a prolonged siege without discomfort. The observers were particularly struck by the ingenious arrangement of a series of gates one within the other, connected by narrow and tortuous passages, which would have placed any force attempting to storm the fortress completely at the mercy of the defenders.

But the most wonderful works of this strange people were without doubt their roads, bridges and aqueducts. The roads were carried for hundreds of miles across the country (some of them for more than a thousand miles), with a splendid disregard of natural difficulties that would extort admiration from the boldest modern engineers. Everything was done on a colossal scale, and though the amount of labour involved must in some cases have been almost incalculable, the results achieved were magnificent and permanent. The whole road was paved with flat slabs, much as are the sidewalks of our London streets; but at each side of it all the way along were planted trees for shade, and odoriferous shrubs which filled the air with their fragrance; so that the country was intersected with a network of splendid paved avenues, up and down which were daily passing the messengers of the King. These men were in effect postmen also, since it was part of their duty to carry letters free of charge for any who wished to send them.

It was when the road-constructors came to a ravine or a river that the patient genius and indomitable perseverance of the race were seen at their highest level. As we have said, they were ignorant of the principle of the true arch, and the nearest that they could approach to it in bridge-building was to cause each layer of stones to project slightly beyond that below it, until in this way two piers eventually met, and their wonderful cement hardened the whole fabric into the likeness of solid rock. They knew nothing of coffer-dams and caissons, so they often spent incredible labour in temporarily diverting the course of a river in order that they might bridge it; or, in other cases, they built out a breakwater into the stream until they reached the spot where the pier was to stand, and then, when it was thus completed, knocked away their breakwater. Because of these difficulties they preferred embankment work to bridging, where-ever it was possible; and they would often carry a road or an aqueduct across even a deep ravine with a considerable river in it, by means of a huge embankment with many culverts in it, rather than by an ordinary bridge.

Their system of irrigation was wonderfully perfect, and it was to a great extent carried on even by the later race, so that much of the country which has now relapsed into desert was green and fertile, until the water-supply fell into the still more incompetent hands of the Spanish conquerors. It is probable that no engineering feats in the world have been greater than the making of the roads and aqueducts of ancient Peru. And all this was done not by the forced labour of slaves or captives, but as regularly paid work by the peasantry of the country, assisted to a large extent by the army.

The King maintained a large number of soldiers, in order that he might always be ready to cope with the border tribes; but since their weapons were simple, and they needed comparatively little drill of any sort, they were available by far the greater part of the time for public service of other kinds. The entire charge of the repair of public works of all sorts was confided to their hands, and they also had to supply the constant stream of post-runners who were carrying reports and despatches, as well as private correspondence, all over the Empire. The maintenance of everything was supposed to be well within the power of the army; but when a new road had to be made or a new fort built additional help was generally hired.

Of course it happened sometimes that war broke out with the less civilised tribes on the borders, but in the time of which we are writing these rarely gave any serious trouble. They were readily driven back, and penalties exacted from them; or sometimes, if they seemed amenable to a higher civilisation, their land was annexed to the Empire and they were brought under its regulations. Naturally there was some difficulty with such new citizens at first; they did not understand the customs and often did not see why they should comply with them; but after a short time most of them fell into the routine readily enough, and the incorrigible ones, who would not, were exiled into other countries not yet absorbed into the Empire.

These Peruvians were fairly humane in their wars; as they were almost always victorious over the savage tribes this was comparatively easy for them. They had a saying: "You should never be cruel to your enemy, because to-morrow he will be your friend." In conquering the surrounding tribes they always endeavoured to do so with as little slaughter as possible, in order that the people might willingly come into the Empire, and make good citizens with a fraternal feeling towards their conquerors.

Their principal weapons were the spear, the sword and the bow, and they also made a considerable use of the bolas, an implement which is still employed by the South American Indians of the present day. It consists of two stone or metal balls joined by a rope, and is so thrown as to entangle the legs of a man or a horse, and bring him to the ground. When defending a fort they always rolled down great rocks on the assailants, and the building was specially arranged with a view to permitting this. The sword employed was a short one, more like a large knife, and it was used only when a man's lance was broken, or when he was disarmed. They usually trusted to demoralising their foes by well-sustained flights of arrows, and then charged them with spears before they could recover.

The weapons were well made, for the people excelled in metal-work. They used iron, but did not know how to make it into steel, and it was less valuable to them than copper and various brasses and bronzes, because all these could be made exceedingly hard by alloying them with a form of their remarkable cement, whereas iron would not blend with it so perfectly. The result of this hardening process was remarkable, as even pure copper when subjected to it was capable of taking at least as fine an edge as our best steel, and there is little doubt that some of their alloys were harder than any metal that we can produce at the present day.

Perhaps the most beautiful feature of their metal-work was its exceeding fineness and delicacy. Some of their engraving was truly wonderful—almost too fine to be seen by the naked eye at all, at any rate by our modern eyes. Best of all, perhaps, was the marvellous gossamer-like filigree-work in which they so excelled; it is impossible to understand how it could have been done without a magnifying glass. Much of it was so indescribably delicate that it could not be cleaned at all in the ordinary way. It would have at once destroyed it to rub or dust it, no matter how carefully; so it had to be cleaned when necessary by means of a sort of blow-pipe.

Another manufacture which was rather a specialty was pottery. They contrived, by mixing some chemical with their clay, to turn it out a lovely rich crimson colour, and then they inlaid it with gold and silver in a way which produced effects that we have never seen elsewhere. Here again the exceeding delicacy of the lines was a matter of great wonder to us. Other fine colours were also obtained, and a further modification of that ever-useful flinty cement, when mixed with the prepared clay, gave it a transparency almost equal to that of our clearest glass. It had also the great advantage of being far less brittle than the glass of the present day; indeed, there was much about it which suggested an approach to the 'malleable glass' of which we sometimes read as a mediæval fable. They undoubtedly possessed the art of making a certain kind of thin porcelain which would bend without breaking, as will be seen when we come to deal with their literary achievements.

Since it was the custom of the nation to make so little use of wood, metal-work and pottery had to a great extent to take its place, and they did so with far greater success than we in these days should think possible. There is no doubt that the ancient Peruvians, in their constant researches into chemistry, had discovered some processes which are still a secret to our manufacturers; but as time goes on they will be rediscovered by this fifth Race also, and when once that happens, the pressing need and competition of the present day will force their adaptation to all kinds of objects never dreamt of in old Peru.

The art of painting was practised to a considerable extent, and any child who showed special aptitude for it was encouraged to cultivate his talent to the utmost. The methods adopted were, however, quite different from our own, and their peculiar nature enormously increased the difficulty of the work. Neither canvas, paper nor panel was used as a surface, but thin sheets of a sort of silicious material were employed instead. The exact composition of this was difficult to trace, but it had a delicate, creamy surface, closely resembling in appearance that of fine unglazed porcelain. It was not brittle, but could be bent much as a sheet of tin might be, and its thickness varied according to its size, from that of stout notepaper to that of heavy millboard.

Upon this surface colours of great brilliancy and purity were laid with a brush supplied by Nature herself. It was simply a length cut from the triangular stem of a common fibrous plant. An inch or so at the end of this was beaten out until nothing was left but the fibre, fine as hair but almost as tough as wire; and so the brush was used, the unbeaten portion serving as a handle. Such a brush could, of course, be renewed again and again when worn out, by a process analogous to cutting a lead-pencil; the artist simply cut off the exposed fibre and beat out another inch of the handle. The sharply-defined triangular shape of this instrument enabled the skilful painter to use it either to draw a fine line or to put on a broad dash of colour, employing in the first case the corner, and in the second the side, of his triangle.

The colours were usually in powder, and were mixed as required, neither with water nor oil, but with some vehicle which dried instantaneously, so that a touch once laid on could not be altered. No outline of any sort was drawn, but the artist had to train himself to dash in his effects with sure but rapid strokes, getting the exact tone of colour as well as the form in the one comprehensive effort, much as is done in fresco painting, or in some of the Japanese work. The colours were exceedingly effective and luminous, and some of them surpassed in purity and delicacy any that are now employed. There was a wonderful blue, clearer than the finest ultramarine, and also a violet and a rose colour unlike any modern pigment, by means of which the indescribable glories of a sunset sky could be reproduced far more closely than seems to be possible at the present day. Ornaments of gold, silver and bronze, and of a metal of deep crimson colour which is not now known to science, were represented in a picture by the use of the dust of the metals themselves, much as in mediæval illuminations; and, bizarre as such a method seems to our modern eyes, it cannot be denied that it produced an effect of barbaric richness which was exceedingly striking in its own way.

The perspective was good, and the drawing accurate, and quite free from the clumsy crudity which characterised a later period of Central and South American art. Though their landscape art was distinctly good of its kind, at the time when we were studying them, they did not make it an end in itself, but employed it only as a background for figures. Religious processions were frequently chosen as subjects, or sometimes scenes in which the King or some local Governor took a prominent part.

When the picture was completed (and they were finished with remarkable rapidity by practised artists), it was brushed over with some varnish, which also possessed the property of drying almost instantaneously. The picture so treated was practically indelible, and could be exposed to rain or sun for a long time without any appreciable effect being produced upon it.

Closely associated with the art of the country was its literature, for the books were written, or rather illuminated, on the same material and with the same kind of colours as the pictures. A book consisted of a number of thin sheets, usually measuring about eighteen inches by six, which were occasionally strung together by wire, but far more frequently simply kept in a box from three to five inches in depth. These boxes were of various materials and more or less richly ornamented, but the commonest were made of a metal resembling platinum, and adorned with carved horn, which was somehow fastened to the metal surface by some process of softening, which made it adhere firmly without the use of either rivets or cement.

So far as we could see, nothing of the nature of printing was known; the nearest approach to it was the use of a kind of stencil-plate to produce numerous copies of some sort of official notice for rapid distribution to the Governors all over the Empire. No instance has been observed, however, of any attempt to reproduce a book in this way; and indeed it is evident that such an experiment would have been considered a desecration, for the nation as a whole had a deep respect for its books, and handled them as lovingly as any mediæval monk. To make a copy of a book was regarded as decidedly a work of merit, and many of them were most beautifully and artistically written.

The range of their literature was somewhat limited. There were a few treatises which might have been classed as definitely religious, or at any rate ethical, and they ran mostly on lines not dissimilar from that of the old priest's sermon, a summary of which was given in the preceding chapter. Two or three were even of distinctly mystical tendency, but these were less read and circulated than those which were considered more directly practical. The most interesting of these mystical books was one which so closely resembled the Chinese *Classic of Purity,* that there can be little doubt that it was a version of it with slight variations.

The bulk of the literature might be roughly divided into two parts—scientific information and stories with a purpose. Treatises or manuals existed on every trade or handicraft or art that was practised in the country, and these were of the nature of official handbooks—not usually the work of any one man, but rather a record of the knowledge existing on their subject at the time that they were written. Appendices were constantly issued to these books as further discoveries were made, or old ideas modified, and every person who possessed a copy kept it religiously altered and annotated up to date. As the Governors charged themselves with the dissemination of such information, they were able practically to ensure its reaching everyone who was interested in it; thus the Peruvian monograph on any subject was a veritable compendium of useful knowledge about it, and gave the student in a condensed form the result of all the experience of his predecessors in that particular line.

The stories were almost all of one general type, and were distinctly, as I have said, stories with a purpose. All but invariably the hero was a King, a Governor, or a subordinate official, and the narrative told how he dealt successfully or otherwise with the various emergencies which presented themselves in the course of his work. Many of these stories were classics—household words to the people, as well known among them as biblical stories are among ourselves, constantly referred to and quoted as examples of what ought or ought not to be done. So in almost any conceivable predicament, the man who had to face it had in his mind some sort of precedent to guide his action. Whether all these tales were historical—whether they were all accounts of what had actually happened, or whether some of them were simply fiction—is not certain; but there is no doubt that they were generally accepted as true.

When the scene of such a tale lay in a border province, plenty of wild adventure not infrequently came into it; but (happily for our friends the Peruvians) that wearisome bugbear of the modern novel-reader, the love-story, had not yet made its appearance among them. Many of the situations which arose in the tales were not without humour, and the nation was joyous and laughter-loving; yet the professedly comic story had no place in its literature. Another and more regrettable gap is caused by the complete absence of poetry, as such. Certain maxims and expressions, couched in swinging, sonorous speech, were widely known and constantly quoted, much as some verses of poetry are with us; but, however poetical some of the conceptions may have been, there was nothing definitely rhythmical about their form. "Alliteration's artful aid" was invoked in the case of various short sentences which were given to children to memorise, and in the religious services certain phrases were chanted to music; but even these latter were fitted into the chanting in the same way as we adapt the words of a psalm to the Gregorian tone to which it is sung, not written to suit a definite sort of music, as our hymns are.

This brings us to the consideration of the music of these ancient Peruvians. They had several varieties of musical instruments, among which were noticed a pipe and a kind of harp, from which a wild, sweet, inconclusive, æolian sort of melody was extracted. But their principal and most popular instrument was somewhat of the nature of a harmonium. The sound was produced by the vibration of a tongue of metal, but the wind was forced into the instrument not by the action of the feet, but by an ingenious mechanical arrangement. Instead of keys such as ours, appeared the tops of a cluster of small metal pillars, upon which the fingers of the player pressed, so that a performance upon it irresistibly reminded one of the action of a modern typewriter.

Considerable power and great beauty of expression were attainable with this machine, but the old Peruvian scale in music was the same as that of Atlantis, and it differed so radically from our own that it is almost impossible for us rightly to appreciate the effects produced by its means. So far as we could see no such thing as a *piece* of music, which could be written down and reproduced by anyone at will, was known to these people; each performer improvised for himself, and musical skill among them was not the ability to interpret the work of a master, but simply fertility and resource in improvisation.

Sculpture also was an art fairly well developed among them, though one would perhaps characterise their style rather as bold, dashing and effective than as excelling in grace. Nearly all statues seem to have been of colossal size, and some of them were undoubtedly stupendous pieces of work; but to eyes accustomed to the contemplation of Grecian art, there is a certain air of ruggedness in the massive strength of the old Peruvian sculpture. Fine work was, however, done in bas-relief; this was almost always covered with metal, for the genius of this people turned especially in the direction of metal-work—a line in which the most exquisite decorations were constantly produced.

In connection with the daily life of the nation, and its manners and customs, there are some points which at once attract our attention as unusual and interesting. Their marriage customs, for example, were decidedly peculiar, for marriages took place on only one day in each year. Public opinion expected everyone to marry, unless he had good reason to the contrary, but there was nothing that could be thought of as compulsion in the matter. The marriage of minors was prohibited, but as soon as young people came of age they were as free to choose their own partners as they are among ourselves. The wedding, however, could not take place until the proper day arrived, when the Governor of the district or town made a formal visitation, and all young people who had attained the marriageable age during the previous year were called up before him, and officially notified that they were now free to enter upon the state of matrimony. Some proportion of these had usually already made up their minds to take immediate advantage of the opportunity; they therefore stepped forward before the Governor and preferred their request, and he, after asking a few questions, went through a simple form and pronounced them man and wife. He also made an order rectifying the assignment of land to suit the new circumstances, for the newly-married man and woman now no longer counted as members of their respective fathers' families, but as full-fledged householders on their own account. The married man had therefore twice as much land of his own as the single man, but even so he rarely found the work connected with it at all excessive.

A peculiarity was observed in connection with the principal food of the nation. The people took, of course, various kinds of food, just as men do now. We do not know whether animal flesh was prohibited, but it certainly was not eaten at the period which we were examining. The potato and yam were cultivated, and maize, rice, and milk in various combinations entered largely into their diet. They had, however, one curious and highly artificial kind of food which might have been called their staff of life—which took with them somewhat the place that bread takes with us, as the principal foundation of most of their meals. The basis of this was maize-flour, but various chemical constituents were mixed with it, and the resultant subjected to enormous pressure, so that it came out at the end of the operation as a hard and highly concentrated cake. Its components were carefully arranged, in order that it might contain within itself everything that was necessary for perfect nutrition in the smallest possible compass; and the experiment was so far successful that a tiny slice of it made sufficient provision for a whole day, and a man could carry with him a supply of food for a long journey without the slightest inconvenience.

The simplest method of taking it was to suck it slowly like a lozenge, but, if time permitted, it could be boiled or cooked in various ways, all of which largely increased its bulk. Of itself it had scarcely any taste, but it was the custom to flavour it in various ways in the process of manufacture, and these varieties of flavour were indicated by different colours. A pink cake, for example, was flavoured with pomegranate, a blue one with vanilla, a yellow one with orange, a pink and white striped one with guava, and so on, so that every one's taste might be suited.

This curiously compressed sweetmeat was the staple food of the country, and large numbers of people took practically nothing else, even though there were plenty of other dishes from which to select. It was manufactured in such enormous quantities that it was exceedingly cheap and easily within everybody's reach, and for busy people it had many and obvious advantages. Many fruits were cultivated, and people who liked them took them along with their lozenge, but all these additions were matters of taste and not of necessity.

The race as a whole was fond of pet animals of various kinds, and in the course of ages they had specialised and developed these creatures to an extraordinary degree. Small monkeys and cats were perhaps the most general favourites, and there were many fancy varieties of each, bred almost as much out of all relation to the original creature as are the deformities called dachshunds at the present day. In regard to the cats, they made a great speciality of unusual colours, and they had even succeeded in breeding some of that colour which is so conspicuously absent among quadrupeds—a fairly decided and brilliant blue!

Many people were fond of birds also, as might be expected in a continent where so many magnificently coloured specimens are to be found: indeed, it is by no means impossible that we owe to their care in breeding some of the splendid varieties of bird-life that now inhabit the forests of the Amazon. Some of the richer ladies had huge aviaries with golden wires in the courtyards of their houses, and devoted all their spare time to the endeavour to cultivate the intelligence and affection of their pets.

The national dress was simple and scanty—just a sort of loose flowing garment not at all unlike some of those that are worn in the East in the present day, except that the old Peruvian wore less white and was more addicted to colour than is the average Indian of the present day. A Peruvian crowd on a festal occasion was an exceedingly brilliant sight, perhaps only to be paralleled now among the Burmese. The ladies as a rule exhibited a partiality for blue robes, and a dress closely resembling that often assigned by mediæval painters to the Virgin Mary was one of the commonest at the time of which we are writing. The material was usually cotton, though the fine soft wool of the llama and vicuna was also sometimes used. A sort of cloth of great strength was made from the threads of the maguey, which were chemically treated in some way to make them fit for such use.

The nation had all the facility in the use of purely mechanical methods of rapid calculation which is so characteristic of the Atlantean Race. They employed an abacus, or calculating-frame, closely resembling that used to-day with such dexterity by the Japanese, and they also made a cheaper substitute for such a frame out of a kind of fringe of knotted cord, which may perhaps be the original of the *quipus,* which the Spaniards found in use in the same country thousands of years later.

In studying an ancient civilisation like this, so many points of interest crop up—points of resemblance or of contrast with the life of our own time—that the difficulty is rather to decide what to omit, in trying to give an account of it, than what to include. We cannot convey to our readers the sense of vivid reality which it all bears to those of us who have seen it, but we trust that for some few at least we have been not entirely unsuccessful in making this long-dead past live again for a few brief moments. And be it remembered that we ourselves—many of us who are now living and working in the Theosophical Society—were born at this very time among the inhabitants of old Peru; many dear friends whom we know and love now were friends or relations in that far-off time also; so that the memory of all this that we have tried to describe must lie dormant, deep down within the causal bodies of many of our readers, and it is by no means impossible that in some of them that memory may gradually be revived by quietly thinking over the description. If any should be thus successful, they will realise how curious and interesting it is to look back into those long-forgotten lives, and see what we have gained and what we have failed to gain since then.[1]

At first sight it looks as though in many important ways there had been rather retrogression than advance. The physical life, with all its surroundings, was undoubtedly better managed then, than, so far as we know, it has ever been since. The opportunities for unselfish work and devotion to duty which were offered to the governing class have perhaps never been surpassed; still it must be admitted that nothing in the way of mental struggle or effort was necessary for the less intelligent classes, though when it did show itself it was richly rewarded.

Undoubtedly the condition of public opinion is not so high, nor is the sense of duty so strong, now as it was then. But the comparison is in truth hardly a fair one. We are as yet a comparatively young Race, whereas that which we have been examining was one of the most glorious offshoots of a Race that had long passed its prime. We are passing now, because of our ignorance,

[1] See Appendix IV.

through a period of trial, storm, and stress, but out of it all we too shall, in time, when we have developed a little common-sense, emerge into a season of rest and success, and when that time comes to us, it ought, by the law of evolution, to reach an even higher level than theirs.

We must remember that, beautiful as was their religion, they had, so far as we know, nothing that could really be called Occultism; they had no such grasp of the great scheme of the universe as we have who are privileged to study Theosophy. When our fifth Root Race reaches the same stage of its life, we may assuredly hope to combine physical surroundings as good as theirs with true philosophical teaching, and with a higher intellectual and spiritual development than was possible for us when we formed part of that splendid old relic of Atlantean civilisation, fourteen thousand years ago.

CHAPTER XIII

TWO ATLANTEAN CIVILISATIONS

Turanian, in Ancient Chaldæa, B.C. 19,000

ANOTHER ancient civilisation which has interested us, in its way, almost as much as that of Peru, was one that arose in the part of Asia which was afterwards called Babylonia or Chaldæa. One curious point these two great Empires of old have in common—that each of them in the period of its decadence, many centuries later than the glorious prime at which it is most profitable to study them, was conquered by people much lower in the scale of civilisation, who nevertheless attempted to adopt as far as they could the customs, civil and religious, of the effete race which they had subdued. Just as the Peru discovered by Pizarro was in almost every respect a pale copy of the older Peru which we have tried to describe, so the Babylonia known to the student of archæology is in many ways a kind of degenerate reflection of an earlier and greater Empire.

In many ways, but perhaps not in all. It is possible that at the zenith of its glory the later kingdom may have surpassed its predecessor in military power, in the extent of its territories or its commèrce; but in simplicity of life, in earnest devotion to the tenets of the remarkable religion which they followed, and in real knowledge of the facts of nature, there is little doubt that the older race had the advantage.

Perhaps there could hardly be a greater contrast between any two countries than we find between Peru and Babylonia. In the former the remarkable system of government was the most prominent feature, and religion formed a comparatively small part of the life of the people—indeed, the civil functions of the priests as educators, as doctors, and as agents in the vast scheme of provision for old age, loom much more largely in the mind's eye than their occasional work of praise or preaching in connection with the temple services. In Chaldæa, on the other hand, the system of government was in no way exceptional; the chief factor of life there was emphatically religion, for no undertaking of any sort was ever begun without special reference to it. Indeed, the religion of the people permeated and dominated their life to an extent equalled perhaps only among the Brāhmaṇas of India.

It will be remembered that among the Peruvians the religious cult was a simple but extremely beautiful form of Sun-worship, or rather worship of the Spirit of the Sun; its tenets were few and clear, and its chief characteristic was its all-pervading spirit of joyousness. In Chaldæa the faith was sterner and more mystical, and the ritual far more complicated. It was not the Sun alone that was reverenced there, but all the Host of Heaven, and the religion was in fact an exceedingly elaborate scheme of worship of the great Star-Angels, including within it, as a practical guide to daily life, a comprehensive and carefully worked-out system of Astrology.

Let us postpone for the moment the description of their magnificent temples and their gorgeous ritual, and consider first the relation of this strange religion to the life of the people. To understand its effect we must try to comprehend their view of Astrology, and I think we shall find it on the whole an eminently common-sense view—one which might be adopted with great advantage by professors of the art at the present day.

The idea that it is possible for the physical planets themselves to have any influence over human affairs was of course never held by any of the priests or teachers, nor even, so far as we can see, by the most ignorant of the common people at the early period of which we are now speaking. The theory given to the priests was an exceedingly elaborate mathematical one, probably handed down to them through an unbroken line of tradition from earlier teachers, who had direct and first-hand knowledge of the great facts of nature. The broad idea of their scheme is not difficult to grasp, but it seems impossible in our three dimensions to construct any mathematical figure which will satisfy the requirements of their hypothesis in all its details—at least with the knowledge at present at our disposal.

The entire solar system, then, in all its vast complexity, was regarded as simply one great Being, and all its parts as partial expressions of Him. All its physical constituents—the sun with his wonderful corona, all the planets with their satellites, their oceans, their atmospheres, and the various ethers surrounding them—all these collectively made up His physical body, the expression of Him on the physical plane. In the same way the collective astral worlds (not only the astral spheres belonging to these physical planets, but also the purely astral planets of all the chains of the system—such, for example, as planets B and F of our own Chain) made up His astral body, and the collective worlds of the mental plane were His mental body—the vehicle through which He manifested Himself upon that particular plane.

So far the idea is clear, and corresponds closely with what we have ourselves been taught with regard to the great LOGOS of our system.[1] Now let it be supposed that in these 'bodies' of His at their various levels there are certain different classes or types of matter fairly equally distributed over the whole system. These types do not at all correspond to our usual division into subplanes—a division which is made according to the degree of density of the matter, so that in the

[1] Indeed, we may say at once that the Chaldæan theory upon these subjects was practically that which is held by many Theosophists at the present day. Mr. C. W. Leadbeater, in *A Textbook of Theosophy* and *The Hidden Side of Things*, has made, as the result of his own investigations, a statement on planetary influences which is to all intents and purposes identical with the belief held thousands of years ago (as the result of similar investigations) by the Chaldæan priests.

physical world, for example, we get the solid, liquid, gaseous and etheric conditions of matter. On the contrary, they constitute a totally distinct series of cross-divisions, each containing matter in all these different conditions, so that if we denote the various types by numbers, we should have solid, liquid, and gaseous matter of the first type, solid, liquid, and gaseous matter of the second type, and so on all the way through.

This is the case at all levels, but for the sake of clearness let us for the moment confine our thought to one level only. Perhaps the idea is easiest to follow with regard to the astral. It has often been explained that in the astral body of a man matter belonging to each of the sub-planes is to be found, and that the proportion between the denser and the finer kinds shows how far that body is capable of responding to coarser or more refined desires, and so is to some extent an indication of the degree to which he has evolved himself. Similarly in every astral body there is matter of each of these types or cross-divisions, and in this case the proportion between them shows the disposition of the man—whether he is excitable or serene, sanguine or phlegmatic, patient or irritable, and so on.

Now the Chaldæan theory was that each of these types of matter in the astral body of the LOGOS, and in particular the mass of elemental essence functioning through each type, is to some extent a separate vehicle—almost a separate entity—having its own special affinities, and capable of vibrating under influences which might probably evoke no response from the other types. The types differ among themselves, because the matter composing them originally came forth through different centres of the LOGOS, and the matter of each type is still in the closest sympathy with the centre to which it belongs, so that the slightest alteration of any kind in the condition of that centre is instantly reflected in some way or other in all the matter of the corresponding type.

Since every man has within himself matter of all these types, it is obvious that any modification in, or action of, any one of these great centres must to some degree affect all beings in the system, and the extent to which any particular person is so affected depends upon the proportion of the type of matter influenced which he happens to have in his astral body. That is to say, we find different types of men as well as of matter, and by reason of their constitution, by the very composition of their astral bodies, some of them are more susceptible to one influence, some to another.

The whole solar system, when looked at from a sufficiently high plane, is seen to consist of these great centres, each surrounded by an enormous sphere of influence, indicating the limits within which the force which pours out through it is especially active. Each of these centres has a sort of orderly periodic change or motion of its own, corresponding perhaps on some infinitely higher level to the regular beating of the physical human heart. But since some of these periodic changes are much more rapid than others, a curious and complicated series of effects is produced, and it has been observed that the movement of the physical planets in their relation to one another furnishes a clue to the arrangement of these great spheres at any given moment. In Chaldæa it was held that, in the gradual condensation of the original glowing nebula from which the system was formed, the location of the physical planets was determined by the formation of vortices at certain points of intersection of these spheres with one another and with a given plane.

The influences belonging to these spheres differ widely in quality, and one way in which this difference shows itself is in their action upon the elemental essence both in man and around him. Be it ever remembered that this influence was supposed to be exerted on *all* planes, not only upon the astral, though we are just now confining our attention to that for simplicity's sake. The influences may have, and indeed must have, other and more important lines of action not at present known to us; but this at least forces itself upon the notice of the observer, that each such sphere produces its own special effect upon the manifold varieties of the elemental essence.

One, for example, greatly stimulates the activity and vitality of those kinds of essence which especially appertain to the centre through which it came, while apparently checking and controlling others; the influence of another sphere is strong over quite a different set of essences, which belong to its centre, while apparently not affecting the previous set in the least. There are all sorts of combinations and permutations of these influences, the action of one of them being in some cases greatly intensified, and in others almost neutralised, by the presence of another.

It will inevitably be asked here whether our Chaldæan priests were fatalists—whether having discovered and calculated the exact effect of these influences on the various types of human beings, they believed that these results were inevitable, and that man's will was powerless to resist them. Their answer to this latter question was always most emphatic; the influences have certainly no power to dominate man's will in the slightest degree; all they can do is in some cases to make it easier, or more difficult, for that will to act along certain lines. Since the astral and mental bodies of man are practically composed of this living and vivified matter which we now call elemental essence, any unusual excitation of any of the classes of that essence, or a sudden increase in its activity, must undoubtedly affect to some extent either his emotions or his mind, or both; and it is also obvious that these influences must work differently on different men, because of the varieties of essence entering into their composition.

But it was most clearly stated that in no case can a man be swept away by them into any course of action without the consent of his will, though he may evidently be helped or hindered by them in any effort that he chances to be making. The priests taught that the really strong man has little need to trouble himself as to the influences which happen to be in the ascendant, but that for all ordinary people it is usually worth while to know at what moment this or that force can most advantageously be applied.

They explained carefully that the influences are in themselves no more good or evil than any other of the forces of nature, as we should say now; like electricity or any other great natural force they may be helpful or hurtful, according to the use that is made of them. And just as we should say that certain experiments are more likely to be successful if undertaken when the air is heavily charged with electricity, while certain others under such conditions would most probably fail, so they said that an effort involving the use of the forces of our mental or emotional nature will more or less readily achieve its object according to the influences which predominate when it is made.

It was always understood, therefore, that these factors might be put aside as *une quantité négligeable* by the man of iron determination or the student of real Occultism; but since the majority of the human race still allow themselves to be the helpless sport of the forces of desire, and have not yet developed anything worth calling a will of their own, it was considered that their feebleness permitted these influences to assume an importance to which they had intrinsically no claim.

The fact of a particular influence being in operation can never make it *necessary* that an event should occur, but it makes it more *likely* to occur. For instance, by means of what is called in modern Astrology a Martian influence, certain vibrations of the astral essence are set up which tend in the direction of passion. So it might safely be predicted of a man who had by nature tendencies of a passionate and sensual nature, that when that influence is prominently in action he will probably commit some crime connected with passion or sensuality; not in the least that he is *forced* into such crime, but only that a condition comes into existence in which it is more difficult for him to maintain his balance. For the action upon him is of a double character; not only is the essence *within* him stirred into greater activity, but the corresponding matter of the plane outside is also quickened, and that again reacts upon him.

An example frequently given was that a certain variety of influence may occasionally bring about a condition of affairs in which all forms of nervous excitement are considerably intensified, and there is consequently a general sense of irritability abroad. Under such circumstances disputes arise far more readily than usual, even on the most trifling pretexts, and the large number of people who are always on the verge of losing their temper relinquish all control of themselves on even less than ordinary provocation.

It might even sometimes happen, it was said, that such influences, playing on the smouldering discontent of ignorant jealousy, might fan it into an outburst of popular frenzy from which widespread disaster might ensue. Apparently the warning given thousands of years ago is no less necessary now; for it was just in this way that the Parisians in 1870 were moved to rush about the streets crying "A Berlin!" and just so also has arisen many a time the fiendish yell of "Ḍīn! ḍīn!" which so easily arouses the mad fanaticism of an uncivilised Muhammadan crowd.

The Astrology of these Chaldæan priests therefore devoted itself chiefly to the calculation of the position and action of these spheres of influence, so that its principal function was rather to form a rule of life than to predict the future: or at least such predictions as it gave were rather of tendencies than of special events, while the Astrology of our own day appears to devote itself largely to the latter line of prophecy.

There can be no doubt, however, that the Chaldæans were right in affirming the power of a man's will to modify the destiny marked out for him by his karma. Karma may throw a man into certain surroundings or bring him under certain influences, but it can never force him to commit a crime, though it may so place him that it requires great determination on his part to avoid that crime. Therefore it seems to us that what Astrology could do, then or now, is to warn the man of the circumstances under which at such and such a time he would find himself; but any definite prophecy of his action under those circumstances can, theoretically, only be based upon probabilities—even though we fully recognise how nearly those probabilities become certainties in the case of the ordinary will-less man in the street.

The calculations of these priests of the old time enabled them to draw up a sort of official almanac each year, by which the whole life of the race was largely regulated. They decided the times at which all agricultural operations could most safely be undertaken; they proclaimed the fit moment for arranging the breeding of animals and plants. They were the doctors as well as the teachers of the race, and they knew exactly under what collocation of influences their various remedies could be most efficiently administered.

They divided their followers into classes, assigning each to what would now be called his ruling planet, and their calendar was full of warnings addressed to these different classes; as, for example: "On the seventh day, those who worship Mars should be especially on the watch against causeless irritation;" or: "From the twelfth to the fifteenth days there is unusual danger of rashness in matters connected with the affections, especially for the worshippers of Venus," and so on. That these warnings were of great use to the bulk of their people we cannot doubt, strange as such an elaborate system of provision against minor contingencies may appear to some of us at the present day.

From this peculiar division of the people into types, according to the planets which indicated the position of the centre of influence to which they were most readily susceptible, there arose an equally curious arrangement both of the public temple services and of the private devotions of the worshippers. Certain daily hours of prayer, regulated by the apparent movements of the sun, were observed by all alike; at sunrise, noon, and sunset, certain anthems or verses were chanted by the priests at the temples, and the more religious of the people made a point of being regularly present at these short services, while those who could not conveniently attend them nevertheless observed each of these hours by the recitation of a few pious phrases of praise and prayer.

But, quite apart from these observances, which seem to have been common to all, each person had his own special prayers to offer to the particular Deity to whom by birth he was attached; and the proper time for them varied constantly with the motion of his planet. The moment at which it crossed the meridian appears to have been considered the most favourable of all, and next to that the few minutes immediately after its rising or immediately before its setting. It might, however, be invoked at any time while above the horizon; and even while below it the Deity of the planet was not entirely out of reach, though in this case he was addressed only in some great emergency, and the whole ceremonial employed was entirely different.

The special calendars prepared by the priests for the worshippers of each of these planetary Deities contained full particulars as to the proper hours of prayer and the appropriate verses to be recited at each. What might be described as a kind of periodical prayer-book was issued for each planet, and all those who were attached to that planet were careful to provide themselves with copies of it. Indeed, these calendars were something much more than mere reminders as to hours of prayer; they were prepared under special stellar conditions (each under the influence of its own Deity) and were supposed to have various talismanic properties, so that the devotee of any particular planet always carried its latest calendar about with him.

It followed, therefore, that the religious man of old Chaldæa had not a regular hour of prayer or worship which was always the same, day after day, as would be the case now; but instead of this, his time for meditation and religious exercise was movable, and would occur sometimes in the morning, sometimes at noon, sometimes in the evening, or even at midnight. But whenever it came he did not fail to observe it; however awkwardly the hour might clash with his business, his pleasure or his repose, he would have regarded it as a grave lapse from duty if he had omitted to take advantage of it. So far as we can see, there was no thought in his mind that the Spirit of the planet would in any way resent it if he neglected the hour, or indeed that it was possible for such a Spirit to feel anger at all; the idea was rather that at that moment the Deity was pouring forth a blessing, and that it would be not only foolish but ungrateful to lose the opportunity so kindly offered.

These, however, were only the private devotions of the people; they had great and gorgeous public ceremonies as well. Each of the planets had assigned to it at least two great feast days in the year, and the Sun and Moon appropriated considerably more than two. Each planetary Spirit had his temples in every part of the country, and on ordinary occasions his devotees contented themselves with frequent visits to the nearest; but on the greater festivals to which we have referred, enormous multitudes assembled on a vast plain in the neighbourhood of their capital city, where there was a group of magnificent temples, which were absolutely unique.

These buildings were in themselves worthy of attention as fine examples of a prehistoric style of architecture; but their greatest interest lay in the fact that their arrangement was evidently intended to represent that of the solar system, and that, when the principle of this arrangement was understood, it undoubtedly showed the possession by its designers of a considerable knowledge of the subject. By far the largest and the most splendid of all was the huge temple of the Sun, which it will presently be necessary to describe somewhat more in detail. The others, erected at gradually increasing distances from this, might seem at the first glance to have been built simply as convenience dictated, and not upon any orderly plan.

Closer examination, however, showed that there *was* a plan, and a remarkable one—that not only the gradually increasing distances of these smaller temples from the principal one had a definite ratio and a definite meaning, but even the relative dimensions of certain important parts of these fanes were not accidental, for they typified respectively the sizes of the planets and their distances from the solar orb.

Now it is obvious to anyone who knows anything at all about astronomy that an attempt to construct to scale a model of the solar system in temples would be foredoomed to failure—that is to say, if the temples were to be available for worship in the ordinary way. The difference in size between the Sun and the smaller members of his family is so immense, and the distances between them are so enormous, that unless the buildings were mere dolls' houses no country would be large enough to contain the entire system.

How, then, did the Chaldæan Sage who designed this marvellous group of temples contrive to conquer these difficulties? Precisely as do the illustrators of our modern books of Astronomy—by using two entirely different scales, but preserving the relative proportions in their delineation of each. There is nothing in this wonderful monument of ancient skill to prove to us that its designer knew the absolute sizes and distances of the planets at all, though of course he *may* have done so; what is certain is that he was perfectly well acquainted with their *relative* sizes and distances. He had either been taught, or had himself discovered, Bode's Law; how much further his knowledge went his buildings leave us to conjecture, except that he must certainly have possessed some information as to planetary magnitudes, though his computation of them differed in some ways from that now accepted.

The shrines devoted to the inner planets made a sort of irregular cluster which seemed quite close under the walls of the great Sun-Temple, while those of the giant outer members of the solar family were dotted at ever-increasing intervals over the plain, until the representative of far-away Neptune was almost lost in the distance. The buildings differed in design, and there is little doubt that every variation had its special significance, even though in many cases we were unable to discern it. There was, however, one feature which all shared; each of them possessed a central hemispherical dome, which was evidently intended to bear a special relation to the orb which it typified.

All these hemispheres were brilliantly coloured, each bearing the hues which Chaldæan tradition associated with its particular planet. The principle upon which these colours were selected is far from clear, but we shall have to return to them later when we examine the great festival services. These domes by no means always bore the same relation to the dimensions of their respective temples, but when compared one with another they were found to correspond closely to the sizes of the planets which they symbolised. With regard to Mercury, Venus, the Moon, and Mars, the Chaldæan measurements of relative size corresponded precisely with our own; but Jupiter, Saturn, Uranus, and Neptune, though immensely larger than the inner group, were yet decidedly smaller than they would have been if constructed on the same scale according to our received calculations.

This may have been due to the use of a different standard for these huge globes, but it seems to us far more probable that the Chaldæan proportions were correct, and that in modern astronomy we have considerably over-estimated the size of the outer planets. It is all but established now that the surface which we see in the case of Jupiter or Saturn is that of a deep, dense cloud-envelope, and not the body of the planet at all; and if that be so, the Chaldæan representation of these globes is as accurate as the rest of their scheme. Another point in favour of such a suggestion is that, if it were accepted, the extraordinarily low density commonly assigned by our astronomers to the outer planets would be brought more nearly into agreement with that of the other worlds within our ken.

A number of curious details combined to prove to us the thorough comprehension of the system which must have been possessed by the designer of these beautiful shrines. Vulcan, the intra-Mercurial planet, was duly represented, and the place in the scheme where our earth should have come in was occupied by the temple of the Moon—a large one, though the hemisphere which crowned it seemed disproportionately small, being constructed exactly to the same scale as the rest. Close by this Moon-temple there arose an isolated dome of black marble supported by pillars, which from its size was evidently intended to typify the Earth, but there was no shrine of any kind attached to it.

In the space (quite correctly calculated) between Mars and Jupiter there appeared no temple, but a number of columns, each ending in a tiny dome of the usual hemispherical shape; these we presumed to be intended to represent the asteroids. Every planet which possesses satellites had them carefully indicated by properly proportioned subsidiary domes arranged round the primary, and Saturn's rings were also clearly shown.

On the principal festivals of any of the planets, all the votaries of the corresponding Deities (as we should say now, the people born under those planets) wore over or in place of their ordinary dress a mantle or cope of the colour considered sacred to the planet. These colours were all exceedingly brilliant, and the material worn had a sort of sheen like satin, so that the effect was usually striking, especially as many of the colours had another tint underlying them, as in what is called shot silk. A list of these colours will be of interest, although, as we have before remarked, the reason which dictated their choice is not always obvious.

The dress worn by the followers of the Sun was a beautifully delicate silken material, all interwoven with gold threads, so that it appeared a veritable cloth of gold. But cloth of gold, as we know it now, is of a thick, unbending texture, whereas this fabric was so flexible that it could be folded like muslin.

Vulcan's hue was flame-colour, striking, gorgeous, and distinctive—possibly typical of the extreme propinquity of Vulcan to the Sun, and the fiery physical conditions that must obtain there.

Mercury was symbolised by a brilliant orange hue, shot with lemon-colour—shades not infrequently to be seen in the auras of his adherents as well as in their vestments; but though in some cases the predominant auric colours seem a possible explanation of these selections, there are others to which this would hardly apply.

The votaries of Venus appeared in a lovely pure sky-blue, with an underlying thread of light green, which gave to the whole a quivering iridescent effect when the wearer moved.

The garments of the Moon were naturally of white material, but so interwoven with threads of silver that practically it might be called cloth of silver, as the Sun's was cloth of gold. Yet in certain lights this Moon-robe showed beautiful pale violet shades, which much enhanced its effect.

Mars appropriately enough clothed his followers in a splendid brilliant scarlet, but with a strong crimson shade underlying it, and practically taking its place when seen from certain aspects. This colour was quite unmistakable, and totally distinct from those of Vulcan or Mercury. It may have been suggested either by auric appearances or by the ruddy hue of the physical planet.

Jupiter robed his children in a wonderful gleaming blue-violet material, dappled all over with tiny silvery specks. It is not easy to assign any reason for this, unless indeed it may again be attributed to auric associations.

Saturn's votaries were clothed in clear sunset green, with pearl-grey shades underlying it, while those born under Uranus wore a magnificent deep rich blue—that unimaginable colour of the South Atlantic, which no one knows but those who have seen it. The dress appropriated to Neptune was the least noticeable of them all, for it was a plain-looking dark indigo, though in high lights it too developed an unexpected richness.

On the principal festivals of any one of these planets, its adherents appeared in full dress, and marched in procession to its temple, decked with garlands of flowers, bearing banners and gilded staves, and filling the air with sonorous chanting.

But the grandest display of all was at one of the great feasts of the Sun-God, when the people came together, each robed in the gorgeous vestment of his tutelary Deity, and the whole immense multitude performed the solemn circumambulation of the Sun-temple. On such an occasion the worshippers of the Sun filled the vast building to overflowing, while next to the walls marched the bands of Vulcan, next outside them those of Mercury, then the followers of Venus, and so on, each planet being represented in the order of its position with reference to the Sun. The whole mass of people, thus arranged in concentric rings of flashing colour, swept slowly, steadily round like a colossal living wheel, and, under the flood of living light poured down by that all but tropical Sun, they formed perhaps as brilliant a spectacle as the world has ever seen.

In order that some account may be given of the even more interesting ceremonies that took place on such occasions within that great temple of the Sun, it is necessary that we should attempt a description of its appearance and arrangement. Its main plan was cruciform, with a vast circular space (covered by the hemispherical dome) where the arms of the cross met. We shall gain a more correct image if, instead of thinking of the ordinary cruciform church with nave, chancel and transepts, we picture to ourselves a great circular domed chamber like the reading-room of the British Museum, and then imagine four huge naves opening out of it towards the four quarters of the compass; for all the arms of its cross were of equal length. Having fixed that part of the picture firmly, we must then add four other great openings between the arms of the cross, leading into vast halls whose walls curved round and met at the extremity, so as to give their floors the shape of an immense leaf or the petal of a flower. In fact, the ground-plan of the temple might be described as an equal-armed cross laid upon a simple four-petalled flower, so that the arms lay between the petals.

A man standing in the centre under the dome would therefore see long vistas stretching out from him in all directions. The whole structure was carefully oriented, so that the arms of the cross were accurately directed to the cardinal points. The southern end remained open and constituted the principal entrance, facing the great altar which occupied the end of the northern arm. The eastern and western arms contained altars also, of enormous size from our point of view, though much smaller than the main erection at the northern end.

These eastern and western altars seem to have fulfilled something the same purpose as do those dedicated to the Blessed Virgin and to S. Joseph in a Catholic cathedral, for one of them was consecrated to the Sun and the other to the Moon, and some of the regular daily services connected with these two luminaries were celebrated at them. The great northern altar was, however, that round which all the greatest crowds gathered, at which all the grandest ceremonies were performed, and its arrangements and furniture were curious and interesting.

On the wall behind it, in the place occupied by the 'east window' in an ordinary church—

except that this was north—hung an immense concave mirror, far larger than any that we had ever before seen. It was of metal, quite probably of silver, and was polished to the highest possible degree. Indeed it was observed that the care of it, the keeping it bright and free even from dust, was considered to be a religious duty of the most binding nature. How such a huge speculum had been so perfectly cut, how it was that its own enormous weight did not distort it—these are problems that would be serious ones to our modern artificers, but they had been successfully solved by these men of long ago.

Along the centre of the roof of this huge northern arm of the cross there ran a narrow slit open to the sky, so that the light of whatever star happened to be exactly upon the meridian shone straight into the temple and fell upon the great mirror. It is a well-known property of the concave mirror that it forms in the air in front of it, at its focus, an image of whatever is reflected in it, and this principle was cleverly used by the priests in order, as they would probably have put it, to collect and apply the influence of each planet at the moment of its greatest power. A pedestal bearing a brazier was fixed in the floor beneath the focus of the mirror, and just as a planet was coming to the meridian and therefore shining through the slit in the roof, a quantity of sweet-smelling incense was thrown upon the glowing charcoal. A pillar of light grey smoke immediately ascended, and in the midst of it gleamed forth the living image of the star. Then the worshippers bowed their heads, and the glad chant of the priests rang out; in fact, this ceremony reminded us somewhat of the elevation of the Host in a Catholic church.

When necessary another piece of machinery was brought into action—a flat circular mirror which could be lowered from the roof by lines so as to occupy exactly the focus of the great mirror. This caught the reflected image of the planet, and by tilting it the concentrated light received from the concave mirror could be poured down upon certain spots on the floor of the temple. On these spots were laid the sick for whom it was considered that that particular influence would be beneficial, while the priest prayed that the planetary Spirit would pour healing and strength upon them; and undoubtedly cures did frequently reward their endeavours, though it may well be that faith played a large part in obtaining the result.

The lighting of certain sacred fires when the Sun himself crossed the meridian was achieved by means of the same mechanism, though one of the most interesting ceremonies of this nature was always performed at the western altar. Upon this altar burnt always what was called the 'sacred Moon-fire,' and this was allowed to go out only once a year, on the night before the spring equinox. The following morning the rays of the Sun, passing through an orifice above the eastern altar, fell directly upon that at the west end, and by means of a glass globe filled with water which was suspended in their path and acted as a lens, the Sun himself relit the sacred Moon-fire, which was then carefully tended and kept burning for another year.

The inner surface of the great dome was painted to represent the night-sky, and by some complicated mechanism the principal constellations were made to move over it exactly as the real stars were moving outside, so that at any time of the day, or on a cloudy night, a worshipper could always tell in the temple the precise position of any of the signs of the zodiac, and of the various planets in relation to them. Luminous bodies were used to represent the planets, and in the earlier days of this religion, precisely as in the earlier days of the Mysteries, these bodies were real materialisations called into existence by the Adept Teachers, and moving freely in the air; but in both cases in later days, when less evolved men had to take the place of these exalted Beings, it was found difficult or impossible to make the materialisations work properly, and so their place was filled by ingenious mechanical contrivances—a kind of orrery on a gigantic scale. The outside of this huge dome was thinly plated with gold; and it was noteworthy that a peculiar dappled effect was produced on the surface, evidently intended to represent what are called the 'willow-leaves' or 'rice-grains' of the Sun.

Another interesting feature of this temple was an underground room or crypt, which was reserved for the exclusive use of the priests, apparently with a view to meditation and self-development. The only light admitted came through thick plates of a crystal-like substance of various colours, which were let into the floor of the temple, but arrangements were made to reflect the sun's rays through this medium when necessary, and the priest who was practising his meditation allowed this reflected light to fall upon the various centres in his body—sometimes upon that between the eyes, sometimes upon the base of the spine, and so on. This evidently aided in the development of the power of divination, of clairvoyance and of intuition; and it was evident that the particular colour of light used depended not only upon the object sought, but upon the planet or type to which the priest belonged. It was also noticed that the thyrsus, the hollow rod charged with electric or vital fire, was used here, just as it was in the Grecian Mysteries.

An interesting part of the study of this old-world religion is the endeavour to understand exactly what its teachers meant when they spoke of the Star-Angel, the Spirit of a star. A little careful investigation shows that the terms, though sometimes synonymous, are not always so, for they seem to have included at least three quite different conceptions under the one title 'the Spirit of a planet'.

First they believed in the existence, in connection with each planet, of an undeveloped, semi-intelligent yet exceedingly potent entity, which we can perhaps best express in our Theosophical terminology as the collective elemental essence of that planet, regarded as one huge creature. We know how, in the case of a man, the elemental essence which enters into the composition of his astral body becomes to all intents and purposes a separate entity, which has sometimes been called the desire-elemental: how its many different types and classes combine into a temporary unity, capable of definite action in its own defence, as for example against the disintegrating process which sets in after death. If in just the same way we can conceive of the totality of the elemental kingdoms in a particular planet energising as a whole, we shall have grasped exactly the theory held by the ancient Chaldæans with regard to this first variety of planetary Spirit, for which 'planetary elemental' would be a far more appropriate name. It was the influence (or perhaps the magnetism) of this planetary elemental which they tried to focus upon people suffering from certain diseases, or to imprison in a talisman for future use.

The priests held that the physical planets which we can see serve as pointers to indicate the position or condition of the great centres in the body of the LOGOS Himself, and also that through each of these great centres poured out one of the ten types of essence out of which, according to them, everything was built. Each of these types of essence, when taken by itself, was identified with a planet, and this also was frequently called the Spirit of the planet, thus giving another and quite different meaning to the term. In this sense they spoke of the Spirit of each planet as omnipresent throughout the solar system, as working within each man and showing itself in his actions, as manifesting through certain plants or minerals and giving them their distinctive properties.

Naturally it was this 'Spirit of the planet' within man which could be acted upon by the condition of the great centre to which it belonged, and it was with reference to this that all their astrological warnings were issued.

When, however, the Chaldæans invoked the blessing of the Spirit of a planet, or endeavoured by earnest and reverent meditation to raise themselves towards Him, they were using the expression in yet another sense. They thought of each of these great centres as giving birth to and working through a whole hierarchy of great Spirits, and at the head of each of these hierarchies stood one great One who was called pre-eminently '*The* Spirit of the planet,' or more frequently the Star-Angel. It was His benediction that was sought by those who were more especially born under His influence, and He was regarded by them much as the great Archangels, the "seven Spirits before the throne of God," are regarded by the devout Christian—as a mighty Minister of the divine power of the LOGOS, a channel through which that ineffable splendour manifests itself. It was whispered that when the festival of some particular planet was being held in that great temple, and when at the critical moment the image of the Star shone out brightly amid the incense-cloud, those whose eyes were opened by the fervour of their devotion had sometimes seen the mighty form of the Star-Angel hovering beneath the blazing orb, so that it shone upon his forehead as he looked down benignantly upon those worshippers with whose evolution he was so closely connected.

It was one of the tenets of this ancient faith that it was in rare cases a possibility for highly developed men, who were full of heartfelt devotion to their Angel, to raise themselves by stress of long-continued meditation out of their world into His—to change the whole course of their evolution, and secure their next birth not on this planet any more, but on His; and the temple records contained accounts of priests who had done this, and so passed beyond human ken. It was held that once or twice in history this had happened with regard to that still greater order of stellar Deities, who were recognised as belonging to the fixed stars far outside of the solar system altogether; but these latter were thought of as daring flights into the unknown, as to the advisability of which even the greatest of the high priests were silent.

Strange as these methods may seem to us now, widely as they may differ from anything that is being taught to us in our Theosophical study, it would be foolish for us to criticise them, or to doubt that, for those to whom they appeal, they may be as efficacious as our own. We know that in the great White Brotherhood there are many Masters, and that though the Qualifications required for each step of the Path are the same for all candidates, yet each great Teacher adopts for His pupils that method of preparation which He sees to be best suited for them; and as all these paths alike lead to the mountain-top, it is not for us to say which is the shortest or the best for our neighbour. For each man there is one path which is shortest; but which that is depends upon the position from which he starts. To expect everyone to come round to our starting-point and use our path would be to fall under the delusion, born of conceit and ignorance, which blinds the eyes of the bigoted religionist. *We* have not been taught to worship the great Star-Angels, or to set before ourselves as a goal the possibility of joining the Ḍeva evolution at a comparatively early stage; but we should always remember that there are other lines of Occultism besides that particular form of it to which Theosophy has introduced us, and that we know but little yet even of our own line.

It would perhaps be better to avoid the use of the word 'worship' when describing the feeling of the Chaldæans toward the Star-Angels, for in the West it always leads to misconception; it was rather the deep affection and veneration and loyalty which we feel towards the Masters of Wisdom.

This Chaldæan religion lay close to the hearts of its people, and undoubtedly produced in the case of the majority really good and upright lives. Its priests were men of great learning in their own way along certain lines; their studies in history and astronomy were profound, and they not unnaturally took these two sciences together, always classifying the events of history according to their supposed connection with the various astronomical cycles. They were fairly well versed in chemistry also, and utilised some of its effects in their ceremonies. We noticed a case in which a priest was seen standing upon the flat roof of one of the temples and invoking in private devotion one of the planetary Spirits.[1] He held in his hand a long staff tipped with some bituminous-looking substance, and he began his invocation by marking with this staff the astrological sign of the planet upon the pavement in front of him, the substance leaving a brilliant phosphorescent mark behind it upon the stone or plaster surface.

As a rule each priest took up a special line of study to which he more particularly devoted himself. One group became proficient in medicine, constantly investigating the properties of various herbs and drugs when prepared under this or that combination of stellar influences; another turned its attention exclusively to agriculture, deciding what kind of soil was best suited to certain crops, and how it could be improved—working also at the culture of all kinds of useful plants, and the production of new varieties, testing the rapidity and strength of their growth under differently-coloured glass, and so on. This idea of the use of coloured light to promote growth was common to several of the old Atlantean races, and was part of the teaching originally given in Atlantis itself. Another section constituted themselves into a kind of weather bureau, and foretold with considerable accuracy both the ordinary changes of weather, and also any special disturbances such as storms, cyclones, or cloud-bursts. Later this became a sort of Government Department, and priests who predicted inaccurately were deposed as incapable.

[1] Erato, one of the Fellows of the Theosophical Society, some of whose lives are given in 'Rents in the Veil of Time' in *The Theosophist.*

Enormous importance was attached to pre-natal influences, and a mother was directed to seclude herself and to live a sort of semi-monastic life for some months both before and after the birth of a child. The educational arrangements of the country were not, as in Peru, directly in the hands of the priests, although it was they who decided by their calculations—evidently aided in some cases by clairvoyant insight—to which planet a child belonged. The children attached to a particular planet attended the school of that planet, and were under teachers of the same type as themselves, so that the children of Saturn would by no means be permitted to attend one of the schools of Jupiter, or the children of Venus to be taught by a worshipper of Mercury. The training appointed for these various types differed considerably, the intention being in each case to develop the good qualities and to counteract the weaknesses which long experience had prepared the instructors to expect in that especial kind of boy or girl.

The object of education with them was almost entirely the formation of character; the mere imparting of knowledge took quite a subordinate position. Every child was taught the curious hieroglyphic script of the country, and the rudiments of simple calculation, but beyond this nothing that we should recognise as a school subject was taken up at all. Numerous religious or rather ethical precepts were learnt by heart, all indicating the conduct expected from 'a son of Mars,' the planet—or Venus or Jupiter as the case might be—under various conditions that might arise;

and the only literature studied was an endlessly voluminous commentary upon these, full of interminable stories of adventures and situations in which the heroes acted sometimes wisely, sometimes foolishly. These the children were taught to criticise, giving their reasons for the opinions they formed, and describing in what way their own action in similar circumstances would have differed from that of the hero.

Though children passed many years in the schools, the whole of their time was spent in familiarising themselves (not only theoretically, but as far as might be practically also) with the teachings of this unwieldy *Book of Duty*, as it was called. In order to impress the lessons upon the minds of the children, they were expected to impersonate the various characters in these stories, and act out the scenes as though in a theatre. Any young man who developed a taste for history, mathematics, agriculture, chemistry or medicine, could, upon leaving school, attach himself as a kind of apprentice to any priest who had made a specialty of one of those subjects; but the school curriculum did not include any of these, nor provide any preparation for their study, beyond the general preparation which was supposed to fit everybody for anything that might turn up.

The literature of the race was not extensive. Official records were kept with great care, transfers of land were registered, and the decrees and proclamations of the Kings were always filed for reference; but though these documents offered excellent, even if somewhat dry, material for the historian, there is no trace that any connected history was written. It was taught orally by tradition, and certain episodes of it were tabulated in connection with the astronomical cycles; but these records were merely chronological tables, not histories in our sense of the word.

Poetry was represented by a series of sacred books, which gave a highly symbolical and figurative account of the origin of the worlds and of mankind, and also by a number of ballads or sagas celebrating the deeds of legendary heroes. These latter, however, were not written down, but simply handed on from one reciter to another. The people were exceedingly fond, like so many Oriental races, of listening to and improvising stories, and a great deal of traditional matter of this sort had been handed down through the centuries from what must obviously have been a remote period of far ruder civilisation.

From some of these earlier legends it is possible to reconstruct a rough outline of the early history of the race. The great bulk of the nation were clearly of Turanian stock, belonging to the fourth sub-race of the Atlantean Root-Race. They had apparently been originally a number of petty tribes, always at feud among themselves, living by agriculture of a primitive kind, and knowing little of architecture or culture of any sort.[1] To them in this semi-savage condition came, in B. C. 30,000, a great leader from the East, Theodoros, a man of another race, who

[1] This was the condition in which they were about B. C. 75,000, when Vaivasvaṭa Manu led His small caravan through them.

after the Āryan conquest of Persia and Mesopotamia, and the establishment of the rule of the Manu over those districts, was sent as Governor by Him, under Corona, His grandson, who succeeded Him as Ruler of Persia.[1]

From Theodoros descended the royal line of ancient Chaldæa—a line differing widely in appearance from their subjects, strong-faced, with bronzed complexion and deep-set gleaming eyes. The far later Babylonian sculptures which we know give us a fair idea of this royal type, though at that date the Āryan blood had permeated almost the entire race, whereas in the time of which we are speaking it had scarcely tinged it at all.

After a long period of splendour and prosperity this mighty Empire of Chaldæa slowly waned and decayed, until at last it was utterly destroyed by the incursion of hordes of fanatical barbarians, who, holding some ruder faith and hating with true puritanical fervour all evidence of a religious feeling nobler and more beautiful than their own, destroyed every trace of the glorious temples which had been erected with such loving care for that worship of the Star-Angels which we have tried to describe. These spoilers were in their turn driven out by the Akkads from the northern hill-country—Atlanteans still, but of the sixth sub-race; and these, coalescing gradually with the remnants of the old race and with other tribes of Turanian type, made up the Sumiro-Akkad nation out of which the later Babylonian Empire developed. As it grew, however, it became more and more strongly

[1] See Chapter xviii

affected by the mixture of Āryan blood, first from the Arabian (Semitic) and then from the Iranian sub-races, until when we come to what are commonly called historical times there is scarcely a trace of the old Turanian left in the faces that are pictured for us in the sculptures and mosaics of Assyria.

This later race had, in its beginnings at least, a strong tradition of its grander predecessor, and its endeavour was always to revive the conditions and the worship of the past. Its efforts were but partially successful: tinged by an alien faith, hampered by reminiscences of another and more recent tradition of the predominant partner in the combination, it produced but a pale and distorted copy of the magnificent cult of the Star-Angels, as it had flourished in the Golden Age which we have been attempting to describe.

Faint and unreal as these pictures of the past must be except to those who see them at first-hand, yet the study of them is not only of deep interest to the occult student, but of great use to him. It helps to widen out his view; it gives him now and then a passing glimpse into the working of that vast whole in which all that we can imagine of progress and evolution is but as one tiny wheel in a huge machine, as one small company in the great army of the King. Something is it also of encouragement to him to know a little of the glory and the beauty that have been on this grand old earth of ours, and to know that that is but a pale forecasting of the glory and the beauty that are yet to be.

But we must not leave this trifling sketch of two vignettes from the Golden Age of the past

—introduced, as an inset, into the huge picture of the world-story—without referring to a thought that must inevitably occur to one who studies them. We who love humanity—we who are trying, however feebly, to help it on its arduous way—can we read of conditions such as those of ancient Chaldæa, and perhaps still more of ancient Peru, conditions under which whole nations lived a happy and religious life, free from the curse of intemperance, free from the horror of grinding poverty—can we read of such conditions without a lurking doubt, without putting to ourselves the question: "Can it be that mankind is really evolving? Can it be for the good of humanity that when such civilisations have been attained, they should be allowed to crumble and fall, and leave no sign; and that after them we should come to *this*?"

Yes; for we know that the law of progress is a law of cyclic change, and that under that law personalities, races, empires, and worlds pass away, and come not again—in that form; that all forms must perish, however beautiful, in order that the life within them may grow and expand. And we know that that law is the expression of a Will—the divine Will of the LOGOS Himself; and therefore to the uttermost its working must be for the good of the humanity that we love. None ever loved man as He does—He who sacrificed Himself that man might be; He knows the whole evolution, from the beginning to the end; and He is satisfied. It is in His hand—the hand that blesseth man—that the destinies of man are lying; is there any heart among us not content to leave them there—not satisfied to its inmost core to hear Him say, as a great Master once said to His pupil: "What I do thou knowest not now, but thou shalt know hereafter"?

CHAPTER XIV

BEGINNINGS OF THE FIFTH ROOT RACE

THE statement in *The Secret Doctrine* that the fifth Root Race began one million years ago appears, as already stated, to refer to the beginning of the choosing of materials by the Lord Vaivasvaṭa, the Race Manu. He was a Lord of the Moon, taking the first step in Initiation on Globe G of the seventh round, where also He attained Arhaṭship. About a million years ago, then, He chose out from the ship-load which included our 1,200-year group, a few people whom He hoped to shape for His Race, and with whom He therefore kept up a connection. Four hundred thousand years later, He picked out some more. It was rather like looking over a flock of sheep, and choosing out the most suitable. Of these, numbers would be dropped out on the way, and the selection would be thus narrowed down from time to time.

The isolation of a tribe from the white fifth sub-race (the moon-coloured race, as the Stanzas of Dzyān poetically describe it) which lived in the mountains to the north of Ruṭa, was the first decisive step in the building of the Race, and this took place about 100,000 B. C. The fifth sub-race, it may be said in passing, was addicted to mountains generally, and the Kabyles of the Atlas Mountains are its best modern representatives. Their religion was different from that of the Toltecs living in the plains, and the Manu took advantage of this to isolate the sub-race. Then His Brother the Boḍhisaṭṭva, who became later the Lord Gauṭama Buḍḍha, founded a new religion; and people coming into that were segregated off, and bidden to keep apart, inter-marriage with other tribes being forbidden. His disciples went out into other lands and gathered a few together, who, later, joined the main body. They were told that one day they would journey far away into another land, which became to them 'the promised land,' and that they were under a King and Lord, physically unknown to them; they were thus kept in a state of preparation for the coming of the great One who was to lead them forth; He was going to guide His people to a place of safety, where they would escape the coming catastrophe—that of 75,025 B.C.[1] Some of the Hebraic story was probably derived from these facts, although the separation of the people who were known in history as Hebrews came later. These ancestors of theirs were literally a 'chosen people,' set aside for a great purpose.

The immediate cause of the emigration was the impending subdual of the white sub-race by the Dark Ruler, and the wish of the Manu to withdraw His people from that influence. So, in 79,797 B.C., He called them to the coast, that they might be shipped off through the Sahara Sea,

[1] Usually called that of 80,000 B. C.

whence they travelled forwards on foot by the south of Egypt to Arabia. A small fleet of ships, thirty in number, was provided; the largest did not seem to be over 500 tons, and three were cutter-like vessels, carrying only provisions. They were clumsy-looking ships, sailing fairly well on a wind, but tacking very badly. Some had oars as well as sails, and these were certainly not well adapted for a long sea-voyage. However, they had to cross open water only as far as the mouth of the Sahara Sea (which was a crooked sort of bight opening into the Atlantic), and then to sail along its almost land-locked waters. The fleet carried over about two thousand nine hundred persons, deposited them on the shore at the eastern end of the Sahara Sea, and returned to the place of embarkation for another set. The voyage was performed three times, and the little nation, made up to nine thousand men, women and children by the additional few from elsewhere, set forth eastwards on foot.[1] They had with them a number of animals also, looking like a cross between a buffalo and an elephant with something of the pig, reminding one rather of a tapir, a half-and-half sort of beast. These were used for food when other supplies ran short, but were regarded as too valuable for such use ordinarily. The whole process of embarkation, debarcation, settling down to wait for their comrades, and preparing for the journey on foot, occupied some

[1] Five-sixths of the nine thousand were from the fifth sub-race: one-twelfth were Akkadian, and one-twelfth Toltec, each the best of its kind.

years, and the Manu, with some other great Officials, was then sent by the Head of the Hierarchy to lead them to the high plateau of Arabia, where they were to remain for a time.

[The Atlanteans had conquered Egypt and were ruling the country at this period. They had built the pyramids, on which Cheops put his name many thousands of years later: when Egypt was swamped by a flood, some seventy-seven thousand years ago, the people tried to climb these pyramids for safety, as the waters rose, but failed in consequence of the smoothness of their sides. This great Atlantean civilisation perished; then came the flood, and a negroid domination, and another Atlantean Empire, and an Āryan (B. C. 13,500)—all perhaps before that which history recognises as 'Egyptian'. But we must not follow this fascinating by-way.]

Suffice it that a splendid Toltec civilisation was flourishing in Egypt when our emigrants passed along its borders, and the Egyptian Ruler, following the Toltec tradition that other races existed in order that the Toltecs might exploit them, tried to bribe them into remaining in his land. Some succumbed to the temptation and remained in lower Egypt, in defiance of the Manu's command, to become, a little later, slaves to the dominant Toltecs.

The rest reached Arabia by way of the route which is now the Suez Canal, and were settled down by the Manu in groups, in the various valleys of the great Arabian highlands. The country was sparsely inhabited by a negroid race, and the valleys were fertile when irrigated. But the emigrants did not much like their new quarters, and while the majority of the people, who had been prepared by Vaivasvaṭa Manu in Ruṭa, were even fanatically devoted to Him, the younger generation did a good deal of grumbling, for it was pioneer work, not a 'personally conducted Cook's tour'.

We found in one of the valleys a large number of the 1200 and 700 years' groups, including many members of 'the family,' and their devotion certainly ran into violent fanaticism. They proposed to kill all the people who were not wholly devoted to the Manu, and prepared to fight the deserters, who had settled down comfortably in Egypt. This drew down upon them the wrath of the Egyptians and a considerable slaughter followed, our fanatics being completely wiped out. Mars and Corona gallantly resisted the Egyptian onslaught, while a side party, with Herakles—a young unmarried man—among them, mistaking the direction of the enemy, was annihilated by the Egyptians ; Vaivasvaṭa Manu came up with reinforcements and turned the fortunes of the day, driving back the Egyptians ; a side party of them, in turn, was attacked by a larger force, among which Sirius, the father of Herakles, was prominent, furious at finding his son among the dead; knowing the country, they shepherded the Egyptians into a crater-like depression, with steep sides covered with loose rocks; these rocks they joyfully hurled down on their surrounded foes, and the last we saw of Sirius on this occasion was his ride down the steep slope on an avalanche of stones, waving his spear, and shouting a war-song of an uncomplimentary nature, to become part of the gory mass of crushed men and heavy stones which filled the lowest part of the crater.

The few Egyptian soldiers who finally escaped and reached Egypt were incontinently put to death, as having disgraced the army by their defeat.

After this there was peace for a time for the colonists, and they cultivated their valleys, which were rather cold in winter, and blazingly hot in summer. They had brought seeds of various kinds from Atlantis, and some of these were suitable to their new home: they grew some tasteless fruits resembling apples, and, on the slopes of the hot part of the valley, they raised a very large fruit, as large as a man's head, which, in stickiness and general messiness, was like a date. A kind of crater, where the sun was reflected from the rocks, served as a forcing-house, and they produced there a fruit of the size of a cocoa-nut, of which they seemed to be inordinately proud. It was nutritious, and, boiled in water, it yielded sugar by evaporation of the water, while the residuum of the fruit gave a flour, which the people made into a sort of sweet bun. Sirius had two of these buns in his cloth when he rode down the hill-side of death.

In a succeeding incarnation, Herakles appeared as a tall, slim, and rather striking-looking young woman, hanging a somewhat squawky baby-brother —Sappho—up to a tamarind-like tree in a bark cradle.

The selection from the fifth Atlantean sub-race grew and multiplied exceedingly, and became a nation of several millions in about two thousand years; they were quite isolated from the world in general by a belt of sand, which could only be crossed by caravans carrying with them plenty of water, and there was only one way across it with grass and water, about where Mecca now stands. From time to time emigrants left the main body, some settling in the south of Palestine and some in the south of Egypt; and these movements were encouraged by the representatives of the Manu, for the plateau was limited in size and became crowded to an uncomfortable extent. The least desirable types were sent away as emigrants, while He preserved unmixed within His belt of desert the most promising. Suggestions were made from time to time that a caravan of settlers should go off, make a colony, or found a city: among one of these the horse was developed. Occasionally He Himself incarnated, and His descendants formed a class apart of a somewhat improved type. But generally He was not physically present, but directed affairs through His lieutenants, of whom Jupiter and Mars were the most prominent.

The people were pastoral and agricultural, not settling in large cities, and the plateau became thickly populated till, at the end of about three thousand years, it resembled a single huge village; then He sent out a very large number of people to Africa to found a big colony, so as to reduce the numbers in the central settlement. This colony was, later, quite exterminated.

It was only a few years before the catastrophe of 75,025 B. C. that—on receipt of a message from the Head of the Hierarchy—He selected about seven hundred of His own descendants to lead them northwards. He had made these people once more into an unorthodox sect, stricter in their lives than those around them, and they were not looked on favourably by the orthodox among whom they lived; He advised them therefore to follow Him to a land where they might live in peace, escaping from the persecutions of the orthodox, a land which was distant several years' journey. Even His own lieutenants were not apparently admitted to His confidence, but were simply following out His directions: among these were several who are now Masters, and others who have passed onwards, away from our Earth.

The number of His followers being small, they made a single caravan, and the Manu sent a message to the Ruler of the Sumiro-Akkad Empire, praying for peaceful passage through his dominions —including the present Turkey in Asia, Persia and the countries beyond: He reached the borders of that Empire without difficulty, and the Emperor proved friendly: his passport carried Him right into Turkestan, and then He had to treat with a Confederation of Turanian feudatory States, including what is now Tibet. He passed between mountain-ranges, of which the present Tianshan range was one: these marked the boundaries of the Gobi Sea, and stretched up to the Arctic Ocean. He had passed through Mesopotamia and Babylonia, slanting north, and the mountains He had to cross were not of great height; the Turanian Confederation gave permission for His passage, partly because His people were not numerous enough to cause apprehension, and partly because He stated that He was carrying out a mission imposed upon Him by the Most High. After some years of journeying He reached the shores of the Gobi Sea, but, bearing in mind the message He had received, He did not remain in the plain, but turned into the hills to the north, where a great shallow sea stretched northward to the Arctic Ocean and thus to the Pole. The Lemurian Star was much broken up by this time, and its nearest point was about a thousand miles to the north. He posted some of His followers on a promontory looking out to the north-east, but the greater number settled down in a fertile crater-like depression, something like the 'Devil's Punch-bowl' in Surrey, but much larger: this was more inland, though from an adjoining peak they could catch sight of the sea. From this promontory, which stood high, they could see the Gobi Sea, and the land where later they were to settle. This was to be their dwelling until after the great catastrophe, then close at hand. The White Island was to the south-east and was entirely out of sight, though later, when covered with lofty temples, it became visible from this spot. The promontory and adjoining land were formed of shelves of rock, which would be very little harmed by earthquakes, unless the whole land was broken up. Here He was to remain till all danger was passed; and a few years were left in which to settle down. Many of the people died on the journey and after arrival, and He Himself reincarnated to improve the type more quickly.

These people, as said above, were really His own family, being His physical descendants, and, as bodies died, He packed the egos into new and improved ones.

In Atlantis the reincarnated Metal-Man was again ruling, none the wiser, apparently, for his previous experiences. He was in possession of the City of the Golden Gates, and the nobler types of the Atlanteans were much oppressed.

The City was suddenly destroyed by the rushing in of the sea through huge fissures caused by explosions of gas; but, unlike the catastrophe in which the island of Poseidonis sank within twenty-four hours, these convulsions continued over a period of two years. Further explosions occurred, new cracks were made, earthquakes shook the land, for each explosion led to a further disturbance. The Himālayas were heaved up a little higher; the land to the south of India was submerged with its population; Egypt was drowned, and only the pyramids were left standing; the tongue of land which stretched from Egypt to what are now Morocco and Algeria disappeared, and the two countries remained as an island, washed by the Mediterranean and the Sahara Sea. The Gobi Sea became circular, and land was thrown up, now Siberia, separating it from the Arctic Ocean; Central Asia rose, and many torrents, caused by the unprecedented rainfall, cut deep ravines through the soft earth.

While these seismic changes were in progress, the Manu's community was left undisturbed by absolute cleavage or change of surface; but the people were constantly terrified by the recurring earthquakes, and were almost paralysed by the fear that the sun (which had been rendered invisible for a year by masses of cloud, largely composed of fine dust) had gone out for ever. The weather was unspeakable. Terrible rains fell almost incessantly: masses of steam and clouds of dust enveloped the earth and darkened the air. Nothing would grow properly, and they were exposed to severe privations: the community, originally composed of seven hundred people, which had increased to a thousand, was reduced by these hardships to about three hundred. Only the stronger survived: the weaker were killed off.

At the end of five years, they had again become settled: the punch-bowl depression had become a lake; some years of warm weather followed the years of disturbance: much virgin soil had been thrown up, and they were able to cultivate the land. But the Manu was growing old, and an order came to Him to bring His people to the White Island. To hear was to obey.

There, by the Head of the Hierarchy Himself, the great plan of the future was unrolled before Him, stretching over thousands upon tens of thousands of years. His people were to live on the mainland, on the shores of the Gobi Sea, and they were to increase and grow strong. The new Race was to be founded on the White Island itself, and when it had increased, a mighty City was to be built on the opposite shore for its dwelling, and the plan of the City was suggested. There was a mountain range running along the shores of the Gobi Sea, some twenty miles distant, and low hills stretched out from that range to the shore; there were four great valleys, running from within the ranges to the sea, entirely separated from each other by the intervening hills; He was to plant certain selected families in these valleys, and develop therein four separate sub-races, which then were subsequently to be sent to different parts of the world. Also He was to send some of His own people to be born elsewhere, and then bring them back, and thus form new admixtures—for they would have to marry into His family; and when the type was ready, He would have again to incarnate in it and to fix it. For the Root Race also some admixture was needed, as the type was not quite satisfactory.

Thus a main type and several sub-types had to be formed, and the differences were to be started in the comparatively early days, thus obtaining five groups to develop on different lines. It is interesting to notice that after refining His people for generations and forbidding marriage with those outside themselves, He yet found it necessary, later, to introduce a little foreign blood, and then to separate off the posterity of that foreign ancestor.

The Manu proceeded to settle His people (about 70,000 B. C.), bidding them build villages on the mainland, there to increase and multiply for some thousands of years. They had not to begin at the beginning like savages, for they were already a civilised people, and used a good deal of labour-saving machinery. In one of the towns dotted rather widely along the coast-line, we noticed a number of familiar faces. Mars, a grandson of the Manu, was the head of the community, and, with his wife Mercury and his family—among whom were Sirius and Alcyone—lived in a pleasant house, surrounded by a large garden and fine trees.[1] Corona was there, and Orpheus, an elderly and stately gentleman, very dignified and much respected. Jupiter was the ruler of the province—if we may so call the whole settlement of the embryonic Race numbering about seven thousand souls—wielding an authority which was delegated to him by the Manu, the recognised King of the community, residing at Shamballa.

As we were observing this town, there came galloping in a tumultuous band of men, who had evidently been out on a foray; they were riding on rough-looking animals, resembling horses, and were headed by Vajra; they drew up at the house of Mars, who was Vajra's brother, soon after galloping off again, as tumultuously as they came; and we followed them to another town, also on the shores of the Gobi, where we found Virāj as Chief. His son, Herakles, was in the band of raiders, wherein also we observed Ulysses.

More familiar faces were seen here; Cetus and Ulysses were at feud; they had first quarrelled over an animal, which both claimed to have killed, then over some land which both wanted, and finally over a woman whom both desired. Pollux and Herakles were great friends, Pollux having saved the life of Herakles in a foray, at the imminent risk of his own. One of the daughters of Herakles, Psyche, a big bouncing girl, attracted our attention at the age of fourteen; for she was carrying in her arms a small brother, Fides, when she was attacked by a large goat; the goat had big horns, curling at the base and spiked at the

[1] See Appendix III.

top, but the girl was not daunted; she seized the goat by the horns and turned it head over heels, and then, picking it up by the hind-legs, she banged it vigorously on the ground. The child Fides seemed to be rather a family pet, as we noticed Herakles carrying him about on his shoulder.

Much excitement was caused some years later by the Manu, who was then a very old man, sending for Jupiter, Corona, Mars and Vajra; on their return, obeying His order, they selected some children from the settlement, and sent them over to Shamballa; these children were the best in the community and have since risen to the position of Masters. They were Alcyone's sons, Uranus and Neptune, and his daughters Sūrya and Bṛhaspaṭi; Saturn and Vulcan, boys, and Venus, a girl, were also selected. A few women were sent with them to take care of them, and the children were brought up in Shamballa; in due course Saturn married Sūrya, and the Manu was reborn as their eldest son, to restart the Race on a higher level.

For meanwhile things had been moving on the mainland. Soon after the removal of the above-named children, the Turanians swept down on the community like a devastating flood, for this was the event of which the Manu had forewarned His lieutenants and from which the children were saved; the assailants were bravely beaten back several times, but horde succeeded horde. At last the bulk of the fighting men were killed, and the battle became a mere massacre, not a man, woman or child being left alive. Our old friend Scorpio was the Chief of one tribe, once more renewing his perennial conflict with Herakles. A number of promising children were cut off. but, after all, it did not much matter, for they all went out of earth-life together, grandparents, parents and children, and were ready to come back when the Manu founded His family. Mars returned earlier, and was born in Shamballa as a younger brother of the Manu, while Virāj was His sister.

Then, everything began over again, but on a higher level: they invented. or re-invented, many useful things, and in some thousands of years there was a populous and flourishing civilisation. Our old friends were there among the pioneers, Herakles, this time, as the son of Mars. Those of the group of Servers then in birth worked hard under the direction of their leaders, trying to carry out their will. Thick-headed and stupid they often were, and they made many mistakes, but loyal and whole-hearted they always were, and that bound them closely to those they served.

Houses were built of great size, to accommodate several generations (in fact, all the members of a family), and were strongly fortified, with only one entrance, and the windows opening into a large courtyard in the middle, where the women and children could be in safety. After a time, strong walls were built round villages and round towns, as additional defences, for the savage Turanians were constantly hovering on the outskirts of the community, terrifying the inhabitants by their wild yells and sudden onslaughts. The outlying villages were in a continual state of alarm, the dwellers on the sea-coast being left more at peace.

When the Race had again grown to the proportions of a small nation, there was another determined onslaught of the Turanians, and finally another massacre, with only, once more, a few children and their nurses saved and brought up in Shamballa. It is noteworthy that even the bloodthirsty Turanians did not attack the White Island, for they held it in the deepest veneration. Thus the Race-type was ever preserved, even when the bulk of it was twice swept away, and on each occasion the Manu and His lieutenants incarnated in it as soon as possible and purified it still further, ever approaching the type at which He aimed.

CHAPTER XV

THE BUILDING OF THE GREAT CITY

AFTER the second destruction, the Manu thought that a little more of the Toltec infusion was needed in His Race, which had, it will be remembered, only one-twelfth of Toltec strain in it; so He sent Mars, who had been killed in the beginning of the last war, to incarnate in the purest of the Toltec families in Poseidonis, and called him to return to His infant community at the age of twenty-five. The fairest and best of the Manu's own daughters, who had escaped the second massacre in her childhood, was given to Mars as wife—his age-long friend and teacher, Jupiter. Of these two Virāj was born—a splendid specimen of all that was best in the two Races whence he sprang. He married Saturn, and Vaivasvaṭa Manu took birth again as their son. From this point the Fifth, or Āryan Root-Race, as a really successful foundation, may be said to begin, for after this it was never again destroyed. This was about B. C. 60,000. The civilisation which rose slowly from that tiny seed was a fine and pure one, and, shut away as it was to a large extent from the rest of the world, it flourished exceedingly.

The descendants of the Manu remained on the Island until they numbered one hundred; it had been decreed by the Manu that when they reached that number they should go over to the mainland, and begin to work at the City which He had planned as the future capital of His Race. The plan was fully worked out, as He wished it to be when finished, all the streets marked in, their width stated, the size of the chief buildings given, and so on. The White Island was the centre on which the great main streets converged, so that if they had crossed the intervening sea they would have ended on the Island. Low cliffs rose from the sea, and from these the land sloped gradually up to the lovely purple hills twenty miles away: it was a splendid site for a city, though open to cold winds from the north; the city spread out fan-like round the edge of the shore, extending over this great gentle slope, and the main streets were so wide that even from their extreme ends towards the hills the White Island could be seen. It was the most prominent object, and seemed to dominate all the City's life, when the whole splendid plan was complete. The City was built a thousand years in advance of the people who were to live in it; it did not grow disjointedly, like London; and the little group of one hundred—the children and grand-children of the Manu—looked almost absurdly inadequate for the immense task which they were to begin, and which their descendants would finish. They put up temporary quarters for themselves in a way which did not interfere with the plan, and had, of course, to cultivate enough of the land to enable them to live. All the time which they were not compelled to give to their own support, they devoted to preparation for building; they measured the land and marked out the wide streets according to the plan, cutting down many trees, the wood of which they used for their own quarters. Presently some were sent to the hills to look for suitable stone and metals, and they sank mines and dug out quarries. Out of these they hewed white, grey, red and green stone, stone which looked like marble, but seemed to be harder than the marble we know; it may be that they had some secret for hardening it, since they came from Atlantis, where architecture was carried to great perfection. Later on, they went further afield, and found some porphyry of a splendid purple colour, which they used with great effect.

It was a strange sight to see these builders of a future city at work. Descendants of the Manu, similar in education and training, they felt and acted like one family, even when they had increased to thousands. Doubtless the presence of the Manu and of His lieutenants kept this feeling alive, and made the growing community a real brotherhood, each member knowing the rest. They worked because they were glad to work, and felt that they were carrying out the wishes of Him who was at once their Father and their King. They worked in the fields, they ground corn—they seemed to have wheat, rye and oats—they cut and shaped the huge stones brought from the hills; all was done joyfully, as a religious duty and as bringing merit, and any form of work was willingly taken up.

The style of architecture was cyclopean, enormous stones being used, larger even than those at Karnac. They used machinery, and slung great stones on rollers; sometimes, in difficulties, the Manu gave instructions which rendered the work easier, possibly by some methods of magnetisation. They were allowed to use their utmost strength and ingenuity in managing these immense stones, some of them 160 feet long, and they succeeded in dragging them along the roads. But for lifting them into their destined places, the Manu and His lieutenants lightened them by occult means. Some of these lieutenants, above the rank of Masters, were Lords of the Moon, who had become Chohans of Rays. They moved about among the people superintending their work, and were spoken of under the general name of Maharṣhis. Some names sounded very guttural, as Rhuḍhra; another name heard was Vāsukhya.[1] The buildings were on the Egyptian scale, but were much lighter in appearance; and this was specially noticeable in the buildings on the White Island, where the domes were not great spheres, but were bulging at the base, and went up to a point, like a tightly closed lotus-bud, in which the folded-in leaves had been given a kind of twist. It was as though two helices, right-handed and left-handed, had been superposed, so

[1] We were much surprised at finding what was evidently a form of Samskṛṭ existing such an enormous time ago in a recognisable form. It appeared that the language brought from Venus by the Lords of the Flame was this mother-Samskṛṭ—truly a 'divine language'—and, while the people were in touch with Them, it persisted without much change.

that the lines should cross each other, and that this was worked on to the lotus-bud, bulging at the base. There was immense solidity in the lower parts of the huge buildings; then a crown-work of minarets and arches, arches with a peculiar and very graceful curve, and then, on the top, the fairy-like lotus-bud of a dome.

The whole building was a matter of many hundreds of years, but the White Island, when complete, was a marvel. The Island itself sloped up to a central point, and the builders took advantage of this. They built stupendous Temples on it, all of white marble with inlaid work of gold, and these covered the whole Island, making it a single sacred City. These rose towards the huge Temple in the centre, which was crowned with the minarets and arches mentioned above, with the lotus-bud dome in the middle. The dome was over the great Hall, wherein the Four Kumāras appeared on special occasions, great religious festivals, and ceremonies of national importance.[1]

From a distance—say at the end of one of the City streets, ten miles away—the effect of the white and golden City, like a white dome set in the midst of the blue Gobi Sea,[2] all the buildings seeming to spring upwards into the clear air towards the centre, and to be crowned with the

[1] Readers of 'Rents in the Veil of Time,' *The Theosophist*, July, 1910, will remember in Alcyone's Life, X., the description of the gathering of the Chiefs of the emigration in this Hall, and the appearing of the four Kumāras.

[2] The Gobi Sea, at that time, was a little smaller than the present Black Sea in Europe.

fairy dome, almost floating in the atmosphere, was extraordinarily beautiful and impressive. Rising above it in the air, as in a balloon, and looking down, we could see the White City like a circle, divided by a cross, for the streets were arranged as four radii, meeting at the central Temple. Looked at from the north-west, from the promontory of the earlier settlement, an extraordinary effect was produced. which could hardly have been accidental. The whole looked like the great Eye of Masonic symbolism, being foreshortened so that the curves became cylindrical, and the darker lines of the city on the mainland made the iris.

Both inside and outside, the Temples on the White Island were adorned with many carvings. A large number of these contained Masonic symbols, for Masonry inherits its symbols from the Mysteries, and all Āryan Mysteries were derived from this ancient centre of Initiation. In one room attached to the central Temple, apparently used for teaching, there was a series of carvings, beginning with the physical atom and going on to the chemical atoms, arranged in order, and with explanatory lines marking the various combinations. Verily, there is nothing new under the sun.[1]

In another room were many models, in one of which Crookes' lemniscates were arranged across each other, so as to form an atom with a fourfold rose. Many things were modelled in alto-relievo,

[1] If the present writers had known at the time of the existence of these carvings, they might have saved themselves much trouble in their researches into occult Chemistry.

such as the prāṇic atom, the oxygen snake, the nitrogen balloon.

Alas! for the great catastrophe which shook these mighty buildings into ruins. But for that, they might have lasted for thousands upon thousands of years.

The City of the mainland was built of the various-coloured stone hewn out of the mountain quarries, some of the buildings being very effective with the grey and red intermixed. Pink and green was another favourite combination, and here and there the purple porphyry was introduced with striking success. Looking forward through many centuries, we saw the building still going on, though with many more workers, until the great City grew into its full magnificence, a capital, building through a thousand years, for a people that was to become imperial. The workers moved outwards, as their numbers expanded, bringing more land, which was very fertile, under cultivation for their support, now working in the fields, now at their huge Temples. Century after century this expansion continued along the shores of the Gobi Sea and up the great slope towards the hills, ever following the Manu's original plan.

There were gold mines in the hills, and mines for jewels and precious stones of all sorts. Gold was much used on the buildings, especially on those made of white marble, and gave an effect of extraordinary and chaste richness. Jewels were also largely introduced into decorations, inset as brilliant points in schemes of colour; slabs of chalcedony entered into decorative designs, and a precious stone, resembling Mexican onyx, was worked into patterns. One favourite and most effective device in the ornamenting of large public buildings was a combination of dark green jade and the purple porphyry.

Carving was largely employed, both outside and inside buildings, but no paintings were observed, nor drawings on a flat surface, and no perspective. There were long friezes, representing processions, in alto-relievo, all the figures being of the same size, no idea of distance being introduced by reducing the size of the figures. There were no trees or clouds as background, and no impression of space was given. These friezes recalled the Elgin marbles, and were exceedingly well done and very natural. Figures in these friezes were often painted, as were also separate statues, of which there were many, both in the public streets and the private houses.

The City was connected with the White Island by a massive and splendid bridge—a structure so remarkable that it gave its name to the City, called, because of it, the City of the Bridge.[1] It was a cantilever Bridge, the form very graceful, outlined with hewn work of massive scrolls, and decorated with great groups of statuary, where its ends rested on the cliff of the mainland and on the Island itself. The stones of the causeway were 160 feet in length and wide in proportion—a noble structure, worthy even of the Island to which it was the sole approach.

The City was at its zenith in B. C. 45,000, when it was the capital of an immense Empire, which included the whole of East and Central Asia, from Tibet to the coast and from Manchuria to Siam, besides claiming suzerainty over all the islands

[1] Called also Manova, the City of Manu.

from Japan to Australia. Traces of its domination are still to be seen in some of these countries; the ineffaceable stamp of the Āryan blood is set upon races so primitive as the Hairy Ainus of Japan and the Australian so-called aborigines.

In the zenith of its glory it had the magnificent architecture we have described, of the cyclopean style as to size, but finished with great delicacy. and polished to a remarkable degree. We have seen that its builders erected the marvellous Temples whose colossal ruins are the wonder of all who have seen them at Shamballa to-day:[1] it was they who dowered the world with that unequalled Bridge which once linked the Sacred Island with the shore—which may still be seen standing, mighty as ever, though now only the shifting desert sand flows beneath it. Its sculpture too was noble, as we have seen, its colouring brilliant, its mechanical genius considerable. In its prime it compared not ignobly with Atlantis, and though its luxury was never so great, its morals were distinctly purer.

Such was the mighty City planned by Vaivasvaṭa Manu and built by His children. Many and great were the cities of Asia, but the City of the Bridge outshone them all. And over it ever brooded the mighty Presences who had, and still have, Their earthly dwelling-place on the sacred White Island, giving to this one, out of all the cities of earth, the ever-abiding benediction of Their immediate proximity.

[1] Shamballa is still the Imperishable Sacred Land, where dwell the four Kumāras, and where gather, every seven years, Initiates of all nations.

CHAPTER XVI

EARLY ĀRYAN CIVILISATION AND EMPIRE

THE children of Manu were in no sense a primitive people, beginning, as they did, with many hundreds of thousands of years of civilisation behind them in Atlantis, and thousands of years under their own Manu, in Arabia and northern Asia. The population could all read and write, including all those who did what we should call the lowest work; for all work was regarded as honourable, being done for the Manu, as His work, no matter what it was. We noticed a man who was cleaning the streets, and as a very dignified and gorgeously-clothed priest, evidently in high office, came along, he addressed the sweeper courteously as a brother, as an equal, as one of the brotherhood of the great family of the Manu's children. The feeling cultivated was that of the brotherhood of the Race, a wonderful fundamental equality—like that which may sometimes be seen among Freemasons—and a mutual courtesy; there was at the same time a full recognition of personal merit, a looking up to the greater people and much gratitude to them for their help, and a complete absence of rude self-assertion. There was a kindly feeling of taking everyone at his best, of taking it for granted that the other man meant well: and so quarrels were avoided. This Āryan civilisation was in this extraordinarily different from the more elaborate and luxurious Atlantean one, where each sought his own comfort, and recognition for himself, and where people distrusted each other and were mutually suspicious. In this the people trusted one another —a man's word was sufficient; it would have been un-Āryan to break it.

Another curious thing was the number of people everyone seemed to know. As now in a small village, so there in a large town, for centuries all the people seemed to know each other, more or less. As the population increased, and this became impossible, it was the duty of the officials to know the people of their districts, and the knowledge of a large number of people was one of the qualifications for office.

The feeling of brotherhood, however, was of a brotherhood of Race; it did not extend outside the Āryan people themselves, as, for instance, to the Turanians. They were of a different stock, and a different culture; they were crafty and cunning, and not to be depended on. Towards them they showed a marked and very dignified reserve; they were not hostile to foreigners, nor did they despise them, but they treated them with reserve, as not of the family. People of other nations were not allowed into the inner parts of their houses, but only into the outer courts. There were special houses and courtyards set apart for the lodging of strangers, of whom, however, there were few; caravans of merchants came occasionally, and embassies from other nations, and these were received courteously and hospitably, but always with that quiet reserve which indicated a barrier not to be crossed.

In governing foreign nations, as they came to do later, they were occasionally hard: this was observed in a Governor, set over Turanians; he was not cruel nor oppressive, but was stern and somewhat hard. This stern attitude seemed to be rather characteristic of their foreign rule, and it was compatible with the warmest feeling of brotherhood to their own Race.

It would seem that here, as everywhere else, a physical-world-brotherhood demanded a certain common ground of education and culture, of morality and honour. A man was 'an Āryan,' a 'noble man,' and that fact implied a code of honour and of customs which could not be disregarded. He must be, as we should now say, 'a gentleman,' living up to a certain standard of social obligation. He might do any kind of work, he might rise to any grade of learning, but there was a certain minimum of good behaviour and good manners below which he must not fall. Out of this grew the feeling of reserve towards all 'outside the pale,' as to whose manners and customs, morals and qualities, nothing was known. The children of Manu were a nation of aristocrats, in the true sense of the word, proud of their high descent, and fully recognising the demands it made upon them. For them, *Noblesse oblige* was no empty phrase.

The civilisation was a very bright and happy one, with much music, dancing and gaiety, and to this their religion conduced, for it was eminently one of praise and thanksgiving. The people were constantly singing hymns of praise, and they recognised Ḍevas behind all natural forces. The Dawn-Maidens were joyously hymned with each morning, and the Spirit in the Sun was the chief object of worship. The four Kumāras were regarded as Gods, and Their Presence was evidently felt by a people living so near to Nature as to be sensitive and psychic. Behind the throne of the Chief of the Kumāras in the large Hall of the central Temple was an immense golden Sun, a half sphere, projecting from the wall, and, on days of ceremony, this glowed out with dazzling light. The planet Venus was also imaged as an object of worship, perhaps in consequence of the tradition that it was from Venus that the Lords of the Flame had descended. The Sky itself was worshipped, and at one time there was worship given to the Atom, as the origin of all things, and a manifestation of the Deity in miniature.

An annual ceremony may serve as an example of one of their greater religious festivals.

At an early hour the people—men, women and children—were seen marching in procession along the converging streets into the great crescent which faced the mighty Bridge. Rich silken cloths fluttered from windows and flag-staffs, and the roads were strewn with blossoms; great braziers sent up clouds of incense, and the people were clad in silks of many colours, often heavily jewelled, and wore splendid coral ornaments, and wreaths and garlands of flowers—a fairyland of colour—and they marched with clashing of metal plates and blasts of horns.

Across the Bridge they passed in orderly succession, but all sounds sank to silence as they set foot upon the Bridge; and in the silence they passed on between the mighty Temples to the central Fane, and onwards into the Hall itself. The great throne hewn out of living rock, gold-encrusted, jewelled richly, stood on its rocky platform, over which great symbols, wrought in gold, were scattered, and before it stood an altar, now piled high with fragrant woods. Above, the huge golden Sun gleamed faintly, and the planet Venus hung in air, high in the vault above.

When the Hall was filled to its utmost extent, save in a space in front and at the sides of the great throne, a stately group entered from the back, and filled this space, and all bowed low in homage; there stood the three Manus, arrayed in Their robes of office, and the Mahāguru, the Boḍhisaṭṭva of the time, Vyāsa, standing beside Vaivasvaṭa. And there was Sūrya, close behind His mighty Brother and Predecessor, and nearest to the throne the three Kumāras; unseen by the crowd probably, but surely dimly felt, hung in the air, in a great semi-circle, gorgeous purple and silver Ḍevas, watchful also, attendant. Then over the whole vast assemblage fell an utter silence, as though men could hardly bear to breathe; and softly, sweetly, scarce seeming to break the silence, stole out an exquisite strain of music, supporting a chant, intoned by those Mightiest and Holiest who stood around the throne, an invocation to the

Lord, the Ruler, to come among His own. The solemn hushed accents died into silence, and then rang out a single silvery note, as though in answer; the great golden Sun blazed out in dazzling splendour, and below it, just over the throne, flashed out a brilliant Star, its beams like lightning shooting forth above the heads of the waiting throng; and HE was there, the supreme Lord of the Hierarchy, seated on the throne, more radiant than Sun and Star, which indeed seemed to draw their lustre from Him; and all fell on their faces, hiding their eyes from the blinding glory of His Presence.

Then, in His gentleness, He softened that glory, so that all might lift their eyes, and see Him, Sanaț Kumāra, the 'Eternal Virgin,'[1] in all the beauty of His unchanging Youth, who was yet the Ancient of Days. And a deep breath of awe and wonder came from the adoring crowd, and a luminous smile, rendering the exquisite strong beauty of the Face yet more entrancing, answered their simple reverent gaze of love and worship.

Then He stretched forth His Hands towards the altar in front of Him, and fire blazed forth upon it, the flames rising high in air. And then He was gone—the throne was empty, the Star had vanished, the golden Sun glowed but faintly, and only the Fire which He had given leapt unchanged upon the Altar. From this a glowing

[1] The name, translated from the Samskṛt, means 'Eternal Virgin,' the termination showing that 'Virgin' is masculine.

fragment of wood was given to the priests for the altars of the various Temples, and to each head of a household present there,[1] and he received it in a vessel with a lid which closed above it, wherein it remained, live fire, unquenchable, till it had been carried to the altar of the home.

The processions re-formed and left the Holy Place in silence, again passing to the Bridge and by it reaching the City. Then came an outburst of joyous singing, and hand-in-hand the people passed along, and congratulations were exchanged, and the elders blessed the youngers, and all were very glad. The sacred fire was placed on the family altar, to set alight the flame which was to be kept alive through the year, and brands lighted at it were taken to the houses of those who had not been present, for until the recurrence of the festival when another year had run its course, such fire could not be had to hallow the family shrine. After this, there was music, and feasting, and dancing, until the happy City sank to sleep.

Such was the Festival of the Sacred Fire, held on every Midsummer Day in the City of the Bridge.

Some of the people devoted themselves almost wholly to study, and reached great proficiency in occult science, in order to devote themselves to certain branches of the public service. They became clairvoyant, and gained control of various natural forces, learning to make thought-forms, and to leave their physical bodies at will. Mindful of

[1] In later time, when the population of the City had grown very large, officials received it, to distribute to the houses in their districts.

the melancholy results in Atlantis of occult power divorced from unselfishness and morality, the instructors in these studies chose their pupils with extreme care, and one of the lieutenants of the Manu maintained a general supervision over such classes. Some of the students, when proficient, had it as their special duty to the State to keep the different parts of the Empire in touch with each other; there were no newspapers, but they conducted what may be called a news department. News was not published as a rule, but anyone who wanted news about anyone else in any part of the Empire could go to this central office and obtain it. Thus, there were Commissioners for the various countries, each of whom gave information about the country in his charge, obtaining it by occult means. Expeditions sent out on errands of peace or war were thus followed and news was given of them, as in modern days by wireless or other telegraphy.

On one occasion, when Corona was ruling a distant country, the Manu was not able to impress him with His directions; so He bade one of these trained students to leave his physical body, go astrally to Corona, and materialise himself on arrival; by this device, the message was delivered to Corona in his waking consciousness. In this way the Manu remained as the real Ruler, no matter how far the Empire extended.

Writing was done on various substances; one man was observed writing with a sharp instrument on a waxy-looking surface in an oblong case, as though he were etching; then he went over it again with a hollow pen, out of which flowed a coloured liquid which hardened as it dried, leaving the script embedded in the wax. Occasionally a man would strike out a method of his own.

Machinery was not carried to the point reached in Atlantis: it was simpler, and more of the work was done by hand. The Manu evidently did not desire the extreme luxury of Atlantis to be reproduced among His people.

From the small beginning of 60,000 B. C., there gradually grew up a thickly populated kingdom, which surrounded the Gobi Sea, and obtained dominion by degrees over many neighbouring nations, including the Turanians who had so mercilessly massacred its forefathers. This was the root-stock of all the Āryan nations, and from it went out—from 40,000 B. C., onwards—the great migrations which formed the Āryan sub-races. It remained in its cradle-land until it had sent out four of these migrations westwards, and had also sent many huge bands of conquering emigrants into India, who subdued the land and possessed it; its last remnants only left their home and joined their forerunners in India shortly before the sinking of Poseidonis, 9,564 B. C.; [1] they were sent away, in fact, in order that they might escape the ruin wrought by that tremendous cataclysm.

[1] This root-stock is usually called 'the first sub-race' in Theosophical literature, but it must not be forgotten that this is the original Root Race from which all the branches, or sub-races, went out. The *first migration* is called the *second sub-race*, and so on. The emigrants to India all came from this Asian stock, and are the 'first sub-race'.

From 60,000 B. C. to 40,000 B. C. the parent-stock grew and flourished exceedingly, reaching the zenith of its first glory at about 45,000 B. C. It conquered China and Japan, peopled chiefly by Mongols—the seventh Atlantean sub-race—going northward and eastward till stopped by the cold: it also added to its Empire Formosa and Siam, which were populated by Turanians and Tlavatli—fourth and second Atlantean sub-races. Then the Āryans colonised Sumatra and Java and the adjoining islands—not quite so much broken up as now: for the most part they were welcomed in these regions by the people, who looked on the fair-faced strangers as Gods, and were more inclined to worship than to fight them. An interesting remnant of one of their settlements, still left in Celebes, is a hill tribe called Toala. This island, to the east of Borneo, came under their sway, and they stretched down over what is now the Malay Peninsula, and over the Philippines, the Liu-Kiu Islands, the Eastern Archipelago, and Papua, the islands on the way to Australia, and over Australia itself, which was still thickly populated with Lemurians—third Root Race.

We found Corona, about 50,000 B. C., ruling over a large kingdom in these island-studded seas; he had been born in that region, and made for himself a kingdom, recognising the Manu as Overlord, and obeying any directions which he received from Him. Over all the huge Empire with its many kingdoms, the Manu was Suzerain. Whether He was in incarnation or not, the Kings ruled in His name, and He sent directions from time to time as to the carrying on of the work.

By 40,000 B. C., the Empire began to show signs of decline, and the islands and the outer provinces were asserting a barbarian independence. The Manu still occasionally incarnated, but usually directed things from higher planes. The central kingdom, however, remained splendid in civilisation, contented and quiescent, for another twenty-five thousand years and more, while activities were chiefly carried on in directions further afield, in the building up of sub-races, and in their spreading in all directions.

CHAPTER XVII

THE SECOND SUB-RACE, THE ARABIAN

IT will be remembered that when the Manu went to Shamballa—after leading His little flock from Arabia to their temporary northern resting-place, and, after the great catastrophe of B. C. 75,025, bringing them to the White Island—He was shown by the Head of the Hierarchy the plan which was to be followed in the shaping of His Race.[1] Four long valleys—running back through the mountain range which lay twenty miles from the shore of the Gobi Sea, separated from each other by intervening hills—were to be used by Him for the segregation and training of four distinct sub-races. This work was now to begin.

The Manu started by picking out from the great band of Servers—who had been developing in the noble Āryan civilisation—a few families, willing to act as pioneers, and, leaving the glorious City of the Bridge, to go out into the wilderness and found His new colony. A large group of people who, for the most part, are or have been in the Theosophical Society of our own times, were selected by Him for this pioneer work,[2] and of

[1] See Chapter XIV, p. 249.

[2] They are doing, over again, what they have done so often before, breaking open the way for a new type

these a few families were sent out to lead the way. In the third generation Mars and Mercury took birth among the descendants of these, and then the Manu and some of the great people incarnated there to specialise the type, the Manu preparing a special body of the type at which He was aiming, and incarnating in it, when He had brought it to the desired point.

This latter group of highly developed Personages set the type whenever a new sub-race is founded, and the type is then seen at its best; it is the Golden Age to which each nation looks back in later days. Then the younger egos come in and carry it on, unable, of course, to keep at the level set. There is in each case, a group of younger egos sent to prepare the way; then some older ones come, of the rank which now includes Masters; from these the greater people take bodies and set the new type. The juniors then flock in and do the best they can with it, at first led by some of their seniors, and then later left to themselves to learn their lessons by experience.

Among the juniors chosen to form the first pioneer families, we noticed Herakles—a son of Corona and Theodoros—with Sirius as wife, Sirius a tall, rather muscular woman, a notable housewife, and very kind to her rather large family, among whom we observed Alcyone, Mizar, Uranus,

of humanity and of civilisation. They are the pioneers, the sappers and miners, of a great advancing army, for which they are clearing away jungles, making roads, bridging rivers. The work may be thankless, but it is necessary, and to many congenial.

Selene and Neptune.[1] Herakles had brought some Tlavatli nobles as captives from a foray, and the son of one of these, Apis, married his niece Gemini, much to the anger of the proud Āryan family, that looked on this marriage as a *mésalliance*—an unworthy mixing of their pure blood: but doubtless it was quietly arranged by the Manu, in order that a Tlavatli intermixture might be brought in! They had Spica and Fides as twins, a quaint little pair. Hector and Aurora were another married pair of the emigrant families, and their daughter Albireo married Selene: they had Mercury as child. Uranus married Andromeda, and Mars and Venus were born to them, and Vulcan appeared as a son of Alcyone.

It will be noticed here that two who are now Masters, Uranus and Neptune, were born in the second generation: Mars and Venus, both now Masters, were born in the family of these in the third; Mercury, now a Master, was also born in the third, a child of Selene; and Vulcan, also now a Master, in the third, a child of Alcyone. In the fourth generation the Manu appeared, as a son of Mars and Mercury.

At this time some of our friends were living in the City of the Bridge—Castor among them, married to Rhea. They thought the people who went to the valley were behaving very foolishly, for the existing civilisation was a very fine one, and there was no sense in going off to make a new one, and to plant turnips in an unreclaimed valley, instead of living in the culture and order

[1] See Appendix vii, for the complete lists.

of the City. Besides the new religion followed by the valley-dwellers was quite unnecessary, the old one being much better. Another of the friends who accompany Castor through the ages, Lachesis, was a ponderous merchant, with Velleda as a hasty short-tempered son, who was impolite to customers, much to the displeasure of his courteous father. Lachesis had married Amalthea, and she ran away with Calypso, a proceeding which was considered to be most improper. As she and her lover were not received in the City, they went to the valley, but met there with no warmer welcome.

The visit of a Toltec Prince from Poseidonis to the City showed an old friend, Crux, in his person, and among his suite was another old friend, Phocea.

For some centuries the people in the valley increased and multiplied, the careful specialisation going on, until in B. C. 40,000 the Manu thought them sufficiently numerous and sufficiently prepared to be sent out into the world. He sent them out under the leadership of Mars, supported by Corona and Theodoros, to retrace the way by which so many thousands of years ago they had come, to try to Āryanise the descendants of the Arabs whom they had left behind, for these, of all the Atlanteans, were the nearest to the possession of the new characteristics. These Arabs were still where He had settled them—a number of half-civilised tribes occupying the whole of the Arabian peninsula, and with a few settlements on the Somali coast. A strong and friendly power existed at that time in the region now called Persia and Mesopotamia, and the Manu—who had later joined the emigrants and headed His forces—had no difficulty in obtaining permission to march His host through it along a carefully indicated and guarded route. It is noteworthy that this migration differs in character from those of later years. In those which descended into India the entire tribe moved, from the old men and women to the babies: but in this case the old and those with many young children were advised to stay behind, and the migration was confined to men of fighting age, with their wives and a comparatively small number of children. Many also were young unmarried men. The number of fighters was about 150,000, and the women and children may have added another 100,000 to the party.

The Manu had sent messengers two years before to prepare the Arab tribes for His coming, but the news had not been altogether favourably received, and He was by no means sure of a welcome. When He had crossed the belt of desert which then, as now, separated Arabia from the rest of the world, and came in sight of the first of the Arab settlements, a body of armed horsemen appeared in front of Him and incontinently attacked the van of His army. He easily repulsed them, and, capturing some of them, endeavoured to make them understand that His mission was peaceful. The language had changed so much that they had great difficulty in understanding one another at all, but He contrived to reassure His captives and sent them to arrange an interview with their Chief. After some trouble and the interchange of more messages, the Chief came, suspicious and unconciliatory: but a long conversation and full explanations somewhat changed his attitude, and it occurred to him that he might use this unusual sort of invasion for his own purposes. He was at deadly feud with a neighbouring tribe, and while he had no force fit to cope with the Manu's capable-looking army, he felt that if he could enlist these strangers on his side he could make short work of his ancient enemies. So he temporised, and agreed to allow the visitors to establish themselves in a great desolate valley on the borders of his territory.

They thankfully accepted this offer, and very soon changed the whole aspect of that valley. Coming as they did from a highly-civilised nation, they knew all about the science of well-boring, and they presently had the entire valley efficiently irrigated, and a great stream flowing down the middle of it. Within a year the whole of their tract of country was thoroughly cultivated and some good crops had already been obtained; in three years they were fully established as a prosperous and self-supporting community.

The Chieftain who had received them, however, was by no means satisfied; he cast a jealous eye upon the improvements they had made, and felt that, as this was part of his territory, his own people and not strangers ought to reap the advantages of it. Also, when asked to join in predatory expeditions, the Manu had said quite plainly that although He was grateful to His host and ready at any time to defend him from aggression, He would be no party to an unprovoked attack upon peaceable people. This made the Chief very angry—the more so as he did not see his way to enforcing his commands. At last he patched up a peace with his hereditary enemy, and induced him to join him in an endeavour to exterminate the new-comers.

This little scheme, however, came hopelessly to grief: the Manu defeated and killed both the Chiefs, and made Himself Ruler over their combined States. Their subjects, when once the battle was over, philosophically accepted a new Ruler, and soon found that they were much more prosperous and happy under the improved régime, though it involved less fighting and more regular work. Thus the Manu made secure his footing in Arabia, and promptly proceeded to Āryanise his new subjects as rapidly as possible. Other tribes attacked Him now and then, but were so invariably defeated with heavy loss that they presently came to recognise the wisdom of letting Him alone. As years rolled on His kingdom prospered mightily, and grew ever stronger, while constant internecine struggles enfeebled and impoverished the other tribes. The natural result followed; by degrees, by taking opportunities as they offered, He absorbed tribe after tribe, usually without bloodshed and with the full consent of the majority. Before His death, forty years later, the upper half of Arabia owned his sway, and might be regarded as definitely Āryan. He might have acquired sovereignty over the south as well, but for the advent of a religious fanatic, who reminded his people that they were a chosen race; this man—whom, as he will reappear later, and therefore needs a distinguishing name, we will call Alastor—took his stand on the directions of their Manu, given in ancient days, forbidding them to intermarry with aliens. They must therefore on no account intermingle their blood with that of these Gentiles, who came no one knew whence, with their pretended civilisation and their odious tyranny, which denied to man even his inalienable right to kill his fellow-man freely, whenever he pleased. This appealed to the fierce impatience of control which is a prominent feature of the Arab character, and the southern tribes, who had for centuries squabbled viciously among themselves, actually united now to oppose their re-incarnated Leader. And they opposed Him in His own name, making His original order as to purity of race their rallying cry against Him.

It was quaint that Vaivasvaṭa Manu should thus be used against Himself, but Alastor was really only an anachronism, set in a groove from which he could not be moved. When the Manu had needed a separate people He had forbidden intermarriage with outsiders: when He wished to Āryanise the descendants of his old followers, intermarriage became essential. But to Alastor—as to many of his ilk—growth and adaptation were heresy, and he played on the fanaticism of his followers.

While this long struggle was going on, the Manu had the joy, in one of the intervals of comparative peace, of receiving a visit from His mighty Brother, the Mahāguru—the Buḍḍha-to-be—who came to the second sub-race ere it began its long career of conquest—to indoctrinate it with the new religion which He had been teaching in Egypt as a reform of the ancient faith there prevailing.

The great Atlantean Empire in Egypt—which had quarrelled with Vaivasvaṭa Manu when He was leading His people away from the catastrophe of B. C. 75,025 to settle in Arabia—had perished in that cataclysm, when Egypt went under water. When the swamps later became inhabitable, a negroid people possessed the land for awhile, and left behind them incongruous flints and other such barbarous remains to mark their occupation. After these, came the second Atlantean Empire with a great dynasty of Divine Kings, and with many of the heroes whom Greece later regarded as demi-gods, such as Herakles of the twelve labours, whose tradition was handed on to Greece. This Atlantean Empire lasted until about B. C. 13,500, when the Āryans came from southern India and made there an Empire of the Āryan root-stock. This Atlantean Empire was therefore ruling in B. C. 40,000, when the Manu was again in Arabia, and had attained to a very high state of civilisation, stately and splendid; it had immense Temples, such as that of Karnac, with long and very gloomy passages, and a very ornate ritual, with elaborate religious teaching.

The Egyptians were a profoundly religious race, and they lived through the stories belonging to their faith with an intensity of reality of which only a faint reflection is now seen among Roman and Anglican Catholics on such days as Good Friday. They were psychic, and felt the play of super-physical influences, and hence were without scepticism as to the existence of higher beings and higher worlds; their religion was their very life. They built their huge Temples to produce the impression of vastness and greatness, to instil reverence into the minds of the lower-class people. All the colour and splendour of life circled round their religion. The people normally wore white, but the religious processions were gorgeous rivers of splendid colour, glittering with gold and gems. The ceremonies accompanying the celebration of the death of Osiris palpitated with reality; the mourning for the murdered God was real mourning; the people wept and wailed aloud, the whole multitude being carried away with passionate emotion, and calling on Osiris to return.

It was to this people that the Mahāguru came as Tehuṭi or Thoth, called later by the Greeks Hermes. He came to teach the great doctrine of the 'Inner Light' to the priests of the Temples, to the powerful sacerdotal hierarchy of Egypt, headed by its Pharaoh. In the inner court of the chief Temple He taught them of "the Light that lighteth every man that cometh into the world"—a phrase of His that was handed down through the ages, and was echoed in the fourth Gospel in its early Egyptian-coloured words. He taught them that the Light was universal, and that Light, which was God, dwelt in the heart of every man: "I am that Light," He bade them repeat, "that Light am I". "That Light," He said, "is the true man, although men may not recognise it, although they neglect it. Osiris is Light; He came forth from the Light; He dwells in the Light; He is the Light. The

Light is hidden everywhere: it is in every rock and in every stone. When a man becomes one with Osiris the Light, then he becomes one with the whole of which he was part, and then he can see the Light in everyone, however thickly veiled, pressed down, and shut away. All the rest is not; but the Light is. The Light is the life of men. To every man—though there are glorious ceremonies, though there are many duties for the priest to do, and many ways in which he should help men—that Light is nearer than aught else, within his very heart. For every man the Reality is nearer than any ceremony, for he has only to turn inwards, and then will he see the Light. That is the object of every ceremony, and ceremonies should not be done away with, for I come not to destroy but to fulfil. When a man knows, he goes beyond the ceremony, he goes to Osiris, he goes to the Light, the Light Amun-Ra, from which all came forth, to which all shall return."

And again: "Osiris is in the heavens, but Osiris is also in the very heart of men. When Osiris in the heart knows Osiris in the heavens, then man becomes God, and Osiris, once rent into fragments, again becomes one. But see! Osiris the Divine Spirit, Isis, the Eternal Mother, give life to Horus, who is Man, Man born of both, yet one with Osiris. Horus is merged in Osiris, and Isis, who had been Matter, becomes through him the Queen of Life and Wisdom. And Osiris, Isis, and Horus are all born of the Light."

"Two are the births of Horus. He is born of Isis, the God born into humanity, taking flesh of the Mother Eternal, Matter, the Ever-Virgin. He is born again into Osiris, redeeming his Mother from her long search for the fragments of her husband scattered over the earth. He is born into Osiris when Osiris in the heart sees Osiris in the heavens, and knows that the twain are one."

So taught He, and the wise among the priests were glad.

To Pharaoh, the Monarch, He gave the motto: "Look for the Light," for He said that only as a King saw the Light in the heart of each could he rule well. And to the people He gave as motto: "Thou art the Light. Let that Light shine." And He set that motto round the pylon in a great Temple, running up one pillar, and across the bar, and down the other pillar. And this was inscribed over the doors of houses, and little models were made of the pylon on which He had inscribed it, models in precious metals, and also in baked clay, so that the poorest could buy little blue clay models, with brown veins running through them, and glazed. Another favourite motto was: "Follow the Light," and this became later: "Follow the King," and this spread westward and became the motto of the Round Table. And the people learned to say of their dead: "He has gone to the Light."

And the joyous civilisation of Egypt grew yet more joyous, because He had dwelt among them, the embodied Light. The priests whom He had taught handed on His teachings and His secret instructions which they embodied in their Mysteries, and students came from all nations to learn the

'Wisdom of the Egyptians,' and the fame of the Schools of Egypt went abroad to all lands.

At this time He went over to Arabia, to teach the leaders of the sub-race settled there. Deep was the joy in each as the mighty Brothers clasped hands and smiled into each other's eyes, and thought, in Their exile, of Their far-off home, of the City of the Bridge and of white Shamballa. For even the Great Ones must be sometimes weary, when They are living in the midst of the littleness of ignorant men.

Thus to the second sub-race came the Supreme Teacher, and gave to them the doctrine of the Inner Light.

To return to the history of the growth of this people in Arabia. In consequence of the opposition raised against the Manu by Alastor in the south, the peninsula of Arabia was divided into two parts, and the Manu's successors, for many generations, were satisfied to maintain their kingdom without seeking to increase its borders. After some centuries, a more ambitious Ruler succeeded to the throne, and, taking advantage of local dissensions in the south, marched his armies clear down to the ocean, and proclaimed himself Emperor of Arabia. He allowed his new subjects to retain their own religious ideas, and as the new Government was in many ways an improvement over the old, there was no lasting opposition to the conqueror.

A certain fanatical section of the southerners, however, felt it their duty to protest against what they considered the triumph of evil; and under a prophet of rude and fiery eloquence, they abandoned their conquered fatherland and settled as a community on the opposite Somali coast.

There, under the rule of the prophet and his successors, they lived for some centuries, greatly increasing in numbers, until an event occurred which caused a serious rupture. It was discovered that the ruling prophet of the period, while proclaiming fanatical purity of race, had himself formed an attachment to a young Negress from the interior. When this came to light there was a great uproar, but the prophet was equal to the occasion, and promulgated as a new revelation the idea that the stern prohibition against intermarriage was intended only to prevent them from mingling with the new-comers from the north, and did not at all apply to the Negroes, who indeed were to be regarded as slaves, as goods and chattels rather than as wives. This bold pronouncement divided the community; the majority accepted it, at first hesitatingly and then with enthusiasm, and black 'slaves' were purchased with avidity. But a fairly large minority rebelled against the revelation, and denounced it as merely a clumsy artifice to shield a licentious priest (as indeed it was); and when they saw themselves outvoted they drew apart in horror, and declared that they could no longer dwell amongst heretics who had abandoned all principle. An ambitious preacher, who had always yearned to be a leader, put himself at their head, and they made themselves into a huge caravan and departed in virtuous indignation. They wandered round the shore of the Gulf of Aden and up the coast of the Red Sea, eventually finding their way into Egyptian territory. Their curious story happened to take the fancy of the Pharaoh of the period, and he offered them an outlying district of his kingdom if they chose to settle there. They accepted, and lived there peacefully enough for centuries, flourishing under the beneficent Egyptian Government, but never in any way intermingling with its people.

Eventually some Pharaoh made a demand upon them for additional taxation and forced work, which they considered an infringement of their privileges; so once more they undertook a wholesale migration, and this time settled in Palestine, where we know them as the Jews, still maintaining as strongly as ever the theory that they are a chosen people.

But the majority, left behind in Somaliland, had their adventures also. Now that, owing to the slave-traffic, they became better known to the tribes of the interior, whom they had always previously kept rigidly outside their bounds, the savages realised the wealth to be obtained from robbing the semi-civilised, and the tribes began a series of descents upon the colony, which so harassed its members that, after fighting them for many years, losing thousands of lives, and finding their territory more and more circumscribed every decade, they too decided to abandon their homes, and migrate once more across the Gulf to the land of their forefathers. They were received in a friendly manner, and were soon absorbed into the general mass of the population. They had called themselves 'the true Arabs,' though they deserved that title less than any; and even to-day there is a tradition that the true

Arabs landed at Aden, and slowly spread northwards: even to-day may be seen among the Hamyaritic Arabs of the southern part of the country the indelible traces of that admixture of negroid blood so many thousands of years ago; even to-day we may hear a legend that the Mostareb or adscititious Arabs of the northern half went away somehow for a long time into Asia, far away beyond Persia, and then returned, bearing with them many marks of their stay in foreign lands.

The second sub-race grew and increased, flourishing exceedingly for many thousands of years, and extending its dominion over nearly the whole of Africa, except that part which was in the hands of Egypt. Once, very much later, they invaded Egypt, and for a short time ruled as the Hyksos Kings, but their palmy days were when they ruled the great Algerian island, pushed their way down the east coast to the very Cape of Good Hope itself, and founded a kingdom which included all Matabeleland and the Transvaal and the Lorenzo Marques district.

Our band of pioneers, after several births in Arabia, took part in the building of this South African Empire, and we found Mars there as Monarch, with His faithful Herakles as ruler of a province under him. Sirius was also born in Mashonaland, where he married Alcyone, and among their negro servants we find the faithful hand-maiden of many lives, Boreas. The scenery in Matabeleland was beautiful, and there were valleys full of fine trees, and studded with herds of antelopes. Great cities were made of the favourite massive type, and huge Temples, and the civilisation gradually built up was by no means an unworthy one. But the gulf between the two peoples, the native Africans and the Arab conquerors, was too wide to be spanned, and the Africans remained labourers and domestic servants, kept entirely in subjection.

The Arabs made settlements also on the West Coast of Africa, but there they came into collision with men from Poseidonis, and were in the end entirely driven back. Madagascar was invaded, the southern Empire trying to occupy it, but it succeeded only in maintaining for a time settlements on different parts of the coast.

When the great Sumero-Akkad Empire of Persia, Mesopotamia and Turkestan finally broke up into small States and disorder, an Arab monarch conceived the bold idea of reuniting it under his own leadership. He led his armies against it, and, after twenty years of strenuous fighting, made himself master of the plains of Mesopotamia and of almost the whole of Persia, up to the great salt lake of Khorasan, where the desert now is. But he could not conquer Kurdistan, nor could he subdue the mountain tribes who harassed his armies on their way. Then he died, and his son wisely set himself to consolidate rather than to extend his Empire. It held together well for some centuries, and might have endured much longer, but for the fact that dynastic troubles broke out in Arabia itself, and the governor of Persia, a cousin of the Arab King, seized the opportunity to proclaim himself independent. The Arab dynasty which he thus founded lasted two hundred years, but amidst incessant warfare: then again came a period of upheaval and of small tribes, and frequent raids from the savage Central Asian nomads, who play so prominent a part in the history of that region. One Arab King was tempted by reports which reached him of the fabulous wealth of India to send a fleet across to attack it; but that was a failure, for his fleet was promptly destroyed and his men killed or taken prisoners.

After the final collapse of the Arabian Empire of Persia and Chaldæa, there were centuries of anarchy and bloodshed, and the countries were becoming almost depopulated; so the Manu at last determined to come to their rescue, and sent forth to them His third sub-race, which established the great Persian Empire of the Iranians.

CHAPTER XVIII

THE THIRD SUB-RACE, THE IRANIAN

AGAIN we return to the City of the Bridge, still great, though decreasing in splendour, for we have come to the year B. C. 30,000. An interval of ten thousand years elapsed after the despatch of the second sub-race before the Manu sent forth the third. The men for this work had been carefully prepared through many centuries, like the others; He had kept them apart in one of His mountain-valleys, and developed them until they showed as quite a distinct type. In His original selection in Atlantis, He had included a small proportion of the best of the sixth Atlantean sub-race, and He now utilised the families which had preserved most of that Akkadian blood, sending into incarnation in them His group of pioneers. One or two of them were sent further afield to bring back a strain of Akkadian blood from its home in more western countries. Thus we observed Herakles, a strong good-looking young man, arriving at the City of the Bridge in a caravan from Mesopotamia, his birthplace; he was dolichocephalous, an Akkadian of pure blood. He had joined the caravan from a mere spirit of adventure, the desire of high-spirited youth to see the world, and certainly had not the faintest idea that he had been sent to Mesopotamia to take birth, and was being drawn back to Central Asia to rejoin his old friends in their accustomed pioneer work. He was immensely attracted by the beauty and splendour of the ancient and ordered civilisation into which he came, and promptly anchored himself therein by falling in love with Orion, a daughter of Sirius.

This proceeding was frowned upon by Sirius and his wife Mizar, for Sirius was a younger son of Vaivasvaṭa Manu and Mercury, and he disapproved of the introduction of a young Akkadian into his family circle. But a hint from his Father was enough to ensure his compliance, for he was, as ever, promptly obedient to authority, and the Manu was at once his Father and his King. In order to comply with the law which the Manu Himself had established, it was necessary that Herakles should be adopted into an Āryan family, so he was accepted into that of Osiris, an older brother of Sirius.

The Manu was very old, and as Sirius was not wanted for the succession, he was packed off to the valley selected for the building up of the third sub-race, with his family, including his son-in-law, Herakles, and his children.[1] Pallas—the Plato of later history—was there as a priest, and Helios as a priestess, a tall commanding figure, with dignified gestures.

The people of this valley, as they multiplied, were more pastoral than agricultural, keeping large herds of sheep and cattle and numbers of horses.

[1] See Appendix viii, for complete list.

The Manu who, on this occasion, had largely modified His appearance, came into the sub-race in the fifth generation, and He allowed the people to multiply for some two thousand years until there was available an army of three hundred thousand fighting men, fit to undergo hardship and strenuous marching. He then sent into incarnation Mars, Corona, Theodoros, Vulcan and Vajra, fit captains for His host, and He led it forth Himself. This time it was no ordinary migration; it was simply an army on the march. The women and children were left behind in the valley, where Neptune, the wife of Mars, and Osiris, the wife of Corona, strong and noble matrons, took into their hands the direction of affairs, and ruled the community well.[1]

A fine body-guard of young unmarried men acted as staff to the leaders, ready to be sent off with messages in any direction; they were very proud of themselves and very gay, enthusiastic over the idea that they were going out for a real good fight under the Manu Himself.

But it was no holiday march, for the route lay through a difficult country; some of the passes across the end of the Tian-shan range, where it curves round into the Kashgar district, were nine thousand feet in height; for part of the way they followed the course of a river which passed through ravines and valleys. The Manu poured His great army of three hundred thousand splendid fighting men into Kashgar, defeating easily such of the nomad hordes as ventured to attack Him as He crossed their deserts. These tribes buzzed round the fringe of the army, and there were many

[1] See Appendix ix.

skirmishes, but no battles of any account. The weapons used were long and short lances and spears, short strong swords, slings and bows. The horsemen used lances and swords, and had round shields slung across their backs; the footmen carried spears, and there were bodies of archers and slingers, the former marching in the centre, and the archers and slingers on the outside.

Sometimes, as they neared a village, the villagers—who dreaded and hated the warlike hill tribes—would meet and welcome them, bringing cattle and food of all sorts. Long harassed by forays, often attacked, robbed and massacred, the people of the plains were inclined to welcome a power which would restore and maintain order.

Persia was overrun without much difficulty in the course of two years, and then Mesopotamia was subdued. The Manu established military posts at frequent intervals, dividing the country among His chiefs. Forts were built, first of earth and later of stones, until a network was made over Persia to prevent raids from the mountains. No attempt was made to conquer the warlike tribes, but they were practically confined within their fastnesses, and were no longer permitted to plunder the peaceable inhabitants of the plains.

The body-guard, now bearded and seasoned warriors, accompanied their Chiefs everywhere, and the land was conquered right down to the desert of the south, and up to the Kurdish mountains on the north. For some years there was occasional fighting, and it was not until the country was quite peaceful and settled that the Manu called to it the vast caravan of the wives and children of the soldiers, left behind in the valley of the third sub-race.

The arrival of the caravan was a matter of great rejoicing, and marriages became the order of the day. Herakles and Alcyone fell in love with the same young woman, Fides, a handsome girl with a decided nose: she preferred Alcyone, and the disconsolate Herakles decided to commit suicide, life being no longer worth living; his father, Mars, however, came down upon him, bidding him not to be a fool, and sent him off on an expedition against an insurgent chief, Trapezium; under these conditions Herakles recovered, defeated his adversary, came back quite contented, and married Psyche, a niece of Mars, who had been adopted by him after her father was slain in battle.

For the next fifty years the Manu kept this new Empire under His direct rule, visiting it several times, and appointing members of His family as its Governors; but just before His death He resigned His own throne in Central Asia to His grandson Mars, appointed Mars' next brother, Corona, as the independent King of Persia, with Theodoros under him as Governor of Mesopotamia. From this time the third sub-race quickly increased in power. In a few centuries it dominated the whole of western Asia from the Mediterranean to the Pamirs, and from the Persian Gulf to the Sea of Aral. With certain changes its Empire lasted until about B. C. 2,200.

In this long period of twenty-eight thousand years, one event stands out as of supreme importance—the coming of the Mahāguru as the first Zaraṭhustra, the founding of the Religion of the Fire, in B. C. 29,700.

The country had become fairly settled under the reigns of the Kings who had succeeded Corona, of whom Mars, the Ruler of the time—of course in a new body—was the tenth. Military rule had passed away, though occasional raids reminded the inhabitants of their turbulent neighbours on the further side of the ring of forts, now well-built and strong. It was in the main an agricultural country, though large numbers of herds and flocks were kept, and it was these which specially tempted descents from the hills.

The second son of Mars was Mercury, and his body was chosen as the vehicle for the Supreme Teacher; Sūrya was the Chief Priest, the Hierophant, of the time, at the head of the State religion, a mixture of Nature and Star Worship, and he wielded an immense authority, chiefly because of his office, but also partly because he was of the blood royal. The fact that Mercury had been chosen to surrender his body for the use of the Mahāguru had been communicated to his father as well as to the Chief Priest, and from his childhood he had been carefully trained in view of his glorious destiny, Sūrya taking charge of his education, and the father co-operating in every way in his power.

The day arrived when the first public appearance of the Mahāguru was to be made; He had come from Shamballa in His subtle body, and had taken possession of the body of Mercury, and a great procession started from the Royal Palace to the chief Temple of the city. In it walked, on the right, under a golden canopy, the stately figure of the King; the jewelled canopy of the High Priest glittered on the left: and between them was carried, shoulder-high so that all might see, a golden chair, in which sat the well-known figure of the King's second son. But what was there that caused a murmur of surprise, of wonder, as he passed along? Was that really the Prince, whom they had known from childhood? Why was he carried high as the centre of the procession, while King and Hierophant walked humbly beside him? What was this new stateliness, this unknown dignity, this gaze, so piercing yet so tender, that swept across the crowd? Not thus had held himself, not thus had looked at them, the Prince who had grown up among them.

The procession swept on and entered the huge courtyard of the Temple, crowded with people in the many-coloured garments of festival days, when each wore a mantle of the colour of his ruling planet; down the sides of the steps which rose to the platform in front of the great door of the Temple were ranged the priests in long white garments, and rainbow-coloured over-robes of silk; in the midst of the platform an altar had been erected, and on it wood was piled, and fragrant gums, and incense, but no smoke arose—for the pile, to the people's surprise, was unlighted.

The procession passed on to the foot of the steps, and there all halted, save the three central figures; they ascended the steps, the King and the Hierophant placing themselves to the right and left of the altar, and the Prince, who was the Mahāguru, in the centre, behind it.

Then Sūrya, the Hierophant, spoke to the priests and to the people, telling them that He who stood there behind the altar was no longer the Prince they had known, but that He was the Messenger from the Most High and from the Sons of the Fire who dwelt in the far East, whence their forefathers had come forth. That He had brought Their word to Their children, to which all should yield reverence and obedience, and he bade them listen while the great Messenger spake in Their Name. As the Head of their faith, he humbly bade Him welcome.

Then over the listening throng rang the silver voice of the Mahāguru, and none there was who could not hear it as though spoken to him alone. He told them that He had come from the Sons of the Fire, the Lords of the Flame, who dwelt in the sacred City of the White Island, in far Shamballa. He brought them a revelation from Them, a symbol which should ever keep Them in their minds. He told them how the Fire was the purest of all elements and the purifier of all things, and that thereafter it should be for them the symbol of the Holiest. That the Fire was embodied in the Sun in the heavens, and burned, though hidden, in the heart of man. It was heat, it was light, it was health and strength, and in it and by it all had life and motion. And much He told them of its deep meaning, and how in all things they should see the hidden presence of the Fire.

Then He lifted up His right hand, and behold! there shone in it a Rod, as of lightning held in bondage, yet shooting out its flashes on every side; and He pointed the Rod to the East of the Heavens, and cried some words aloud in an unknown tongue; and the heavens became one sheet of flame, and Fire fell blazing down upon the altar, and a Star shone out above His Head and seemed to bathe Him in its radiance. And all the priests and the people fell upon their faces, and Sūrya and the King bowed down in homage at His feet, and the clouds of fragrant smoke from the altar veiled the three for a few moments from sight.

Then, with His hand upraised in blessing, the Mahāguru descended the steps, and He, with the King and the Hierophant, returned with the procession to the Palace whence they had come. And the people marvelled greatly and rejoiced, because the Gods of their forefathers had remembered them, and had sent them the Word of Peace. And they carried home the flowers which had rained down upon them from the sky when the Fire had passed, and kept them in their shrines as precious heirlooms for their descendants.

The Mahāguru remained for a considerable time in the city, going daily to the Temple to instruct the priests; He taught them that Fire and water were the purifiers of all else, and must never be polluted, and that even the water was purified by the Fire; that all fire was the Fire of the Sun, and was in all things and might be released as fire; that out of the Fire and out of the water all things come, for the Fire and the water were the two Spirits, Fire being life and water form.[1]

The Mahāguru had round Him a quite august assemblage of Masters, and others less advanced. He left these to carry on His teaching when He departed.

His departure was as dramatic as His first preaching.

The people were gathered together to hear Him preach, as He was wont to do occasionally, and they knew not that it was for the last time. He stood, as before, on the great platform, but there was no altar. He preached, inculcating the duty of gaining knowledge and of practising love, and bade them follow and obey Sūrya, whom He left in His place as Teacher. And then He told them that He was going, and He blessed them, and lifting up His arms to the eastern sky He called aloud; and out of the sky came down a whirling cloud of flame, and enwrapped Him as He stood, and then, whirling still, it shot upwards and fled eastwards, and—He was gone.

Then the people fell on their faces and cried out that He was a God, and they exulted exceedingly that He had lived among them; but the King was very sad, and mourned for His departure many days. And Mercury, who, in his subtle body, had ever remained near Him, at His service, returned with Him to the Holy Ones, and rested for awhile in peace.

[1] Possibly out of this arose the later teaching of Ormuzd and Ahriman. There are passages which show that the double of Ormuzd was not originally an evil power, but rather matter, while Ormuzd was Spirit.

After He had gone, Star-worship did not at once disappear, for the people regarded His teaching as a reform. not as a substitution, and still worshipped the Moon, and Venus, and the constellations, and the planets; but the Fire was held sacred as the image, the emblem, and the being of the Sun, and the new religion rather enfolded the old one than replaced it. Gradually the Faith of the Fire grew stronger and stronger; Star-worship retreated from Persia to Mesopotamia, where it remained the dominant faith, and took a very scientific form. Astrology there reached its zenith, and scientifically guided human affairs, both public and private. Its priests possessed much occult knowledge, and the wisdom of the Magi became famed throughout the East. In Persia, the Religion of the Fire triumphed, and later Prophets carried on the work of the great Zaraṭhustra, and built up the Zoroastrian Faith and its literature; it has endured down to our own day.

The third sub-race numbered about a million souls when they settled down in Persia and Mesopotamia, and they multiplied rapidly under the favourable conditions of their new home, and also incorporated in their nation the sparse population which existed in the country when they entered it.

In the twenty-eight thousand years of the Persian Empire there were naturally many fluctuations; most of the time Persia and Mesopotamia were under separate rulers, of whom sometimes the one, sometimes the other, was nominally Overlord; sometimes the two countries were split up into smaller States, owing a kind of loose feudal allegiance to the central King. All through their history they had constantly recurring difficulties with the nomad Mongolians on one hand, and the mountaineers of Kurdistan and the Hindū Kush on the other. Sometimes the Iranians drew back for a time before these tribes; sometimes they pushed the frontier of civilisation further forward, and drove the savages back. At one period they ruled most of Asia Minor, and made temporary settlements in several of the countries bordering the Mediterranean; at one time they held Cyprus, Rhodes and Crete; but on the whole in that part of the world the Atlantean power was too strong for them, and they avoided conflict with it. At this western boundary of their kingdom powerful Scythian and Hittite confederations disputed their dominion at various points of their history; once at least they conquered Syria, but seem to have found it a useless acquisition and soon abandoned it; and twice they embroiled themselves with Egypt, against which they could do but little. During most of this long period they kept up a high level of civilisation, and many relics of their mighty architecture lie buried beneath desert sands. Various dynasties arose among them, and several different languages prevailed in the course of their chequered history. They avoided hostilities with India, being separated from it by a wild territory—a sort of no-man's-land; Arabia troubled them but little, for there again a useful belt of desert intervened. They were great traders, merchants, manufacturers—a much more settled people than the second sub-race, and with more definite religious ideas. The best specimens of the Pārsīs of the present day give a fair idea of their appearance. The present inhabitants of Persia have still much of their blood in them, though largely commingled with that of their Arab conquerors. The Kurds, the Afghans, and the Baluchis are also mainly descended from them, though with various admixtures.

CHAPTER XIX

THE FOURTH SUB-RACE, THE KELTIC[1]

By this time the great Central Asian Race was far on the road to its decline, but the Manu had been careful to preserve dignity, power, and pristine vigour in two branches to which He had given much special training—the seed of the fourth and fifth sub-races. His arrangements for them had been somewhat different from those of the earlier segregations. The type of the Root Race, the points in which it varied from the Atlantean, were now thoroughly established, so He was able to devote his attention to another kind of specialisation.

Those who were to constitute the fourth sub-race were drawn apart as usual, into a large valley in the mountains, not far from the capital; the Manu selected a number of the most refined people whom He could find in the City as the nucleus of the new sub-race, and a division of classes arose in the colony; for the Manu was striving to develop certain new characteristics, to awaken imagination and artistic sensibility, to encourage poetry, oratory, painting and music, and the people who

[1] Our band of Servers took no part in the founding of the fourth and fifth sub-races. They were at work in many countries, and may be met in the *Lives of Alcyone.*

responded to this could not do agricultural and other hard manual labour. Anyone who showed any artistic talent in the schools was drafted off for special culture; thus Neptune was observed reciting, and was given special attention in order to develop the artistic faculty revealed in his recitation. He was remarkably handsome, and physical beauty was a marked characteristic of the sub-race, especially among this artistic class. The people were also trained to be enthusiastic, and to be devoted to their leaders. Great pains were taken for many centuries to develop these characteristics, and so effective was the work that they remain the special marks of the Kelt. The valley was managed practically as a separate State, and great predominance was given to the arts already named, art of all kinds being endowed in various ways. Under this special treatment the sub-race, as time rolled on, grew somewhat conceited, and looked down upon the rest of the kingdom as being what we should now call 'Philistine'. And, indeed, they had much justification for their vanity, for they were an extraordinarily handsome people, cultured and refined in their tastes, and with much artistic talent.

The time chosen to send them forth was about 20,000 B.C., and their instructions were to proceed along the northern frontier of the Persian Kingdom, and to win for themselves a home among the mountains which we now call the Caucasus, at that time occupied by a number of wild tribes of predatory nature who were a constant annoyance to Persia. By taking advantage of this, the Manu was able to make arrangements with the Persian Monarch not only to allow free passage and food to His enormous host, but also to send with them a strong army to assist in subduing the mountaineers. Even with this help this proved no easy task. The new-comers soon conquered for themselves a place in which to live, and they easily defeated the tribes when the latter could be persuaded to risk a pitched battle; but when it came to guerilla warfare they were by no means so successful, and many a year had passed before they could consider themselves reasonably secure from attack. They established themselves first somewhere in the district of Erivan, on the shores of Lake Sevanga, but as the centuries rolled on and their number greatly increased, they gradually exterminated the tribes or reduced them to submission, until eventually the whole of Georgia and Mingrelia was in their hands. Indeed in two thousand years they were occupying Armenia and Kurdistan as well, and later on Phrygia also came under their domination, so that they held nearly all Asia Minor as well as the Caucasus. In their mountain home they flourished greatly and became a mighty nation.

They formed rather a federation of tribes than an Empire, for their country was so broken up into valleys that free communication was impossible. Even after they had begun to colonise the Mediterranean coast, they looked back to the Caucasus as their home, and it was really a second centre from which the sub-race went forth to its glorious destiny. By 10,000 B. C. they began to resume their westward march, travelling not as a nation, but as tribes. So it was only in comparatively small waves that they finally arrived in Europe, which it was their destiny to occupy.

Even a tribe did not go as a whole, but left behind it in its valley many of its members to carry on the work of cultivation; these intermarried with other races, and their descendants, with some intermixture of Semitic blood in their veins, are the Georgians of to-day. Only in the cases in which a tribe proposed to settle in a country already in the hands of their sub-race did they depart from their old home in a body.

The first section to cross into Europe from Asia Minor were the ancient Greeks—not the Greeks of our 'Ancient History,' but their far-away ancestors, those who are sometimes called Pelasgians. It will be remembered that the Egyptian priests are mentioned in Plato's *Timœus* and *Critias* as having spoken to a later Greek of the splendid race which had preceded his own people in his land; how they had turned back an invasion from the mighty nation from the West, the conquering nation that had subdued all before it, until it shivered itself against the heroic valour of these Greeks. In comparison with these, it was said, the modern Greeks —the Greeks of our history who seem to us so great—were as pigmies. From these sprang the Trojans who fought with the modern Greeks, and the city of Agadé in Asia Minor was peopled by their descendants.

These, then, had held for a long time the sea-board of Asia Minor and the islands of Cyprus and Crete, and all the trade of that part of the world was carried in their vessels. A fine civilisation was gradually built up in Crete, which endured for thousands of years, and was still flourishing in B. C. 2,800. The name of Minos will ever be remembered as its founder or chief builder, and he was of these elder Greeks, even before B. C. 10,000. The final cause of their definite entry into Europe as a power was an aggressive movement on the part of the Emperor of Poseidonis.

The Mediterranean coasts and islands had for many centuries been in the hands of a number of small nations, most of them Etrurian or Akkadian, but some Semitic; and, except for occasional squabbles, these people were usually peaceful merchantmen. But it occurred one day to the Emperor of Poseidonis to annex all these States, by way of extending his realm and rivalling the traditions of his forefathers. So he prepared a great army and a mighty fleet, and started on his career of conquest. He subdued without difficulty the large Algerian island; he ravaged the coasts of Spain, Portugal and Italy, and forced all those peoples to submit to him; and Egypt, which was not a great naval power, was already debating whether to propose a treaty with him, or to anger him by a resistance which it was feared would be hopeless. Just when he felt secure of the success of his plans, a difficulty arose from an entirely unexpected quarter. The Greek sailors of the Levant declined altogether to be impressed by his imposing forces, and defied him to interfere with their trade. He had been so sure of victory that he had divided his fleet, and had only half of it immediately available; but with that half he at once attacked the presumptuous Greeks, who inflicted upon him a serious defeat, drowning thousands of his soldiers, and leaving not one ship afloat of the great number that attacked them. The battle was not unlike the destruction by the English of the great Spanish Armada; the Greek vessels were smaller than the Atlantean, and not so powerfully armed, but they were faster and far easier to handle. They knew their seas thoroughly, and in several cases decoyed their enemies into positions where the loss of the larger ship was certain. The weather helped them, too, as in the case of the Spanish Armada. The Atlantean ships had great banks of oars, and were clumsy, lumbering things, quite unfitted for heavy weather, and shipping water easily. They also could only navigate deep water, and the agile Greek vessels fled into channels navigable enough for them but fatal to their heavy antagonists, which promptly ran aground.

The second half of the Atlantean fleet was hastily collected and another attack was made, but it was no more successful than the first, though the Greeks lost heavily in repelling it. The Atlantean Monarch himself escaped, and contrived to land in Sicily, where some of his troops had established themselves; but as soon as it became known that his fleet had been destroyed, the conquered populations rose against him, and he had to fight his way home through the whole length of Italy. He withdrew as he went the various garrisons which he had established, but, nevertheless, by the time he reached the Riviera, he had but a few utterly exhausted followers. He made his way in disguise across the south of France, and eventually reached his own kingdom in a merchant ship. Naturally he vowed direst vengeance against the Greeks, and at once ordered preparations for another vast expedition; but the news of the total loss of his fleet and army emboldened various discontented tribes in his own island to raise the standard of rebellion, and during the rest of his reign he never again found himself in a position to undertake foreign aggression.

The success of the Greeks immensely strengthened their position in the Mediterranean, and within the next century they had established settlements on many of its shores. But a worse enemy than the Emperor of Poseidonis now assailed them, and for the moment conquered them, although in the end it proved beneficial. It was the terrible tidal wave created by the sinking of Poseidonis, in B. C. 9,564, which destroyed most of their settlements, and seriously injured the remainder. Both the Gobi Sea and the Sahara Sea became dry land, and the most appalling convulsions took place.

This, however, affected the main stock of the sub-race in its highland home but slightly; messengers from the almost destroyed emigrants arrived in the Caucasus, begging urgently for help, and they went from tribe to tribe, haranguing the people, and urging them to send help to their suffering brethren. Partly from fellow-feeling, and partly with the wish of bettering their own condition and furthering their fortunes by commerce, the tribes combined, as soon as it seemed certain that the catastrophe was over, to send exploring expeditions to ascertain the fate of their brethren beyond the seas, and, when those returned, further relief was organised on a large scale.

The early Greek settlements had been all on the sea-coast, and the colonists were daring sailors; the populations of the interior were not always friendly, though overawed by the dash and valour of the Greeks. But when these latter were almost all destroyed by the cataclysm, the few survivors were often persecuted, and even in some cases enslaved, by the interior races. When the bottom of the Sahara Sea was heaved up, its waters poured out through the great gap between Egypt and Tunis, where Tripoli now stands, and the tidal wave destroyed the sea-coasts, though the interior suffered but little; it was just those sea-coasts on which the Greeks had settled, so that they were the chief sufferers. The Sahara gradually sank down again, and a new coast line rose, assuming the configuration known to us along the African coast, the great Algerian island joining the mainland, and forming with the new land the northern coast of Africa.

Almost all shipping had been simply annihilated, and new navies had to be built; yet so great was the energy of the Greeks that within a few years all the ports of Asia Minor were once more in working order, and streams of new ships went forth from them to see what help was needed across the seas, to re-establish the colonies, and to redeem the honour of the Greek name by delivering those who bore it from a foreign yoke. In a surprisingly short time this was done, and the fact that these ancient Greeks were the first to recover from the shock of the great cataclysm gave them the opportunity of annexing all the best harbours of the new coast line, and since most of the trade of Egypt also was in their hands, the Mediterranean remained for centuries practically a Greek sea. There came a time when Phœnicians and Carthaginians divided the trade with them, but that was much later. They even carried their trade eastward, an expedition going as far as Java, and founding a colony in that island, with which a connection was long kept up.

The Phœnicians were a fourth Race people derived from the Semites and Akkadians, the fifth and sixth Atlantean sub-races, the Akkadian blood much predominating. The Carthaginians, later, were also Akkadian, intermixed with Arab, and with a dash of negro blood. Both were trading peoples, and in the much later days, when Carthage was a mighty city, its troops were almost entirely mercenaries, recruited among the African tribes, the Libyans and Numidians.

The emigration from Asia Minor into Europe was almost continuous, and it is not easy to divide it into distinct waves. If we take these ancient Greeks as our first subdivision, we may perhaps count the Albanians as the second, and the Italian race as the third, both of these latter occupying about the same countries as those in which we know them now. Then after an interval came a fourth wave of astonishing vitality—that to which modern ethnologists restrict the name 'Keltic'. This slowly became the predominant race over the north of Italy, the whole of France and Belgium and the British Isles, the western part of Switzerland, and Germany west of the Rhine. The Greeks of our 'Ancient History' were a mixture, derived from the first wave, mingled with settlers from the second, third and fourth, and with an infusion of the fifth sub-race, coming down from the north and settling in Greece. These gave the rare, and much admired, golden hair and blue eyes, occasionally found among the Greeks.

The fifth wave practically lost itself in the north of Africa, and only traces can now be found of its blood, much mingled with the Semitic—the fifth sub-race of the Atlantean to which the name originally belonged, and the second sub-race of the Āryan, the Arabian, sometimes also called Semitic—among the Berbers, the Moors, the Kabyles, and even the Guanches of the Canary Islands, in this last case mingled with the Tlavatli. This wave encountered the fourth and intermingled with it in the Spanish peninsula, and at a later stage of its existence—only about two thousand years ago—it contributed the last of the many elements which go to make up the population of Ireland; for to it belonged the Milesian invaders who poured into that island from Spain—some of them founding a dynasty of Milesian Kings in France—and bound it under curious forms of magic.

But a far more splendid element of the Irish population had come into it before: that from the sixth wave, which left Asia Minor in a totally different direction, pushing north-west until they reached Scandinavia, where they intermingled to some extent with the fifth sub-race, the Teutonic, of which we shall speak in the next chapter. They thus descended upon Ireland from the north, and are celebrated in its history as the Tuatha-de-Danaan, who are spoken of more as Gods than men. The slight mixture with the Teutonic sub-race gave this last wave some characteristics, both of disposition and of personal appearance, in which they differed from the majority of their sub-race.

But, on the whole, we may describe the men of this fourth, or Keltic sub-race, as having brown or black hair and eyes, and round heads. They were, as a rule, not tall in stature, and their character showed clearly the result of the Manu's efforts thousands of years before. They were imaginative, eloquent, poetical, musical, capable of enthusiastic devotion to a leader, and splendidly brave in following him, though liable to quick depression in case of failure. They seemed to lack what we call business qualities, and they had but scant regard for truth.

The first Athens—or the city built upon the site where Athens now stands—was built B. C. 8,000. (The Athens of our histories was begun about B. C. 1,000, the Parthenon being built in B. C. 480.) After the catastrophe of B. C. 9,564, some of the old Greeks settled down in Hellas, occupying the country, and it was there that the Mahāguru, the Supreme Teacher, came to them, Orpheus, the Founder of the most ancient Orphic Mysteries, from which the later Mysteries of Greece were derived. About B. C. 7,000 He came, living chiefly in the forests, where He gathered His disciples round Him. There was no King to bid Him welcome, no gorgeous Court to acclaim Him. He came as a Singer, wandering through the land, loving the life of Nature, her sunlit spaces and her shadowed forest retreats, averse to cities and to the crowded haunts of men. A band of disciples grew around Him, and He taught them in the glades of woodland, silent save for the singing of the birds and the sweet sounds of forest life, that seemed not to break the stillness.

He taught by song, by music, music of voice and instrument, carrying a five-stringed musical instrument, probably the origin of Apollo's lyre, and He used a pentatonic scale. To this He sang, and wondrous was His music, the Devas drawing nigh to listen to the subtle tones; by sound He worked upon the astral and mental bodies of His disciples, purifying and expanding them; by sound He drew the subtle bodies away from the physical, and set them free in the higher worlds. His music was quite different from the sequences repeated over and over again by which the same result was brought about in the Root-stock of the Race, and which it carried with it into India. Here He worked by melody, not by repetition of similar sounds; and the rousing of each etheric centre had its own melody, stirring it into activity. He showed His disciples living pictures, created by music, and in the Greek Mysteries this was wrought in the same way, the tradition coming down from Him. And He taught that Sound was in all things, and that if man would harmonise himself, then would the Divine Harmony manifest through him, and make all

Nature glad. Thus He went through Hellas singing, and choosing here and there one who should follow Him, and singing also for the people in other ways, weaving over Greece a network of music, which should make her children beautiful and feed the artistic genius of her land. One of His disciples was Neptune, a youth of exquisite beauty, who followed Him everywhere, and often carried His lyre.

Traditions of Him came down among the people and spread far and wide. He became the God of the Sun, Phœbus-Apollo, and, in the North, Balder the Beautiful; for the sixth Keltic wave, as we have seen, went northward to Scandinavia, and carried with it the legend of the Singer of Hellas.

As we think over the symbolism used by this Supreme Teacher, coming as Vyāsa, as Hermes, as Zaraṭhustra, as Orpheus, we recognise the unity of the teaching under the variety of the symbols. Ever He taught the Unity of Life, and the oneness of God with His world. For Vyāsa it was the Sun, that warmed all and gave life; for Hermes it was the Light, that shone alike in heaven and in earth; for Zaraṭhustra it was the Fire, that lay hidden in all things; for Orpheus it was the Harmony, in which all vibrated together. But Sun, Light, Fire, Sound, all gave but a single message: the One Life, the One Love, that was above all, and through all, and in all.

From Hellas some of the disciples went to Egypt, and fraternised with the teachers of the Inner Light, and some went teaching as far afield as Java. And so the Sound went forth, even to the ends of the world. But not again was the Supreme Teacher to come to the teaching of a sub-race. Nearly seven thousand years later He came to His ancient people, came for the last time, and in a body taken from them in India He reached final Illumination, He finished His lives on earth, He became a Buḍḍha.

CHAPTER XX

THE FIFTH SUB-RACE, THE TEUTONIC

WE must now turn back again to B. C. 20,000, in order to trace from its cradle the fifth sub-race, for it was prepared simultaneously with the fourth, although in a different way. For it the Manu had set apart a valley far from His capital, away on the northern side of the Gobi Sea, and into it He had sparingly introduced factors which had not appeared in the fourth. He brought back to it a few of the best specimens of His third sub-race from Persia, where it was by that time thoroughly specialised, and He called also for a few Semites from Arabia. He chose for it especially men who were tall and fair, and when He Himself was born in it He always used a body showing markedly those characteristics. It must be remembered that the Manu starts each sub-race just as he does the Root-Race—by incarnating in it Himself; and the form which He chooses to take largely determines what the appearance of the sub-race shall be. This fifth sub-race was of a very strong and vigorous type, much larger than the preceding one, and was tall and fair, long-headed, with light hair and blue eyes. The character was also very different from that of the Keltic sub-race; it was dogged and persevering, with little of the dash of the fourth: its virtues were not of the artistic type, but rather of the business and common-sense practical sort, blunt and truthful, plain-spoken and straightforward, caring for the concrete rather than for the poetic.

While the fourth was developing its beautiful and artistic type in its own valley, the sterner fifth was also building up its type in its appointed abiding-place, the two different evolutions being thus carried on simultaneously. By the time that they were both ready to start on their migration, the difference between them was clearly marked; and though they left Central Asia together, 20,000 B. C., and passed together through Persia, their eventual destinies were quite different.

The fifth sub-race, small in number, was directed to move further along the shores of the Caspian Sea, and it settled itself in the Territory of Daghestan. There it slowly grew for thousands of years, gradually extending itself along the northern slopes of the Caucasian Range, and occupying the Terek and Kuban districts. There its people remained until after the great cataclysm of 9,564 B. C.; indeed, it was nearly a thousand years after that before they began their great march to world-dominion. They had not been idle during this long time of waiting, for they had already differentiated themselves into several distinct types.

Then, as with one accord, now that the swamps of the great Central European plain were becoming habitable, they moved north-westward in one mighty army as far as what is now Cracow in Poland. There they rested for some centuries for the marshes were not yet dry enough for safe habitation, and disease fell upon them and thinned their ranks. It was chiefly from this secondary centre that the final radiations took place. The first of them was the Slavonic, and it branched off into two main directions. One party turned east and north, and from it come largely the modern Russians; the other took a more southerly direction, and is now represented by the Croatians, Servians, and Bosnians. The second wave was the Lettish, though its members did not travel far; it gives us the Letts, the Lithuanians and the Prussians. The third was the Germanic, and part at least of that went further afield, for if those called especially the Teutons spread themselves over Southern Germany, the other branches, called the Goths and Scandinavians, swept to the northern point of Europe. The later descent of the Scandinavians upon Normandy, and of the Goths upon Southern Europe, the spreading of this fifth sub-race over Australia, North America and South Africa, and its dominance in India, where the Root-stock of its people is settled, belong to modern history.

It has yet to build, like its predecessors, its World-Empire, though the beginnings of it are before our eyes. The terrible blunder of the eighteenth century, which rent away from Great Britain its North American Colonies, may be remedied by an offensive and defensive alliance between the severed halves, and a similar alliance with Germany, the remaining great section of the Teutonic sub-race, would weld the whole sufficiently into one to make a federated Empire. Late events show the rising of

India into her proper place in this extending Empire, destined to be mighty in the East as well as in the West.

As this World-Empire rises to its zenith during the coming centuries, the group composed of men of the mightiest genius, spoken of on p. 69 will be sent to take incarnation in it, to lift it to the highest pinnacle of literary and scientific glory, till it overtops the vanished Empires of the Arabians, the Persians, the Romans, those of the second, third, and fourth sub-races of the Āryan stock. For the resistless course of ages, unrolling the Divine Plan, must accomplish its purpose, until the fifth Race shall have played its part, and the sixth and the seventh shall have followed it, shaping such human perfection as belongs to the story of our earth in this fourth Round of our terrene Chain. What heights of unimaginable splendour lie hidden in the further future, no tongue of half-evolved man may tell.

CHAPTER XXI

THE ROOT-STOCK AND ITS DESCENT INTO INDIA

WE have traced, roughly and in broad outlines, the migration out of Central Asia of the second, third, fourth and fifth sub-races of the Āryan Root-stock. We have seen its magnificent civilisation, and the vast extent of its Empire, and that from B. C. 40,000 onwards it had been slowly declining. From B. C. 40,000 to B. C. 20,000, the chief work of Vaivasvaṭa Manu lay with His sub-races, and He and His immediate group, during these twenty thousand years, had been incarnating in the special districts set apart for the preparation of those sub-races. The original Empire, having long passed its prime, had been wearing away, as do all human institutions, while its sub-races were going out to play their appointed parts, and the process of disintegration had already gone far. The Mongolian and Turanian races, over whom it had so long ruled, had asserted their independence, and the Kingdom centring round the City of the Bridge was now but a small one. The people built no more—they lived in the ruins of the great work of their forefathers. The egos showing genius and straining after high education were incarnating in the great daughter civilisations, so in the Mother State the level of learning steadily sank. Trade had fallen almost to zero, and the people were becoming agricultural and pastoral only. The central Kingdom still held together, but outlying districts had broken off and become independent.

But now, B. C. 18,800, the toilsome work of building up and sending out the sub-races was, for the time, over. The Manu had managed all His migrations, and seen His sub-races definitely established, and He now turned His attention once more to the Root Race, because He wished to get it away by degrees from its ancestral home, and to establish it in India, the land chosen for its further evolution. In India the splendid Atlantean civilisation had developed from the time that huge Atlantean hosts, pouring through the Himālayan passes, after the land was sufficiently dry for settlement, had occupied the country; before that, a vast Atlantean Kingdom had existed in the far south, and had spread to the ocean which, before the catastrophe of B. C. 75,025, bounded it on the north. This civilisation, over-luxurious, had now become effete, and the higher classes, belonging to the Toltec sub-race, were indolent and self-seeking; much, however, remained of a noble literature, and there was a great tradition of occult knowledge, both of which were needed for the work of the future and therefore had to be preserved. The warrior spirit had largely died out, and the wealth of the country, enormously and lavishly displayed, invited conquest from a more virile people, who should inherit and carry on all that deserved perpetuation.

The entire removal of the Race from its Central Asian Home was necessary so that (1) Shamballa should be left in the required solitude; the work carried on in close contact with the outer world was finished for the time, and the Race must be left to grow without external supervision; (2) India should be Āryanised; (3) the Race should be out of the way before the coming cataclysm, as the Central Asian region would be much altered.

The Manu had not incarnated in the Root Race since He led away the fourth and fifth sub-races, that is for about one thousand two hundred years; for, as said above, we are now at B. C. 18,800. He had therefore become rather a myth in Central Asia, and there had been differences of opinion, a few centuries earlier, as to whether His rules as to intermarriage still held good. Some held that they were obsolete, their object having been obtained, and some families had married into those of some of the Tartar rulers. A schism had thus occurred, and those who favoured the new departure had left the Kingdom and set themselves up as a separate community. They went no further, however, along the road of intermarriage, and it may be opined that the few outside marriages which had occurred had been brought about in order to gain a slight, but necessary, infusion of other blood, and perhaps also to cause the desired separation. The disappearance of the original cause of disunion did not draw the communities nearer together, and, indeed, they became more hostile as centuries went by, and the increasing numbers in the Central Kingdom pressed the seceders further and further back into the valleys of the northern hills. Mars, at the date mentioned above, was King of one of the tribes of the seceders, who were suffering much from the incursions of the larger nation; continual fighting barely enabled his tribe to hold its own, and its eventual destruction was certain; his teacher, Jupiter, advised him not to fight, but this did not help him, and he thought and prayed desperately to find a way of safety for his people, so brave, so loyal, but so hopelessly over-matched.

Then, in the crisis of his perplexity, the Manu appeared to him in a dream, and bade him lead his tribe westward and southward—the vanguard of the greatest migration that had ever occurred—into the sacred land of India, which was assigned to the Race as dwelling. He was told to fight as little as he could on his way to his future home, to attack none who would let him pass in peace, and to press on to the southern extremity of India. In the future all the Race would follow, and in the coming migrations he would frequently take part; and at a future time he and his wife Mercury would do such work as He, the Manu, was then doing.

Thus encouraged, and full of joy, Mars set to work to prepare, telling his people of his dream, and bidding them get ready for the march. Nearly all believed him, but our old Arabian friend, Alastor, had turned up again, and he headed a small party who refused to follow Mars, saying that he was not going to leave the old land and the old teachings because of the hysterical dream of an overwrought and despairing man. So he stayed behind, betrayed the route of his people to their enemies, and was put to death after the failure of the pursuing expedition.

Mars started in B. C. 18,875[1] and followed the appointed road, and after many hardships and not a little fighting—for though he never attacked, he was frequently assailed—he reached the great plains of India, and for a while enjoyed the hospitality of his comrade in many lives, Virāj, who was ruling as King Podishpar over the greater part of northern India. The alliance was cemented by the marriage of Corona, the son of Podishpar, to Bṛhaspaṭi, a daughter of Mars and the widow of Vulcan, who had been killed in a battle during the journey. Southern India was then a large Kingdom under King Huyaranda, or Lahira—our Saturn—the High Priest of the Kingdom being our Sūrya, under the name Byarsha, and the Deputy High Priest being Osiris. Sūrya had told Saturn that the strangers were coming at the command of the Gods, some years before their arrival, so that the King sent the Crown Prince, Crux, to meet them, and gave them welcome, settling them in his land. Later, Sūrya declared that "the high-nosed strangers from the north" were fitted to be priests, and that they should hold the priestly office hereditarily; those who agreed to this became priests, and were the ancestors of the Brāhmaṇas of Southern India, abstaining from intermarriage with the earlier inhabitants, and living as a separate class.

Others intermarried with the Toltec aristocracy, thus gradually Āryanising the whole upper classes

[1] See Appendix X.

of the country, and the south of India passed peacefully under Āryan rule; for Crux, who succeeded Saturn, died without issue, and Herakles, the second son of Mars, was elected by the people to the vacant throne, establishing an Āryan dynasty. From this migration forward, all the immigrants into India are spoken of as the 'first sub-race,' since the whole Root Race, the ancient stock, passed over into India. Births into this are reckoned as births into the first sub-race, whether taking place in India itself or in the countries colonised and Aryanised by it.

We find a number of old friends in this migration, in addition to those already named; Mars' eldest son was Uranus, who became a hermit in the Nilghiris, and his third son was Alcyone, who became Deputy High Priest on the resignation—due to old age—of Osiris. His second daughter was Demeter.[1] A curious instance of bringing friends in from abroad was the arrival of a young Mongolian chieftain, Taurus, who fled from his elder brother's anger, and took refuge with Mars in his Central Asian Kingdom; he brought Procyon with him as his wife, and Cygnus, whom he married to Aries, was one of his daughters.

From the South Indian Āryan Kingdom went out, about B. C. 13,500, an important mission to Egypt; the order came from the Head of the Hierarchy through the Manu, and the expedition travelled via Ceylon, by water up the Red Sea, then hardly more than an inlet. It was not intended to colonise, since Egypt was already a

[1] See Appendix X.

mighty Empire, but rather to settle there under the Egyptian Government, a great and beneficent, as well as highly civilised, power.

Mars was at the head of the expedition, and Sūrya was a High Priest in Egypt as he had been in southern India nearly three thousand years before: as then, he smoothed the way for the coming Aryans, and he told the Pharaoh of their approach, and advised him to welcome them. His advice was taken, and a little later he counselled the Pharaoh to marry his daughter to Mars, and to name the latter his successor. This was duly done, and thus peaceably but effectively was an Āryan dynasty established in Egypt at the death of the ruling Pharaoh. It reigned gloriously for many thousand years, until the sinking of Poseidonis, when it, with the Egyptian people, was driven to the hills by the flooding of Egypt. The flood, however, retreated comparatively soon, and the country recovered ere long. Manetho's history apparently deals with this Āryan dynasty; he makes Unas—whose date is given as B. C. 3,900, while we make it 4,030 B. C.—the last King of the Fifth dynasty. The Arab Hyksos Kings are put at B. C. 1,500. Under the Āryan Pharaohs the great Schools of Egypt became even more famous, and for long it led the learning of the western world.

It was the second mighty Empire of the first sub-race, if we count the Empire of the Root Race as the first. From Egypt was introduced Āryan blood into several East African tribes; it would seem as though a low type of body were sometimes required for little-advanced egos, who had gone through many previous sub-races without making much progress, and were thrown into contact with a higher race in order to force them forward. Some of the lowest types of dwellers in the slums of civilised fourth and fifth Āryan sub-races are obviously less advanced than Zulus. On the other hand, a touch of Āryan blood in an uncivilised tribe would give certain characteristics required for its improvement.

The South Indian Kingdom was used by the Manu as a subsidiary centre of radiation on other occasions than this of the Āryanising of Egypt. He sent out from it colonists to Java, to Australia and to the islands of Polynesia, which accounts for the Āryan strain to be observed even to-day in what are called the brown Polynesians, in contradistinction to the Melanesians.

While these arrangements were being carried out in the south of India, the Manu still worked at the gradual transportation of His Race from Central Asia into the northern parts of India. One of the early immigrations settled itself in the Panjab, and after much fighting made terms of peace with the inhabitants, partly plundering and partly defending them. Another, turning eastwards, had established itself in Assam and northern Bengal. The expedition immediately preceding one on which we may pause for a few minutes had taken place about B. C. 17,520; part of it reached its destination safely by the route followed by Mars, more than a thousand years before, while a smaller division, seeking to penetrate through what is now called the Khyber Pass, was annihilated. In B. C. 17,455 a third[1] was sent out, led by Mars, the eldest son

[1] See Appendix XI.

black people of Lemurian descent, whom they regarded with horror, they called Ḍaiṭyas and Ṭakṣhaks.

There were some intermarriages between the more liberal Āryans and the Toltecs, and we found Alcyone, about B. C. 12,850, much attached to Psyche, the son of Orpheus, an Atlantean dignitary, and marrying the latter's daughter, Mizar, though his own father, Algol, was a fanatical Āryan, hating the Atlanteans and their civilisation. While, under these circumstances, he and his young wife became fugitives, yet an Āryan leader, Vesta, head of an invading band, gave them shelter, and a relative of his, Draco, with his wife Cassiopeia members of a band settled longer in India, helped them to the possession of an estate, where he was on very friendly terms with Aletheia, - a rich Atlantean. It was evident, therefore, that in some cases, at least, friendly relations existed between the races, and these were not disturbed by the irruption of a large host of Āryans, once more under Mars, who passed through the neighbourhood on his way to carve himself out an Empire in Central India.[1]

By these constant migrations the Central Asian Kingdom was drained of its inhabitants by about 9,700 B.C. The convulsions attending the catastrophe of B. C. 9,564 shattered the City of the Bridge into ruins, and wrought the destruction of most of the great Temples on the White Island. The latest bands did not reach India easily; they were delayed in Afghanistan and Baluchistan for some two thousand years, and many were massacred by Mongol

[1] See Appendix XIII.

raiders; the rest slowly found their way down to the plains, already thickly populated.

When His people were thus finally conveyed into India, a danger arose that the Āryan blood might become a mere trace amidst the enormous majority of the Atlanteans and Atlanto-Lemurians, so the Manu again forbade inter-marriage, and about B. C. 8,000 ordained the caste system, in order that no further admixture might be made, and that those already made might be perpetuated. He founded at first only three castes—Brāhmaṇa, Rājan and Vish. The first were pure Āryans, the second Āryan and Toltec, the third Āryan and Mongolian.

The castes were hence called the Varṇas, or colours, the pure Āryans white, the Āryan and Toltec intermixture red, and the Āryan and Mongolian yellow. The castes were allowed to intermarry among themselves, but a feeling quickly grew up that marriages should be restricted within the caste. Later, those who were not Āryan at all were included under the general appellation of Shūḍras, but even here in many cases a certain small amount of Āryan blood may appear. Many of the hill tribes are partly Āryan—some few are wholly so, like the Siaposh people and the Gipsy tribes.

During the emigrations into India, one tribe had gone off in a direction different from that of the others, and had contrived to establish itself in a valley in the Susamir district. There, forgotten by the rest of the world, it enjoyed its primitive pastoral life for many centuries. About 2,200 B. C., there arose a great military leader amongst the

Mongol tribes, and they devastated all of Asia that they could reach, utterly destroying, among others, the remnants of the Persian Empire. The Tartar leader was finally overthrown, and his hordes scattered, but he had left utter desolation behind him. Somehow in a hundred years or so, news of a fertile but unoccupied land reached our Āryans in their valley; they sent out spies to report, and when the story was confirmed, they migrated bodily into Persia. These were the speakers of Zend, and their late arrival accounts for the curiously unsettled state of the country even in the time of the last Zoroaster. Such remnants of the third sub-race as had been only driven from their homes, and had escaped the general massacre, came back and made common cause with our tribe, and from these beginnings gradually developed the latest Persian Empire.

MAN :

WHITHER

FOREWORD

THE following pages are an attempt to sketch the early beginnings of the sixth Root Race, comparable to the early stage of the fifth Root Race in Arabia. Ere the sixth Race comes to its own, and takes possession of its continent, now rising slowly, fragment after fragment, in the Pacific, many, many, thousands of years will have rolled away. North America will have been shattered into pieces, and the western strip on which the first Colony will be settled will have become an easternmost strip of the new continent.

While this little Colony is working at the embryonic stage, the fifth Race will be at its zenith, and all the pomp and glory of the world will be concentrated therein. The colony will be a very poor thing in the eyes of the world, a gathering of cranks, slavishly devoted to their Leader.

This sketch is reprinted from *The Theosophist*, and is wholly the work of my colleague.

A. B.

CHAPTER XXII

THE BEGINNINGS OF THE SIXTH ROOT RACE

THE VISION OF KING ASHOKA

Introductory

SOME twelve years ago the present writers engaged in an examination of some of the earlier lives of Colonel H. S. Olcott. Most members of the Society are aware that in the incarnation preceding this last one he was the great Buḍḍhist King Ashoka; and those who have read a little memorandum upon his previous history (written for an American Convention) will remember that when the end of that life was approaching he had a time of great depression and doubt, to relieve which his Master showed him two remarkable pictures, one of the past and the other of the future. He had been mourning over his failure to realise all of his plans, and his chief doubt had been as to his power to persevere to the end, to retain his link with his Master until the goal should be attained. To dispel this doubt the Master first explained to him by a vision of the past how the connection between them had originally been established long ago in Atlantis, and how the promise had then been given that that link should never be broken; and then, by another vision of the future, He showed Himself as the Manu of the sixth Root Race, and King Ashoka as a lieutenant serving under Him in that high office.

The scene was laid in a beautiful park-like country, where flower-covered hills sloped down to a sapphire sea. The Master M. was seen standing surrounded by a small army of pupils and helpers, and even while the fascinated King watched the lovely scene, the Master K. H. entered upon it, followed by His band of disciples. The two Masters embraced, the groups of pupils mingled with joyous greetings, and the wondrous picture faded from before our entranced eyes. But the impression which it left has remained undimmed, and it carries with it a certain knowledge, strange beyond words and full of awe. The sight which we were then using was that of the causal body, and so the egos composing that crowd were clearly distinguishable to our vision. Many of them we instantly recognised; others, not then known to us, we have since met on the physical plane. Strange beyond words, truly, to meet (perhaps on the other side of the world) some member whom physically we have never seen before, and to exchange behind his back the glance which telegraphs our recognition of him—which says: "Here is yet another who will be with us to the end."

We know also who will *not* be there; but from that, thank God, we are not called upon to draw any deductions, for we know that large numbers who are not at the inception of the Race will join it later, and also that there are other centres of activity connected with the Master's work. This particular centre at which we were looking will exist for the special purpose of the foundation of the new Root Race, and therefore will be unique: and only those who have by careful previous self-training fitted themselves to share in its peculiar work can bear a part in it. It is precisely in order that the nature of that work, and the character of the education necessary for it, may be clearly known, that we are permitted to lay before our members this sketch of that future life. That self-training involves supreme self-sacrifice and rigorous self-effacement, as will be made abundantly clear as our story progresses; and it involves complete confidence in the wisdom of the Masters. Many good members of our Society do not yet possess these qualifications, and therefore, however highly developed they may be in other directions, they could not take their place in this particular band of workers; for the labours of the Manu are strenuous, and He has neither time nor force to waste in arguing with recalcitrant assistants who think they know better than He does. The exterior work of this Society will, however, still be going on in those future centuries, and in its enormously extended ramifications there will be room enough for all who are willing to help, even though they may not yet be capable of the total self-effacement which is required of the assistants of the Manu.

Nothing that we saw at that time, in that vision shown to the King, gave us any clue either to the date of the event foreseen or to the place where it is to occur, though full information on these points is now in our possession. Then we knew only that the occasion was an important one connected with the founding of the new Race—indeed, that much was told to King Ashoka; and, knowing as we did the offices which our two revered Masters are to hold in the sixth Root Race, we were easily able to associate the two ideas.

So the matter remained until much later, and we had no expectation that any further elucidation of it would be vouchsafed to us. Suddenly, and *apparently* by the merest accident, the question was re-opened, and an enquiry in a department of the teaching utterly remote from the founding of the sixth Root Race was found to lead straight into the very heart of its history, and to pour a flood of light upon its methods.

The remainder of the story is told by the one who was chosen to transmit it.

THE ḌEVA HELPER

I was talking to a group of friends about the passage in the *Jñāneshvari* which describes the yogī as "hearing and comprehending the language of the Ḍevas," and trying to explain in what wonderful ecstasies of colour and sound certain orders of the great Angels express themselves, when I was aware of the presence of one of them, who has on several previous occasions been good enough to give me some help in my efforts to understand the mysteries of their glorious existence. Seeing, I suppose, the inadequacy of my attempts at description, he put before me two singularly vivid little pictures, and said to me: "There, describe this to them."

Each of the pictures showed the interior of a great Temple, of architecture unlike any with which I am familiar, and in each a Ḍeva was acting as priest or minister, and leading the devotions of a vast congregation. In one of these the officiant was producing his results entirely by the manipulation of an indescribably splendid display of colours, while in the other case music was the medium through which he on the one hand appealed to the emotions of his congregation, and on the other expressed their aspirations to the Deity. A more detailed description of these Temples and of the methods adopted in them will be given later; for the moment let us pass on to the later investigations of which this was only the starting-point. The Ḍeva who showed these pictures explained that they represented scenes from a future in which Ḍevas would move far more freely among men than they do at present, and would help them not only in their devotions but also in many other ways. Thanking him for his kind assistance, I described the lovely pictures as well as I could to my group, he himself making occasional suggestions.

SEEING THE FUTURE

When the meeting was over, in the privacy of my chamber I recalled these pictures with the greatest pleasure, fixed them upon my mind in the minutest detail, and endeavoured to discover how far it was possible to see in connection with them other surrounding circumstances. To my great delight, I found that this was perfectly possible—that I could, by an effort, extend my vision from the Temples to the town and country surrounding them, and could in this way see and describe in detail this life of the future. This naturally raises a host of questions as to the type of clairvoyance by which the future is thus foreseen, the extent to which such future may be thought of as foreordained, and how far, if at all, what is seen is modifiable by the wills of those who are observed as actors in the drama; for if all is already arranged, and they cannot change it, are we not once more face to face with the wearisome theory of predestination? I am no more competent to settle satisfactorily the question of freewill and predestination than any of the thousands of people who have written upon it, but at least I can bear testimony to one undoubted fact—that there *is* a plane from which the past, the present, and the future have lost their relative characteristics, and each is as actually and absolutely present in consciousness as the others.

I have in many cases examined the records of the past, and have more than once described how utterly real and living those records are to the investigator. He is simply living in the scene, and he can train himself to look upon it from the outside merely as a spectator, or to identify his consciousness for the time with that of some person who is taking part in that scene, and so have the great advantage of contemporary opinion on the subject under review. I can only say that in this, the first long and connected vision of the future which I have undertaken, the experience was precisely similar; that this future also was in every way as actual, as vividly present, as any of those scenes of the past, or as the room in which I sit as I write: that in this case also precisely the same two possibilities existed—that of looking on the whole thing as a spectator, or of identifying oneself with the consciousness of one who was living in it, and thereby realising exactly what were his motives and how life appeared to him.

As, during part of the investigation, I happened to have present with me in the physical body one of those whom I clearly saw taking part in that community of the future, I made some special effort to see how far it may be possible for that ego, by action in the intervening centuries, to prevent himself from taking part in that movement or to modify his attitude with regard to it. It seemed clear to me, after repeated and most careful examination, that he can *not* avoid or appreciably modify this destiny which lies before him; but the reason that he cannot do this is that the Monad above him, the very Spirit within him, acting through the as yet undeveloped part of himself as an ego, has already determined upon this, and set in motion the causes which must inevitably produce it. The ego has unquestionably a large amount of freedom in these intervening, centuries. He can move aside from the path marked out for him to this side or to that; he can hurry his progress along it or delay it;

but yet the inexorable compelling power (which is still at the same time his truest Self) will not permit such absolute and final divergence from it as might cause him to lose the opportunity which lies before him. The Will of the true man is already set, and that Will will certainly prevail.

I know very well the exceeding difficulty of thought upon this subject, and I am not in the least presuming to propound any new solution for it; I am simply offering a contribution to the study of the subject in the shape of a piece of testimony. Let it be sufficient for the moment to state that I for my part know this to be an accurate picture of what will inevitably happen; and, knowing that, I put it thus before our readers as a matter which I think will be of deep interest to them and a great encouragement to those who find themselves able to accept it; while at the same time I have not the slightest wish to press it upon the notice of those who have not as yet acquired the certainty that it is possible to foresee the distant future even in the minutest detail.

C. W. L.

CHAPTER XXIII

THE BEGINNINGS OF THE SIXTH ROOT RACE

IT was discovered that these gorgeous Temple services do not represent what will be the ordinary worship of the world at that period, but that they will take place among a certain community of persons living apart from the rest of the world; and but little further research was necessary to show us that this is the very same community, the foundation of which had formed the basis of the vision shown so long ago to King Ashoka. This community is in fact the segregation made by the Manu of the sixth Root Race; but instead of carrying it away into remote desert places inaccessible to the rest of the world—as did the Manu of the fifth Root Race—our Manu plants it in the midst of a populous country, and preserves it from admixture with earlier races by a moral boundary only. Just as the material for the *fifth* Root Race had to be taken from the *fifth* sub-race of the Atlantean stock, so the material bodies from which the *sixth* Root Race is to be developed are to be selected from the *sixth* sub-race of our present Āryan Race. It is therefore perfectly natural that this community should be established, as it was found to be, on the great continent of North America, where even already steps are being taken towards the development of the sixth sub-race. Equally natural is it that the part of that continent chosen should be that which in scenery and climate approaches most nearly to our ideal of Paradise, that is to say, Lower California. It is found that the date of the events portrayed in the vision of King Ashoka—the actual founding of the community—is almost exactly seven hundred years from the present time; but the pictures shown by the Ḍeva (and those revealed by the investigations which sprang from them) belong to a period about one hundred and fifty years later, when the community is already thoroughly established and fully self-reliant.

FOUNDING THE COMMUNITY

The plan is this. From the Theosophical Society as it is now, and as it will be in the centuries to come, the Manu and the High-Priest of the coming Race—our Mars and Mercury—select such people as are thoroughly in earnest and devoted to Their service, and offer to them the opportunity of becoming Their assistants in this great work. It is not to be denied that the work will be arduous, and that it will require the utmost sacrifice on the part of those who are privileged to share in it.

The LOGOS, before He called into existence this part of His system, had in His mind a detailed plan of what He intended to do with it—to what level each Race in each Round should attain, and in what particulars it must differ from its predecessors. The whole of His mighty thought-form exists even now upon the plane of the Divine Mind; and when a Manu is appointed to take charge of a Root Race, His first proceeding is to materialise this thought-form down to some plane where He can have it at hand for ready reference. His task is then to take from the existing world such men as most nearly resemble this type, to draw them apart from the rest, and gradually to develop in them, so far as may be, the qualities which are to be specially characteristic of the new Race.

When He has carried this process as far as He thinks possible with the material ready to His hand, He will Himself incarnate in the segregated group. Since He has long ago exhausted all hindering karma, He is perfectly free to mould all His vehicles, causal, mental and astral, exactly to the copy set before Him by the LOGOS. No doubt He can also exercise a great influence even upon His physical vehicle, though He must owe that to parents who, after all, belong still to the fifth Root Race, even though themselves specialised to a large extent.

Only those bodies which are physically descended in a direct line from Him constitute the new Root Race; and since He in His turn must obviously marry into the old fifth Root Race, it is clear that the type will not be absolutely pure. For the first generation His children must also take to themselves partners from the old Race, though only within the limits of the segregated group; but after that generation there is no further admixture of the older blood, intermarriage outside of the newly constituted family being absolutely forbidden. Later on, the Manu Himself will re-incarnate, probably as His own great-grandchild, and so will further purify the Race, and all the while He will never relax His efforts to mould all their vehicles, now including even the physical, into closer and closer resemblance to the model given to Him by the LOGOS.

GATHERING THE MEMBERS

In order that this work of special moulding should be done as quickly and as completely as possible, it is eminently necessary that all the egos incarnating in these new vehicles should themselves fully understand what is being done, and be utterly devoted to the work. Therefore the Manu gathers round Him for this purpose a large number of His pupils and helpers, and puts them into the bodies which He Himself provides, the arrangement being that they shall wholly dedicate themselves to this task, taking up a new body as soon as they find it necessary to lay aside the old one. Therefore, as we have said, exceedingly arduous labour will be involved for those who become His assistants; they must take birth again and again without the usual interval on other planes; and further, every one of this unbroken string of physical lives must be absolutely unselfish—must be entirely consecrated to the interests of the new Race without the slightest thought of self or of personal interest. In fact, the man who undertakes this must live not for himself but for the Race, and this for century after century.

This is no light burden to assume; but on the other side of the account it must be said that those who undertake it will inevitably make abnormally rapid progress, and will have not only the glory of taking a leading part in the evolution of humanity, but also the inestimable privilege of working through many lives under the immediate physical direction of the Masters whom they love so dearly. And those who have already been so blest as to taste the sweetness of Their presence know well that in that presence no labour seems arduous, no obstacles seem insurmountable; rather all difficulties vanish, and we look back in wonder at the stumbles of yesterday, finding it impossible to comprehend how we could have felt discouraged or despairing. The feeling is exactly that which the Apostle so well expressed when he said: "I can do all things through Christ who strengtheneth me."

Entering the Estate

When the time draws near which in His judgment is the most suitable for the actual founding of the Race, He will see to it that all these disciples whom He has selected shall take birth in that sixth sub-race. When they have all attained maturity He (or they jointly) will purchase a large estate in a convenient spot, and all will journey thither and commence their new life as a community. It was this scene of the taking possession of the estate which was shown to King Ashoka, and the particular spot at which the two Masters were seen to meet is one near the boundary of the estate. They then lead their followers to the central site which has already been selected for the principal city of the community, and there they take possession of the dwellings which have been previously prepared for them. For, long before this, the Manu and His immediate lieutenants have supervised the erection of a magnificent group of buildings in preparation for this occasion—a great central Temple or cathedral, vast buildings arranged as libraries, museums and council-halls, and, surrounding these, perhaps some four hundred dwelling-houses, each standing in the midst of its own plot of ground. Though differing much in style and detail, these houses are all built according to a certain general plan which shall be described later.

All this work has been done by ordinary labourers working under a contractor—a large body of men, many of whom are brought from a distance; and they are highly paid in order to ensure that the work shall be of the best. A great deal of complicated machinery is required for the work of the colony, and in their early days men from without are employed to manage this and to instruct the colonists in its use; but in a few years the colonists learn how to make and repair everything that is necessary for their well-being, and so they are able to dispense with outside help. Even within the first generation the colony becomes self-supporting, and after this no labour is imported from outside. A vast amount of money is expended in establishing the colony and bringing it into working order, but when once it is firmly established it is entirely self-supporting and independent of the outer world. The community does not, however, lose touch with the rest of the world, for it always takes care to acquaint itself with all new discoveries and inventions, and with any improvements in machinery.

CHILDREN OF THE MANU

The principal investigations which we made, however, concern a period about one hundred and fifty years later than this, when the community has already enormously increased, and numbered somewhere about a hundred thousand people, all of them direct physical descendants of the Manu, with the exception of a few who have been admitted from the outer world under conditions which shall presently be described. It at first seemed to us improbable that the descendants of one man could in that period amount to so large a number; but such cursory examination as could be made of the intervening period showed that all this had happened quite naturally. When the Manu sees fit to marry, certain of His pupils selected by Him stand ready voluntarily to resign their old bodies as soon as He is able to provide them with new ones. He has twelve children in all ; it is noteworthy that He arranges that each shall be born under a special influence—as astrologers would say—one under each sign of the Zodiac. All these children grow up in due course, and marry selected children of other members of the community.

Every precaution is taken to supply perfectly healthy and suitable surroundings, so that there is no infant mortality, and what we should call quite large families are the rule. At a period of fifty years after the founding of the community one hundred and four grandchildren of the Manu are already living. At eighty years from the commencement, the number of descendants is too great to be readily counted: but taking at random ten out of the hundred and four grandchildren, we find that those ten, by that time, have between them ninety-five children, which gives us a rough estimate of one thousand direct descendants in that generation, not including the original twelve children and one hundred and four grandchildren. Moving on another quarter of a century—that is to say one hundred and five years from the original founding of the community, we find fully ten thousand direct descendants, and it then becomes clear that in the course of the next forty-five years there is not the slightest difficulty in accounting for fully one hundred thousand.

Government

It is now necessary to describe the government and the general conditions of our community, to see what are its methods of education and of worship, and its relation with the outer world. This last appears entirely amicable; the community pays some quite nominal tax for its land to the general government of the country, and in return it is left almost entirely alone, since it makes its own roads and requires no services of any sort from the outside government.

It is popularly regarded with great respect: its members are considered as very good and earnest people, though unnecessarily ascetic in certain ways. Visitors from outside sometimes come in parties, just as tourists might in the twentieth century, to admire the Temples and other buildings. They are not in any way hindered, though they are not in any way encouraged. The comment of the visitors generally seems to be along the lines: "Well, it is all very beautiful and interesting, yet I should not like to have to live as they do!"

As the members have been separated from the outside world for a century and a half, old family connections have fallen into the background. In a few cases such relationships are still remembered, and occasionally visits are interchanged. There is no restriction whatever upon this; a member of the colony may go and visit a friend outside of it, or may invite a friend quite freely to come and stay with him. The only rule with regard to these matters is that intermarriage between those within the community and those outside is strictly forbidden. Even such visits as have been described are infrequent, for the whole thought of the community is so entirely one-pointed that persons from the outside world are not likely to find its daily life interesting to them.

THE SPIRIT OF THE NEW RACE

For the one great dominant fact about this community is the spirit which pervades it. Every member of it knows that he is there for a definite purpose, of which he never for a moment loses sight. All have vowed themselves to the service of the Manu for the promotion of the progress of the new Race. All of them definitely mean business; every man has the fullest possible confidence in the wisdom of the Manu, and would never dream of disputing any regulation which He made. We must remember that these people are a selection of a selection. During the intervening centuries many thousands have been attracted by Theosophy, and out of these the most earnest and the most thoroughly permeated by these ideas have been chosen. Most of them have recently taken a number of rapid incarnations, bringing through to a large extent their memory, and in all of those incarnations they have known that their lives in the new Race would have to be entirely lives of self-sacrifice for the sake of that Race. They have therefore trained themselves in the putting aside of all personal desires, and there is consequently an exceedingly strong public opinion among them in favour of unselfishness, so that anything like even the slightest manifestation of personality would be considered as a shame and a disgrace.

The idea is strongly engrained that in this selection a glorious opportunity has been offered to them, and that to prove themselves unworthy of it, and in consequence to leave the community for the outer world, would be an indelible stain upon their honour. In addition, the praise of the Manu goes to those who make advancement, who can suggest anything new and useful and assist in the development of the community, and not to anyone who does anything in the least personal. The existence among them of this great force of public opinion practically obviates the necessity of laws in the ordinary sense of the word. The whole community may not inaptly be compared to an army going into battle; if there are any private differences between individual soldiers, for the moment all these are lost in the one thought of perfect co-operation for the purpose of defeating the enemy. If any sort of difference of opinion arises between two members of the community, it is immediately submitted either to the Manu, or to the nearest member of His Council, and no one thinks of disputing the decision which is given.

The Manu and His Council

It will be seen therefore that government in the ordinary sense of the term scarcely exists in this community. The Manu's ruling is undisputed, and He gathers round Him a Council of about a dozen of the most highly developed of His pupils, some of them already Adepts at the Asekha level, who are also the Heads of departments in the management of affairs, and are constantly making new experiments with a view to increasing the welfare and efficiency of the Race. All members of the Council are sufficiently developed to function freely on all the lower planes, at least up to the level of the causal body; consequently we may think of them as practically in perpetual session—as constantly consulting, even in the very act of administration.

Anything in the nature either of courts of law or a police force does not exist, nor are such things required; for there is naturally no criminality nor violence amongst a body of people so entirely devoted to one object. Clearly, if it were conceivable that any member of the community could offend against the spirit of it, the only punishment which would or could be meted out to him would be expulsion from it; but as that would be to him the end of all his hopes, the utter failure of aspirations cherished through many lives, it is not to be supposed that anyone would run the slightest risk of it.

In thinking of the general temper of the people it must also be borne in mind that some degree of psychical perception is practically universal, and that in the case of many it is already quite highly developed; so that all can see for themselves something of the working of the forces with which they have to deal, and the enormously greater advancement of the Manu, the Chief Priest and Their Council is obvious as a definite and indubitable fact, so that all have before their eyes the strongest of reasons for accepting their decisions. In ordinary physical life, even when men have perfect confidence in the wisdom and good-will of a ruler, there still remains the doubt that that ruler may be misinformed on certain points, and that for that reason his decisions may not always be in accordance with abstract justice. Here, however, no shadow of such a doubt is possible, since by daily experience it is thoroughly well-known that the Manu is practically omniscient as far as the community is concerned, and that it is therefore impossible that any circumstances can escape His observation. Even if His judgment upon any case should be different from what was expected, it would be fully understood by His people that that was not because any circumstances affecting it were unknown to Him, but rather because He was taking into account circumstances unknown to *them*.

Thus we see that the two types of people which are perpetually causing trouble in ordinary life do not exist in this community—those who intentionally break laws with the object of gaining something for themselves, and those others who cause disturbance because they fancy themselves wronged or misunderstood. The first class cannot exist here, because only those are admitted to the community who leave self behind and entirely devote themselves to its good; the second class cannot exist here because it is clear to all of them that misunderstanding or injustice is an impossibility. Under conditions such as these the problem of government becomes an easy one.

CHAPTER XXIV

RELIGION AND THE TEMPLES

THIS practical absence of all regulations gives to the whole place an air of remarkable freedom, although at the same time the atmosphere of one-pointedness impresses itself upon us very forcibly. Men are of many different types, and are moving along lines of development through intellect, devotion and action; but all alike recognise that the Manu knows thoroughly well what He is doing, and that all these different ways are only so many methods of serving Him—that whatever development comes to one comes to him not for himself, but for the Race, that it may be handed on to his children. There are no longer different religions in our sense of the word, though the one teaching is given in different typical forms. The subject of religious worship is, however, of such great importance that we will now devote a special section to its consideration, following this up with the new methods of education, and the particulars of the personal, social and corporate life of the community.

THEOSOPHY IN THE COMMUNITY

Since the two Masters who founded the Theosophical Society are also the leaders of this community, it is quite natural that the religious opinion current there should be what we now call Theosophy. All that we now hold—all that is known in the innermost circles of our Esoteric Section—is the common faith of the community, and many points on which as yet our own knowledge is only rudimentary are thoroughly grasped and understood in detail. The outline of our Theosophy is no longer a matter of discussion but of certainty, and the facts of the life after death and the existence and nature of the higher worlds are matters of experimental knowledge for nearly all members of the colony. Here, as in our own time, different branches of the study attract different people; some think chiefly of the higher philosophy and metaphysics, while the majority prefer to express their religious feelings along some of the lines provided for them in the different Temples. A strong vein of practicality runs through all their thinking, and we should not go far wrong in saying that the religion of this community is to do what it is told. There is no sort of divorcement between science and religion, because both alike are bent entirely to the one object, and exist only for the sake of the State. Men no longer worship various manifestations, since all possess accurate knowledge as to the existence of the Solar Deity. It is still the custom with many to make a salutation to the Sun as he rises, but all are fully aware that he is to be regarded as a centre in the body of the Deity.

THE ḌEVAS

One prominent feature of the religious life is the extent to which the Ḍevas take part in it. Many religions of the twentieth century spoke of a Golden Age in the past in which Angels or Deities walked freely among men, but this happy state of things had then ceased because of the grossness of that stage of evolution. As regards our community this has again been realised, for great Ḍevas habitually come among the people and bring to them many new possibilities of development, each drawing to himself those cognate to his own nature. This should not surprise us, for even in the twentieth century much help was being given by Ḍevas to those who were able to receive it. Such opportunities of learning, such avenues of advancement, were not then open to the majority, but this was not because of the unwillingness of the Ḍevas, but because of man's backwardness in evolution. We were then much in the position of children in a primary class in this world-school. The great professors from the universities sometimes came to our school to instruct the advanced students, and we sometimes saw them pass at a distance; but their ministrations were as yet of no direct use to us simply because we were not at the age or state of development at which we could make any use of them. The classes were being held. The teachers were there, quite at our disposal as soon as we grew old enough. Our community has grown old enough, and therefore it is reaping the benefit of constant intercourse with these great beings and of frequent instruction from them.

THE TEMPLE SERVICES

These Ḍevas are not merely making sporadic appearances, but are definitely working as part of the regular organisation under the direction of the Chief Priest, who takes entire control of the religious development of the community, and of its educational department. For the outward expression of this religion we find that various classes of Temple services are provided, and that the management of these is the especial function of the Ḍevas. Four types of these Temples were observed, and though the outline and objects of the services were the same in all, there were striking differences in form and method, which we shall now endeavour to describe.

The key-note of the Temple service is that each man, belonging as he does to a particular type, has some one avenue through which he can most easily reach the Divine, and therefore be most easily reached in turn by divine influence. In some men that channel is affection, in others devotion, in others sympathy, in yet others intellect. For these four kinds of Temples exist, and in each of them the object is to bring the prominent quality in the man into active and conscious relationship with the corresponding quality in the LOGOS, of which it is a manifestation, for in that way the man himself can most easily be uplifted and helped. Thereby he can be raised for a time to a level of spirituality and power far beyond anything that is normally possible for him; and every such effort of spiritual elevation makes the next similar effort easier for him, and also raises slightly his normal level. Every service which a man attends is intended to have a definite and calculated effect upon him, and the services for a year or series of years are carefully ordered with a view to the average development of the congregation, and with the idea of carrying its members upward to a certain point. It is in this work that the co-operation of the Ḍeva is so valuable, since he acts as a true priest and intermediary between the people and the LOGOS, receiving, gathering together and forwarding their streams of aspirational force, and distributing, applying and bringing down to their level the floods of divine influence which come as a response from on high.

THE CRIMSON TEMPLE

The first Temple entered for the purposes of examination was one of those which the Ḍeva originally showed in his pictures—one of those where progress is principally made through affection, a great characteristic of the services of which is the splendid flood of colour which accompanies them, and is in fact their principal expression. Imagine a magnificent circular building somewhat resembling a cathedral, yet of no order of architecture at present known to us, and much more open to the outer air than it is possible for any cathedral to be in ordinary European climates. Imagine it filled with a reverent congregation, and the Ḍeva-priest standing in the centre before them, on the apex of a kind of pyramidal or conical erection of filigree work, so that he is equally visible from every part of the great building.

It is noteworthy that every worshipper as he enters takes his seat on the pavement quietly and reverently, and then closes his eyes and passes before his mental vision a succession of sheets or clouds of colour, such as sometimes pass before one's eyes in the darkness just before falling asleep. Each person has an order of his own for these colours, and they are evidently to some extent a personal expression of him. This seems to be of the nature of the preliminary prayer on entering a church of the twentieth century, and is intended to calm the man, to collect his thoughts, if they have been wandering, and to attune him to the surrounding atmosphere and the purpose which it subserves. When the service commences the Ḍeva materialises on the apex of his pyramid, assuming for the occasion a magnificent and glorified human form, and wearing in these particular Temples flowing vestments of rich crimson (the colour varies with the type of Temple, as will presently be seen).

His first action is to cause a flashing-out above his head of a band of brilliant colours somewhat resembling a solar spectrum, save that on different occasions the colours are in different order and vary in their proportions. It is practically impossible to describe this band of colours with accuracy, for it is much more than a mere spectrum: it is a picture, yet not a picture; it has within it geometrical forms, yet we have at present no means by which it can be drawn or represented, for it is in more dimensions than are known to our senses as they are now constituted. This band is the keynote or text of that particular service, indicating to those who understand it the exact object which it is intended to attain, and the direction in which their affection and aspiration must be outpoured. It is a thought expressed in the colour-language of the Ḍevas, and is intelligible as such to all the congregation. It is materially visible on the physical plane, as well as on the astral and mental, for although the majority of the congregation are likely to possess at least astral sight, there may still be some for whom such sight is only occasional.

Each person present now attempts to imitate this text or key-note, forming by the power of his will in the air in front of himself a smaller band of colours as nearly like it as he can. Some succeed far better than others, so that each such attempt expresses not only the subject indicated by the Ḍeva but also the character of the man who makes it. Some are able to make this so definitely that it is visible on the physical plane, while others can make it only at astral and mental levels. Some of those who produce the most brilliant and successful imitations of the form made by the Ḍeva do not bring it down to the physical plane.

The Ḍeva, holding out his arms over the people, now pours out through this colour-form a wonderful stream of influence upon them—a stream which reaches them through their own corresponding colour-forms and uplifts them precisely in the proportion in which they have been successful in making their colour-forms resemble that of the Ḍeva. The influence is not that of the Ḍeva-priest alone, for above and altogether beyond him, and apart from the Temple or the material world, stands a ring of higher Devas for whose forces he acts as a channel. The astral effect of the outpouring is remarkable. A sea of pale crimson light suffuses the vast aura of the Ḍeva and spreads out in great waves over the congregation, thus acting upon them and stirring their emotions into greater activity. Each of them shoots up into the rose-coloured sea his own particular form, but beautiful though that is, it is naturally of a lower order than that of the Ḍeva, individually coarser and less brilliant than the totality of brilliancy in which it flashes forth, and so we have a curious and beautiful effect of deep crimson flames piercing a rose-coloured sea—as one might imagine volcanic flames shooting up in front of a gorgeous sunset.

To understand to some extent how this activity of sympathetic vibration is brought about we must realise that the aura of a Ḍeva is far more extensive than that of a human being, and it is also far more flexible. The feeling which in an ordinary man expresses itself in a smile of greeting, in a Ḍeva causes a sudden expansion and brightening of the aura, and manifests not only in colour but also in musical sound. A greeting from one Ḍeva to another is a splendid chord of music, or rather an arpeggio; a conversation between two Ḍevas is like a fugue; an oration delivered by one of them is a splendid oratorio. A Rūpaḍeva of ordinary development has frequently an aura of many hundred yards in diameter, and when anything interests him or excites his enthusiasm it instantly increases enormously.

Our Ḍeva-priest therefore is including the whole of his congregation within his aura, and is consequently able to act upon them in a most intimate manner—from within as well as from without. Our readers may perhaps picture to themselves this aura, if they recollect that of the Arhaṭ in *Man Visible and Invisible*; but they must think of it as less fixed and more fluidic, more fiery and sparkling —as consisting almost entirely of pulsating fiery rays, which yet give much the same general effect of arrangement of colour. It is as though those spheres of colour remain, but are formed of fiery rays which are ever flowing outward, yet as they pass through each section of the radius they take upon themselves its colour.

THE LINKS WITH THE LOGOS

This first outpouring of influence upon the people has the effect of bringing each person up to his highest level, and evoking from him the noblest affection of which he is capable. When the Ḍeva sees that all are tuned to the proper key, he reverses the current of his force, he concentrates and defines his aura into a smaller spherical form, out of the top of which rises a huge column reaching upwards. Instead of extending his arms over the people he raises them above his head, and at that signal every man in the congregation sends towards the Ḍeva-priest the utmost wealth of his affection and aspiration—pours himself out in worship and love at the feet of the Deity. The Ḍeva draws all those fiery streams into himself, and pours them upward in one vast fountain of many-coloured flame, which expands as it rises and is caught by the circle of waiting Ḍevas, who pass it through themselves and, transmuting it, converge it, like rays refracted through a lens, until it reaches the great chief Ḍeva of their Ray, the mighty potentate who looks upon the very LOGOS Himself, and represents that Ray in relation to Him.

That great Chieftain is collecting similar streams from all parts of his world, and he weaves these many streams into one great rope which binds the earth to the Feet of its GOD; he combines these many streams into the one great river which flows around those Feet, and brings our petal of the lotus close to the heart of the flower. And He answers. In the light of the LOGOS Himself shines forth for a moment a yet greater brilliancy; back to the great Ḍeva Chieftain flashes that instant recognition; through him on the waiting ring below flows down that flood of power; and as through them it touches the Ḍeva-priest expectant on his pinnacle, once more he lowers his arms and spreads them out above his people in benediction. A flood of colours gorgeous beyond all description fills the whole vast cathedral; torrents as of liquid fire, yet delicate as the hues of an Egyptian sunset, are bathing every one in their effulgence; and out of all this glory each one takes to himself that which he is able to take, that which the stage of his development enables him to assimilate.

All the vehicles of each man present are vivified into their highest activity by this stupendous down-rush of divine power, and for the moment each realises to his fullest capacity what the life of God really means, and how in each it must express itself as love for his fellow-man. This is a far fuller and more personal benediction than that poured out at the beginning of the service, for here is something exactly fitted to each man, strengthening him in his weakness and yet at the same time developing to its highest possibility all that is best in him, giving him not only a tremendous and transcendent experience at the time, but also a memory which shall be for him as a radiant and glowing light for many a day to come. This is the daily service—the daily religious practice of those who belong to this Ray of affection.

Nor does the good influence of this service affect only those who are present; its radiations extend over a large district, and purify the astral and mental atmospheres. The effect is distinctly perceptible to any moderately sensitive person even two or three miles from the Temple. Each such service also sends out a huge eruption of rose-coloured thought-forms which bombard the surrounding country with thoughts of love, so that the whole atmosphere is full of it. In the Temple itself a vast crimson vortex is set up which is largely permanent, so that anyone entering the Temple immediately feels its influence, and this also keeps up a steady radiation upon the surrounding district. In addition to this each man as he goes home from the service is himself a centre of force of no mean order, and when he reaches his home the radiations which pour from him are strongly perceptible to any neighbours who have not been able to attend the service.

THE SERMON

Sometimes, in addition to this, or perhaps as a service apart from this, the Ḍeva delivers what may be described as a kind of colour-sermon, taking up that colour-form which we have mentioned as the key-note or text for the day, explaining it to his people by an unfolding process, and mostly without spoken words, and perhaps causing it to pass through a series of mutations intended to convey to them instruction of various kinds. One exceedingly vivid and striking colour-sermon of this nature was intended to show the effect of love upon the various qualities in others with which it comes into contact. The black clouds of malice, the scarlet of anger, the dirty green of deceit, or the hard brown-grey of selfishness, the brownish-green of jealousy, and the heavy dull-grey of depression, were all in turn subjected to the glowing crimson fire of love. The stages through which they pass were shown, and it was made clear that in the end none of them could resist its force, and all of them at last melted into it and were consumed.

INCENSE

Though colour is in every way the principal feature in this service which we have described, the Ḍeva does not disdain to avail himself of the channels of other senses than that of sight. All through his service, and even before it began, incense has been kept burning in swinging censers underneath his golden pyramid, where stand two boys to attend to it. The kind of incense burnt varies with the different parts of the service. The people are far more sensitive to perfumes than we of earlier centuries; they are able to distinguish accurately all the different kinds of incense, and they know exactly what each kind means and for what purpose it is used. The number of pleasant odours available in this way is much larger than that of those previously in use, and they have discovered some method of making them more volatile, so that they penetrate instantly through every part of the building. This acts upon the etheric body somewhat as the colours do upon the astral, and bears its part in bringing all the vehicles of the man rapidly into harmony. These people possess a good deal of new information as to the effect of odours upon certain parts of the brain, as we shall see more fully when we come to deal with the educational processes.

Sound

Naturally every change of colour is accompanied by its appropriate sound, and though this is a subordinate feature in the colour-temple which we have described, it is yet by no means without its effect. We shall now, however, attempt to describe a somewhat similar service in a Temple where music is the predominant feature, and colour comes only to assist its effect, precisely as sound has assisted colour in the Temple of affection. In common parlance, these Temples in which progress is made principally by the development of affection are called 'crimson Temples'—first because everyone knows that crimson is the colour in the aura which indicates affection, and therefore that is the prevailing colour of all the splendid outpourings which take place in it; and secondly, because in recognition of the same fact all the graceful lines of the architecture are indicated by lines of crimson, and there are even some Temples entirely of that hue. The majority of these Temples are built of a stone of a beautiful pale grey with a polished surface much like that of marble, and when this is the case only the external decorations are of the colour which indicates the nature of the services performed within. Sometimes, however, the Temples of affection are built entirely of stone of a lovely pale rose-colour, which stands out with marvellous beauty against the vivid green of the trees with which they are always surrounded. The Temples in which music is the dominant factor are similarly known as 'blue Temples,' because since their principal object is the arousing of the highest possible devotion, blue is the colour most prominent in connection with their services, and consequently the colour adopted for both exterior and interior decoration.

The Blue Temple

The general outline of the services in one of the blue Temples closely resembles that which we have already described, except that in their case sound takes the place of colour as the principal agent. Just as the endeavour in the colour-Temple was to stimulate the love in man by bringing it consciously into relation with the divine love, so in this Temple the object is to promote the evolution of the man through the quality of devotion, which by the use of music is enormously uplifted and intensified and brought into direct relation with the LOGOS who is its object. Just as in the crimson Temple there exists a permanent vortex of the highest and noblest affection, so in this music-Temple there exists a similar atmosphere of unselfish devotion which instantly affects everyone who enters it.

Into this atmosphere come the members of the congregation, each bringing in his hand a curious musical instrument, unlike any formerly known on earth. It is not a violin; it is perhaps rather of the nature of a small circular harp with strings of some shining metal. But this strange instrument has many remarkable properties. It is in fact much more than a mere instrument; it is specially magnetised for its owner, and no other person must use it. It is tuned to the owner; it is an expression of the owner—a funnel through which he can be reached on this physical plane. He plays upon it, and yet at the same time he himself is played upon in doing so. He gives out and receives vibrations through it.

THE DEVOTIONAL SERVICE

When the worshipper enters the Temple, he calls up before his mind a succession of beautiful sounds—a piece of music which fulfils for him the same office as the series of colours which pass before the eyes of the man in the colour-Temple at the same stage of the proceedings. When the Ḍeva materialises he also takes up an instrument of similar nature, and he commences the service by striking upon it a chord (or rather an arpeggio) which fulfils the function of the keynote in colour which is used in the other Temple. The effect of this chord is most striking. His instrument is but a small one and apparently of no great power, though wonderfully sweet in tone: but as he strikes it, the chord seems to be taken up in the air around him as though it were repeated by a thousand invisible musicians, so that it resounds through the great dome of the Temple and pours out in a flood of harmony, a sea of rushing sound, over the entire congregation. Each member of the congregation now touches his own instrument, and very softly at first, but gradually swelling out into a greater volume, until everyone is taking part in this wonderful symphony. Thus, as in the colour-Temple, every member is brought into harmony with the principal idea which the Ḍeva wishes to emphasise at this service, and in this case, as in the other, a benediction is poured over the people which raises each to the highest level possible for him, and draws from him an eager response which shows itself both in sound and in colour.

Here also incense is being used, and it varies at different points of the service, much as in the other case. Then when the congregation is thoroughly tuned, each man begins definitely to play. All are clearly taking recognised parts, although it does not seem that this has been arranged or rehearsed beforehand. As soon as this stage is in full operation the Ḍeva-priest draws in his aura, and begins to pour his sound inwards instead of out over the people. Each man is putting his very life into his playing, and definitely aiming at the Ḍeva, so that through him it may rise. The effect on the higher emotions of the people is most remarkable, and the living aspiration and devotion of the congregation is poured upwards in a mighty stream through the officiating Ḍeva to a great circle of Ḍevas above, who, as before, draw it into themselves, transmuting it to an altogether higher level, and send it forward in a still mightier stream towards the great Ḍeva at the head of their Ray. Upon him converge thousands of such streams from all the devotion of the earth, and he in his turn gathers all these together and weaves them into one, which, as he sends it upwards, links him with the solar LOGOS Himself.

In it he is bearing his share in a concert which comes from all the worlds of the system, and these streams from all the worlds make somehow the mighty twelve-stringed lyre upon which the LOGOS Himself plays as He sits upon the Lotus of His system. It is impossible to put this into words; but the writer has seen it, and knows that it is true. He hears, He responds, and He Himself plays upon His system. Thus for the first time we have one brief glimpse of the stupendous life which He lives among the other LOGOI who are His peers; but thought fails before this glory; our minds are inadequate to comprehend it. At least it is clear that the great music-Devas, taken in their totality, represent music to the LOGOS, and He expresses Himself through them in music to His worlds.

THE BENEDICTION

Then comes the response—a downpouring flood of ordered sound too tremendous to be described, flowing back through the Chieftain of the Ray to the circle of Ḍevas below, and from them to the Ḍeva-priest in the Temple, transmuted at each stage to lower levels, so that at last it pours out through the officiant in the Temple in a form in which it may be assimilated by his congregation—a great ocean of soft, sweet, swelling sound, an outburst of celestial music which surrounds, enwraps, overwhelms them, and yet pours into them through their own instruments vibrations so living, so uplifting, that their higher bodies are brought into action and their consciousness is raised to levels which in their outer life it could not even approach. Each man holds out his instrument in front of him, and it is through that that this marvellous effect is produced upon him. It seems as though from the great symphony each instrument selected the chords appropriate to itself—that is to say, to the owner whose expression it is. Yet each harp somehow not only selects and responds, but also calls into existence far more than its own volume of sound.

The whole atmosphere is surcharged by the Ganḍharvas, or music-Ḍevas, so that veritably every sound is multiplied, and for every single tone is produced a great chord of overtones and undertones, all of unearthly sweetness and beauty. This benedictory response from on high is an utterly amazing experience, but words completely fail when we endeavour to find expression for it. It must be seen and heard and felt before it can in any way be understood.

This magnificent final swell goes sounding home with the people, as it were; it lives inside them still even though the service is over, and often the member will try to reproduce it in a minor degree in a kind of little private service at home. In this Temple also there may be what corresponds to a sermon, but in this case it is delivered by the Ḍeva through his instrument and received by the people through theirs. It is clear that it is not the same to all—that some get more and some less of the meaning of the Ḍeva and of the effect which he intends to produce.

INTELLECT

All the effects which are produced in the crimson Temple through affection by the gorgeous seas of colour are attained here through devotion by this marvellous use of music. It is clear that in both cases the action is primarily on the intuitional and emotional bodies of the people—on the intuitional directly, in those who have developed it to the responsive stage, and on the intuitional through the emotional for others who are somewhat less advanced. The intellect is touched only by reflection from these planes, whereas in the next variety of Temple to be described this action is reversed, for the stimulation is brought to bear directly upon the intellect, and it is only through and by means of that that the intuitional is presently to be awakened. Eventual results are no doubt the same, but the order of procedure is different.

THE YELLOW TEMPLE

If we think of the men of the crimson Temple as developing through colour, and those of the blue as utilising sound, we might perhaps put form as the vehicle principally employed in the yellow Temple—for naturally yellow is the colour of the Temple especially devoted to intellectual development, since it is in that way that it symbolises itself in the various vehicles of man.

Once more the architecture and the internal structure of the Temple are the same, except that all decorations and outlinings are in yellow instead of blue or crimson. The general scheme of the service, too, is identical—the text or key-note first, which brings all into union, then the aspiration or prayer or effort of the people, which calls down the response from the LOGOS. The form of instruction which, for want of a better name, I have called the sermon also has its part in all the services. All alike use incense, though the difference between the kind used in this yellow Temple and that of the blue and the crimson is noticeable. The vortex in this case stimulates intellectual activity, so that merely to enter the Temple makes a man feel more keenly alive mentally, better able to understand and to appreciate.

These people do not bring with them any physical instruments, and instead of passing before their eyes a succession of clouds of colour, they begin, as soon as they take their seats, to visualise certain mental forms. Each man has his own form, which is clearly intended to be an expression of himself, just as was the physical instrument of the musician, or the special colour-scheme of the worshipper in the Temple of affection. These forms are all different, and many of them distinctly imply the power to visualise in the physical brain some of the simpler four-dimensional figures. Naturally the power of visualisation differs; so some people are able to make their figures much more complete and definite than others. But, curiously, the indefiniteness seems to show itself at both ends of the scale. The less educated of the thinkers—those who are as yet only learning how to think—often make forms which are not clearly cut, or even if at first they are able to make them clear they are not able to maintain them so, and they constantly slip into indefiniteness. They do not actually materialise them, but they do form them strongly in mental matter, and almost all of them, even at quite an early stage, seem to be able to do this. The forms are evidently at first prescribed for them, and they are told to hold them rather as a means than as an object of contemplation. They are clearly intended to be each an expression of its creator, whose further progress will involve modifications of the form, though these do not change it essentially. He is intended to think through it and to receive vibrations through it, just as the musical man received them through his instrument, or the member of the colour congregation through his colour-form. With the more intelligent persons the form becomes more definite and more complicated; but with some of the most definite of all it is again taking on an appearance suggesting indefiniteness, because it is beginning to be so much upon a still higher plane—because it is taking on more and more of the dimensions, and is becoming so living that it cannot be kept still.

The Intellectual Stimulus

When the Ḍeva appears he also makes a form—not a form which is an expression of himself, but, as in the other Temples, one which is to be the keynote of the service, which defines the special object at which on this occasion he is aiming. His congregation then project themselves into their forms, and try through those to respond to his form and to understand it. Sometimes it is a changing form—one which unfolds or unveils itself in a number of successive movements. Along with the formation of this, and through it, the Ḍeva-priest pours out upon them a great flood of yellow light which applies intense stimulus to their intellectual faculties along the particular line which he is indicating. He is acting strongly upon both their causal and mental bodies, but very little comparatively on the emotional or the intuitional. Some who have not normally the consciousness of the mental body have it awakened in them by this process, so that for the first time they can use it quite freely and see clearly by its means. In others, who have it not normally, it awakens the power of four-dimensional sight for the first time; in others less advanced it only makes them see things a little more clearly, and comprehend temporarily ideas which are usually too metaphysical for them.

INTELLECTUAL FEELING

The mental effort is not entirely unaccompanied by feeling, for there is at least an intense delight in reaching upwards, though even that very delight is felt almost exclusively through the mental body. They all pour their thoughts through their forms into the Ḍeva-priest, as before, and they offer up these individual contributions as a kind of sacrifice to the LOGOS of the best that they have to give. Into him and through him they give themselves in surrender to the burning Light above; they merge themselves, throw themselves, into him. It is the white heat of intellectuality raised to its highest power. As in the other Temples, the Ḍeva-priest synthesises all the different forms which are sent to him, and blends together all the streams of force, before forwarding it to the circle above him, which this time consists of that special class which for the present we will call the yellow Ḍevas—those who are developing intellect, and revel in assisting and guiding it in man.

As before, they absorb the force, but only to send it out again at a higher level and enormously increased in quantity to the great Chieftain who is the head of their Ray, and a kind of centre for the exchange of forces. The intellect aspect of the LOGOS plays upon him and through him from above, while all human intellect reaches up to him and through him from below. He receives and forwards the contribution from the Temple, and in turn he opens the flood-gates of divine intelligence which, lowered through many stages on the way, pours out upon the waiting people and raises them out of their every-day selves into what they will be in the future. The temporary effect of such a down-pouring is almost incalculable. All egos present are brought into vigorous activity, and the consciousness in the causal body is brought into action in all of those in whom it is as yet in any way possible. In others it means merely greatly increased mental activity; some are so lifted out of themselves that they actually leave the body, and others pass into a kind of Samāḍhi, because the consciousness is drawn up into a vehicle which is not yet sufficiently developed to be able to express it.

The response from above is not merely a stimulation. It contains also a vast mass of forms —it would seem all possible forms along whatever is the special line of the day. These forms also are assimilated by such of the congregation as can utilise them, and it is noteworthy that the same form means much more to some people than to others. For example, a form which conveys some interesting detail of physical evolution to one man may to another represent a whole vast stage of cosmic development. For many people it is as though they were seeing in visible form the Stanzas of Dzyān. All are trying to think on the same line, yet they do it in different ways, and consequently they attract to themselves different forms out of the vast ordered system which is at their disposal. Each man draws out of this multitude that which is most suited to him. Some people, for example, are simply getting new lights on the subject, substituting for their own thought-form another which is in reality in no way superior to it, but simply another side of the question.

Men are evidently raised into the intuitional consciousness along these lines. By intense thinking, by comprehension of the converging streams, they attain first an intellectual grasp of the constitution of the universe, and then by intense pressure upwards they realise it and break through. It usually comes with a rush and almost overwhelms the man—all the more so as along his line he has had little practice before in understanding the feelings of humanity. From his intellectual point of view he has been philosophically examining and dissecting people, as though they were plants under a microscope; and now, in a moment, it is borne in upon him that all these also are divine as himself, that all these are full of their own feelings and emotions, understandings and misunderstandings, that these are more than brothers, since they are actually within himself and not without. This is a great shock for the man to whom it comes, and he needs time to readjust himself and to develop some other qualities which he has been hitherto to some extent neglecting. The service ends much as the others did, and each man's mental form is permanently somewhat the better for the exercise through which he has passed.

MENTAL MAGIC

Here also we have the form of instruction which we have called the sermon, and in this case it is usually an exposition of the changes which take place in a certain form or set of forms. In this case the Ḍeva occasionally makes use of spoken words, though only few of them. It is as though he were showing them changing magic-lantern pictures, and naming them as they pass before them. He materialises strongly and clearly the special thought-form which he is showing them, and each member of the congregation tries to copy it in his own mental matter. In one case which is observed, that which is described is the transference of forms from plane to plane—a kind of mental magic which shows how one thought can be changed into another. On the lower mental plane he shows how a selfish thought may become unselfish. None of his people are crudely selfish, or they would not be in the community; but there may still remain subtle forms of self-centred thought. There is a certain danger also of intellectual pride, and it is shown how this can be transmuted into worship of the wisdom of the LOGOS.

In other cases most interesting metamorphoses are shown—forms changing into one another by turning inside out like a glove. In this way, for example, a dodecahedron becomes an icosahedron. Not only are these changes shown, but also their inner meaning on all the different planes is explained, and here also it is interesting to see the unfoldment of the successive esoteric meanings and to notice how some members of the congregation stop at one of these, feeling it to the highest possible degree, and well satisfied with themselves for being able to see it, while others go on one, two or more stages beyond them, further into the real heart of the meaning. What is applied only as a transmutation of their own thoughts by the majority of the congregation may be to the few who have gone further a translation of cosmic force from one plane to another. Such a sermon is a veritable training in mental intensity and activity, and it needs a closely sustained attention to follow it.

In all these Temples alike a great point is made of the training of the will which is necessary in order to keep the attention focused upon all the different parts of their variations in the pictures, the music, or the thought-forms. All this is shown most prominently by the intense glow of the causal bodies, but it reacts upon the mental vehicles and even upon the physical brain, which appears on the whole to be distinctly larger among these pioneers of the Sixth Root Race than with men of the fifth. It used to be thought by many that much study and intellectual development tended greatly to atrophy or destroy the power of visualisation, but that is not at all the case with the devotees of the yellow Temple. Perhaps the difference may be that in the old days study was so largely a study of mere words, whereas in the case of all these people they have for many lives been devoting themselves also to meditation, which necessarily involves the constant practice of visualisation in a high degree.

THE GREEN TEMPLE

Yet one more type of Temple remains to be described—a type which is decorated in a lovely pale green, because the thought-forms generated in it are of precisely that colour. Of the Temples already mentioned the crimson and the blue seem to have many points in common, and a similar link seems to join the yellow and the green. One might perhaps say that the blue and the crimson correspond to two types of what in India is called Bhakṭi-yoga; in that case the yellow Temple might be thought of as offering us the Jñāna-yoga, and the green Temple the Karma-yoga; or in English we might characterise them as the Temples of affection, devotion, intellect and action respectively. The congregation of the green Temple works also chiefly on the mental plane, but its particular line is the translating of thought into action—to get things done. It is part of its regular service to send out intentionally arranged thought-currents, primarily towards its own community, but also through them to the world at large. In the other Temples too they think of the outside world, for they include it in their thoughts of love and devotion or treat it intellectually; but the idea of these people of the green Temple is action with regard to everything, and they consider that they have not surely grasped an idea until they have translated it into action.

The people of the yellow Temple, on the other hand, take the same idea quite differently, and consider it perfectly possible to have the fullest comprehension without action. But the devotees of this green Temple cannot feel that they are really fulfilling their place in the world unless they are constantly in active motion. A thought-form to them is not an effective thought-form unless it contains some of their typical green—because, as they say, it is lacking in sympathy—so that all their forces express themselves in action, action, action, and in action is their happiness, and through the self-sacrifice in the action they attain.

They have powerful and concentrated plans in their minds, and in some cases it is noticed that many of them combine to think out one plan and to get the thing done. They are careful to accumulate much knowledge about whatever subject they take up as a speciality. Often each one takes some area in the world into which he pours his thought-forms for a certain object. One, for example, will take up education in Greenland, or social reform in Kamchatka. They are naturally dealing with all sorts of out-of-the-way places like these, because by this time everything conceivable has already been done in every place of which we have ever heard in ordinary life. They do not use hypnotism, however; they do not in any way try to dominate the will of any man whom they wish to help; they simply try to impress their ideas and improvements on his brain.

THE LINE OF THE HEALING-DEVAS

Once more, the general scheme of their service is like that of the others. They do not bring with them any physical instruments, but they have their mental forms just as the intellectual people have, only in this case they are always plans of activity. Each has some special plan to which he is devoting himself, though at the same time through it he is devoting himself to the LOGOS. They hold their plans and the realisation of them before them, just in the same way as the other men do their thought- or colour-forms. It is noteworthy that these plans are always carried to a great height of conception. For example, a man's plan for the organisation of a backward country would include and be mainly centred in the idea of the mental and moral uplifting of its inhabitants. These devotees of the green Temple are not actually philanthropical in the old sense of the word, though their hearts are filled with sympathy with their fellow-men which expresses itself in the most beautiful shade of their characteristic colour. Indeed, from what glimpses have been caught of the outer world it seems evident that ordinary philanthropy is quite unnecessary, because poverty has disappeared. Their schemes are all plans for helping people, or for the improvement of conditions in some way.

Suggestions of all kinds and sorts of activity find their place here, and they appeal to the active or healing-Ḍevas, the type identified by Christian Mystics with the hierarchy of the Archangel Raphael. Their Ḍeva-priest puts before them as his text, or as the dominant idea of the service, something which will be an aspect of all their ideas and will strengthen every one of them. They try to present clearly their several schemes, and through that they gain development for themselves in trying to sympathise with and help other people. After the preliminary tuning up and the opening benediction, there comes once more the offering of their plans. The opening benediction may be thought of as bringing the sympathy of the Ḍevas for all their schemes and the identification of the Ḍeva-priest with each and all of them.

When the time of aspiration comes, each offers his plan as something of his own which he has to give, as his contribution, as the fruit of his brain, which he lays before the Lord, and also he has the thought that thus he throws himself and his life into his schemes as a sacrifice for the sake of the LOGOS. Once more we get the same magnificent effect, the splendid sheet and fountains, the great glowing sea of pale luminous sunset green, and among it the flames of darker green shooting up from the sympathetic thought of each member present. Just as before, all this is gathered into a focus by the Ḍeva-priest, is sent up by him to a circle of healing-Ḍevas above, and through them to the Chieftain of their Ray, who once more presents this aspect of the world to the LOGOS.

When they thus offer themselves and their thoughts, there comes back the great flow of response, the outpouring of good-will and of blessing, which in turn illuminates the sacrifice which they have offered through the line to which each has directed himself. The great Ḍevas seem to magnetise the man and increase his power along this and cognate lines, raising it to higher levels, even while they increase it. The response not only strengthens such thoughts of good as they already have, but also opens up to them the conception of further activities for their thoughts. It is a definite act of projection, and it is done by them in a time of silent meditation after the reception of the blessing.

There are many types among these people; they bring different chakrams or centres in the mental body into activity, and their streams of thought-force are projected sometimes from one chakram and sometimes from another. In the final benediction it seems as though the LOGOS pours Himself through His Ḍevas into them, and then again out through them to the objects of their sympathy, so that an additional transmutation of the force takes place, and the culmination of their act is to be an active agent for His action. Intense sympathy is the feeling most cultivated by these people; it is their key-note, by which they gradually rise through the mental and causal bodies to the intuitional, and there find the acme of sympathy, because there the object of sympathy is no longer outside themselves, but within.

The sermon in this case is frequently an exposition of the adaptability of various types of elemental essence to the thought-force which they require. Such a sermon is illustrated as it goes on, and the thought-forms are constructed before the congregation by the Ḍeva and materialised for them, so that they may learn exactly the best way to produce them and the best materials of which to build them.

INDEPENDENTS

In the special lines of development of these Temples there seems a curious half-suggestion of the four lower sub-planes of the mental plane as they present themselves during the life after death, for it will be remembered that affection is the chief characteristic of one of these planes, devotion of another, action for the sake of the Deity of a third, and the clear conception of right for right's sake of the fourth. It is, however, quite evident that there is no difference in advancement between the egos who follow one line and those who follow another; all these paths are clearly equal, all alike are stairways leading from the level of ordinary humanity to the Path of Holiness which rises to the level of Adeptship. To one or other of these types belong the great majority of the people of the community, so that all these temples are daily filled with crowds of worshippers.

A few people there are who do not attend any of these services, simply because none of these are to them the most appropriate ways of development. There is not, however, the slightest feeling that these few are therefore irreligious or in any way inferior to the most regular attendants. It is thoroughly recognised that there are many paths to the summit of the mountain, and that each man is absolutely at liberty to take that which seems best to him. In most cases a man selects his path and keeps to it, but it would never occur to him to blame his neighbour for selecting another, or even for declining to select any one of those provided. Every man is trying his best in his own way to fit himself for the work that he will have to do in the future, as well as to carry out to the best of his ability the work at present before him. Nobody harbours the feeling: "I am in a better way than so-and-so," because he sees another doing differently. The habitual attendants of one Temple also quite often visit the others; indeed, some people try them all in turn rather according to their feeling of the moment, saying to themselves: "I think I need a touch of yellow this morning to brighten up my intellect"; or: "perhaps I am becoming too metaphysical, let me try a tonic of the green Temple"; or on the other hand: "I have been straining hard lately along intellectual lines; let me now give a turn to affection or devotion."

Congregation of the Dead

Many people also make a practice of attending the magnificent, though more elementary, services which are frequently held in the Temples, ostensibly for children; these will be described in detail when we come to the subject of education. It is interesting to observe that the peculiar nature of the Temple services of this community has evidently attracted much attention in the astral world, for large numbers of dead people make a practice of attending the services. They have discovered the participation of the Ḍevas and the tremendous forces which are consequently playing through them, and they evidently wish to partake of the advantages. This congregation of the dead is recruited exclusively from the outside world; for in the community there are no dead, since every man, when he puts aside one physical body, promptly assumes another in order to carry on the work to which he has devoted himself.

The Master of Religion

The religious and educational side of the life of the community is under the direction of the Master K. H.; and He Himself makes it a point to visit all the Temples in turn, taking the place of the officiating Ḍeva, and in doing so showing the fact that He combines within Himself in the highest possible degree all the qualities of all the types. The Ḍevas who are doing work connected with religion and education are all marshalled under His orders. Some members of the community are being specially trained by the Ḍevas, and it seems probable that such men will in due course pass on to the line of the Ḍeva evolution.

CHAPTER XXV

EDUCATION AND THE FAMILY

THE EDUCATION OF CHILDREN

AS we should naturally expect, much attention is paid in this community to the education of the children. It is considered of such paramount importance that nothing which can in any way help is neglected, and all sorts of adjuncts are brought into play; colour, light, sound, form, electricity are all pressed into the service, and the Ḍevas who take so large a part in the work avail themselves of the aid of armies of nature-spirits. It has been realised that many facts previously ignored or considered insignificant have their place and their influence in educational processes—that, for example, the surroundings most favourable for the study of mathematics are not at all necessarily the same that are best suited for music or geography.

People have learnt that different parts of the physical brain may be stimulated by different lights and colours—that for certain subjects an atmosphere slightly charged with electricity is useful, while for others it is positively detrimental. In the corner of every class-room, therefore, there stands a variant upon an electrical machine, by means of which the surrounding conditions can be changed at will. Some rooms are hung with yellow, decorated exclusively with yellow flowers, and permeated with yellow light. In others, on the contrary, blue, red, violet, green or white predominates. Various perfumes are also found to have a stimulating effect, and these also are employed according to a regular system.

Perhaps the most important innovation is the work of the nature-spirits, who take a keen delight in executing the tasks committed to them, and enjoy helping and stimulating the children much as gardeners might delight in the production of especially fine plants. Among other things they take up all the appropriate influences of light and colour, sound and electricity, and focus them, and as it were spray them upon the children, so that they may produce the best possible effect. They are also employed by the teachers in individual cases; if, for example, one scholar in a class does not understand the point put before him, a nature-spirit is at once sent to touch and stimulate a particular centre in his brain, and then in a moment he is able to comprehend. All teachers must be clairvoyant; it is an absolute prerequisite for the office. These teachers are members of the community—men and women indiscriminately; Ḍevas frequently materialise for special occasions or to give certain lessons, but never seem to take the entire responsibility of a school.

The four great types which are symbolised by the Temples are seen to exist here also. The children are carefully observed and treated according to the results of observation. In most cases they sort themselves out at a quite early period into one or other of these lines of development, and every opportunity is given to them to select that which they prefer. Here again there is nothing of the nature of compulsion. Even tiny children are perfectly acquainted with the object of the community, and fully realise that it is their duty and their privilege to order their lives accordingly. It must be remembered that all these people are immediate reincarnations, and that most of them bring over at least some memory of all their past lives, so that for them education is simply a process of as rapidly as possible getting a new set of vehicles under control and recovering as quickly as may be any links that may have been lost in the process of transition from one physical body to another.

It does not of course in any way follow that the children of a man who is on (let us say) the musical line need themselves be musical. As their previous births are always known to the parents and schoolmasters, every facility is given to them to develop either along the line of their last life or along any other which may seem to come most easily to them. There is the fullest co-operation between the parents and schoolmasters. A particular member who was noticed took his children to the schoolmaster, explained them all to him in detail, and constantly visited him to discuss what might be best for them. If, for example, the schoolmaster thinks that a certain colour is especially desirable for a particular pupil he communicates his idea to the parents, and much of that colour is put before the child at home as well as at school; he is surrounded with it, and it is used in his dress and so on. All schools are under the direction of the Master K. H., and every schoolmaster is personally responsible to Him.

TRAINING THE IMAGINATION

Let me take as an example the practice of a school attached to one of the yellow Temples, and see how they begin the intellectual development of the lowest class. First the master sets before them a little shining ball, and they are asked to make an image of it in their minds. Some who are quite babies can do it really well. The teacher says:

"You can see my face; now shut your eyes; can you see it still? Now look at this ball; can you shut your eyes and still see it?"

The teacher, by the use of his clairvoyant faculty, can see whether or not the children are making satisfactory images. Those who can do it are set to practise day by day, with all sorts of simple forms and colours. Then they are asked to suppose that point moving, and leaving a track behind it as a shooting star does; then to imagine the luminous track, that is to say, a line. Then they are asked to imagine this line as moving at right angles to itself, every point in it leaving a similar track, and thus they mentally construct for themselves a square. Then all sorts of permutations and divisions of that square are put before them. It is broken up into triangles of various sorts, and it is explained to them that in reality all these things are living symbols with a meaning. Even quite the babies are taught some of these things.

"What does the point mean to you?"

"One."

"Who is One?"

"God."

"Where is He?"

"He is everywhere."

And then presently they learn that two signifies the duality of Spirit and matter, that three dots of a certain kind and colour mean three aspects of the Deity, while three others of a different kind mean the soul in man. A later class has also an intermediate three which obviously mean the Monad. In this way, by associating grand ideas with simple objects, even tiny little children possess an amount of Theosophical information which would seem quite surprising to a person accustomed to an older and less intelligent educational system. An ingenious kind of kindergarten machine was observed, a sort of ivory ball—at least it looked like ivory—which, when a spring is touched, opens out into a cross with a rose drawn upon it like the Rosicrucian symbol, out of which come a number of small balls each of which in turn subdivides. By another movement it can be made to close again, the mechanism being cleverly concealed. This is meant as a symbol to illustrate the idea of the One becoming many, and of the eventual return of the many into the One.

More Advanced Classes

For a later class that luminous square moves again at right angles to itself and produces a cube, and then still later the cube moves at right angles to itself and produces a tesseract, and most of the children are able to see it and to make its image clearly in their minds. Children who have a genius for it are taught to paint pictures, trees and animals, landscapes and scenes from history, and each child is taught to make his picture living. He is taught that the concentration of his thought can actually alter the physical picture, and the children are proud when they can succeed in doing this. Having painted a picture as well as they can, the children concentrate upon it and try to improve it, to modify it by their thought. In a week or so, working at the concentration for some time each day, they are able to produce considerable modifications, and a boy of fourteen can, from much practice, do it quite rapidly.

Having modified his picture, the child is taught to make a thought-form of it, to look at it, to contemplate it earnestly, and then to shut his eyes and visualise it. He takes, first, ordinary physical pictures; then a glass vessel containing a coloured gas is given to him, and by the effort of his will he has to mould the gas into certain shapes—to make it take a form by thought—to make it become, inside its vessel, a sphere, a cube, a tetrahedron or some such shape. Many children can do this easily after a little practice. Then they are asked to make it take the shape of a man, and then that of the picture at which they have previously been looking. When they can manage this gaseous matter fairly easily they try to do it in etheric, then in astral, and then in purely mental matter. The teacher himself makes materialisations for them to examine when necessary, and in this way they gradually work upward to more advanced acts of thought-creation. All these classes are open to visits from parents and friends, and often many older people like to attend them and themselves practise the exercises set for the children.

THE SCHOOL SYSTEM

There is nothing in the nature of the boarding-school, and all children live happily at home and attend the school which is most convenient for them. In a few cases the Ḍeva-priests are training children to take their places; but even in these cases the child is not taken away from home, though he is usually surrounded by a special protective shell, so that the influence which the Ḍeva pours in upon him may not be interfered with by other vibrations.

A child does not belong to a class at all in the same way as under older methods; each child has a list of numbers for different subjects; he may be in the first class for one subject, in the third for another, in the fifth for some other. Even for small children the arrangement seems to be far less a class than a kind of lecture-room. In trying to comprehend the system, we must never for a moment forget the effect of the immediate reincarnations, and that consequently not only are these children on the average far more intelligent and developed than other children of their age, but also they are unequally developed. Some children of four remember more of a previous incarnation, and of what they learnt then, than other children of eight or nine; and again some children remember a certain subject fully and clearly, and yet have almost entirely lost their knowledge of some other subjects which seem quite as easy. So that we are dealing with entirely abnormal conditions, and the schemes adopted have to be suited to them.

At what corresponds to the opening of the school, they all stand together and sing something. They get four lessons into their morning session, but the lessons are short, and there is always an interval for play between them. Like all their houses, the school-room has no walls, but is supported entirely on pillars, so that practically the whole life of the children, as well as of the rest of the community, is lived in the open air; but nevertheless the children are turned out even from that apology for a room after each of the lessons, and left to play about in the park which surrounds the school. Girls and boys are taught together promiscuously. This morning session covers all of what would be called the compulsory subjects —the subjects which everybody learns; there are some extra lessons in the afternoon on additional subjects for those who wish to take them, but a considerable number of the children are satisfied with the morning work.

The Curriculum

The school curriculum is different from that of the twentieth century. The very subjects are mostly different, and even those which are the same are taught in an entirely different way. Arithmetic, for example, has been greatly simplified; there are no complex weights and measures of any kind, everything being arranged on a decimal system; they calculate but little, and the detailed working-out of long rows of figures would be denounced as insufferably tedious. Nothing is taught but what is likely to be practically useful to the average person in after-life; all the rest is a matter of reference. In earlier centuries they had books of logarithms, by reference to which long and complicated calculations could be avoided; now they have the same system immensely extended, and yet, at the same time, much more compressed. It is a scheme by which the result of practically any difficult calculation can be looked up in a few moments by a person who knows the book. The children know how to calculate, just as a man may know how to make his own logarithms, and yet habitually use a book for them to avoid the waste of time in tedious processes involving long rows of figures.

Arithmetic with them is hardly a subject in itself, but is taken only as leading up to calculations connected with the geometry which deals with solid figures and the higher dimensions. The whole thing is so different from previous ideas that it is not easy to describe it clearly. For example, in all the children's sums there is no question of money, and no complicated calculation. To understand the sum and know how to do it is sufficient. The theory in the schoolmaster's mind is not to cram the brains of the children, but to develop their faculties and tell them where to find facts. Nobody, for example, would dream of multiplying a line of six figures by another similar line, but would employ either a calculating machine (for these are common), or one of the books to which I have referred.

The whole problem of reading and writing is far simpler than it used to be, for all spelling is phonetic, and pronunciation cannot be wrong when a certain syllable must always have a certain sound. The writing has somewhat the appearance of shorthand. There is a good deal to learn in it, but at the same time, when he has learnt it, the child is in possession of a finer and more flexible instrument than any of the older languages, since he can write at least as fast as any ordinary person can speak. There is a large amount of convention about it, and a whole sentence is often expressed by a mark like a flash of lightning.

The language which they are speaking is naturally English, since the community has arisen in an English-speaking country, but it has been modified considerably. Many participial forms have disappeared, and some of the words are different. All subjects are learnt so differently now. Nobody learns any history, except isolated interesting stories, but everyone has in his house a book in which an epitome of all history can be found. Geography is still learnt to a limited extent. They know where all the different races live, and with great precision in what these races differ, and what qualities they are developing. But the commercial side has dropped; no one bothers about the exports of Bulgaria; nobody knows where they make woollen cloth, or wants to know. All these things can be turned up at a moment's notice in books which are part of the free furniture of every house, and it would be considered a waste of time to burden the memory with such valueless facts.

The scheme is in every respect strictly utilitarian; they do not teach the children anything which can be easily obtained from an encyclopædia. They have developed a scheme of restricting education to necessary and valuable knowledge. A boy of twelve usually has behind him, in his physical brain, the entire memory of what he knew in previous lives. It is the custom to carry a talisman over from life to life, which helps the child to recover the memory in the new vehicles—a talisman which he wore in his previous birth, so that it is thoroughly loaded with the magnetism of that birth and can now stir up again the same vibrations.

CHILDREN'S SERVICES

Another interesting educational feature is what is called the children's service at the Temple. Many others than children attend this, especially those who are not yet quite up to the level of the other services already described. The children's service in the music-Temple is exceedingly beautiful;

the children perform a series of graceful evolutions, and both sing and play upon instruments as they march about. That in the colour-Temple is something like an especially gorgeous Drury Lane pantomime, and has evidently been many times carefully rehearsed.

In one case they are reproducing the choric dance of the priests of Babylon, which represents the movement of the planets round the sun. This is performed upon an open plain, as it used to be in Assyria, and groups of children dress in special colours (representing the various planets) and move harmoniously, so that in their play they have also an astronomical lesson. But it must be understood that they fully feel that they are engaging in a sacred religious rite, and that to do it well and thoroughly will not only be helpful to themselves, but that it also constitutes a kind of offering of their services to the Deity. They have been told that this used to be done in an old religion many thousands of years ago.

The children take great delight in it, and there is quite a competition to be chosen to be part of the Sun! Proud parents also look on, and are pleased to be able to say: "My boy is part of Mercury to-day," and so on. The planets all have their satellites—more satellites in some cases than used to be known, so that astronomy has evidently progressed. The rings of Saturn are remarkably well represented by a number of children in constant motion in a figure closely resembling the 'grand chain' at the commencement of the fifth figure of the Lancers. An especially interesting point is that even the inner 'crape' ring of Saturn is represented, for those children who are on the inside of the next ring keep a gauzy garment floating out so as to represent it. The satellites are single children or pairs of children waltzing outside the ring. All the while, though they enjoy it immensely, they never forget that they are performing a religious function and that they are offering this to God. Another dance evidently indicates the transfer of life from the Moon Chain to the Earth Chain. All sorts of instruction is given to the children in this way, half a play and half a religious ceremony.

SYMBOLIC DANCES

There are great festivals which each Temple celebrates by special performances of this kind, and on these occasions they all do their best in the way of gorgeous decoration. The buildings are so arranged that the lines are picked out in a kind of permanent phosphorescence, not a line of lamps, but a glow which seems to come from the substance. The lines of the architecture are graceful, and this has a splendid effect. The children's service is an education in colours. The combinations are really wonderful, and the drilling of the children is perfect. Great masses of them are dressed identically in the most lovely hues, delicate and yet brilliant, and they move in and out among one another in the most complicated figures. In their choric dance they are taught that they must not only wear the colour of the star for spectacular purposes, but must also try mentally to make the same colour. They are instructed to try to fancy themselves that colour, and try to think that they actually are part of the planet Mercury or Venus, as the case may be. As they move they sing and play, each planet having its own special chords, so that all the planets as they go round the sun may produce an imitation of the music of the spheres. In these children's services also the Ḍevas often take part, and aid with the colours and the music. Both kāma and rūpa Ḍevas move quite freely among the people, and take part in daily life.

The children's service in connection with the yellow Temple is exceedingly interesting. Here they dance frequently in geometrical figures, but the evolutions are difficult to describe. One performance, for example, is exceedingly pretty and effective. Thirty-two boys wearing golden brocaded robes are arranged in a certain order, not all standing on the same level, but on raised stages. They evidently represent the angles of some solid figure. They hold in their hands thick ropes of a golden-coloured thread, and they hold these ropes from one to another so as to indicate the outline of a certain figure—say a dodecahedron. Suddenly, at a preconcerted signal, they drop one end of the rope or throw it to another boy, and in a moment the outline has changed into that of an icosahedron. This is wonderfully effective, and gives quite a remarkable illusory effect of changing solid figures one into another. All such changes are gone through in a certain order, which is somehow connected with the evolution of the matter of the planes at the commencement of a solar system. Another evolution is evidently to illustrate something of the formation of atoms out of bubbles. The children represent bubbles. A number of them rush out from the centre and arrange themselves in a certain way. Then they rush back again to the centre and again come still further out, and group themselves in quite a different way. All this needs much training, but the children appear most enthusiastic about it.

THE UNDERLYING IDEA

The education and the religion are so closely mingled that it is difficult clearly to differentiate one from the other. The children are playing in the Temple. The underlying idea which is kept before them is that all this is only the physical side of something far greater and grander, which belongs to higher worlds, so that they feel that to everything they do there is an inner side, and they hope to realise this and to be able to see and comprehend it directly; and this is always held before them as the final reward of their efforts.

BIRTH AND DEATH

The various influences which take such a prominent part in the education of the children are brought to bear upon them even before birth. Once more we must reiterate that when a birth is about to take place the father and mother and all parties concerned are quite aware what ego is to come to them, and therefore they take care that for months before the actual birth takes place the surroundings shall in every way be suitable to that ego, and such as may conduce to a perfect physical body. Great stress is laid upon the influence of beautiful surroundings. The future mother has always before her eyes lovely pictures and graceful statues. The whole of life is pervaded with this idea of beauty—so much so that it would be considered a crime against the community that any object should be ugly or ungraceful. In all architecture this beauty of line as well as of colour is the first consideration, and the same is true with regard to all the minor accessories of life. Even before the child's birth preparation will be made for him; his mother dresses chiefly in certain colours, and surrounds herself with flowers and lights of what are considered the most appropriate kind.

Parentage is a matter of arrangement between all parties concerned, and death is usually voluntary. As the members of this community live entirely healthy lives, and have surrounded themselves with perfect sanitary conditions, disease has been practically eliminated, so that except in the rare case of an accident no one dies except of old age, and they do not drop the body as long as it is useful. They do not feel at all that they are giving up life, but only that they are changing a worn-out vehicle. The absence of worry and unhealthy conditions has certainly tended on the whole to lengthen physical life. Nobody looks at all old until at least eighty, and many pass beyond the century.

When a man begins to find his powers failing him, he also begins to look round him for a desirable re-birth. He selects a father and mother whom he thinks would suit him, and goes round to call upon them to ask whether they are willing to take him. If they are, he tells them that he expects to die soon, and then hands over to them his personal talisman which he has worn all his life, and also sends to them any personal effects which he wishes to carry over to his next life. The talisman is usually a jewel of the particular type appropriate to the ego, according to the sign of the Zodiac to which as an ego he belongs, the influence under which he attained individuality. This charm he always wears, so that it may be fully impregnated with his magnetism, and he is careful to make arrangements that it may be handed over to him in his next birth, in order to help in the arousing in the new body of the memory of past lives, so as to make it easier to keep unbroken the realisation of life as an ego. This amulet is always correspondent to his name as an ego—the name which he carries with him from life to life. In many cases men are already using this name in ordinary life, though in others they have perpetuated the name which they bore when they entered the community, carrying it on from life to life and altering its termination so as to make it masculine or feminine according to the sex of the moment. Each person has therefore his own name, his permanent name, and in addition in each incarnation he takes that of the family into which he happens or chooses to be born.

The personal effects do not include anything of the nature of money, for money is no longer used, and no man has more than a life-interest in houses or land, or in other property. But he has sometimes a few books or ornaments which he wishes to preserve, and if so he hands them over to his prospective father and mother, who, when they hear that his death is approaching, can begin to prepare for him. He does not alter his ordinary mode of life; he does nothing which in the slightest degree resembles committing suicide; but he simply loses the will to live—lets his life go, as it were—and generally passes away peacefully in sleep within a short period of time. Usually, indeed, he takes up his abode with the prospective father and mother as soon as the agreement is made, and dies at their house.

There is no funeral ceremony of any sort, as death is not regarded as an event of any importance. The body is not cremated, but is instead placed in a kind of retort into which some chemical is poured—probably a strong acid of some sort. The retort is then hermetically sealed, and a power resembling electricity, but far stronger, is passed through it. The acid fizzes vigorously, and in a few minutes the whole body is entirely dissolved. When the retort is opened and the process is completed there is nothing left but a fine grey powder. This is not preserved or regarded with any reverence. The operation of disposing of the body is easily performed at the house, the apparatus being brought there when desired. There is no ceremony of any kind, and the friends of the deceased do not assemble for the occasion. They do, however, come round and pay him a visit soon after his rebirth, as the sight of them is supposed to help to reawaken the memory in the new baby body. Under these circumstances there are of course no prayers or ceremonies of any kind for the dead, nor is there any need of help upon the astral plane, for every member of the community remembers his past lives and knows perfectly well the body which he is about to take as soon as it can be prepared for him. Many members of the community continue to act as invisible helpers to the rest of the world, but within the community itself nothing of that kind is necessary.

The Manu has a careful record kept of all the successive incarnations of each of the members of His community, and in some rare cases He interferes with an ego's choice of his parents. As a general rule all the members of the community have already disposed of such grosser karma as would limit them in their choice, and they also know enough of their own type and of the conditions which they require not to make an unsuitable selection, so that in almost every case they are left perfectly free to make their own arrangements. The matter is, however, always within the knowledge of the Manu, so that He may alter the plan if He does not approve.

As a rule the dying man is at liberty to select the sex of his next birth, and many people seem to make a practice of taking birth alternately as man and as woman. There is no actual regulation as to this, and everything is left as free as possible; but at the same time the due proportion of the sexes in the community must be maintained, and if the number of either sex falls temporarily below what it should be, the Manu calls for volunteers to bring things once more into harmony. Parents usually arrange to have ten or twelve children in the family, and generally the same number of girls as boys. Twins, and even triplets, are not at all uncommon. Between the birth of one child and the next there is mostly an interval of two or three years, and there are evidently theories with regard to this matter. The great object is to produce perfect children, and no cripples or deformed persons are to be seen, nor is there any infant mortality. It is manifest that the labour of childbirth has diminished almost to vanishing-point; indeed, there seems to be scarcely any trouble, except perhaps a little with the first child.

MARRIAGE

This brings us to the question of marriage. There is no restriction placed upon this, except the one great restriction that no one must marry outside the community; but it is generally regarded as rather undesirable that people of the same type of religious feeling should intermarry. There is no rule against it, but it is understood that on the whole the Manu prefers that it should not take place. There is a certain all-sufficing expression which practically puts any matter beyond the limits of discussion: "It is not His wish."

People choose their own partners for life—fall in love, in fact—much as they used to do, but the dominant idea of duty is always supreme, and even in matters of the heart no one permits himself to do anything or feel anything which he does not think to be for the best for the community. The great motive is not passion, but duty. The ordinary sex passions have been dominated, so that people now unite themselves definitely with a view to carrying on the community and to creating good bodies for the purpose. They regard married life chiefly as an opportunity to that end, and what is necessary for such production is a religious and magical action which needs to be carefully directed. It forms part of the sacrifice of themselves to the LOGOS, so that no one must lose his balance or his reason in connection with it.

When people fall in love, and, as we should say, engage themselves, they go to the Manu Himself and ask Him for a benediction on their union. Usually they also arrange with a prospective son or daughter, so that when they go to the Manu they say that such and such a man wishes to be born from them, and ask that they may be permitted to marry. The Manu examines them to see whether they will suit each other, and if He approves He pronounces for them a formula: "Your life together shall be blessed." Marriage is regarded almost entirely from the point of view of the prospective offspring. Sometimes it is even arranged by them. One man will call on another and say:

"I am expecting to die in a few weeks, and I should like to have you and Miss X. for my father and mother, as I have some kārmic ties with both of you that I should like to work off; would that be agreeable to you?"

Not infrequently the suggestion seems to be accepted, and the plan works out well. One man, who was taken at random for the purpose of investigation, was found to have three egos desiring to incarnate through him, so that when he took his prospective wife to the Manu he asked:

"May we two marry, with these three egos waiting to take birth through us?"

And the Manu gave His consent. There is no other marriage ceremony than this benediction given by the Manu, nor is a wedding made the occasion of feasting or the giving of presents. There is nothing in the nature of a marriage contract. The arrangements are exclusively monogamous, and there is no such thing as divorce, though the agreement is always terminable by mutual consent. People marry distinctly with a view of furnishing a vehicle for a certain soul, and when that is safely done it seems to be entirely at their option whether they renew their agreement or not. Since the parents are selected with care, in the majority of cases the agreement is renewed, and they remain as husband and wife for life; but there are cases in which the agreement is terminated, and both parties form other alliances. Here also, as in everything else, duty is the one ruling factor, and everyone is always ready to yield his personal preference to what is thought to be best for the community as a whole. There is therefore far less of passion in these lives than in those of the older centuries; and the strongest affection is probably that between parents and children.

There are cases in which the unwritten rule as to not marrying a person of the same type is abrogated, as, for example, when it is desired to produce children who can be trained by the Devas as priests for a particular Temple. In the rare case where a man is killed by some accident, he is at once impounded in the astral body and arrangements are made for his re-birth. Large numbers of people desire to be born as children of the members of the Council; those, however, have only the usual number of children, lest the quality should be deteriorated. Birth in the family of the Manu Himself is the greatest of all honours; but of course He selects His children Himself. There is no difference of status between the sexes, and they take up indifferently any work that is to be done. On this matter it may be interesting to record the opinion of a mind of that period which was examined for that special purpose. This man does not seem to think much of the difference between man and woman. He says that there must be both, in order that the Race may be founded, but that we know there is a better time coming for the women. He feels that in bearing children the women are taking a harder share of the work, and are therefore to be pitied and protected. The Council, however, is composed entirely of men, and, under the direction of the Manu, its members are making experiments in the creation of mind-born bodies. They have produced some respectable copies of humanity, but have not yet succeeded in satisfying the Manu.

CHAPTER XXVI

BUILDINGS AND CUSTOMS

RACIAL CHARACTERISTICS

IN appearance the community is still like the sixth sub-race from which it sprang—that is to say, it is a white Race, although there are among it people with darker hair and eyes and a Spanish or Italian complexion. The stature of the Race has distinctly increased, for none of the men are under six feet, and even the women are but little short of this. The people are all muscular and well-proportioned, and much attention is paid to exercise and the equal development of the muscles. It is noteworthy that they preserve a free and graceful carriage even to extreme old age.

PUBLIC BUILDINGS

It was mentioned in the beginning that when the community was founded a vast block of central buildings was erected, and that the houses of the first settlers were grouped round that, though always with ample space between them for beautiful gardens. By this time many subordinate towns have sprung up in the district—though perhaps the word town may mislead a twentieth-century reader, since there is nothing in the least resembling the sort of town to which he is accustomed. The settlements may rather be called groups of villas thinly scattered amidst lovely parks and gardens; but at least all such settlements have their Temples, so that every inhabitant is always within easy reach of a Temple of the variety which he happens to prefer. The inhabited part of the estate is not of great size, some forty or fifty miles in diameter, so that even the great central buildings are, after all, quite easily available for anyone who wishes to visit them. Each Temple has usually in its neighbourhood a block of other public buildings—a sort of public hall, an extensive library, and also a set of school-buildings.

Houses

The houses built for the community before its foundation were all on the same general plan and, though a good deal of individual taste has been shown in those erected since, the broad principle is still the same. The two great features of their architecture which much differentiate it from almost all that preceded it, are the absence of walls and of corners. Houses, temples, schools, factories, all of them are nothing but roofs supported upon pillars—pillars in most cases as lofty as those of the Egyptian Temples, though far lighter and more graceful. There is, however, provision for closing the spaces between the pillars when necessary—something distantly resembling the patent automatic rolling shop-blinds of earlier centuries, but they can be made transparent at will. These devices, however, are rarely employed, and the whole of the life of the people, night and day, is in reality spent in the open air.

Domes of many shapes and sizes are prominent features. Some of them are of the shape of that of S. Peter's, though smaller; some are low and broad, like those of San Giovanni degli Eremiti, in Palermo; some with the lotus-bud shape of those of a Muhammadan mosque. These domes are full of windows, or are often themselves built of some transparent substance of various colours. Every Temple has a great central dome, and every house has one at least. The general scheme of the house is to have a sort of great circular or oval hall under the dome, which is the general living room. Fully three-fourths of its circumference is quite open, but behind the fourth part are often built rooms and offices of various kinds, which usually rise to only half the height of the columns, having above them other small rooms which are used as bedrooms. All those rooms, though separated from one another by partitions, have no outside walls, so that in them also people are still practically in the open air. There are no corners anywhere, every room being circular or oval. There is always some part of the roof upon which it is possible to walk. Every house is full of flowers and statues, and another striking feature is the abundance of water everywhere; there are fountains, artificial cascades, miniature lakes and pools in all directions.

The houses are always lighted from the roof. No lamps or lanterns are seen, but the dome is made to glow out in a mass of light, the colour of which can be changed at will, and in the smaller rooms a section of the ceiling is arranged to glow in the same way. All the parks and streets are thoroughly lighted at night with a soft and moon-like but penetrating light—a far nearer approach to daylight than anything previously secured.

FURNISHING

Furniture is principally conspicuous by its absence. There are scarcely any chairs in the houses, and there are no seats of any sort in the Temples or public halls. The people recline upon cushions somewhat in the oriental style, or rather perhaps like the ancient Romans, for they do not sit cross-legged. The cushions, however, are curious; they are always either air-cushions or entirely vegetable products stuffed with some especially soft fibrous material, not altogether unlike cocoanut fibre. These things are washable, and indeed are constantly being washed. When going to the Temple, to the library or to any public meeting each person usually carries his own air-cushion with him, but in the houses large numbers are seen lying about which may be used by anybody. There are small low tables—or perhaps they are rather to be described as book-rests, which can be so arranged as to be flat like a table. All the floors are of marble, or of stone polished like marble—often a rich crimson hue.

Beds, filled either with air or water, or made of the same vegetable material as that used for the cushions,. are laid upon the floor, or sometimes suspended like hammocks, but no bedsteads are used. In the few cases where there are comparatively permanent walls, as for example between the bed-rooms and offices and the great hall, they are always beautifully painted with landscapes and historic scenes. Curiously, all these things are interchangeable, and there is a department which is always prepared to arrange exchanges—a kind of circulating library for decorations, through the medium of which any person can change the wall-panels or statues which decorate his house, whenever he wishes to do so.

DRESS

The dress of the people is simple and graceful, but at the same time strictly utilitarian. Most of it is not unlike that of India, though we sometimes see an approach to the ancient Greek dress. There is no uniformity about it, and people wear all sorts of different things. But there is nothing inharmonious; all is in perfect taste. Colours both brilliant and delicate are worn by both men and women alike, for there seems to be no distinction between the clothing of the sexes. Not a single article is made of wool; it is never worn. The substance employed is exclusively linen or cotton, but it is steeped in some chemical which preserves its fibres so that the garments last for a long time, even though all are washed daily.

The chemical process imparts a glossy satin-like surface, but does not interfere in the least with the softness or flexibility of the material. No shoes or sandals or any other foot-coverings are worn by the members of the community, and scarcely any people wear hats, though there are a few something like the panama, and one or two small linen caps were seen. The idea of distinctive clothes for certain offices has disappeared; no uniforms of any sort are worn, except that the officiating Ḍeva always materialises round himself robes of the colour of his Temple, while conducting a service; and the children, as before described, dress themselves in certain colours when they are about to take part in the religious festivals.

Food

The community is entirely vegetarian, because it is one of the standing rules that nothing must be killed. Even the outer world is by this time largely vegetarian, because it has begun to be recognised that the eating of flesh is coarse, vulgar, and above all unfashionable! Comparatively few people take the trouble of preparing their own meals, or eat in their own houses, though they are perfectly free to do so if they wish. Most go to what may be called restaurants, although, as they are practically entirely in the open air, they may be supposed rather to resemble tea-gardens. Fruit enters largely into the diet of the period. We have a bewildering variety of fruits, and centuries of care have been devoted to scientific crossing of fruits, so as to produce the most perfect forms of nourishment and to give them at the same time remarkable flavours.

If we look in at a fruit-farm we see that the section devoted to each kind of fruit is always divided into smaller sections, and each section is labelled as having a particular flavour. We may have, for example, grapes or apples, let us say, with a strawberry flavour, a clove flavour, a vanilla flavour, and so on—mixtures which would seem curious from the point of view of those who are not accustomed to them. This is a country where there is almost no rain, so that all cultivation is managed by means of irrigation, and as they irrigate these different sections they throw into the water what is called 'plant-food' and by variations in this they succeed in imparting different flavours. By varying the food, growth can be intensified or retarded, and the size of the fruits can also be regulated. The estate of the community runs up into the hills, so they have the opportunity at different levels of cultivating almost all possible kinds of fruit.

The food which is most eaten is a sort of substance somewhat resembling blanc-mange. It is to be had in all kinds of colourings, and the colouring indicates the flavour, just as it used to do in ancient Peru. There is a large selection. Perhaps the choice of different flavours in the food may to some extent take the place of many habits which have now disappeared, such as smoking, wine-drinking, or the eating of sweets. There is also a substance which looks like cheese, but is sweet. It is certainly not cheese, for no animal products are used, and no animals are kept in the colony except as pets. Milk is used, but it is exclusively the vegetable milk obtained from what is sometimes called the cow-tree, or an exact imitation made from some kind of bean. Knives and forks do not appear, but spoons are still used, and most people bring their own with them. The attendant has a sort of weapon like a hatchet with which he opens fruits and nuts. It is made of an alloy which has all the qualities of gold but has a hard edge, which apparently does not need resharpening. It is possibly made of one of the rarer metals, such as iridium. In these restaurant gardens also there are no chairs, but each person half-reclines in a marble depression in the ground, and there is a marble slab which can be turned round in front of him so that he can put his food upon it, and when he has finished he turns this up and water flows over it.

On the whole people eat distinctly less than in the twentieth century. The usual custom is to have one regular meal in the middle of the day, and to take a light refection of fruit in the morning and evening. Everybody is at breakfast just after sunrise, for people are always up then or a little before. The light evening meal is at about five o'clock, for most people go to bed fairly early. So far as has been seen, no one sits down to a heavy meal in the evening; but there is complete individual freedom with regard to all these matters, so that people follow their own taste. The drinking of tea or coffee has not been observed; indeed there seems to be but little drinking of any sort, possibly because so much fruit is eaten.

Plenty of water is available everywhere, even though there is almost no rain. They have enormous works for the distillation of sea-water, which is raised to a great height and then sent out on a most liberal scale. It is worthy of note, however, that the water specially sent out for drinking is not the pure result of the distillation, but they add to it a small proportion of certain chemicals—the theory being that pure distilled water is not the most healthy for drinking purposes. The manager of the distillation-works explains that they use natural spring water as far as it will go, but they cannot get nearly enough of it, and so it has to be supplemented by the distilled water; but then it is necessary to add the chemicals to this in order to make it fresh and sparkling and really thirst-quenching.

LIBRARIES

The literary arrangements are curious but perfect. Every house is provided, gratis and as part of its permanent fittings, with a sort of encyclopædia of the most comprehensive nature, containing an epitome of practically all that is known, put as tersely as possible and yet with great wealth of detail, so as to contain all the information that an ordinary man is ever likely to want on any subject. If, however, for some reason he needs to know more, he has only to go to the nearest district-library, of which there is one connected with each Temple. There he finds a far fuller encyclopædia, in which the article on any given subject contains a careful epitome of every book that has ever been written upon it—a most colossal work. If he wants to know still more, or if he wants to consult original books printed in the old languages or the ancient Roman type now disused, he has to go to the central library of the community, which is on a scale commensurate with that of the British Museum. Translations into the English of the day printed in this shorthand-like script, are always appended to these originals.

Thus it is possible for a man to study to the fullest any subject in which he is interested, for all instruments of research and books are provided free in this way. New books are being written all the time on all conceivable subjects. The fiction of the day is almost entirely based upon reincarnation, the characters always passing from life to life and exemplifying the working of karma; but a novelist in these days writes not with a view to fame or money, but always to the good of the community. Some people are writing short articles, and these are always on view at their own district Temple hall. Anyone may go and read them there, and anyone who is interested has only to go and ask for a copy and it is given to him. If a man is writing a book it is exhibited in this way, chapter by chapter; the whole life is in this way communal; the people share with their neighbours what they are doing while they are doing it.

NEWSPAPERS

The daily newspaper has disappeared—or perhaps we may rather say that it survives in a much amended form. To make it comprehensible it must be premised that in each house there is a machine which is a kind of combination of a telephone and recording tape-machine. This is in connection with a central office in the capital city, and is so arranged that not only can one speak through it as through a telephone, but that anything written or drawn upon a specially prepared plate and put into the box of the large machine at the central office will reproduce itself automatically upon slips which fall into the box of the machine in each of the houses. What takes the place of the morning newspaper is managed in this way. It may be said that each person has his newspaper printed in his own house. When any news of importance arrives at any time it is instantly forwarded in this way to every house in the community; but a special collection of such news is sent early each morning and is commonly called the *Community Breakfast Chat*. It is a comparatively small affair and has a certain resemblance to a table of contents and an index, for it gives the briefest epitome of the news, but attaches a number to each item, the different departments being printed upon different colours. If any person wants full information as to any of the items, he has only to ring up the central office and ask for details of number so-and-so, and all that is available is at once sent along his wire and dropped before him. But the newspaper differs greatly from those of older times. There is hardly any political news, for even the outer world has changed in many ways. There is a great deal of information upon scientific subjects, and as to new theories. There are still notes of the private doings of royal people, but they are quite brief. There is a department for community news, but even that is chiefly concerned with scientific papers, inventions and discoveries, although it also records marriages and births.

The same instrument is also used for adding to the household encyclopædias whenever it is necessary. Extra slips are sent out daily whenever there is anything to say, so that just as the newspaper is being delivered in slices all day, so now and then come little slips to be added to the various departments of the encyclopædia.

PUBLIC MEETINGS

In connection with each Temple there is a definite scheme of educational buildings, so that broadly speaking the school-work of each district is done under the ægis of its Temple. The great central Temple has in connection with it the huge open-air places of assembly, where, when necessary, almost the entire community can be gathered together. More usually, when the Manu desires to promulgate some edict or information to all His people He Himself speaks in the great central Temple, and what He says is simultaneously produced by a sort of altogether improved phonographic system in all the other Temples. It would seem that each of the district Temples has a sort of representative phonograph in the central Temple, which records at the other end of the line all that takes place there, so that all particulars are in this way immediately reproduced.

SCIENCE DEPARTMENTS

Mention has already been made of the great central library in connection with the central Temple. In addition to that, as another part of the same great mass of buildings, there is a complete and well-appointed museum, and also what may be called a university. Many branches of study are taken up here, but they are pursued by methods different from those of old. The study of animals and plants, for example, is entirely and only done by means of clairvoyance, and never by destruction of any kind, only those being professors and students of these arts who have developed sufficient sight to work in this manner. There is a department of what we may call physical geography, which has already mapped out the entire earth in a vast number of large-scale models, which show by coloured signs and inscriptions not only the nature of the surface soil, but also what is to be found in the way of minerals and fossils down to a considerable depth.

There is also an elaborate ethnographical department in which there are life-size statues of all races of men which have ever existed on the earth, and also models of those existing on other planets of this chain. There is even a department with reference to the other chains of the solar system. For each of the statues there is an exhaustive description with diagrams showing in what way his higher vehicles differ. The whole is tabulated and arranged from the point of view of the Manu, to show what the development of mankind has been in the various Races and sub-races. A good deal is also shown of the future, and models with detailed explanations are given for them also. In addition to this there is also the anatomical department, dealing with the whole detailed anatomy of the human and animal bodies in the past, the present and the future. There is not exactly any medical department, for illness no longer exists; it has been eliminated. There is still, however, surgery for cases of accident, though even that has been much improved. Few professors of that art are needed, for naturally accidents are rare. There is nothing corresponding to the great hospitals of former times, but only a few light and airy rooms, in which the victims of accidents can be temporarily laid if necessary.

Connected with the centre of learning is also an elaborate museum of all sorts of arts and crafts which have existed in the world from the beginning onwards. There are also models of all kinds of machinery, most of which is new to us, since it has been invented between the twentieth century and the twenty-eighth. There is also much Atlantean machinery which had long been forgotten, so that there is a complete arrangement for any kind of study along these lines.

History is still being written, and it has been in process of production for more than a hundred years; but it is being written from a reading of the records. It is illustrated by a method which is quite new to us—a method which precipitates a scene from the records when it is considered important. We have in addition a series of models illustrating the history of the world at all periods. In the central library there are certain small rooms somewhat like telephone-cabinets, into which students can take the record of any prominent event in history, and by putting it into a machine and setting that in motion they can have the whole scene reproduced audibly and visibly, with the exact presentment of the appearance of the actors, and their words in the very tones in which they were spoken.

There is also an astronomical department, with most interesting machinery indicating the exact position at any moment of everything visible in the sky. There is a great mass of information about all these worlds. There are two departments, one for direct observation by various means and another for the tabulation of information acquired by testimony. Much of this information has been given by Ḍevas connected with various planets and stars; but this is always kept entirely apart from the results of direct observation. Chemistry has been carried to a wonderful height and depth. All possible combinations are now fully understood, and the science has an extension in connection with elemental essence, which leads on to the whole question of nature-spirits and Ḍevas as a definite department of science, studied with illustrative models. There is also a department of talismans, so that any sensitive person can by psychometry go behind the mere models, and see the things in themselves.

ARTS

It does not seem that lecturing holds at all a prominent place. Sometimes a man who is studying a subject may talk to a few friends about it, but beyond that, if he has anything to say he submits it to the officials and it gets into the daily news. If anybody writes poetry or an essay he communicates it to his own family, and perhaps puts it up in the district hall. People still paint, but only as a kind of recreation. No one now devotes the whole of his time to that. Art, however, permeates life to a far greater extent than ever before, for everything, even the simplest object for daily use, is artistically made, and the people put something of themselves into their work and are always trying new experiments.

There is nothing corresponding to a theatre, and on bringing the idea to the notice of an inhabitant, a definition of it comes into his mind as a place in which people used to run about and declaim, pretending to be other than they were, and taking the parts of great people. They consider it as archaic and childish. The great choric dances and processions may be considered as theatrical, but to them these appear as religious exercises.

Games and athletics are prominent in this new life. There are gymnasiums, and much attention is given to physical development in women as well as in men. A game much like lawn-tennis is one of the principal favourites. The children play about just as of old, and enjoy great freedom.

WILL-POWER

The force of will is universally recognised in the community and many things are performed by its direct action. Nature-spirits are well-known, and take a prominent part in the daily life of the people, most of whom can see them. Almost all children are able to see them and to use them in various ways, but they often lose some of this power as they grow up. The use of such methods, and also of telepathy, is a kind of game among the children, and the grown-up people recognise their superiority in this respect, so that if they want to convey a message to some friend at a distance they often call the nearest child and ask him to send it rather than attempt to do it themselves. He can send the message telepathically to some child at the other end, who then immediately conveys it to the person for whom it is intended, and this is a quite reliable and usual method of communication. Adults often lose the power at the time of their marriage, but some few of them retain it, though it needs a far greater effort for them than it does for the child.

ECONOMIC CONDITIONS

Some effort was made to comprehend the economic conditions of the colony, but it was not found easy to understand them. The community is self-supporting, making for itself everything which it needs. The only importations from outside are curiosities such as ancient manuscripts, books and objects of art. These are always paid for by the officials of the community, who have a certain amount of the money of the outside world, which has been brought in by tourists or visitors. Also they have learnt the secret of making gold and jewels of various kinds by alchemical means, and these are often used for payment for the few goods imported from the outside. If a private member wishes for something which can only be bought from the outer world, he gives notice of his desire to the nearest official, and work of some sort is assigned to him in addition to the daily work which he is normally doing, so that by that he may earn the value of whatever he desires.

Everybody undertakes some work for the good of the community, but it is usually left entirely to each to choose what it is to be. No one kind of work is esteemed nobler than any other kind, and there is no idea of caste of any sort. The child at a certain age chooses what he will do, and it is always open to him to change from one kind of work to another by giving due notice. Education is free, but the free tuition of the central university is given only to those who have already shown themselves specially proficient in the branches which they wish to pursue. Food and clothing are given freely to all—or rather, to each person is distributed periodically a number of tokens in exchange for one of which he can obtain a meal at any of the great restaurant-gardens anywhere all over the colony. Or if he prefers it he can go to certain great stores and there obtain food-materials, which he can take home and prepare as he wishes. The arrangement appears complicated to an outsider, but it works perfectly simply among those who thoroughly understand it.

All the people are working for the community, and among the work done is the production of food and clothing, which it then proceeds to hand round. Take, for example, the case of a cloth factory. It is the Government's factory, and it is turning out on an average so much cloth, but the output can be increased or decreased at will. The work is chiefly in the hands of girls, who join the factory voluntarily; indeed, there is a competition to get in, for only a certain number are needed. If things are not wanted they are not made. If cloth is wanted the factory is there to produce it; if not, it simply waits. The superintendent in charge of the cloth-store of the Government calculates that in a certain time he will need so much cloth, that he has in stock so much, and therefore requires for renewal so much, and he asks for it accordingly; if he does not want any, he says he has enough. The factory never closes, though the hours vary considerably.

In this cloth factory the workers are mostly women, quite young, and they are doing little but superintending certain machines and seeing that they do not go wrong. Each of them is managing a kind of loom into which she has put a number of patterns. Imagine something like a large clock-face with a number of movable studs on it. When a girl starts her machine she arranges these studs according to her own ideas, and as the machine goes on its movements produce a certain design. She can set it to turn out fifty cloths, each of different pattern, and then leave it. Each girl sets her machine differently—that is where their art comes in; every piece is different from every other piece, unless she allows the machine to run through its list over again after it has finished the fifty. In the meantime, after having started the machines the girls need only to glance at them occasionally, and the machinery is so perfect that practically nothing ever goes wrong with it. It is arranged to run almost silently, so that while they are waiting one of the girls reads from a book to the rest.

The New Power

One feature which makes an enormous difference is the way in which power is supplied. There are no longer any fires anywhere, and therefore no heat, no grime, no smoke, and hardly any dust. The whole world has evolved by this time beyond the use of steam, or any other form of power which needs heat to generate it. There seems to have been an intermediate period when some method was discovered of transferring electrical power without loss for enormous distances, and at that time all the available water-power of the earth was collected and syndicated; falls in Central Africa and in all sorts of out-of-the-way places were made to contribute their share, and all this was gathered together at great central stations and internationally distributed. Tremendous as was the power available in that way, it has now been altogether transcended, and all that elaborate arrangement has been rendered useless by the discovery of the best method to utilise what the late Mr. Keely called dynaspheric force—the force concealed in every atom of physical matter.

It will be remembered that as long ago as 1907, Sir Oliver Lodge remarked that "the total output of a million-kilowatt station for thirty million years exists permanently and at present inaccessibly in every cubic millimetre of space". (*Philosophical Magazine,* April, 1907, p. 493.) At the period which we are now describing, this power is no longer inaccessible, and consequently unlimited power is supplied free to everyone all over the world. It is on tap, like gas or water, in every house and every factory in this community, as well as everywhere else where it is needed, and it can be utilised for all possible purposes to which power can be turned. Every kind of work all over the world is now done in this way. Heating and lighting are simply manifestations of it. For example, whenever heat is required, no one in any civilised country dreams of going through the clumsy and wasteful process of lighting a fire. He simply turns on the force and, by a tiny little instrument which can be carried in the pocket, converts it into heat at exactly the point required. A temperature of many thousands of degrees can be produced instantly wherever needed, even in an area as small as a pin's head.

By this power all the machines are running in the factory which we inspected, and one result of this is that all the workers emerge at the end of the day without having even soiled their hands. Another consequence is that the factory is no longer the ugly and barren horror to which in earlier ages we were painfully accustomed. It is beautifully decorated—all the pillars are carved and wreathed with intricate ornament, and there are statues standing all about, white and rose and purple—the last being made of porphyry beautifully polished. Like all the rest of the buildings, the factory has no walls, but only pillars. The girls wear flowers in their hair, and indeed flowers plentifully decorate the factory in all directions. It is quite as beautiful architecturally as a private house.

Conditions of Work

A visitor who calls to look over the factory obligingly asks some questions from the manageress —a young girl with black hair and a gorgeous garland of scarlet flowers in it. The latter replies:

"Oh, we are told how much we are to do. The manager of the community cloth-stores considers that he will want so many cloths by such a time. Sometimes few are wanted, sometimes many, but always some, and we work accordingly. I tell my girls to come to-morrow according to this demand—for one hour, or two, or four according to what there is to do. Usually about three hours is a fair average day's work, but they have worked as long as five hours a day when there was a great festival approaching. Oh, no, not so much because new clothes were required for the festival, but because the girls themselves wanted to be entirely free from work for a week, in order to attend the festival. You see we always know beforehand how much we are expected to turn out in a given week or month, and we calculate that we can do it by working, say, two and a half hours each day. But if the girls want a week's holiday for a festival, we can compress two weeks' work into one by working five hours a day for that week, and then we can close altogether during the next one, and yet deliver the appointed amount of cloth at the proper time. Of course, we rarely work as much as five hours; we should more usually spread the work of the holiday-week over some three previous weeks, so that an hour extra each day would provide all that is needed. An individual girl frequently wants such a holiday, and she can always arrange it by asking some one to come and act as a substitute for her, or the other girls will gladly work a few minutes longer so as to make up for the amount which she would have done. They are all good friends and thoroughly happy. When they take a holiday they generally go in to visit the central library or cathedral, to do which comfortably they need a whole day free."

A visitor from the outside world wonders that anyone should work at all where there is no compulsion, and asks why people do so, but meets with little sympathy or comprehension from the inhabitants:

"What do you mean?" says one of them, in answer, "we are here to work. If there is work to do, it is done for His sake. If there is no work, it is a calamity that it happens so, but He knows best."

"It is another world!" exclaims the visitor.

"But what other world is possible?" asks the bewildered colonist; "for what does man exist?"

The visitor gives up the point in despair, and asks:

"But who tells you to work, and when and where?"

"Every child reaches a certain stage," replies the colonist. "He has been carefully watched by teachers and others, to see in what direction his strength moves most easily. Then he chooses accordingly, perfectly freely, but with the advice of others to help him. You say work must begin at this time or at that time, but that is a matter of agreement between the workers, and of arrangement each day."

There is a certain difficulty in following this conversation, for though the language is the same a good many new words have been introduced, and the grammar has been much modified. There is, for example, a common-gender pronoun, which signifies either 'he' or 'she'. It is probable that the invention of this has become a necessity because of the fact that people remember and frequently have to speak of incarnations in both sexes.

At all the various kinds of factories visited the methods of work are of much the same kind. In every place the people work by watching machines doing the work, and occasionally touching adjusting buttons or setting the machine going anew. In all, the same short hours of labour are the rule, except that the arrangements at the restaurant gardens are somewhat different. In this case the staff cannot altogether absent itself simultaneously, because food has to be ready at all times, so that there are always some workers on duty, and no one can go away for a whole day without previous arrangement. In all places where perpetual attendance is necessary, as it is at a restaurant, and at certain repairing shops, and in some other departments, there is an elaborate scheme of substitution. The staff is always greatly in excess of the requirements, so that only a small proportion of it is on duty at any one time. The cooking or arrangement of food, for example, at each of the restaurants is done by one man or one woman for each meal—one for the big meal in the middle of the day, another for morning breakfast, another for tea, each being on duty something like three hours.

Cooking has been revolutionised. The lady who does this work sits at a kind of office-table with a regular forest of knobs within her reach. Messages reach her by telephone as to the things that are required; she presses certain knobs which squirt the required flavour into the blanc-mange, for example, and then it is shot down a kind of tube and is delivered to the attendant waiting in the garden below. In some cases the application of heat is required, but that also she does without moving from her seat, by another arrangement of knobs. A number of little girls hover about her and wait upon her—little girls from eight to fourteen years old. They are evidently apprentices, learning the business; they are seen to pour things out of little bottles, and also to mix other foods in little bowls. But even among these little girls, if one wants a day or a week off, she asks another little girl to take her place, and the request is always granted; and though of course the substitute is likely to be unskilled, yet the companions are always so eager to help her that no difficulty ever arises. There is always a large amount of interplay and exchange in all these matters; but perhaps the most striking thing is the eager universal good-will which is displayed—everybody anxious to help everybody else, and no one ever thinking that he is being unfairly treated or 'put upon'.

It is also pleasant to see, as has been already mentioned, that no class of work is considered as inferior to any other class. But indeed there is no longer any mean or dirty labour left. Mining is no longer undertaken, because all that is needed can be as a rule alchemically produced with much less trouble. The knowledge of the inner side of chemistry is such that almost anything can be made in this way, but some things are difficult and therefore impracticable for ordinary use. There are many alloys which were not known to the older world.

All agricultural work is now done by machinery, and no person any longer needs to dig or to plough by hand. A man does not even dig his own private garden, but uses instead a curious little machine which looks something like a barrel on legs, which digs holes to any required depth, and at any required distance apart, according to the way in which it is set, and shifts itself along a row automatically, needing only to be watched and turned back at the end of the row. There is no manual labour in the old sense of the word, for even the machinery itself is now made by other machinery; and though machinery still needs oiling, even that appears to be done in a clean manner. There is really no low or dirty labour required. There are not even drains, for everything is chemically converted and eventually emerges as an odourless grey powder, something like ashes, which is used as a manure for the garden. Each house has its own converter.

There are no servants in this scheme of life, because there is practically nothing for them to do; but there are always plenty of people ready to come and help if necessary. There are times in the life of every lady when she is temporarily incapacitated from managing her household affairs; but in such a case some one always comes in to help—sometimes a friendly neighbour, and at other times a kind of ladies' help, who comes because she is glad to help, but not for a wage. When any such assistance is required, the person who needs it simply applies through the recognised means of communication, and some one at once volunteers.

Private Property

There is but little idea of private property in anything. The whole colony, for example, belongs to the community. A man lives in a certain house, and the gardens are his so that he can alter or arrange them in any way that he chooses, but he does not keep people out of them in any way, nor does he encroach upon his neighbours. The principle in the community is not to own things, but to enjoy them. When a man dies, since he usually does so voluntarily, he takes care to arrange all his business. If he has a wife living, she holds his house until her death or her remarriage. Since all, except in the rarest cases, live to old age, it is scarcely possible that any children can be left unprotected, but if such a thing does happen, there are always many volunteers anxious to adopt them. At the death of both parents, if the children are all married, the house lapses to the community, and is handed over to the next young couple in the neighbourhood who happen to marry. It is usual on marriage for the young couple to take a new house, but there are cases in which one of the sons or daughters is asked by the parents to remain with them and take charge of the house for them. In one case an extension is built on to a house for a grand-child who marries, in order that she may still remain in close touch with the old people; but this is exceptional.

There is no restriction to prevent people from gathering portable property, and handing it over before death to the parents selected for the next life. This is always done with the talisman, as has already been said, and not infrequently a few books accompany it, and sometimes perhaps a favourite picture or object of art. A man, as we have mentioned, can earn money if he wishes, and can buy things in the ordinary way, but it is not necessary for him to do so, since food, clothing and lodging are provided free, and there is no particular advantage in the private ownership of other objects.

A Park-Like City

Although in this community so large a number of people are gathered together into one central city and other subordinate centres, there is no effect of crowding. Nothing now exists in the least like what used to be meant by the central part of a city in earlier centuries. The heart of the great central city is the cathedral, with its attendant block of museum, university and library buildings. This has perhaps a certain resemblance to the buildings of the Capitol and Congressional Library at Washington, though on a still larger scale. Just as in that case, a great park surrounds it. The whole city and even the whole community exists in a park—a park abundantly interspersed with fountains, statues and flowers. The remarkable abundance of water everywhere is one of the striking features. In every direction one finds splendid fountains, shooting up like those at the Crystal Palace of old. In many cases one recognises with pleasure exact copies of old and familiar beauties; for example, one fountain is exactly imitated from the Fontana di Trevi at Rome. The roads are not at all streets in the old sense of the word, but more like drives through the park, the houses always standing well back from them. It is not permitted to erect them at less than a certain minimum distance one from another.

There is practically no dust, and there are no street sweepers. The road is all in one piece, not made of blocks, for there are no horses now to slip. The surface is a beautiful polished stone with a face like marble and yet an appearance of grain somewhat like granite. The roads are broad, and they have at their sides slight curb-stones; or rather it would be clearer to say that the road is sunk slightly below the level of the grass at each side, and that the curb-stones rise to the level of the grass. The whole is thus a kind of shallow channel of polished marble, which is flooded with water every morning, so that the roads are thus kept clean and spotless without the necessity of the ordinary army of cleaners. The stone is of various colours. Most of the great streets are a lovely pale rose-colour, but some are laid in pale green.

Thus there is really nothing but grass and highly polished stone for the people to walk upon, which explains the fact that they are always able to go bare-footed, not only without inconvenience but with the maximum of comfort. Even after a long walk the feet are scarcely soiled, but notwithstanding, at the door of every house or factory, there is a depression in the stone—a sort of shallow trough, through which there is a constant rush of fresh water. The people, before entering the house, step into this and their feet are instantly cooled and cleansed. All the Temples are surrounded by a ring of shallow flowing water, so that each person before entering must step into this. It is as though one of the steps leading up to the Temple were a kind of shallow trough, so that no one carries into the Temple even a speck of dust.

LOCOMOTION

All this park-like arrangement and the space between the houses make the capital of our community emphatically a 'city of magnificent distances' This however does not cause the slightest practical inconvenience, since every house possesses several light running cars of graceful appearance. They are not in the least like any variety of motor-car —they rather resemble bath-chairs made of light metal filigree work, probably aluminium, with tyres of some exceedingly elastic substance, though apparently not pneumatic. They run with perfect smoothness and can attain a high speed, but are so light that the largest size can be readily pushed with one finger. They are driven by the universal power; a person wishing to start on a journey charges from the power-tap a sort of flat shallow box which fits under the seat. This gives him sufficient to carry him clear across the community without recharging, and if he wishes for more than that, he simply calls at the nearest house, and asks to be allowed to attach his accumulator to its tap for a few moments. These little cars are perpetually used; they are in fact the ordinary means of locomotion, and the beautiful hollow polished roads are almost entirely for them, as pedestrians mostly walk along the little paths among the grass. There is little heavy transport—no huge and clumsy vehicles. Any large amount of goods or material is carried in a number of small vehicles, and even large beams and girders are supported on a number of small trolleys which distribute the weight. Flying machines are observed to be commonly in use in the outer world, but are not fashionable in the community, as the members feel that they ought to be able to get about freely in their astral bodies, and therefore rather despise other means of aerial locomotion. They are taught at school to use astral consciousness, and they have a regular course of lessons in the projection of the astral body.

Sanitation and Irrigation

There is no trouble with regard to sanitation. The method of chemical conversion, mentioned some time ago, includes deodorisation, and the gases thrown off from it are not in any way injurious. They seem to be principally carbon and nitrogen, with some chlorine, but no carbon dioxide. The gases are passed through water, which contains some solution, as it has a sharp acid feeling. All the gases are perfectly harmless, and so is the grey powder, of which only a little is present. All bad smells of every kind are against the law now, even in the outer world. There is not what we should call a special business-quarter in the town, though certain factories are built comparatively near one another, for convenience in interchanging various products. There is, however, so little difference between a factory and private house that it is difficult to know them apart, and as the factory makes no noise or smell it is not in any way an objectionable neighbour.

One great advantage which these people have is their climate. There is no real winter, and in the season corresponding to it the whole land is still covered with flowers just as at other times. They irrigate even where they do not cultivate; the system has been extended in a number of cases into fields and woods and the country in general, even where there is no direct cultivation. They have specialised the eschscholtzia, which was so common in California even centuries ago, and have developed many varieties of it, scarlet as well as brilliant orange, and they have sown them all about and allowed them to run wild. They have evidently in the beginning imported seeds of all sorts extensively from all parts of the world. People sometimes grow in their gardens plants which require additional heat in winter, but this is not obtained by putting them in a green-house, but by surrounding them with little jets of the power in its heat form. They have not yet needed to build anywhere near the boundary line of the community, nor are there any towns or villages for some distance on the other side of that boundary. The whole estate was a kind of huge farm before they bought it, and it is surrounded principally by smaller farms. The laws of the outside world do not trouble or affect the community, and the Government of the continent does not in any way interfere with it, as it receives a nominal yearly tribute from it. The people of the community are well-informed as regards the outside world; even school-children know the names and location of all the principal towns in the world.

CHAPTER XXVII

CONCLUSION

THE FEDERATION OF NATIONS

THE whole object of this investigation was to obtain such information as was possible about the beginnings of the Sixth Root-Race and the community founded by the Manu and the High-Priest for that purpose. Naturally therefore no special attention was directed to any other part of the world than this. Notwithstanding, certain glimpses of other parts were obtained incidentally, and it will perhaps be interesting to note these; but they are put down without attempt at order or completeness, just as they were observed.

Practically the whole world has federated itself politically. Europe seems to be a Confederation with a kind of Reichstag, to which all countries send representatives. This central body adjusts matters, and the Kings of the various countries are Presidents of the Confederation in rotation. The rearrangement of political machinery by which this wonderful change has been brought about is the work of Julius Cæsar, who reincarnated some time in the twentieth century in connection with the coming of the Christ to reproclaim the WISDOM.

Enormous improvements have been made in all directions, and one cannot but be struck with the extraordinary abundance of wealth that must have been lavished upon these. Cæsar, when he succeeds in forming the Federation and persuades all the countries to give up war, arranges that each of them shall set aside for a certain number of years half or a third of the money that it has been accustomed to spend upon armaments, and devote it to certain social improvements which he specifies. According to his scheme the taxation of the entire world is gradually reduced, but notwithstanding, sufficient money is reserved to feed all the poor, to destroy all the slums, and to introduce wonderful improvements into all the cities. He arranges that those countries in which compulsory military service has been the rule shall for a time still preserve the habit, but shall make their conscripts work for the State in the making of parks and roads and the pulling down of slums and the opening up of communications everywhere. He arranges that the old burdens shall be gradually eased off, but yet contrives with what is left of them to regenerate the world. He is indeed a great man; a most marvellous genius.

There seems to have been some trouble at first and some preliminary quarrelling, but he gets together an exceedingly capable band of people—a kind of cabinet of all the best organisers whom the world has produced—reincarnations of Napoleon, Scipio Africanus, Akbar and others—one of the finest bodies of men for practical work that has ever been seen. The thing is done on a gorgeous scale. When all the Kings and prime ministers are gathered together to decide upon the basis for the Confederation, Cæsar builds for the occasion a circular hall with a great number of doors so that all may enter at once, and no one Potentate take precedence of another.

The Religion of the Christ

Cæsar arranges all the machinery of this wonderful revolution, but his work is largely made possible by the arrival and preaching of the Christ Himself, so we have here a new era in all senses, not merely in outward arrangement, but in inner feeling as well. All this is long ago from the point of view of the time at which we are looking, and the Christ is now becoming somewhat mythical to the people, much as He was to many people at the beginning of the twentieth century. The religion of the world now is that which He founded; that is *the* Religion, and there is no other of any real importance, though there are still some survivals, of which the world at large is somewhat contemptuously tolerant, regarding them as fancy religions or curious superstitions. There are a few people who represent the older form of Christianity—who in the name of the Christ refused to receive Him when He came in a new form. The majority regard these people as hopelessly out-of-date. On the whole the state of affairs all the world over is obviously much more satisfactory than in the earlier civilisations. Armies and navies have disappeared, or are only represented by a kind of small force used for police purposes. Poverty also has practically disappeared from civilised lands; all slums in the great cities have been pulled down, and their places taken, not by other buildings, but by parks and gardens.

The New Language

This curious altered form of English, written in a kind of short-hand with many grammalogues, has been adopted as a universal commercial and literary language. Ordinarily educated people in every country know it in addition to their own, and indeed it is obvious that among the upper and commercial classes it is rapidly superseding the tongues of the different countries. Naturally the common people in every country still speak their old tongue, but even they recognise that the first step towards getting on in the world is to learn the universal language. The great majority of books, for example, are printed only in that, unless they are intended especially to appeal to the uneducated. In this way it is now possible for a book to have a much wider circulation than it could ever have had before. There are still university professors and learned men who know all the old languages, but they are a small minority, and all the specially good books of all languages have long ago been translated into this universal tongue.

In every country there is a large body of middle and upper class people who know no other language, or know only the few words of the language of the country which are necessary in order to communicate with servants and labourers. One thing which has greatly contributed to this change is this new and improved method of writing and printing, which was first introduced in connection with the English language and is therefore more adapted to it than others. In our community all books are printed on pale sea-green paper in dark blue ink, the theory being apparently that this is less trying to the eyes than the old scheme of black on white. The same plan is being widely adopted in the rest of the world. Civilised rule or colonisation has spread over many parts of the world which formerly were savage and chaotic; indeed almost no real savages are now to be seen.

THE OLD NATIONS

People have by no means yet transcended national feelings. The countries no longer fight with one another, but each nation still thinks of itself with pride. The greatest advantage is that they are not now afraid of one another, and that there is no suspicion, and therefore far greater fraternity. But on the whole, people have not changed much; it is only that now the better side of them has more opportunity to display itself. There has not as yet been much mingling of the nations; the bulk of the people still marry in their own neighbourhood, for those who till the soil almost always tend to stay in the same place. Crime appears occasionally, but there is much less of it than of old, because the people on the whole know more than they did, and chiefly because they are much more content.

The new religion has spread widely and its influence is undoubtedly strong. It is an entirely scientific religion, so that though religion and science are still separate institutions, they are no longer in opposition as they used to be. Naturally people are still arguing, though the subjects are not those which we know so well. For example, they discuss the different kinds of spirit-communion, and quarrel as to whether it is safe to listen to any spooks except those who have been authorised and guaranteed by the orthodox authorities of the time. Schools exist everywhere, but are no longer under the control of the Church, which educates no one except those who are to be its own preachers. Ordinary philanthropy is not needed, since there is practically no poverty. There are still hospitals, and they are all Government institutions. All necessaries of life are controlled, so that there can be no serious fluctuations in their price. All sorts of luxuries and unnecessary things are still left in the hands of private trade—objects of art, and things of that kind. But even with this, there is not so much competition as division of business; if a certain man opens a shop for the sale of ornaments and such things, another one is not likely to start in business close by, simply because there would not be enough trade for the two; but there is no curtailing of liberty with regard to that.

Land and Mines

The conditions as to the ownership of private land and of mines and factories are much changed. A large amount at least of the land is held nominally from the King, on some sort of lease by which it reverts to him unconditionally at the end of a thousand years, but he has the right to resume it at any intervening period if he chooses, with certain compensations. In the meantime it may descend from father to son, or be sold or divided, but never without the consent of the authorities. There are also considerable restrictions as to many of these estates, referring to what kind of buildings may be erected on them. All factories for necessaries are State property, but still there is no restriction which prevents anyone from starting a similar factory if he likes. There is still some mining, but much less than of old. The cavities and galleries of many of the old mines in the northern parts of Europe are now used as sanatoria for the rare cases of consumption or bronchial or other affections, because of their equal temperature in summer and winter. There are also arrangements for raising metal from great depths, which cannot exactly be called mines, for they are much more like wells. This may be considered a modern and improved type of mine. Little of the work is done down below by human beings; rather machines excavate, cut out huge slices and lift them. All these are State property in the ultimate, but in many cases private owners rent them from the State. Iron is burnt out of various earths in some way, and the material is obtained with less trouble than of old.

The Government of Britain

The Government of England has been considerably changed. All real power is in the hands of the King, though there are ministers in charge of separate departments. There is no parliament, but there is a scheme the working of which is not easy fully to comprehend in the rapid glimpse which is all that we had. It is something more or less of the nature of the referendum. Everybody has a right to make representations, and these pass through the hands of a body of officials whose business it is to receive complaints or petitions. If these representations show any injustice, it is rapidly set right without reference to the higher authorities. Every such petition is attended to if it can be shown to be reasonable, but it does not usually penetrate to the King himself, unless there are many requests for the same thing. The Monarchy is still hereditary, still ruling by the claim of descent from Cerdic. The British Empire appears to be much as in the twentieth century, but it was an earlier federation than the greater one, and it naturally acknowledges permanently one King, while the World-Federation is constantly changing its President. Some of what used to be Colonial Governors now hold their offices by heredity, and are like tributary Monarchs.

London

London still exists, and is larger than ever, but much changed, for now all over the world there are no fires, and consequently no smoke. Some of the old streets and squares are still recognisable in general outline, but there has been a vast amount of pulling-down, and improvements upon a large scale. S. Paul's Cathedral is still there, preserved with great care as an ancient monument. The Tower has been partly reconstructed. The introduction of one unlimited power has produced great effects here also, and most things that are wanted seem to be supplied on the principle of turning on a tap. Here also few people any longer cook in private houses, but they go out for meals much as they do in the community, although things are served here in a different manner.

Other Places

Taking a passing glance at Paris, it also is seen to be much changed. All the streets are larger and the whole city is, as it were, looser. They have pulled down whole blocks, and thrown them into gardens. Everything is so hopelessly different. Glancing at Holland, we see a country so thickly inhabited that it looks like almost a solid city. Amsterdam is, however, still clearly distinguishable, and they have elaborated some system by which they have increased the number of canals and contrive to change all the water in all of them every day. There is not any natural flow of water, but there is some curious scheme of central suction, a kind of enormous tube system with a deep central excavation. The details are not clear; but they somehow exhaust the area and draw into that all sewage and such matters, which are carried in a great channel under the sea to a considerable distance and are then spouted out with tremendous vigour. No ships pass anywhere near that spot, as the force is too great. Here also, as in the community, they are distilling sea-water and extracting things from it—obtaining products from which many things are made—articles of food among others, and also dyes. In some of the streets they grow tropical trees in the open air by keeping round them a constant flow of the power in its heat aspect.

Centuries ago they began by roofing in the streets and keeping them warm, like a green-house; but when the unlimited power appeared they decided to dispense with the roofs, about which there were many inconveniences. In passing glimpses at other parts of the world, hardly anything worth chronicling was seen. China appears to have had some vicissitudes. The race is still there and it does not seem to have diminished. There is a good deal of superficial change in some of the towns, but the vast body of the race is not really altered in its civilisation. The great majority of the country people still speak their own tongue, but all the leading people know the universal language.

India is another country where but little change is observable. The immemorial Indian village is an Indian village still, but there are no famines now. The country groups itself into two or three big kingdoms, but is still part of the one great Empire. There is evidently far more mixture in the higher classes than there used to be, and much more intermarriage with white races; so that it is clear that among a large section of the educated people the caste system must to a great extent have been broken down. Tibet seems to have been a good deal opened up, since easy access is to be had to it by means of flying machines. Even these, however, meet with occasional difficulties, owing to the rarity of the air at a great height. Central Africa is radically changed, and the neighbourhood of the Victoria Nyanza has become a sort of Switzerland full of great hotels.

ADYAR

Naturally it is interesting to see what has happened by this time to our Headquarters at Adyar, and it is delightful to find it still flourishing, and on a far grander scale than in older days. There is still a Theosophical Society; but as its first object has to a large extent been achieved, it is devoting itself principally to the second and third. It has developed into a great central University for the promotion of studies along both these lines, with subsidiary centres in various parts of the world affiliated to it.

The present Headquarters building is replaced by a kind of gorgeous palace with an enormous dome, the central part of which must be an imitation of the Tāj Mahāl at Agra, but on a much larger scale. In this great building they mark as memorials certain spots by pillars and inscriptions, such as: "Here was Madame Blavatsky's room"; "Here such and such a book was written"; "Here was the original shrine-room"; and so on. They even have statues of some of us, and they have made a copy in marble of the statues of the Founders in the great hall. Even that marble copy is now considered as a relic of rémote ages. The Society owns the Adyar River now, and also the ground on the other side of it, in order that nothing may be built over there that may spoil its prospect, and it has lined the river-bed with stone of some sort to keep it clean. They have covered the estate with buildings, and have acquired perhaps an additional square mile along the sea-shore. Away beyond Olcott Gardens they have a department for occult chemistry, and there they have all the original plates reproduced on a larger scale and also exceedingly beautiful models of all the different kinds of chemical atoms. They have a magnificent museum and library, and a few of the things which were here at the beginning of the twentieth century are still to be seen. One fine old enamelled manuscript still exists, but it is doubtful whether there are any books going back as far as the twentieth century. They have copies of *The Secret Doctrine,* but they are all transcribed into the universal language.

THE THEOSOPHICAL SOCIETY

The Society has taken a great place in the world. It is a distinct department in the world's science, and has a long line of specialities which no one else seems to teach. It is turning out a vast amount of literature, possibly what we should call texts, and is keeping alive an interest in the old religions and in forgotten things. It is issuing a great series somewhat resembling the old 'Sacred Books of the East,' but on a more magnificent scale. The volume just issued is number 2,159. There are many paṇḍiṭs who are authorities on the past. Each man appears to specialise on a book. He knows it by heart and knows all about it, and has read thoroughly all the commentaries upon it. The literary department is enormous, and is the centre of a world-wide organisation. Though they still use English, they speak it differently, but they keep the archaic motto of the Society written in its original form. The Society's dependencies in other parts of the world are practically autonomous—big establishments and universities in all the principal countries; but they all look up to Adyar as the centre and origin of the movement and make it a place of pilgrimage. Colonel Olcott, though working in the community in California as a lieutenant of the Manu, is the nominal President of the Society, and visits its Headquarters at least once in every two years. He comes and leads the salutations before the statues of the Founders.

Three Methods of Reincarnation

As in the examination of the Californian community a great many people were seen who were clearly recognisable as friends of the twentieth century, it seems desirable to enquire how they manage to be there—whether they have been taking a number of rapid incarnations, or have calculated their stay in the heaven-world so as to arrive at the right moment.

The enquiry leads in unexpected directions and gives more trouble than had been anticipated, but at least three methods of occupying the intermediate time have been discovered. First, some of the workers do take the heaven-life, but greatly shorten and intensify it. This process of shortening but intensifying produces considerable and fundamental differences in the causal body; its effects cannot in any way be described as better or worse, but they are quite certainly different. It is a type which is much more amenable to the influence of the Devas than the other, and this is one of the ways in which modifications have been introduced. That shorter heaven-life is not shut in in a little world of its own, but is to a great extent open to this Deva influence. The brains of the people who come along that line are different, because they have preserved lines of receptivity which in other cases have been atrophied. They can be more easily influenced for good by invisible beings, but there is a corresponding liability to less desirable influences. The personality is less awake, but the man inside is more awake in proportion. Those who take the longer heaven-life focus practically all their consciousness in one place at once, but people of this other type do not. Their consciousness is more equally distributed on the different levels, and consequently they are usually less concentrated upon the physical plane and less able to achieve in connection with it.

There are others to whom a different opportunity has been offered, for they were asked whether they felt themselves able to endure a series of rapid incarnations of hard work devoted to the building of the Theosophical Society. Naturally, such an offer is made only to those who bring themselves definitely to a point where they are useful—those who work hard enough to give satisfactory promise for the future. To them is offered this opportunity of continuing their work, of taking incarnation after incarnation without interval, in different parts of the world, to carry the Theosophical Movement up to the point where it can provide this large contingent for the community. The community at the time when it is observed is much larger than the Theosophical Society of the twentieth century; but that Society has increased by geometrical progression during the intervening centuries—so much so that although practically all the hundred thousand members of the community have passed through its ranks (most of them many times), there is still a huge Society left to carry on the activities at Adyar and the other great centres all over the world.

We have seen already two methods by which persons who are in the Society in the twentieth century may form part of the community of the twenty-eighth century—by the intensification of the heaven-life, and by the taking of special and repeated incarnations. Another method is far more remarkable than either of these—one which is probably applied in only a limited number of instances. The case which drew attention to this was that of a man who had pledged himself to the Master for this work towards the conclusion of his twentieth century incarnation, and unreservedly devoted himself to preparation for it. The preparation assigned was indeed most unusual, for he needed development of a certain kind in order to round off his character and make him really useful—development which could only be obtained under the conditions existing in another planet of the chain. Therefore he was transferred for some lives to that planet and then brought back again here—a special experiment made by permission of the Mahā-Chohan Himself. The same permission was in some cases obtained by other Masters for Their pupils, though such an extreme measure is rarely necessary.

Most of the members of the community have been taking a certain number of special incarnations, and therefore have preserved through all those lives the same astral and mental bodies. Consequently they have retained the same memory, and that means that they have known all about the community for several lives, and had the idea of it before them. Normally such a series of special and rapid incarnations is arranged only for those who have already taken the first of the great Initiations. For them it is understood that an average of seven such lives should bring them to the Arhaṭ Initiation, and that after that is attained seven more should suffice to cast off the remaining five fetters and attain the perfect liberation of the Asekha level. This number, fourteen incarnations, is given merely as an average, and it is possible greatly to shorten the time by especially earnest and devoted work, or, on the other hand, to lengthen it by any lukewarmness or carelessness. The preparation for the work of the community is an exception to ordinary rules, and although all its members are definitely aiming at the Path, we must not suppose that all of them have attained as yet to the greater heights.

A certain small number of persons from the outside world, who are already imbued with the ideals of the community, sometimes come and desire to join it, and some at least of these are accepted. They are not allowed to intermarry with the community, because of the especial purity of race which is exacted, but they are allowed to come and live among the rest, and are treated exactly like all the others. When such members die they reincarnate in bodies belonging to the families of the community.

The Manu has advanced ideas as to the amount of progress which He expects the community as a whole to make in a given time. In the principal Temple He keeps a kind of record of this, somewhat resembling a weather-chart, showing by lines what He has expected and how much more or less has been achieved. The whole plan of the community was arranged by our two Masters, and the light of Their watchful care is always hovering over it. All that has been written gives only a little gleam of that light—a partial foreshadowing of that which They are about to do.

How to Prepare Ourselves

It is certainly not without definite design that just at this time in the history of our Society permission has been given thus to publish this, the first definite and detailed forecast of the great work that has to be done. There can be little doubt that at least one of the objects of the great Ones in allowing this is not only to encourage and stimulate our faithful members, but to show them along what lines they must specially develop themselves, if they desire the inestimable privilege of being permitted to share in this glorious future, and also what (if anything) they can do to pave the way for the changes that are to come. One thing that can be done here and now to prepare for this glorious development is the earnest promotion of our first object, of a better understanding between the different nations and castes and creeds.

In that everyone of us can help, limited though our powers may be, for every one of us can try to understand and appreciate the qualities of nations other than our own; every one of us, when he hears some foolish or prejudiced remark made against men of another nation, can take the opportunity of putting forward the other side of the question—of recommending to notice their good qualities rather than their failings. Every one of us can take the opportunity of acting in an especially kindly manner toward any foreigner with whom we happen to come into contact, and feeling the great truth that when a stranger visits our country all of us stand temporarily to him in the position of hosts. If it comes in our way to go abroad—and none to whom such an opportunity is possible should neglect it—we must remember that we are for the moment representatives of our country to those whom we happen to meet, and that we owe it to that country to endeavour to give the best possible impression of kindliness and readiness to appreciate all the manifold beauties that will open before us, while at the same time we pass over or make the best of any points which strike us as deficiencies.

Another way in which we can help to prepare is by the endeavour to promote beauty in all its aspects, even in the commonest things around us. One of the most prominent characteristics of the community of the future is its intense devotion to beauty, so that even the commonest utensil is in its simple way an object of art. We should see to it that, at least within the sphere of our influence, all this is so with us at the present day; and this does not mean that we should surround ourselves with costly treasures, but rather that, in the selection of the simple necessaries of every-day life, we should consider always the question of harmony, suitability and grace. In that sense and to that extent we must all strive to become artistic; we must develop within ourselves that power of appreciation and comprehension which is the grandest feature of the artist's character.

Yet, on the other hand, while thus making an effort to evolve its good side, we must carefully avoid the less desirable qualities which it sometimes brings with it. The artistic man may be elevated clear out of his ordinary every-day self by his devotion to his art. By the very intensity of that, he has not only marvellously uplifted himself, but he also uplifts such others as are capable of responding to such a stimulus. But unless he is an abnormally well-balanced man, this wonderful exaltation is almost invariably followed by its reaction, a correspondingly great depression. Not only does this stage usually last far longer than the first, but the waves of thought and feeling which it pours forth affect nearly everybody within a considerable area, while only a few (in all probability) have been able to respond to the elevating influence of the art. It is indeed a question whether many men of artistic temperament are not, on the whole, thus doing far more harm than good; but the artist of the future will learn the necessity and the value of perfect equipoise, and so will produce the good without the harm; and it is at this that we must aim.

It is obvious that helpers are needed for the work of the Manu and the Chief Priest, and that in such work there is room for all conceivable diversities of talent and of disposition. None need despair of being useful because he thinks himself lacking in intellect or ecstatic emotion; there is room for all, and qualities which are lacking now may be speedily developed under the special conditions which the community will provide. Good-will and docility are needed, and perfect confidence in the wisdom and capability of the Manu; and above all the resolve to forget self utterly and to live only for the work that has to be done in the interests of humanity. Without this last, all other qualifications "water but the desert".

Those who offer themselves to help must have in some sort the spirit of an army—a spirit of perfect self-sacrifice, of devotion to the Leader and of confidence in Him. They must above all things be loyal, obedient, painstaking, unselfish. They may have many other great qualities as well, and the more they have the better; but these at least they must have. There will be scope for the keenest intelligence, the greatest ingenuity and ability in every direction; but all these will be useless without the capacity of instant obedience and utter trust in the Masters. Self-conceit is an absolute barrier to usefulness. The man who can never obey an order because he always thinks that he knows better than the authorities, the man who cannot sink his personality entirely in the work which is given to him to do and co-operate harmoniously with his fellow-workers —such a man has no place in the army of the Manu, however transcendent his other qualifications may be. All this lies before us to be done, and it will be done, whether we take our share in it or not; but since the opportunity is offered to us surely we shall be criminally foolish if we neglect it. Even already the preparatory work is beginning; the harvest truly is plenteous, but as yet the labourers are all too few. The Lord of the Harvest calls for willing helpers; who is there among us who is ready to respond?

EPILOGUE

It is obvious that the outline of the Californian community and of the world of the twenty-eighth century is but an infinitesimal fragment of the 'Whither' of the road along which humanity will travel. It is an inch or two of the indefinite number of miles which stretch between us and the goal of our Chain, and even then a longer 'Whither' stretches beyond. It tells of the first small beginnings of the sixth Root Race, beginnings which bear much the same proportion to the life of that Race, as the gathering of the few thousands on the shore of the sea that washed the south-eastern part of Ruṭa bore to the great fifth Root Race that is now leading the world. We do not know how long a time is to elapse from those peaceful days to the years during which America will be rent into pieces by earthquakes and volcanic outbursts, and a new continent will be thrown up in the Pacific, to be the home of the sixth Root Race. We see that later the strip in the far west of Mexico, on which the community exists will become a strip on the far east of the new continent, while Mexico and the United States will be whelmed in ruin. Gradually will that new continent be upheaved, with many a wild outburst of volcanic energy, and the land that was once Lemuria will arise from its age-long sleep, and lie again beneath the sun-rays of our earthly day.

It may be supposed that a very long period will be occupied by these great seismic changes, ere the new land will be ready for the new Race, and its Manu and its Boḍhisaṭṭva will lead it thither.

Then will come the ages during which its seven sub-races will rise, and reign, and decay; and from the seventh the choosing of the germs of the seventh Root Race by its future Manu, and the long labours of that new Manu and of His Brother the new Boḍhisaṭṭva, until it shall, in turn, grow into a definite new Race and inherit the earth. It also will have its seven sub-races, to rise, and reign, and vanish—vanishing as the earth itself falls asleep, and passes into its fourth obscuration.

The Sun of Life will rise on a new earth, the planet Mercury, and that fair orb will pass through its day of ages, and again that Sun will set and the night will fall. A new rising, a new setting, on the globes F and G of our Round, and the ending of the Round, and the gathering of its fruits into the bosom of its Seed Manu.

Then, after long repose, the fifth, sixth and seventh Rounds, ere our terrene Chain shall vanish into the past. Then, onwards yet, after an Inter-Chain Nirvāṇa, and still there are fifth and sixth and seventh Chains yet to come and to pass away, ere the Day of the High Gods shall decline to its setting, and the soft still Night shall brood over a resting system, and the great Preserver shall repose on the many-headed serpent of Time.

But even then the 'Whither' stretches onward into the endless ages of Immortal Life. The dazzled eyes close; the numbed brain is still. But above, below, on every side, stretches the illimitable Life who is GOD, and in Him will ever live and move and exist the children of men.

PEACE TO ALL BEINGS

APPENDIX

I

THE MOON CHAIN

THE names of individuals who have been traced through the ages—adopted from 'Rents in the Veil of Time,' with many subsequent additions—have been as far as possible relegated to Appendices. In a book intended for the general public, too many of these names would be wearisome. On the other hand, they are of great interest to Fellows of the Theosophical Society, many of whom may thus trace some of their former incarnations. We have retained these names in the text where the exigencies of the story required it, and have added large numbers, family relationships, etc., in the form of Appendices.

P. 33. Individualised on Globe D, in the fourth Round of the Moon Chain: MARS and MERCURY; probably many others who have become Masters in the Earth Chain. Yet loftier Beings individualised in earlier Chains. Thus, the MAHĀGURU and SŪRYA dropped out of globe D of the seventh Round of the second Chain at its Day of Judgment, and came to globe D of the third, or Moon Chain, in the fourth Round—as primitive men, with second Chain animals ready for individualisation. JUPITER was probably with these, and VAIVASVAṬA MANU—Manu of the fifth Race on the fourth Round of the Earth Chain.

P. 36. Individualised on globe D, in the fifth Round: Herakles, Sirius, Alcyone, Mizar, and probably all those later called Servers, who worked together through the ages—see the next paragraph. Many others, who have made great progress along other lines, probably individualised during this Round. Also individualised on globe D, in the fifth Round: Scorpio, and many of that ilk; but they dropped out again at the Day of Judgment in the sixth Round. These were first noticed in the sixth Round, evidently at the same stage as Herakles, Sirius, Alcyone and Mizar; and therefore must have individualised in the fifth Round.

II

IN THE CITY OF THE GOLDEN GATE ABOUT B. C. 220,000

IN these lists all the people recognised up to the time of writing will be named, whether given in the text or not, so as to enable the reader to draw, without much trouble, a genealogical chart, if he likes to do so.

MARS was Emperor, the Crown Prince Vajra, the Hierophant of the State, Mercury. Ulysses was Captain of the Palace Guard. In the Imperial Guard were recognised: Herakles, Pindar, Beatrix, Gemini, Capella, Lutetia, Bellona, Apis, Arcor, Capricorn, Theodorus, Scotus, Sappho. Herakles had as servants three Tlavatli youths,—Alcmene, Hygeia and Boötes—who had been captured in battle by his father, and given to him.

III

ANCIENT PERU

WHEN the articles on ancient Peru appeared in the *Theosophical Review*, Mr. Leadbeater wrote the following introduction to them, and it is useful to reprint it here. It was written in 1899.

When, in writing on the subject of clairvoyance, I referred to the magnificent possibilities which the examination of the records of the past opened up before the student of history, several readers suggested to me that deep interest would be felt by our Theosophical public in any fragments of the results of such researches which could be placed before them. That is no doubt true, but it is not so easy as might be supposed to carry out the suggestion. It has to be remembered that investigations are not undertaken for the pleasure of the thing, nor for the gratification of mere curiosity, but only when they happen to be necessary for the due performance of some piece of work, or for the elucidation of some obscure point in our study. Most of the scenes from the past history of the world which have so interested and delighted our enquirers have come before us in the course of the examination of one or other of the lines of successive lives which have been followed far back into earlier ages, in the endeavour to gather information as to the working of the great laws of karma and reincarnation; so that what we know of remote antiquity is rather in the nature of a series of glimpses than in any way a sustained view—rather a gallery of pictures than a history.

Nevertheless, even in this comparatively casual and desultory manner, much of exceeding interest has been unveiled before our eyes—much not only with regard to the splendid civilisations of Egypt, of India and of Babylonia, as well as to the far more modern States of Persia, Greece, and Rome, but to others on a scale vaster and grander far even than these—to which, indeed, these are but as buds of yesterday; mighty Empires whose beginnings reach back into primeval dawnings, even though some fragments of their traces yet remain on earth for those who have eyes to see.

Greatest perhaps of all these was the magnificent and world-embracing dominion of the Divine Rulers of the city of the Golden Gate in old Atlantis; for with the exception of the primary Āryan civilisation round the shores of the Central Asian sea, almost all Empires that men have called great since then have been but feeble and partial copies of its marvellous organisation; while before it there existed nothing at all comparable to it, the only attempts at government on a really large scale having been those of the egg-headed sub-race of the Lemurians, and of the myriad hosts of the Tlavatli mound-builders in the far west of early Atlantis.

Some outline of the polity which for so many thousands of years centred round the glorious City of the Golden Gate has already been given in one of the *Transactions* of the London Lodge; what I wish to do now is to offer a slight sketch of one of its later copies—one which, though on but a small scale as compared to its mighty parent, yet preserved to within almost what we are in the habit of calling historical periods much of the splendid public spirit and paramount sense of duty which were the very life of that grand old scheme.

The part of the world, then, to which we must for this purpose direct our attention is the ancient kingdom of Peru—a kingdom, however, embracing enormously more of the South American continent than the Republic to which we now give that name, or even the tract of country which the Spaniards found in possession of the Incas in the sixteenth century. It is true that the system of government in this later kingdom, which excited the admiration of Pizarro, aimed at reproducing the conditions of the earlier and grander civilisation of which I have now to speak; yet, wonderful as even that pale copy was acknowledged to be, we must remember that it *was* but a copy, organised thousands of years later by a far inferior race, in the attempt to revivify traditions, some of the best points of which had been forgotten.

The first introduction of our investigators to this most interesting epoch took place, as has already been hinted, in the course of an endeavour to follow back long line of incarnations. It was found that after two nobly-borne lives of great toil and stress (themselves the consequence, apparently, of a serious failure in the one preceding them), the subject (Erato) whose history was being followed was born under favourable circumstances in this great Peruvian Empire, and there lived a life which, though certainly as full of hard work as either of its predecessors, yet differed from them in being honoured, happy and successful far beyond the common lot.

Naturally the sight of a State in which most of the social problems seemed to have been solved—in which there was no poverty, no discontent, and practically no crime—attracted our attention immediately, though we could not at the time stay to examine it more closely; but when afterwards it was found that several other lines of lives in which we were interested had also passed through that country at the same period, and we thus began to learn more and more of its manners and customs, we gradually realised that we had come upon a veritable physical Utopia—a time and place where at any rate the physical life of man was better organised, happier, and more useful than it has perhaps ever been elsewhere.

No doubt there will be many who will ask themselves: "How are we to know that this account differs from those of other Utopias—how can we feel certain that the investigators were not deceiving themselves with beautiful dreams, and reading theoretical ideas of their own into the visions which they persuaded themselves that they saw—how, in fact, can we assure ourselves that this is more than a mere fairy-story?"

The only answer that can be given to such enquiries is that for them there *is* no assurance. The investigators themselves are certain—certain by long accumulation of manifold proofs, small often in themselves, perhaps, yet irresistible in combination—certain also in their knowledge, gradually acquired by many patient experiments, of the difference between observation and imagination. They know well how often they have met with the absolutely unexpected and unimaginable, and how frequently and how entirely their cherished preconceptions have been overset.

Outside the ranks of the actual investigators there are a few others who have attained practically equal certainty, either by their own intuitions, or by a personal knowledge of those who do the work; to the rest of the world the results of all enquiry into a past so remote must necessarily remain hypothetical. They may regard this account of the ancient Peruvian civilisation as a mere fairy-tale, in fact; yet even so I think I may hope for their admission, that it is a beautiful fairy-tale.

I imagine that except by these methods of clairvoyance it would be impossible now to recover any traces of the civilisation which we are about to examine. I have little doubt that traces still exist, but it would probably require extensive and elaborate excavations to enable us to acquire sufficient knowledge to separate them with any certainty from those of other and later races. It may be that, in the future, antiquarians and archæologists will turn their attention more than they have hither to done to these wonderful countries of South America, and then perhaps they may be able to sort out the various footprints of the different races which one after another occupied and governed them; but at present all that we know (outside of clairvoyance) about old Peru is the little that was told to us by the Spanish conquerors; and the civilisation at which they marvelled so greatly was but a faint and far distant reflection of the older and grander reality.

The very race itself had changed; for though those whom the Spaniards found in possession were still some offshoot of that splendid third sub-race of the Atlanteans, which seems to have been endued with so much more enduring power and vitality than any of those which followed it, it is yet evident that this offshoot was in many ways in the last stage of decrepitude, in many ways more barbarous, more degraded, less refined, than the much older branch of which we have to speak.

This little leaf out of the world's true history—this glimpse at just one picture in nature's vast galleries—

reveals to us what might well seem an ideal State compared to anything which exists at the present day; and part of its interest to us consists in the fact that all the results at which our modern social reformers are aiming were already fully achieved there, but achieved by methods diametrically opposite to most that are being suggested now. The people were peaceful and prosperous; no such thing as poverty was known, and there was practically no crime; no single person had cause for discontent, for everyone had an opening for his genius (if he had any) and he chose for himself his profession or line of activity, whatever it might be. In no case was work too hard or too heavy placed upon any man; everyone had plenty of spare time to give to any desired accomplishment or occupation; education was full, free, and efficient, and the sick and aged were perfectly and even luxuriously cared for. And yet the whole of this wonderfully elaborate system for the promotion of physical well-being was carried out, and so far as we can see could only have been carried out, under an autocracy which was one of the most absolute that the world has ever known.

IV

PERU, ABOUT B. C. 12,000

THIS is one of the largest of the gatherings of those who are now working in the Theosophical Society. MARS was Emperor at the time, and the lists begin with his father and mother. There were three families of the time among which they were distributed, those descended from JUPITER, SATURN, and Psyche.

JUPITER married VULCAN and had two sons—MARS and URANUS. The family of MARS by his marriage with

BṚHASPAṬI consisted of two sons, Siwa and Pindar, who respectively married Proteus and Tolosa. Siwa and Proteus also had two sons, Corona and Orpheus, Corona marrying Pallas, and having as sons Ulysses and OSIRIS, and as daughter Theodoros—Ulysses marrying Cassiopeia, VIRĀJ being their son; OSIRIS marrying ATHENA, and Theodoros marrying Deneb; Orpheus marrying Hestia, by whom he had two sons—Thor and Rex—who respectively married Iphigenia and Ajax. Pindar and Tolosa had three daughters, Herakles, Adrona and Cetus, and one son—Olympia. Herakles married Castor, Adrona Berenice, Cetus Procyon and Olympia Diana.

URANUS married Hesperia, and had three sons—Sirius, Centaurus and Alcyone—and two daughters—Aquarius and Sagittarius. The wife of Sirius was Spica, and Pollux, Vega and Castor were their sons, and Alcestis and Minerva their daughters. Fides was an adopted son and married Glaucus. Pollux married Melpomene and had three sons—Cyrene, Apis, Flora—and two daughters—Eros and Chamæleon. Apis married Boötes, Eros Pisces, and Chamæleon Gemini. Vega married Pomona and they had one son, Ursa, who espoused Lacerta, and two daughters—Circe and Ajax, the latter marrying Rex. Ursa's family included Cancer (daughter), Alastor (son), Phocea (daughter), and Thetis (son). Of these, Alastor married Clio and had one daughter, Trapezium, and a son, Markab. Castor married Herakles, and they had as issue: Vajra and Aurora (sons), the latter marrying Wenceslas, and daughters Lacerta, Alcmene, and Sappho, who respectively married Ursa, Hygeia and Dorado. Alcestis married Nicosia and they had a son—Formator. Minerva married Beatus. The next son of URANUS was Centaurus, who married Gimel, their son being Beatus. Alcyone had Mizar as his wife, and their children were—Perseus, Leo, Capella, Regulus and Irene (sons), and Ausonia (daughter). Perseus married Alexandros. Leo married Concordia, and they had as children—Deneb, whose wife was Theodoros, Egeria, whose husband was Telemachus, Calliope, whose wife was

Parthenope, Iphigenia, whose husband was Thor, and Daleth, whose husband was Polaris. Capella married Soma and they had two sons—Telemachus and Aquila—and one daughter—Parthenope, who married Calliope. Telemachus married Egeria and they had a son, Beth. Ausonia married Rama. Regulus married Mathematicus, and they had a daughter, Trefoil, who married Aquila. Irene married Flos. Of the daughters of URANUS, Aquarius married Virgo, and Sagittarius Apollo.

The second great family of this period was that of SATURN, who had VENUS as his wife. Their children were six—Hesperia (daughter) who married URANUS; MERCURY (son) who married Lyra (by whom he had two sons, SŪRYA and Apollo, and one daughter, Andromeda, who married Argus); Calypso (son) who married Avelledo, by whom he had one son Rhea (who married Zama and had two sons Sirona and Lachesis) and one daughter, Amalthea; Crux (daughter) married NEPTUNE, by whom there were five children—Melete, son, (married Erato, sons Hebe, Stella), Tolosa, daughter (married Pindar), Virgo, son, (married Aquarius—son Euphrosyne, who married Canopus), Alba, daughter, (married Altair), Leopardus, son, (married Auriga); Selene (son) who married Beatrix, and by whom there were six children, Erato, daughter, who married Melete, Aldebaran, son, who married Orion (children: Theseus, wife Dactyl; Arcor, husband Capricorn—children, Hygeia, wife Alcmene; Boötes, husband Apis; Gemini, wife Chamæleon; Polaris, wife Daleth—Fomalhaut, son; Arcturus, husband Nitocris; and Canopus, husband Euphrosyne); Spica, daughter, who married Sirius, Albireo, son, who married Hector, Leto, son, who married Fons (children: Norma, wife Aulus, Scotus, wife Elsa, Sextans, husband Pegasus) and Elektra; Vesta (son) who married Mira, by whom there was one son, Bellatrix (married Tiphys, sons Juno, who weds Minorca, and Proserpina, who espouses Colossus), and four daughters: Orion, who married Aldebaran, Mizar, who married Alcyone, Achilles, who married Demeter, (children:

Elsa, husband Scotus; Aletheia, wife Ophiuchus, to whom are born two sons, Dorado and Fortuna—who respectively marry Sappho and Eudoxia; Aries and Taurus, sons, and Procyon, wife Cetus) and Philæ, who married Cygnus.

The third family was that of Psyche, whose wife was Libra. To them were born: Rigel—daughter, who married Betelgueuse, and by whom there were six children: Altair, wife Alba (son Ara, marries Pepin); Hector, husband Albireo (sons, Pegasus, wife Sextans, Berenice, wife Adrona); Auriga, husband Leopardus (daughter Flos, married Irene); Viola, wife Elektra (daughter, Aulus, married Norma, son Nitocris, married Arcturus); Cygnus, wife Philae (daughter Minorca, married Juno); and Demeter, whose wife was Achilles—Mira, whose husband was Vesta; and Algol, whose wife was Iris, and by whom there were five children, Helios, wife Lomia (daughter Mathematicus, married Regulus); Draco, wife Phoenix (son Atalanta, married Herminius); Argus, wife Andromeda (daughters, Pepin, married Ara, and Dactyl, married Theseus); Fons, daughter, and Xanthos, son. Boreas is also noticed as one of the characters.

V

ON THE SHORE OF THE GOBI SEA, ABOUT B. C. 72,000

THE MANU had MARS, Vajra, Ulysses, VIRĀJ and Apollo as grandsons; MARS married MERCURY, and they had as sons: Sirius, Achilles, Alcyone, Orion, and one daughter, Mizar. Sirius married Vega, and had as children: Mira, Rigel, Ajax, Bellatrix and Proserpina, all massacred. Achilles married Albireo, and had a daughter, Hector. Alcyone married Leo, and had as sons: URANUS and NEPTUNE, and as daughters SŪRYA and BṚHASPAṬI; all these were saved from the massacre, and, as a woman, SŪRYA married SATURN, saved at the same time, and VAIVASVAṬA MANU, VIRĀJ and MARS were their children; in the next generation, Herakles was the son of MARS. Returning to the children of MARS and MERCURY, Mizar married Herakles, the son of VIRĀJ, and they had three sons: Capricorn, Arcor, Fides, and two daughters, Psyche and Pindar. Corona married Deneb, and had two sons, one of whom was Dorado. Adrona had Pollux as son. Cetus married Clio. Others seen were Orpheus, VULCAN and VENUS, who were both saved, and JUPITER, the head of the community. Vega and Leo were sisters, as were Albireo and Helios, the latter a very pretty and coquettish young lady. Scorpio appeared among the Turanian assailants.

VI

IN SHAMBALLA, ABOUT B. C. 60,000

MARS, a Toltec Prince from Poseidonis, married JUPITER, the daughter of the MANU. They had VIRĀJ as son, who married SATURN and of them VAIVASVAṬA MANU was born.

VII

IN THE CITY OF THE BRIDGE, AND THE VALLEY OF THE SECOND SUB-RACE, ABOUT B. C. 40,000

TWO families chiefly provided the emigrants, Corona and Theodorus, who sent two sons, Herakles and Pindar, and Demeter and Fomalhaut sent their sons Vega and Aurora, and their daughters Sirius and Dorado; their remaining son Mira and daughter Draco remained with them in the City. In the City were also Castor and Rhea. Lachesis, who married Amalthea, had Velleda as son; and Calypso who ran away with Amalthea. Crux, a foreigner, with Phocea, came as visitors.

Herakles married Sirius, and they had as children: Alcyone, Mizar, Orion, Achilles, URANUS, Aldebaran, Siwa, Selene, NEPTUNE, Capricorn, and some others unrecognised. Alcyone married Perseus, and VULCAN, Bellatrix, Rigel, Algol, and Arcturus were their children. Mizar married Deneb, and their children were Wenceslas, Ophiuchus, and Cygnus, with many unrecognised. Orion married Eros, and had Sagittarius, Theseus and Mu in his family. Achilles married Leo, and had as children Ulysses, Vesta, Psyche, and Cassiopeia. URANUS married Andromeda, and MARS and VENUS were born to them. Aldebaran married Pegasus, and Capella and Juno were among their children. Selene married Albireo, and MERCURY appeared in their family; she married MARS, and they had VAIVASVAṬA MANU as son. Capricorn married her first cousin, Polaris, and their children were Vajra, Adrona, Pollux, and Diana.

Pindar married Beatrix, and they had Gemini, Arcor, and Polaris as children. Gemini married a foreigner, Apis, and Spica and Fides were born to them as twins.

The children of Sirius are given above; his brother Vega married Helios, and they had children Leo, Proserpina, Canopus, Aquarius, and Ajax. Aurora married Hector, and one of their children was Albireo. Dorado had a daughter Aletheia, who married Argus.

VIII

IN THE CITY OF THE BRIDGE AND THE VALLEY OF THE THIRD SUB-RACE, ABOUT B. C. 32,000.

THE MANU was married to MERCURY, and had Sirius as a younger son. Sirius married Mizar, and had as children: Alcyone, Orion, VENUS, Ulysses, Albireo and SATURN and went to the valley. Alcyone married Achilles, who was the daughter of Vesta and Aldebaran, and had Libra as a brother. Orion married Herakles, an Akkadian, and they had six sons: the eldest, Capella, was a fine horseman; Fides, a good runner, slim and lightly built; Dorado, a fair rider and first-rate at games, fond of a game like quoits, throwing rings on upright posts; Elektra, Canopus and Arcor, the third, fifth and sixth. As daughters there were: Gemini, who, by a strange repetition of the story of eight thousand years before, married Apis, an Arabian, who had travelled thus far from his home; Fortuna, Draco, Hygeia, a very fat girl, to whom the baby Capricorn clung with much energy, and a passionate child, Polaris, who was seen on her back, screaming vigorously, because an animal had carried off her toy. Albireo married Hector, and Pegasus, Leo and Berenice were found in her family. Pallas and Helios were in the valley, as said in the text.

IX

IN THE EMIGRATION, ABOUT B. C. 30,000

VAIVASVATA MANU as leader: His Captains: MARS (wife NEPTUNE), Corona (wife OSIRIS) his brother, VULCAN (wife VENUS), Theodoros, (wife Aldebaran), VAJRA. In body-guard: Ulysses, Herakles, Sirius, Arcor, Leo, Alcyone, Polaris. MERCURY married Rama, Vajra married URANUS. Ulysses married Spica. Herakles, son of Mars, married Psyche, and had Capella, Dolphin, Lutetia and Canopus, as sons and a daughter Daphne. Sirius married Achilles, and Aurora Dorado. Capella married Bellatrix. Leo married Leto. Alcyone married Fides, and had as children Cygnus, Mira, Perseus, Proserpina, Demeter. Polaris married Minerva. Vega married Helios. Castor married

Aries, and had a son Lachesis who married Rhea. Calypso married Amalthea; Tolosa was among their children. Velleda had among his children Cyrene and Sirona. Markab was a soldier, and married Clio. Vesta, Mizar, Albireo, Orion, Ajax, Hector, Crux and Selene were also seen. Trapezium was an insurgent chief.

X

THE FIRST ĀRYAN IMMIGRATION INTO INDIA, B. C. 18,875

MARS married MERCURY, and had sons URANUS, Herakles, and Alcyone, daughters BṚHASPAṬI and Demeter. BṚHASPAṬI married first VULCAN, and after his death Corona, the son of VIRĀJ, and had one son, Trefoil, who married Arcturus, and five daughters: Fides, who married Betelgueuse; Thor, who married Iphigenia; Rama, who married Perseus; Dædalus, who married Elsa; and Rector who married Fomalhaut. SATURN was King in South India, and had Crux as son; SŪRYA was High Priest, and OSIRIS, Deputy High Priest.

Herakles married Capella, and had as sons Cassiopeia, Altair and Leto, as daughters Argus and Centaurus. Alcyone married Theseus, and had four sons: Andromeda, Betelgueuse, Fomalhaut and Perseus, and three daughters, Draco, NEPTUNE, and Arcturus. Demeter married Wenceslas, and had as sons, Elsa, Iphigenia and Diana, who married respectively, Dædalus, Thor, and Draco. Cassiopeia married Capricorn, and had Cetus, Spica and Adrona as sons, Sirona as daughter; Spica married Kudos, Altair married Polaris, and had Tolosa as son. Leto married Gemini. Argus married Andromeda and had among her sons Arcor, who married Mizar, the daughter of NEPTUNE and Hector; the latter had also Siwa and

Orpheus as sons. Diomede married Orpheus. Regulus and Irene were daughters of Arcor and Mizar. Argus married a second husband, Mathematicus, and had three daughters, Diomede, Judex who married Beatus, and Kudos. Centaurus married Concordia. Of Alcyone's sons: Andromeda married Argus as said, and died early; Betelgueuse married Fides, and had as sons Flos, and Beatus who married Judex. Fomalhaut married Rector, Perseus married Rama, Draco Diana, NEPTUNE Hector, and Arcturus Trefoil. Alcyone's wife, Theseus, was the daughter of Glaucus and Telemachus, and the latter had a sister, Soma. Alastor was in Central Asia. Taurus, a Mongol, had Procyon as wife, and Cygnus as daughter, who married Aries.

XI

AN ARYAN IMMIGRATION INTO INDIA, B. C. 17,455

JUPITER married SATURN and had MARS as his son and MERCURY as his sister. MARS married NEPTUNE, and had sons, Herakles, Siwa and Mizar, daughters OSIRIS, Pindar and Andromeda. Herakles married Cetus, and had, as sons, Gemini and Arcor; as daughters, Polaris who married Diana, Capricorn who married Glaucus, and Adrona. Ṣiwa married Proserpina, Mizar married Rama, and had as sons: Diana and Dædalus; as daughters: Diomede and Kudos. OSIRIS married Perseus.

VULCAN married Corona, and their three daughters, Rama, Rector and Thor, married respectively Mizar, Trefoil and Leto. Psyche, a friend of Mars, married Arcturus, and had as sons, Alcyone, Albireo, Leto and Ajax; as daughters, Beatrix, Procyon and Cygnus. Alcyone married Rigel and had as sons: Cassiopeia who married Diomede; Crux who married Kudos, and Wenceslas who married Regulus. They had also three daughters: Taurus who married Concordia, Irene who married Flos, and Theseus who married Dædalus. Albireo married Hector, and had a daughter Beatus, who married Iphigenia. Leto married Thor, and had a son Flos. Ajax married Elsa, Beatrix Mathematicus, and Cygnus Fomalhaut. Capella, another friend of Mars, married Judex, and had as sons Perseus, who married OSIRIS, and Fomalhaut who married Cygnus. The daughters were Hector, Demeter who married Aries, and Elsa who married Ajax. Vajra married Orpheus, and had Draco and Altair as sons, BṚHASPAṬI, URANUS and Proserpina as daughters. Draco married Argus, and had as son Concordia, who married Taurus. Altair married Centaurus, and their daughter Regulus married Wenceslas. Betelgueuse married Canopus, and had Spica and Olympia as sons, Rigel as daughter. Spica married Telemachus, and had two sons, Glaucus and Iphigenia, whose marriages are mentioned above. Castor married Pollux, and had as sons Aries and Alastor, and three daughters, Minerva, Sirona and Pomona.

XII

AN ĀRYAN IMMIGRATION INTO INDIA, B. C. 15,950

SŪRYA was the father of MARS and MERCURY. MARS married BṚHASPAṬI, and had sons, JUPITER, Siwa and VIRĀJ; daughters, OSIRIS, URANUS, and Ulysses. JUPITER married Herakles, and they had as sons: Beatrix who married Pindar, Aletheia who married Taurus, Betelgueuse; and as daughters: Canopus who married Fomalhaut, Pollux who married Melpomene, and Hector who married NEPTUNE. URANUS married Leo, and Ulysses Vajra; the latter had as sons: Clio who married Concordia, Melpomene, and Alastor, who married Gemini; as daughters: Irene who married Adrona, Sirona who married Spica, and Beatus who married Soma.

MERCURY married SATURN, and their sons were: Selene, Leo, Vajra and Castor, and their daughters, Herakles, Alcyone and Mizar. Selene married Aurora, and had as sons:

Wenceslas who married Crux, Theseus who married Lignus, and Polaris who married Proserpina; as daughters: Taurus who married Aletheia, Arcturus who married Perseus, and Argus who married Draco. Leo married URANUS, and had as sons: Leto, who married Demeter, Draco, Fomalhaut—both married as above—and as daughters: Centaurus who married Altair, Proserpina, and Concordia who married Clio. Castor married Iphigenia. Alcyone married Albireo, and had four sons: NEPTUNE who married Hector, Psyche married Clarion, Perseus married Arcturus, and Ajax Capella; the daughters were Rigel who married Centurion, Demeter who married Leto, and Algol who married Priam. Mizar married Glaucus, and had two sons, Soma and Flos. The daughters, Diomede and Telemachus, married respectively Trefoil and Betelgueuse; VULCAN married Cetus and had one son, Procyon, and three daughters, Olympia, Minerva and Pomona. Arcor married Capricorn and had four sons: Altair, Adrona, Spica, Trefoil, and four daughters: Pindar, Capella, Crux, and Gemini. Corona married Orpheus, and had three sons: Rama who married VENUS, Cassiopeia who married Rector, and Aries; of the daughters, Andromeda married Dædalus, Elsa Mathematicus, and Pallas Diana. Thor married Kudos; his sons were Mathematicus, Diana and Dædalus—who married three sisters as above—and Judex; the daughter was Rector.

At the one pole of human evolution there stood at the date of this immigration the four KUMĀRAS, the MANU and the MAHĀGURU; far down towards the other, Scorpio, the high priest Yā-uli.

XIII

IN NORTHERN INDIA, B. C. 12,800

MARS and MERCURY are brothers. MARS married SATURN, and had two sons, Vajra and VIRĀJ, and two daughters, VULCAN and Herakles. Vajra married Proserpina, and had three sons, Ulysses, Fides and Selene, and three daughters, Beatrix, Hector and Hestia. VIRĀJ married OSIRIS, VULCAN married URANUS, and Herakles Polaris. Ulysses married Philæ, and had three sons: Cygnus who married Diana, Calliope who married Parthenope, and Pisces Ajax; the daughters were Bellatrix who married Thor, Aquarius who married Clarion, and Pepin who married Lignus. Returning to the sons of Vajra we have: Fides who married Iphigenia, and had three sons: Aquila who married Sappho, Kudos Concordia, and Beatus Gimel. They had four daughters: Herminius married to Nicosia, Sextans to Virgo, Sagittarius to Clio, Parthenope to Calliope. Selene married Achilles and had two sons: Aldebaran marrying Elektra, and Helios marrying Lomia. There were five daughters: Vega marrying Leo, Rigel marrying Leto, Alcestis marrying Aurora, Colossus marrying Aries, and Eros marrying Juno. Of Vajra's daughters, Beatrix married Albireo, and had two sons, Berenice who married Canopus, and Deneb. The daughters, Pindar and Lyra, married respectively Capella and Euphrosyne. Hector married Wenceslas, and had as sons: Leo, Leto, Norma marrying Melete, Nicosia marrying Herminius; the daughters were: Ajax married to Pisces, and Crux married to Demeter. Hestia married Telemachus; their sons were: Thor, Diomede married to Chrysos; the daughters were Sappho, Trefoil, Minorca married to Lobelia, and Magnus to Calypso. Herakles, the daughter of MARS, married Polaris; their three sons, Viola, Dorado, and Olympia, married respectively Egeria, Dactyl and Mira; the daughter, Phœnix, married Atalanta. Viola and Egeria had four sons: Betelgueuse married to Iris, Nitocris married to Brunhilda, Taurus to Tiphys and Perseus to Fons; one daughter, Lomia, married Helios, the other, Libra, married Boreas. Dorado and Dactyl had sons: Centurion married to Theodoros, Pegasus to Priam, Scotus to Ausonia; daughters: Arcturus to Rector, and Brunhilda to Nitocris. Olympia married Mira, and had four sons: Clarion married Aquarius, Pollux Cancer, Procyon Avelledo, and Capricorn Zama. The daughter, Arcor, married Centaurus. Phœnix, the daughter of Herakles, who married Atalanta, had three sons: Gemini, Lignus and Virgo, who married Adrona, Pepin and Sextans; there were three daughters: Daleth married Regulus, Dolphin married Formator, and Daphne Apis. That finishes the descendants of MARS.

MERCURY, his brother, married VENUS, and had NEPTUNE and URANUS as sons, OSIRIS, Proserpina and Tolosa as daughters. URANUS married VULCAN, and had two sons, Rama and Albireo, who married Glaucus and Beatrix; and two daughters, BṚHASPAṬI and ATHENA, who married Apollo and JUPITER. Rama and Glaucus had Juno and Ara as sons, who married Eros and Ophiuchus; their daughters were four: Canopus married to Berenice, Diana to Cygnus, Chrysos to Diomede, and Judex to Irene. Albireo, marrying into the family of Vajra, has his children noted above. BṚHASPAṬI and Apollo had three sons: Capella married to Pindar, Corona and Siwa; their daughter Proteus married Rex. OSIRIS married VIRĀJ, and had as sons JUPITER and Apollo, the latter marrying BṚHASPAṬI. The daughter, Pallas, married Castor; they had five sons: Clio who married Sagittarius, Markab who married Cetus, Aries who married Colossus, Aglaia who married Pomona, and Sirona, who married Quies. That finishes the descendants of MERCURY.

Algol married Theseus, and had son Alcyone, who married Mizar, the daughter of Orpheus and sister of Psyche. Alcyone and Mizar had five sons: Fomalhaut who married Alexandros, Altair Alba, Wenceslas Hector, Telemachus Hestia, Soma Flos; their three daughters were: Iphigenia married to Fides, Glaucus to Rama, Philæ to Ulysses. Fomalhaut and Alexandros had three sons: Rex who married Proteus, Rector who married Arcturus, and Leopardus; their three daughters were: Melete who married Norma, Ausonia who married Scotus, and Concordia who married Kudos.

Altair and Alba had three sons: Apis who married Daphne, Centaurus who married Arcor, and Flora; their daughters were Chamæleon, Gimel who married Beatus, and Priam who married Pegasus. The children of Wenceslas are given among the descendants of MARS, as are those of Telemachus, Iphigenia, and Philæ, while those of Glaucus are among the descendants of MERCURY. Soma and Flos had four sons: Alastor married to Melpomene, Boreas to Libra, Regulus to Daleth, Irene to Judex; the two daughters, Phocea and Dædalus, married Zephyr and Leopardus.

Aletheia took Spes to wife, and had two sons, Mona and Fortuna, and four daughters: Achilles, Aulus, Flos and Alba. Mona married Andromeda, and they had as sons: Lobelia who married Minorca, and Zephyr who married Phocea; their daughters were: Adrona who married Gemini, Cetus who married Markab, Melpomene who married Alastor, and Avelledo who married Procyon. Fortuna married Auriga, and their two sons, Hebe and Stella, married Trefoil and Chamæleon; their daughters were: Iris, Tiphys, Eudoxia married to Flora, and Pomona to Aglaia. Aulus married Argus, and they had three sons: Calypso married to Magnus, Formator to Dolphin, and Minerva; the daughters, Elektra and Ophiuchus, married Aldebaran and Ara.

Psyche, the brother of Mizar, married Mathematicus, and they had three daughters: Egeria, Elsa who married Beth, and Mira. Elsa and Beth had Aurora, Demeter and Euphrosyne as sons, who married Alcestis, Crux and Lyra; their daughters were: Theodoros married to Centurion, and Fons to Perseus.

Draco married Cassiopeia; their sons were: Argus Beth, Atalanta and Castor, who married Pallas; his daughters were: Andromeda, Dactyl, Alexandros, Auriga. Vesta was also present.

XIV

THE ĀRYANISATION OF EGYPT

IN the body of this book we have three times referred (on pp. 242, 283, 329) to the expedition sent forth from South India by the MANU for the express purpose of Āryanising the noble families of Egypt. While the book is going through the press some further investigations have been made, which are found to throw additional light upon the subject, and to some extent to link it up with accepted Egyptian history. The earlier part of the book being already in type, all that we can do is to append here an article which has been written to explain the later discoveries.

Referring to our remark on p. 330 that "Manetho's history apparently deals with this Āryan dynasty," we now see that he—quite reasonably—begins with the reunification of Egypt under the MANU, and that the date which our researches assign to that reunification (though not yet verified with perfect exactitude) comes within a few years of 5,510 B. C., which is the latest selection by the most distinguished living Egyptologist for the commencement of the First Dynasty. The new Egyptological theories now make the date of the Pharaoh Unas about two hundred years *earlier* than we do.

Others of our characters, besides the few whom MARS took with Him, are to be found in Egypt in 13,500 B. C.; a full list of all these will be given when the Lives of Alcyone appear in book form.

In the sixth life of Alcyone we followed the first of the great Āryan migrations from the shores of what was then the Central Asian sea to the south of the Indian Peninsula. The religious kingdom that the Āryans established there was, as centuries rolled on, used by the MANU as a subsidiary centre of radiation, as we have already said.

From South India likewise was sent forth the expedition destined to bring about the Āryanisation of Egypt, which was carried out in much the same way and by many of the same egos who five thousand years previously had played their part in the migration from Central Asia to which reference has just been made.

About the year 13,500 B. C. (shortly after the time of the thirteenth life of Alcyone and the twelfth life of Orion, when so many of our characters had taken birth in the Tlavatli race inhabiting the southern part of the Island of Poseidonis) VIRĀJ was ruler of the great South Indian Empire. He had married BṚHASPATI, and MARS was one of their sons. The MANU appeared astrally to the Emperor, and directed him to send MARS over the sea to Egypt by way of Ceylon. VIRĀJ obeyed, and MARS departed upon his long journey, taking with him (according to the instructions received) a band of young men and women, of whom twelve are recognisable: Ajax, Betelgueuse, Deneb, Leo, Perseus and Theodoros among the men, and Arcturus, Canopus, Olympia, VULCAN, Pallas and OSIRIS among the ladies.

On their arrival in Egypt, then under Toltec rule, they were met by JUPITER, the Pharaoh of the time. He had one child only—his daughter SATURN—his wife having died in child-birth. The High-Priest SŪRYA had been directed in a vision by the MAHĀGURU to receive the strangers with honour, and to advise JUPITER to give his daughter to MARS in marriage, which he did; and in a comparatively short time marriages were arranged among the existing nobility for all the new-comers.

Small as was this importation of Āryan blood, in a few generations it had tinged the whole of the Egyptian nobility, for since the Pharaoh had set his seal of august approval upon these mixed marriages, all the patrician families competed eagerly for the honour of an alliance with the sons or daughters of the new-comers. The mingling of the two races produced a new and distinctive type, which had the high Āryan features, but the Toltec colouring—the type which we know so well from the Egyptian monuments. So powerful is the Āryan blood that it still shows its unmistakable traces even after centuries of dilution; and from this time onward an incarnation among the principal classes of Egypt counted as a birth in the first sub-race of the fifth root-race.

Many changes took place as the centuries rolled by, and the impetus given by the Āryan rejuvenation gradually died out. The country never reached so low a level as the parallel civilisation of Poseidonis, chiefly because of the retention of Āryan tradition by a certain clan whose members claimed exclusively for themselves direct descent from the royal line of MARS and SATURN. For more than a thousand years after the Āryanisation this clan ruled the country, the Pharaoh being always its head; but there came a time when for political reasons the reigning monarch espoused a foreign princess, who by degrees acquired over him so great an influence that she was able to wean him from the traditions of his forefathers, and to establish new forms of worship to which the clan as a whole would not subscribe. The country, weary of Āryan strictness, followed its monarch into license and luxury; the clan drew its ranks together in stern disapproval, and thenceforward its members held themselves markedly aloof—not declining offices in the army or in the service of the State, but marrying only among themselves, and making a great point of maintaining old customs and what they called the purity of the religion as well as of the race.

After nearly four thousand years had passed, we find a condition of affairs in which the Egyptian Empire, its religion and even its language were alike degenerate and decaying. Only in the ranks of the conservative clan can we find some pale reflection of the Egypt of earlier days. About this time, among the priests of the clan arose some who were prophets, who re-echoed in Egypt the message that was being given in Poseidonis—a warning that, because of the wickedness of these mighty and long-established civilisations, they were doomed to destruction, and that it behoved the few righteous to flee promptly from the wrath to come. Just as a considerable proportion of the white race of mountaineers left Poseidonis, so the members of the clan in a body shook off the dust of Egypt from their feet, took ship across the Red Sea and found a refuge among the mountains of Arabia.

As we know, in due time the prophecy was fulfilled, and in the year 9564 B. C. the island of Poseidonis sank beneath the Atlantic. The effect of the cataclysm on the rest of the world was of the most serious character, and for the land of Egypt it was specially ruinous. Up to this point Egypt had had an extensive western seaboard, and although the Sahara Sea was shallow, it was sufficient for the great fleets of comparatively small ships which carried the traffic to Atlantis and the Algerian Islands. In this great catastrophe the bed of the Sahara Sea rose, a vast tidal wave swept over Egypt, and almost its entire population was destroyed. And even when everything settled down, the country was a wilderness, bounded on the west no longer by a fair and peaceful sea, but by a vast salt swamp, which as the centuries rolled on dried into an inhospitable desert. Of all the glories of Egypt there remained only the Pyramids towering in lonely desolation—a desolation which endured for fifteen hundred years before the self-exiled clan returned from its mountain refuge, grown into a great nation.

But long before this, half-savage tribes had ventured into the land, fighting their primitive battles on the banks of the great river which once had borne the argosies of a mighty civilisation, and was yet again to witness a revival of those ancient glories, and to mirror the stately temples of Osiris and Amen-ra. Professor Flinders Petrie describes five of these earlier races, which overran different parts of the country and warred desultorily among themselves.

1. An aquiline race of the Libyo-Amorite type, which occupied a large part of the land, and held its own longer than any other, maintaining for centuries a fair level of civilisation.

2. A Hittite race with curly hair and plaited beards.

3. A people with pointed noses and long pigtails—mountaineers, wearing long, thick robes.

4. A people with short and tilted noses, who established themselves for some time in the central part of the country.

5. Another variant of this race, with longer noses and projecting beards, who occupied chiefly the marshland near the Mediterranean. All these are observable by clairvoyance, but they have mingled so much that it is often difficult to distinguish them; and in addition to these, and probably earlier in the field than any of them, a savage negroid race from the interior of Africa, which has left practically no record of its passing.

Into this turmoil of mixed races came our clan, priest-led across the sea from its Arabian hills, and gradually made its footing sure in Upper Egypt, establishing its capital in Abydos, and slowly possessing itself of more and more of the surrounding land, until by weight of its superior civilisation it was recognised as the dominant power. All through its earlier centuries its policy was less to fight than to absorb—to build out of this chaos of peoples a race upon which its hereditary characteristics should be stamped. A thousand years had passed since their arrival, when, in the twenty-first life of Alcyone, we find MARS reigning over an already highly-organised empire; but it was fourteen hundred years later still before the MANU Himself (they have corrupted His name to Menes now) united the whole of Egypt under one rule, and founded at the same time the first dynasty and His great city of Memphis—thus initiating in person another stage of the work begun by His direction in 13,500 B. C.

Clio and Markab were noticed among a group of Egyptian statesmen who disapproved of the Âryan immigration and schemed against it. Clio's wife Adrona, and Markab's wife Avelledo were implicated in their plots. All four of them were eventually exiled, as was also Cancer, the sister of Adrona.

INDEX

THE VASANTA PRESS, ADYAR, MADRAS